Jagdgeschwader 5

Also by Werner Girbig
Six Months to Oblivion: The Defeat of the Luftwaffe Fighter Force over the Western Front, 1944-45

The War Diary of Hauptmann Helmut Lipfert: JG 52 on the Russian Front, 1943-45
(with Helmut Lipfert)

Jagdgeschwader 5
The Luftwaffe's JG 5 "Eismeerjäger" in World War II

Werner Girbig

Translated from the German by David Johnston

Schiffer Military History
Atglen, PA

This book was originally published under the title,
Jagdgeschwader 5 "Eismeerjäger Chronik,
by Motorbuch Verlag, Stuttgart, Germany, 2010.

Book design by Robert Biondi.

Copyright © 2012 by Schiffer Publishing, Ltd.
Library of Congress Catalog Number: 2012939788.

All rights reserved. No part of this work may be reproduced or used in any forms or by any means – graphic, electronic or mechanical, including photocopying or information storage and retrieval systems – without written permission from the publisher.
 The scanning, uploading and distribution of this book or any part thereof via the Internet or via any other means without the permission of the publisher is illegal and punishable by law. Please purchase only authorized editions and do not participate in or encourage the electronic piracy of copyrighted materials.
 "Schiffer," "Schiffer Publishing, Ltd. & Design," and the "Design of pen and ink well" are registered trademarks of Schiffer Publishing, Ltd.

Printed in China.
ISBN: 978-0-7643-4272-1

We are always looking for people to write books on new and related subjects. If you have an idea for a book, please contact us at the address below.

Published by Schiffer Publishing, Ltd. 4880 Lower Valley Road Atglen, PA 19310 Phone: (610) 593-1777 FAX: (610) 593-2002 E-mail: Info@schifferbooks.com. Visit our web site at: www.schifferbooks.com Please write for a free catalog. This book may be purchased from the publisher. Try your bookstore first.	In Europe, Schiffer books are distributed by: Bushwood Books 6 Marksbury Ave. Kew Gardens, Surrey TW9 4JF England Phone: 44 (0)20 8392-8585 FAX: 44 (0)20 8392-9876 E-mail: info@bushwoodbooks.co.uk www.bushwoodbooks.co.uk Try your bookstore first.

Contents

Foreword 7

Chapter 1: Background History 9
On the West Coast of Norway 9
Buildup in Northern Finland 15

Chapter 2: I./JG 5 23
From Stavanger to Targsorul 23
In the Defense of the Reich 30
Major Horst Carganico 36
Successes and Losses – The Invasion 37
The *Gruppe*'s Last Path 43

Chapter 3: JG 5 on the Polar Sea 48
The New *Jagdgeschwader* 5 48
Return from the Snow of the Tundra 54
Murmansk Combat Zone – PQ Convoys 63
Black August 1942 72
Murmashi, Shongui, Varlamovo 76
Turn of the Year 1942-1943 80
The Good and Ill Fortune of *Leutnant* Lüdecke 83
The *Jabostaffel* 90
1943: An Eventful Year 92
The "Hunter of Murmansk" 98
Weißenberger and 7./JG 5 107
The Russian Air Force Becomes More Active 113
Odyssey on the Polar Sea 120
Successful Summer 1944 – Schuck, Norz 127
Captivity 135

Chapter 4: Other Fronts 150
II. *Gruppe* Leaves the Polar Sea Front 150
Defensive Struggle over the Homeland 155
"Westside Story" – Standing Guard over Norway's Fjords 161

Chapter 5: Back on the West Coast 166
Retreat from Finland 166
The Tirpitz Affair 171
Towards the End 176

Chapter 6: Dachshund *Staffel* - the *Zerstörer* 185
First Operational Experiences on the Polar Sea Front 185
Escort to Murmansk 190
Locomotive Hunt on the Murmansk Railway 192
The Rescue of the *Sonderführer* 201
Convoy Escort Missions 207
Back in Norway – The End in Stavanger 214

Appendices
Staffel Family Tree 221
Staffing 222
Operational Aircraft of JG 5 228
The Knight's Cross Holders of JG 5 229
Aerial Victories of JG 5 229
Victory List of *Major* Theo Weißenberger 233
Casualties 237

Photo Section 248

Foreword

This *Geschwader* history was created on the initiative of the *Eismeerjäger* Veterans Association and its completion was only possible thanks to the assistance of many former members in the form of personal memories and records, the evaluation of official documents and chronicles, and surviving *Geschwader* records.

Unlike the other "big" fighter units, relatively little is known about *Jagdgeschwader 5*. And yet JG 5 can point to a very distinguished record. The mission of the fighter pilots who fought in the far north was no less important than that of units stationed in other theaters. As well, because of the location of its area of operations on the Polar Sea, the history of JG 5 may serve to complete a little-known chapter in the history of the German fighter arm and indeed the last war.

In the far north, where the European mainland loses itself in rugged fjords in the Polar Sea 600 kilometers north of the Arctic Circle, the "central heating from the Gulf of Mexico," the Gulfstream, creates favorable living conditions found in no other region of the earth above the 70th parallel. In normal winters the Gulfstream also keeps the port of Murmansk ice free. During the last war, therefore, Murmansk was a strategically important gateway through which considerable quantities of materiel from the western Allies flowed into the Soviet Union, contributing significantly to a resurgence of its already flagging ability to resist. Beginning in the summer of 1941, the Germans attempted to close this gateway. The impassable terrain, the difficult climatic conditions, and the fierce resistance of the Soviets, who were accustomed to the Polar conditions, prevented the capture of Murmansk. The Germans therefore began an intensive aerial campaign against the shipping routes and port facilities of Murmansk, while the Russians responded to this threat by bolstering their flak and fighter defenses.

The west coast of Norway from Oslo to the North Cape, and the Finnish-Norwegian Polar Sea coast from the North Cape, through Murmansk, to the White Sea, made up the area of operations of *Jagdgeschwader 5*, which was created from elements of JG 77 and *Zerstörergeschwader 76* at the beginning of 1942. The new unit had to learn a great deal about flying in the difficult weather conditions encountered in the far north and maintaining highly sophisticated engines in severe cold and primitive conditions. From November until the end of January the sun never rose above the horizon at Christmastime there were just four hours of twilight each day, while in June and July the sun never sank below the horizon day or night. From 1941 until the end of 1943 most of the unit's air battles were fought far out over the Polar Sea or 80 to 100 kilometers beyond the front over Soviet territory. This resulted in high stress levels for the pilots, especially those of single-engine fighters.

Like most other *Geschwader*, JG 5 was never completely unified. Individual *Gruppen* were stationed on the west coast of Norway as well as in Finland, Karelia, and even on the Leningrad and Nevel fronts, and later in the Defense of the Reich. It was therefore not easy to present a chronological sequence of events, and out of necessity, several *Gruppen* had to be dealt with individually. In the first fifty pages the reader will find almost nothing about the Polar Sea Front. The period of the "Polar Sea Hunters" does not begin until the third chapter, the actual heart of the history.

A *Geschwader* history written thirty years after the war can never be complete, for most of the records are missing. The author nevertheless hopes to have created a relatively well-rounded picture of the actions involving the Polar Sea *Geschwader*. It is a picture that could perhaps be drawn somewhat more finely through further suggestions and additions.

I wish to thank the *Traditionsgemeinschaft "Eismeerjäger"*, Rudolf Lüder, who unfortunately died much too soon, Erich Mikat, H.H. Schmidt, Herbert Treppe and the many other members of the *Geschwader* who contributed materials that formed the foundation of this unit history. I would also like to thank Motorbuch Verlag of Stuttgart and Herr Wolfgang Schilling, who made publication of the "*Eismeerjäger*" book possible.

Werner Girbig
Frankfurt/Main, summer 1974

Chapter 1
Background History

On the West Coast of Norway

No history of *Jagdgeschwader 5* would be complete if it did not make mention of the other Luftwaffe units with which JG 5 was closely linked. There was the *I. Gruppe* of JG 77, from which the Polar Sea *Geschwader* arose, as well as IV./JG 4 and III./JG 6, both of which were created from elements of JG 5 after the costly Defense of the Reich period.

Jagdgeschwader 5, which was created in early 1942, had its origins in the German occupation of Denmark and Norway in April 1940, which resulted in fighter and *Zerstörer* units being sent north. At that time the only pure fighter unit in Denmark was II./JG 77 under *Major* Hentschel. The *Gruppe*'s adjutant was *Leutnant* Carganico, who was later transferred to the newly-formed I./JG 77 as a *Staffelkapitän*.

All German aviation units were attached to *Luftflotte 5*, which had been created in Oslo in April. Its first commander, *Generaloberst* Milch, was replaced by *Generaloberst* Stumpff in May 1940. After the last enemy troops had left Norway in June, essentially ending combat operations in the country, the air fleet began developing the existing airfields and laying down new bases undisturbed. This expansion was mainly to prevent British encroachments in Scandinavia and the Baltic but also to improve the *Luftwaffe*'s position for attacks against Great Britain. Today, however, we know that the German command was already involved in preparations for an attack on the Soviet Union, and *Luftflotte 5* ultimately assumed responsibility for defending the German buildup in northern Norway and northern Finland. Because defending Norway's western coast was an absolute necessity, the *Luftwaffe* in the north was forced to fight in two directions at once, as the following narrative will show. And that is the reason why part of the *Geschwader* remained in Norway while the rest of the units found themselves on the Polar Sea.

At the turn of the year 1940-41 a decision was made to establish a new *Jagdgruppe*, which in the coming spring would be stationed in the Stavanger area under commanding officer *Hauptmann* Walter Grommes of Cologne.

Operationally, the *Gruppe* was initially attached to the *Zerstörergeschwader* ZG 76 under *Major* Grabmann and consisted of four *Staffeln*:

1./JG 77	*Oblt.* Carganico in Stavanger
2./JG 77	*Hptm.* Von Wehren in Lister
3./JG 77	*Lt.* Menzel in Herdla
4./JG 77	*Lt.* Senoner in Stavanger

I./JG 77's flight personnel came from a variety of Luftwaffe units and, in addition to Carganico and *Oberleutnant* Wienhusen, included a number of others who would become successful fighter pilots and distinguish themselves while serving in *Jagdgeschwader* 5. Among them were *Oberfeldwebel* Dahmer, *Leutnant* Glöckner, *Leutnant* Jakobi, and *Leutnant* Widowitz. Carganico already had six victories to his credit when he took over the *1. Staffel* while Dahmer, who was transferred to Norway from JG 26, had shot down twelve enemy aircraft in the west.

Formation of the *Gruppe* was deemed completed in May 1941 and the unit registered its first victory on 24 May, when a British reconnaissance aircraft was shot down. Incidentally it was also the same day on which the mighty British battle cruiser *Hood* was sunk off Iceland by the German battleship *Bismarck*, which suffered a similar fate itself a few days later.

In the beginning there was little activity in Norway, as the real war was being fought much farther south. Crete was on the verge of falling after fierce and costly fighting and all attention was focused on the Mediterranean. Among the fighter units engaged there was II./JG 77, which had been transferred to Greece.

Actions in Norway were confined to interceptions of small British formations or lone aircraft. During one such action on 15 June Rudi Glöckner shot down his first enemy aircraft, a Bristol Blenheim. One week later Germany attacked the Soviet Union. By then I./JG 77 had lost three pilots. The first to fall was *Unteroffizier* Kind of the *2. Staffel*, who was shot down in an engagement with four Blenheim bombers over the sea west of Lister. *Oblt.* Reinicke, a pilot transferred from ZG 76 to the *2. Staffel*, was posted missing on 24 April, while *Leutnant* Meissel, who had only joined I./JG 77 in March, was killed when his aircraft crashed into the sea during a transfer flight from Stavanger-Sola to Lister.

There was a reshuffling of the fighter units in June, prior to the invasion of the Soviet Union. *Jagdgruppe Stavanger* under *Major* Seegert was created from 2./JG 77 and a newly-formed 3./JG 77 (Oblt. Wienhusen), plus the new 13./JG 77 (Lt. Senoner), formed in part from elements of the *4. Staffel*. Simultaneously, a new *IV. Gruppe* was supposed to be established. Initially designated *Jagdstaffel*

Kirkenes, it was short-lived. The unit combined the *1.* and *14. Staffel* (the old 3./ JG 77) and the *Zerstörerstaffel*, which was renamed 1.(Z)/JG 77. The *Jagdgruppe z.b.V.* (Special Purpose Fighter Group) had been formed in Petsamo in autumn 1940 and now added to it were the remaining elements of *Hauptmann* Schäfer's *4. Staffel*. The *13. Staffel* also went to the northern front, where it was merged with the *14. Staffel*. The *Jagdgruppe z.b.V.* later became II./JG 5, while the *Zerstörer* unit, renamed 10.(Z)/JG 5, continued to operate as an independent unit.

In order to avoid confusion, we will continue to follow the activities of the units in southern Norway. Their bases remained the same as before the reorganization and would not change until the summer of 1943. But that was a long way off.

The *3. Staffel* suffered its first casualty at the end of June 1941, an accident in which *Leutnant* Rudolf Leow tragically lost his life. On the afternoon of the 24th Leow, an *Oberfähnrich* (officer candidate), was advised by the *Staffelkapitän* that he had been promoted to *Leutnant*. That same evening, during a scramble at Herdla at 21:50 hours, his Bf 109T veered off the north-south runway, crashed and burned. Leow died in the flames.

The aircraft on strength with the elements of JG 77 based in Norway still included a number of Messerschmitt Bf 109T fighters. Built in small numbers by Fieseler, the Bf 109T was a modified version of the *Emil,* which differed from the original in having a landing hook beneath the rear fuselage and an extended wingspan. It had been designed for use on the *Graf Zeppelin*, Germany's first aircraft carrier. When completion of the carrier was delayed indefinitely, the landing hooks were removed and the Bf 109Ts (T = *Trägerflugzeug*, or carrier aircraft) were issued to fighter units on the Reich's North Sea coast or in occupied areas in the north. They served for a long time until they were gradually replaced by the standard Bf 109E, F or Fw 190 types.

Again in July there was no obvious focal point on the west coast apart from the Stavanger area. That is where most *Luftwaffe* units were based and it continued to be the favored target area for the English. The fighter pilots scored steadily, but they also suffered a number of painful losses, including two on 2 July. At about 16:10 a pair of fighters from 13./JG 77, flown by *Unteroffizier* Döpfer and *Unteroffizier* Scheimann, took off over the sea to search for reported enemy aircraft. The air defense corps lost contact with the two Messerschmitt in grid square 5947, and not long afterwards another pair of fighters took off to search for them. The search was fruitless and the two aircraft returned to base. On 9 July Döpfer's body washed up on the shore of Sola Bay, however Scheimann was never found. How the two pilots came to be lost remains a mystery.

On 24 July there was another scramble to intercept several enemy aircraft detected by the air warning service over the sea. It was just four in the morning when *Leutnant* Werner Minz and his wingman *Unteroffizier* Schramm took off and set course for the reported intruders. Approximately ten kilometers southeast of Farsund, Schramm reported that *Leutnant* Minz's "Black 8" had just shot down an enemy machine and that he had subsequently lost sight of him. A search was immediately begun, but once again it was unsuccessful. The only indication that an aircraft had crashed into the sea was a huge oil slick approximately where Minz was last seen. Norwegian fisherman later pulled the oil tank of a Bf 109 from the waves, leaving no doubt that *Leutnant* Minz must have met his death there.

There was a dramatic air battle in the early afternoon of 6 August after air defense personnel in Stavanger-Sola detected a lone Lockheed Hudson heading towards the mainland at an altitude of 1300 meters at 13:58 hours. Five minutes later 13./JG 77 scrambled its alert *Rotte*. *Leutnant* Senoner and *Leutnant* Jakobi initially flew towards the specified grid square but failed to locate the enemy aircraft. Suddenly flak bursts appeared in the sky to the north and the two pilots turned towards them. They sighted the enemy aircraft at 14:13. *Leutnant* Senoner immediately attacked from behind but had to break away as he was too close. Jakobi, too, only managed to get off a few rounds. By that time the *Rottenführer* had set himself up for another pass. The Hudson took violent evasive action and tried to reach the clouds, while its gunner scored several hits on the pursuing Messerschmitts.

One burst struck Senoner's cockpit, wounding him in the eye and forcing him to leave the fight. Meanwhile Jakobi clung to the tail of the enemy machine and chased it through a cloud, only then opening fire. The Hudson's starboard engine immediately caught fire. The British bomber's undercarriage came down and it dropped a wing but immediately leveled out again. Bright flames suddenly enveloped the entire aircraft and seconds later it dove vertically into the sea, its port wing, which had been blown off by an exploding fuel tank, spiraling down after it.

Only then did Jakobi have time to worry about his flight leader, whose freedom of movement had been hampered by his injuries. He joined up with Senoner and guided him back to the airfield. After landing, Senoner climbed from the cockpit, his face covered in blood. It turned out that a small splinter had entered his eye.

Leutnant Jakobi scored a second victory five days later, also over the sea. Once again, at about noon on 11 August, radar had detected a lone English aircraft in the Stavanger area heading towards the coast. Jakobi took off with *Unteroffizier* Scharf and shortly before 13:00 they spotted a Bristol Blenheim flying at about 1000 meters. The bomber's crew obviously saw the Messerschmitts as it immediately turned away towards the north. The two Messerschmitts turned after it and slowly closed in from behind. After a few minutes they were in firing position. There was no return fire from the Blenheim and, when the *Leutnant* opened fire on its port engine, there was still no reaction. The first burst set the engine alight, but the Blenheim flew on in a slightly nose-down attitude, turning gently and trailing a plume of black smoke before suddenly rolling onto its back and diving vertically into the sea. Jakobi's victory, which took place about 15 kilometers southwest of Stavanger, had required just 60 rounds from his two machine-guns.

Aerial activity over the west coast remained limited until the end of the year, however September brought another high point. Sentenced to inactivity, the fighter pilots had not seen an enemy formation for some time. The endless waiting on the ground was a strain on the nerves, and hopes of exchanging fire with the enemy were almost exhausted. The pilots did little flying and used every scramble, every maintenance test flight every circuit to maintain their operational readiness. Then finally, after weeks of waiting, they finally got the opportunity to strike a blow.

Monday, 8 September 1941, was a special date in the history of the German fighter arm, for on that day the first two Boeing B-17 four-engined heavy bombers in European airspace, American aircraft operated by the Royal Air Force, were shot down. *Leutnant* Jakobi was able to lay claim to having shot down the first Flying Fortress.

At about noon, air defense radar detected an enemy formation, reportedly consisting of three bombers and two Defiant fighters, approaching the west coast of Norway at high altitude. I./JG 77 in Stavanger was immediately advised, whereupon a *Schwarm* was ordered to scramble. As their Bf 109T fighters raced down the runway, none of the pilots, who had previously encountered mainly Blenheim and Wellington bombers and occasionally a Hampden, knew exactly what types made up the enemy formation.

Before they arrived in the assigned loitering area the fighter pilots saw condensation trails above them moving west to east. They were themselves flying on a southerly heading but immediately turned towards the enemy. The aircraft continued climbing until they finally reached the altitude of the enemy aircraft, 8600 meters. Jakobi spotted a black dot against the hazy horizon. After twelve minutes at full throttle he finally closed to within 400 meters. The dot had by then turned into a four-engined Boeing, with which the pilots were familiar from intelligence briefings but which they had not yet encountered in action.

The Boeing Fortress I (B-17C), twenty examples of which had been delivered to the RAF, flew its first sorties in Europe in July 1941. The American bombers were used – with little success – as high-altitude bombers, attacking Wilhelmshaven, Rotterdam and Brest. Now the Fortress had also become a reality on the northern front and *Leutnant* Jakobi was the first German fighter pilot to have an opportunity to study this Boeing close up. He had very little time to do so, however, for the English gunners opened fire from their ventral and dorsal gun positions. The *Leutnant* could see the red muzzle flashes quite clearly. He immediately opened fire with all guns and, because of his greater speed, found himself sitting right beside the enemy bomber. From there he could see a large hole in its fuselage and flames licking from the top of its rudder. He then broke away to set up for another firing pass, but just before he did he noticed a thin smoke trail suddenly emanating from the bomber's port outboard engine.

The heavy bomber turned to the left but by then Jakobi was again on its tail. Then he saw the British aircraft jettison six to eight bombs, but the enemy hadn't given up yet. The tail gunner scored hits on the Bf 109's starboard wing. Undeterred, Jakobi attacked again. He scored more hits and saw that a fire had broken out between the two port engines. Pieces flew off and smoke came from the cockpit area. A few seconds later the Boeing's nose dropped and it went down in a steep spiral.

Jakobi radioed a warning to his wingman, who was still following the enemy aircraft: "Careful, it's about to explode!"

The Fortress then went into a steep dive, and 2000 meters below them turned into a fireball. Location of the shoot-down: grid square 7949. The two Defiants observed by the fighter pilots throughout the entire action kept their distance and did nothing to interfere with the attacks on the Boeing. It is unlikely, however, that the two fighters were in fact British, as the RAF had no fighters with the radius of action to reach Norway at that time. The aircraft seen by *Leutnant* Steinicke were probably another pair of Bf 109s.

After landing there was of course a big celebration, especially as another B-17 had been shot down by *Unteroffizier* Woite.* (*According to British records, none of the three Fortresses that took part in the raid on Oslo returned. The serials of the aircraft were AN525, AN533 and AN535, all of No.90 Squadron RAF.).

On 17 September I./JG 77 received the following telex from the Commanding General and commanding officer of *Luftgau Norwegen*, *Generalleutnant* Harmjanz:

> "On 8/9/1941 *Leutnant* Jakobi shot down a Boeing 75 km north of Kristiansand and *Unteroffizier* Woite another 50 km southwest of Stavanger. To these men I wish to express my congratulations and sincerest best wishes."

A few days after the action a special team from the RLM arrived to recover the wreckage of the Boeing that went down near Kristiansand and return it to Germany.

The year 1941 slowly came to an end without any further noteworthy actions. There were a few harassment flights resulting in scrambles, and also several victories, but fortunately no further casualties. Things did not pick up again until the end of December, when the RAF carried out several attacks against German airfields in Norway, all of which were connected with the commando operations against the island of Vaasgö and the Lofotens. The airfield on the island of Herdla was also not spared, and the British probably overlooked the Freya air defense radar stationed there. On 27 December Herdla airfield, which was home to 1.(Z)/JG 77 under *Leutnant* Brandis and *Oberleutnant* Wienhusen's 3./JG 77, was attacked by low-flying Blenheim bombers. Casualties among the non-flying personnel were particularly heavy. The raised command post building and the aircraft hangars, which were camouflaged as farm houses, all sustained damage, while the workshop truck parked at the edge of the airfield was riddled by enemy machine-gun fire. The *Staffel* managed to scramble a number of fighters, which attacked the bombers, and the battle extended far out to sea. As far as is known the Messerschmitts returned without loss. *Feldwebel* Kalweit claimed to have shot down a Blenheim, while *Oberfähnrich* Habermann destroyed another for his second victory.

After 13./JG 77 followed the *Jagdgruppe z.b.V.* to the Polar Sea Front, in January 1942 the *Jagdgruppe Stavanger* was disbanded in order to become the *I. Gruppe* of *Jagdgeschwader 5* during the latter's formation. As a result, 2. and 3./JG 77 became 2. and 3./JG 5. At the same time IV./JG 1 moved from Brest to the north, where its *10. Staffel* was renamed 1./JG 5, while 11. and 12./JG 1 were readied for the expansion of III./JG 5.

As the new *I. Gruppe* of JG 5 initially remained on the west coast and was physically separated from the *Geschwader* for the entire war, it seems appropriate to devote a separate chapter to this *Gruppe*'s history.

Buildup in Northern Finland

Even before German forces occupied the Channel Coast, conquered the Balkans, and fought in North Africa, the German government had decided to enter into a conflict with Stalin. The Soviet Union was the real enemy, not England, and, in the euphoria after the victories in the west, no one was prepared to acknowledge its military strength, determination, and will to resist. The first winter in Russia would show, however, just how severely the German leadership had underestimated the other side this time.

During the extensive studies and preparations for the attack in the east, the German planners of course did not lose sight of the fact that the northern theater would be of significance to the Soviet Union, as it was the country's path to the Atlantic Ocean and also a northern sea route to the Pacific. The ports on the White Sea and the Barents Sea represented important strategic bases. From the beginning, therefore, the ports of Murmansk and Arkhangelsk, which remained ice free in normal winters thanks to the Gulf Stream, would be the focus of operations on the northern front.

In January 1941 Germany approached Finland, seeking permission for German forces to be allowed to mass in Finnish territory in preparation for an attack on the northwestern Soviet Union. Finland initially expressed reluctance, but in May meetings between the Finnish general staff and Jodl, head of the *Wehrmacht* Operations Staff, and Halder, Chief-of-Staff of the Army, produced positive results. The 2nd and 3rd Mountain Divisions would be permitted to mass on the north Finnish border to "defend the Polar region." Command Center Finland was established in Rovaniemi under *General* von Falkenhorst, whose units included the III Finnish Army Corps. The target of the buildup: to take the starting point of the Murmansk railway and the ice-free port of Murmansk. Air support for the land forces would be provided by the Finnish Air Force and *Luftflotte 5*. On the other side, ready to frustrate these plans, was the Soviet 14th Army under Lieutenant-General Frolov, stationed between the Barents Sea and Kandalaksha.

As previously stated, 1./JG 77 left Norway and at the end of May 1941 moved to Kirkenes. This airfield, and later the base in Petsamo, had to be completely rebuilt for the coming *Luftwaffe* operations, and the men of the air force construction companies did outstanding work. Despite the lack of suitable construction machinery, they were able to level the ground, lay down runways and build quarters with astonishing ability to improvise, gradually turning Kirkenes into one of *Luftflotte 5*'s most important bases of operation.

When the *Staffel* arrived, Kirkenes was anything but the important base it would later become. "Back when I was first ordered here", Carganico once said, "I would have preferred a posting back to the Channel, where in my opinion proper operations awaited me. Instead I was sent to this miserable place!" Just a few months later, after he had become the most successful fighter pilot in the north, Carganico revised his statement, stressing that one should never resist fate.

For the fighter unit, which ultimately consisted of 1., 4., and 14./JG 77 and the former 2./ZG 76, now 1.(Z)/JG 77, the Russian Campaign did not begin until six days after the successful attack on 22 June 1941, as Kirkenes was shrouded in dense fog. Then, however, *Oberleutnant* Carganico and *Oberfeldwebel* Dahmer took off on a fog-free afternoon to carry out the first combat sortie in the far north. They strafed a lighthouse on the Fischer Peninsula and then returned to Kirkenes without incident. The second mission, this time in *Staffel* strength, was directed against a Russian airfield discovered near Ura-Guba, which was attacked following evaluation of prewar aerial photographs. The pair of Carganico and Dahmer would often fly together over Russian territory. They went looking for enemy aircraft, which they then had to lure away from their airfield. And so they circled provocatively over the enemy bases until 15 to 20 enemy fighters were in the air. The pair returned with victories almost every time. During one such mission the pair brought down three Ratas which crashed on the Russian airfield right in front of the control tower.

When the *Wehrmacht* attacked the Soviet Union that summer the German and Finnish units of the Lapland Army under *General* von Falkenhorst manned the front in northern Finland. At the same time the Lapland Army was designated the *20. Gebirgs-Armee* (20th Mountain Army). From the beginning, it was this army's purpose and objective to take Murmansk and pinch off the Murmansk railway. Strategically important and almost 1500 km long, it had originally been called the Kirov Railway and had been built at great cost by German and Austrian POWs during the First World War. It soon became apparent, however, that the forces assigned to the northern theater were much too weak. The overall situation was made more difficult by the unfamiliar conditions, the trackless Karelian Forest, and the equally barren tundra. The attack bogged down at the Lisa River, the area before Murmansk and the Louhi River line, and in some places the situation became critical on account of Soviet counterattacks. As a result of all of this, by September 1941 the operations conducted by the 20th Mountain Army had turned into positional warfare.

At the same time the Russians did everything they could to interdict German supply ship traffic around the North Cape to Petsamo. If the ships succeeded in evading the numerous submarines and minefields off the North Cape, prior to sailing into Petsamo Bay at the latest they came under attack from coastal batteries in the area of the Fischer Peninsula, or were attacked by torpedo boats and fighter-bombers. More than a few German ships were lost in this way. The situation forced the Germans to send most of their supplies for the northern front through the Baltic Sea to Kremi in Finland, from where they were sent up the so-called "Polar Sea Road" via Rovaniemi, Vuotso and Ivalo, a much more time-consuming route.

After the capture of Petsamo, Carganico's *Staffel* moved there. At about the same time *Luftflotte 5* was making preparations to establish a new *Jagdgruppe*, IV./JG 77, for the Norway area and, at his own request, *Hauptmann* von Lojewski was sent to Kirkenes. He arrived there on 25 June and initially took over the *14. Staffel*, which essentially consisted of the old 3./JG 77. His initial impressions in the north reflected the situation of those days: "I found a small group of comrades and a few barely serviceable aircraft. On closer examination, in Kirkenes one could make out the outline of a Bf 109 *Staffel* and another of Bf 110s. Through the daily arrivals of pilots and ground personnel, as well as machines and other equipment, a fighter *Gruppe* was supposed to be created from this and the *Staffel* already established in Petsamo under Carganico. I had little time to concern myself with the organizational buildup of the *Gruppe* and its operational readiness – we had to put everything we had into the air. The Russian war had been going on for three days, and we lived in the belief that the war must and would be over in a matter of days, three weeks at the most, and the employment of every even relatively serviceable aircraft was necessary to ensure a successful outcome."

Unfortunately *Hauptmann* von Lojewski was unable to complete his mission in Kirkenes, as he failed to return from a combat mission on 29 June 1941, just three days after his arrival. An evening mission over Kola Bay was scheduled. All went well until the fighters reached the Murmansk area and, then, north of the city, anti-aircraft fire suddenly blanketed the Messerschmitts. The *Hauptmann*'s "Red 4" was riddled but the pilot escaped injury. He immediately jettisoned his canopy as the aircraft was at very low altitude. Somehow von Lojewski brought his aircraft down safely and bailed out unhurt, but he waited in vain for his *Gruppe* to mount a rescue. Or did they think a rescue hopeless? In any case the *Hauptmann* had abandoned his blazing aircraft just above the ground; consequently his comrades had failed to see a parachute. Several days earlier, during a pilot briefing at the base, all the precautions for a forced landing had been discussed and they were told that air-sea rescue aircraft were on standby for such an occurrence.

After twenty-four hours, when no search aircraft appeared over the crash site, von Lojewski made preparations to walk toward the west. Three days later the *Hauptmann*, completely exhausted, came upon some fishermen. At first they welcomed him warmly but in the end they turned him over to Russian soldiers. *Hauptmann* von Lojewski thus became the first German fighter pilot to be captured by the Soviet in the Polar Sea region.

To the fighter pilots sent there, the air war in the north was something completely new and it was inevitable that the experience they had to gain would come at the cost of painful losses. As the sun never reached the horizon during the high summer, the pilots and ground personnel were in action 24 hours a day. As well there were the monotone expanses of the land and its primitive conditions, which had an effect on the mental well-being of the men. Not to be forgotten was the great mental strain imposed on the pilots by flights over the sea or unfamiliar Russian territory in single-engine machines.

In that first Polar summer 1. and 13./JG 77 and the *Zerstörerstaffel* bore the brunt of aerial combat in the northern sector, with their main role being to provide fighter escort for *Stuka-Geschwader 5* during operations over the front and Murmansk. At that time the Ju 87s of I./StG 5 were based in Kirkenes, the Ju 88s of KG 30 in Banak, a tactical reconnaissance flight with Henschel Hs 126s and Focke-Wulf Fw 189s and a long-range reconnaissance flight in Rovaniemi, and the Hs 126s of I.(H)/32 in Alakurtti.

On 5 July *Feldwebel* Hauser was posted missing after he was forced to ditch in the southwest corner of Lake Titovka during a mission by the *14. Staffel*, probably having fallen victim to anti-aircraft fire. The *Staffel* suffered another casualty in an attack on Ura-Guba airfield on 23 August, when *Leutnant* Mahlkuch was shot down by a Russian fighter east of the airfield. Mahlkuch was a successful fighter pilot with 16 victories to his credit. His fate remains uncertain to this day. The enemy was certainly not to be underestimated and it is remarkable that the Soviet fighter pilots, who displayed a lack of skill in the early days and suffered heavy losses, quickly caught up in terms of piloting ability and tactics. On 24 June 1941 the fighter squadron under Lieutenant Safonov claimed the first German aircraft shot down over the northern front.

Meanwhile *Leutnant* Dahmer and his *Schwarm* moved to Kemijärvi, from where it was to operate as an independent unit, providing fighter escort for Stukas attacking the Murmansk railway and attacking Russian forest positions. It developed the so-called "*Sauhaufen* tactic" in which its aircraft made repeated individual attacks from high above against Russian bomber formations and thus scored one victory after another [*Sauhaufen* = "bunch of slobs"]. On 1 August 1941, after his 25th victory, Dahmer became the first "*Eismeerjäger*" to be awarded the Knight's Cross, which he received from the hand of air fleet chief *Generaloberst* Stumpff. There remains one unusual incident to relate from that high summer in Alakurtti. One day the aircraft of Dahmer's *Schwarm* were lined up neatly one beside the other and the mechanics were putting the finishing touches on preparations for the next mission. The pilots were already sitting in their cockpits, when suddenly the light anti-aircraft guns began firing. Streams of tracer were being directed towards the nearby forest edge – and then Russian troops left the cover of the trees and began storming the airfield. As the aircraft with their pilots and ground crews were sitting on the airfield with no cover, presenting prime targets, there was only one choice. The mechanics lifted the tails of the Bf 109s and turned the aircraft to face the enemy, whereupon the pilots opened fire. The failure of the enemy's surprise attack was in no small part due to the unusual defensive measures taken by Dahmer's four Messerschmitts.

In July the German advance toward Murmansk made good progress but then bogged down. A second attack in the direction of the port city was launched at the beginning of September, but it also failed after ten days due to resistance from the Soviet 14th Army. Almost all of the aerial combat on the northern front took place over Soviet territory east of the Kola, as enemy fighters rarely crossed the front lines in the early days. The fighter *Staffeln* on the Polar Sea front were very successful, however. In the first three months of operations, 1./JG 77 scored more than 100 victories. On 25 September 1941 its *Staffelkapitän Oberleutnant* Carganico shot down his 27th enemy aircraft and became the second pilot in the north to receive the Knight's Cross. During this period the *Staffel* lost just one pilot. On 22 August *Unteroffizier* Kastens failed to return from a mission against the Murmansk railway in the Taibola area. Three days later *Unteroffizier* Lehmann's machine was shot up by enemy fighters and he was forced to ditch, sustaining arm and head injuries. 14./JG 77 suffered another casualty on the last day of August, when *Gefreiter* Hans Kobold was killed in a failed ditching attempt off Petsamo.

Meanwhile the English had begun trying to send supplies to their new ally by sea. In August the first convoys sailed for Murmansk, however they only enjoyed air cover for the first part of their voyage. The rest of the way around northern Norway to Murmansk they were unescorted. As they were within range of the German bomber, fighter and *Zerstörer* units based between Tromsö and Petsamo, the English decided to prove their ships in that sector with fighter cover. On 12 September 1941 24 Hawker Hurricanes of 81 and 134 Squadrons, Royal Air Force, took off from the aircraft carrier *Argus*, which had been ordered into the Barents Sea. The British fighters landed at the airfield in Vayenga, located northeast of Murmansk. These aircraft were later handed over to the Soviet air force.

That same day the British-flown Hurricanes of No.81 Squadron flew their first sortie over the front and encountered five Messerschmitts flying escort for an Hs 126 reconnaissance aircraft. The Hurricanes and the surprised Messerschmitts fought an engagement about ten kilometers east of Lisa Bay in which three of the German fighters were shot down. *Leutnant* von der Lühe was killed in the action. Unfortunately it is not known who shot down one of the Hurricanes, for the British reported the loss of Sgt.-Pilot Smith. He would be the only fatal casualty suffered by No.81 Squadron before it handed its Hurricanes over to the Russians.

The appearance of the British pilots and their Hurricanes on the northern front resulted in a change in the pattern of aerial activity there. And the appearance there of new types of aircraft sent to the Russians by their western allies was additional proof of the importance the Russians and their western allies placed on the defense of the city and port of Murmansk.

In an effort to rationalize operations, in September 1941 the German fighter units on the northern front were combined into the *Jagdgruppe z.b.V.* under the command of *Major* Hennig Strümpell with its headquarters unit in Kirkenes.

In November 1941 *Hauptmann* Schäfer's 4./JG 77 came from the west coast to Alakurtti, while Carganico and the *1. Staffel* were transferred to Norway. It would not return to Petsamo until after the formation of JG 5 as 6./JG 5. Finally 13./JG 77 also arrived in the north and was assigned to the *14. Staffel*, which was now under the command of *Oberleutnant* Menzel. In October the *Gruppenstab* moved to a Kemijärvi, then in December to Alakurtti, where 4./JG 77 was already stationed. Like the Stuka units, at the end of October 1941 the *Zerstörerstaffel* moved to Rovaniemi for the dark winter months. Only the *14. Staffel* remained in Petsamo, becoming the first aviation unit to spend the winter 600 kilometers north of the Arctic Circle. The Menzel *Staffel*'s experiences could themselves fill a book. It experimented with that classic winter activity, namely dropping bombs from the Bf 109. *Leutnant* Friedrich Dahn (who had come from heavy fighters), called "Felix" because he wanted to bomb the *Politruk* Building in Murmansk, was reported missing in action. He had 26 victories to his credit when he failed to return [*Politruk* = political commissar attached to military unit].

There is little to say about the actions during the final weeks of the year, as there were no more large-scale operations until the formation of *Jagdgeschwader 5*. At the end of the year *Leutnant* Dahmer returned to the Western Front, where he joined JG 2. The *Jagdgruppe* continued to score on almost every mission but also suffered a number of casualties.

On 17 September *Feldwebel* Stiglmair failed to return from a sortie southeast of Zapad Lisa after he was shot down by Russian fighters about 20 kilometers from Alakurtti. It was the *1. Staffel*'s final casualty before it moved to Norway. 14./JG 77 lost one of its pilots in tragic fashion. On 5 October *Unteroffizier* Keller was on a transfer flight in his aircraft "Red 7". He encountered icing conditions, which resulted in a fatal crash. Finally, on 29 October *Unteroffizier* Erich Kersten was lost. That day observers reported three Russian aircraft approaching, whereupon the alert *Rotte* of *Oberfeldwebel* Hornig and *Unteroffizier* Kersten was scrambled. About ten minutes later Kersten shot down an I-153 but then he encountered heavy Russian anti-aircraft fire. Hornig saw Kersten's "Yellow 17" suddenly go into a vertical dive from a height of no more than 400 meters and crash not far from Louhi.

At first things were also far from rosy on the enemy side. One well-known Soviet pilot, who was then deployed in the Murmansk sector, was Sergey Kursenkov. In his autobiography, which was released in East Germany in 1964, the Russian fighter pilot admitted that his initial experiences on the northern front had been anything but promising. One day, sometime near the end of 1941, Russian lookouts reported that a group of Messerschmitts had overflown the front in the Simnaya Motovka area. A flight of three fighters from Kursenkov's

3rd Squadron subsequently took off to intercept. The fighters climbed away and disappeared beyond the mountains. After several hours, when the three fighters failed to return, the regiment initiated a search in which Kursenkov took part. He had this to say: "Beneath us the frozen, snow-covered lakes shone like mirrors. The mountain peaks in the distance resembled sugar loaves. In places the slopes were covered with pines, their wide-sweeping boughs wearing white caps. We spotted three of our fighter aircraft on a gentle slope. They looked like they had been stuck there. Simonenko's aircraft was near the peak, a second was on the slope and the third was at the base of the mountain. We turned and went as low as we dared. Their cockpits were closed. Apart from three deep trenches caused when the aircraft landed, there were no tracks. A special team was sent to the landing site. It returned several days later. The aircraft had been shot down by fascist fighters, the pilots were no longer alive."

For the German fighter pilots, the turn of the year 1941-42 marked the beginning of a new chapter in the air war on the Polar Sea front. Until then the *Staffeln* of JG 77 had been extraordinarily successful, and Carganico, Dahmer, Mahlkuch, and Salwender were just some of the pilots who had contributed to this success. It should also be mentioned that German losses had so far been quite light: between April and the end of 1941, the elements of JG 77 deployed in the north had lost a total of 20 pilots, of whom one was captured and seven reported missing. As we will see, this victory-loss ratio would change as the German fighter pilots had to deal with an enemy whose strength grew steadily.

Chapter 2
I./JG 5

From Stavanger to Targsorul

The new *Jagdgeschwader 5* was formed on 25 January 1942 under the command of *Oberstleutnant* Handrick. At that time the *Geschwaderstab* was in Petsamo. Under *Major* Seegert, I./JG 5 was created from the former *Jagdgruppe Stavanger* on the Norwegian west coast. Operationally nothing changed, for as *I. Gruppe* of JG 5 the unit's mission continued to be to defend German shipping along the Norwegian coast against attacks by British aircraft. For this reason the fighter pilots were presented few opportunities to engage in aerial combat, while the poor weather conditions in the north, the long flights over water, and the relatively small airfields tested the skills of the pilots attached to the *Staffeln* stationed there. The three *Staffeln*, now equipped with the Messerschmitt Bf 109 F-4, still operated from bases in Trondheim, Herdla, Kristiansand, Lister, Mandal, and Stavanger.

In terms of the aerial situation, his mission, and subordination, the Commander of Fighters in Norway (*Jagdfliegerführer Norwegen*) faced the following scenario: the RAF's activities consisted mainly of regular reconnaissance flights over the waters off the entire coast of Norway to monitor German convoys. The presence of German battleships (e.g. the *Tirpitz* in Trondheim Fiord) and heavy cruisers in Norwegian waters were a thorn in the side of the English, as they saw them as a direct threat to their Murmansk convoys. For this reason they concentrated their reconnaissance efforts on those areas they suspected of harboring German warships. While Sunderland flying boats regularly patrolled the area of North Cape-the Lofotens-Jan Meyen, high-flying Spitfire reconnaissance machines kept a watch on the southern and central coasts of Norway. The British also began mining the area of the Lofotens using aircraft and submarines to hamper German supply traffic by sea and restrict the freedom of action of the heavy German naval units.

Until now I./JG 5 had been solely responsible for defending the vast area from Oslo up to the North Cape. Depending on the situation, the *Gruppe* was only able to station single flights of four fighters (*Schwärme*) at its northern bases in Vaernes, Trondheim-Lade, and Örlandet on a temporary basis. Consequently, in reality the coast of Norway north of Trondheim remained undefended. Not until the *7. Staffel* under *Hauptmann* von Sponeck, part of the *III. Gruppe*, was moved to Bodö in January 1942, was an effort made to close this gap in the defenses of northern Norway.

On the day of its formation, I./JG 5's command positions were held by:

Gruppenkommandeur:	*Major* Seegert
Gruppenadjutant:	*Oblt*. Müller
Technical Officer:	*Oblt*. Hartwein
Signals Officer:	*Lt*. Laskovic
1. Staffel:	*Oblt*. Von Eichel-Streiber
2. Staffel:	*Hptm*. Büchel
3. Staffel:	*Hptm*. Wienhusen

Apart from isolated raids on German bases, until the beginning of May 1942 things stayed relatively quiet on the Norwegian front, and so routine missions alternated with required day-to-day activities. *Gefreiter* Reichard of the *3. Staffel* failed to return from an operational sortie on 30 March and thus became the *Gruppe*'s first fatal casualty after its renaming. The pilot attempted a ditching south of Bergen, but his aircraft sank so quickly that he was unable to escape the cockpit and drowned.

The *2. Staffel* recorded its first casualty on 7 April, when, following aerial combat, *Leutnant* Schumann was forced to go around while attempting to land at Lister. His aircraft stalled and he was killed in the ensuing crash. Seven days later, on 14 April, *Obergefreiter* Klesa of the *2. Staffel* and *Feldwebel* Drossel of the *3. Staffel* lost their lives while on a transfer flight. They were shot down by anti-aircraft fire from German vessels and crashed into the sea south of Bergen.

Also in April the *Gruppe* received a new commanding officer, *Hauptmann* von Wehren, who was wounded in a bombing raid on Stavanger-Sola on 15 May 1942. Then the 17th of May brought the first really big action. In the evening hours a British formation made up of 54 bombers approached the Norwegian coast in several waves. Their target was a northbound German fleet unit, which included the cruiser *Prinz Eugen*. The air observer teams reported 27 Bristol Beauforts, 13 Lockheed Hudsons, 8 Bristol Beaufighters and 6 Bristol Blenheims. The German fighter units were scrambled to intercept the intruders. Beginning at 19:30 hours, a fierce battle ensued west of Stavanger, in the course of which the defending fighters shot down a total of 18 enemy aircraft. It was a major defensive success for the *Gruppe*. The victories were shared as follows:

Fw. Beulig	1. *Staffel*	2 Beauforts
Uffz. Graupner	1. *Staffel*	1 Beaufort
Oblt. Hartwein	*Stab*	1 Hudson
		1 Beaufort
Uffz. Heinsdorf	1. *Staffel*	1 Beaufort
Uffz. Kaddatz	1. *Staffel*	1 Beaufort
Uffz. Käppler	2. *Staffel*	2 Beauforts
Uffz. Leitner	1. *Staffel*	2 Beauforts
Lt. Müller	3. *Staffel*	2 Beauforts
Ofw. Schinzel	1. *Staffel*	1 Beaufort
Lt. Schmidt	1. *Staffel*	2 Beauforts
Fw. Schütze	2. *Staffel*	2 Beauforts

Claims were made for five more bombers, however these were not confirmed by the *Gruppe* for lack of witnesses. The *Gruppe* suffered just a single casualty in return for these 18 victories: *Feldwebel* Josef Reitlinger was killed when his aircraft collided with an obstacle during the scramble from Stavanger.

On 26 May another English formation approached the Norwegian coast and, abeam Sola, attacked a *Kriegsmarine* convoy. I./JG intercepted and claimed two more victories. After this opening act quiet returned; it would last until spring 1943. In the summer of 1942 the *Gruppe* received new fighter aircraft, Fw 190s. There were additional casualties, however. *Unteroffizier* Bruns of the *1. Staffel* lost his life on 10 August 1942 when his Focke-Wulf crashed during a scramble from Örlandet, apparently because of pilot error.

On 25 September the *3. Staffel* recorded a rare success. *Unteroffizier* Erich Klein, one of the unit's more successful pilots, remembers this day very well: "We had flown our four Focke-Wulfs to Oslo to give the city, or rather the participants in the big Quisling rally, a feeling of greater security from air attack. The scene on the Oslo airfield was peaceful. None of us believed that we would meet the enemy there in the hinterland."

Approximately an hour after the *Schwarm* of German fighters had landed, radar detected four twin-engined aircraft in the Skagerrak area heading towards the Swedish coast. Not until it was determined with certainty that the bombers were in fact heading for Oslo did the pilots race to their Focke-Wulfs. There were no electric starter trolleys at Oslo and, to make matters worse, the onboard starters in two of the Fw 190s failed. Because of this only two of the fighter pilots got airborne: *Unteroffizier* Klein in his "Yellow 9" and *Unteroffizier* Fenten. Shortly after takeoff they spotted the four enemy aircraft, approximately 10 km south of Oslo, flying low on the right side of the fjord. At first the German pilots thought the enemy aircraft were Douglas Bostons, however they were much too fast for that. *Unteroffizier* Klein:

"We caught up with them right over the city center. My wingman fired at the trailing machine and I saw its starboard engine burst into flames. I opened fire on aircraft number three. Pieces flew from the center of its fuselage and black smoke began pouring from both engines. I broke away from the burning aircraft, which crashed and exploded while attempting a forced landing in the sea. I then got on the tail of another of the twin-engined machines. At low level I chased it out of the metropolitan area into the mountains. I was a raw beginner in aerial combat and so I tried to fly even lower than the enemy so that I could shoot at it from below as they had taught us in school. A more experienced pilot would probably have positioned himself a little higher and then pressed the firing buttons when a favorable opportunity presented itself. Trying to fly lower almost cost me my life.

"The pursuit led us towards a wooded mountain, where I saw my chance. I wanted to fire when the enemy reached the peak. I descended my 'Inka' a little lower and immediately felt a heavy blow in my left wing. Before me the Englishman made a tight turn to the left, vapor trails coming from his wingtips. I turned with him, but it was a pitiful attempt as I almost stalled over the damaged wing. My speed dropped sharply, making my continued pursuit of the twin-engined machine hopeless. A short time later I landed at Oslo and saw my mishap. I had clipped the top off a tall fir tree, making a big hole in the wing.

"On the evening of 25 September we heard an account of the attack on British radio. The crew of the aircraft whose starboard engine had been set alight by *Unteroffizier* Fenten managed to extinguish the flames and flew home on one engine. Not until later did we discover that my victim had been a Mosquito and not a Boston."* Since August the *Gruppe* had been fortunate with respect to casualties, not least because the enemy rarely showed himself. (*The four Mosquito high-speed bombers were from No.105 Squadron RAF. Their target on 25/9/42 was Gestapo headquarters in Oslo.).

In January 1943 *Unteroffizier* Neldner of the *3. Staffel* and *Unteroffizier* Friedmann of 1./JG 5 were lost in the Stavanger area. Friedmann had taken off on a weather reconnaissance sortie in "Black 12" and later flew into the ground while descending through cloud. On the first day of February *Unteroffizier* Sommeregger of the *1. Staffel* was fired on by friendly anti-aircraft guns during a combat sortie over the sea, suffering burns to his hands and face. On 3 February his *Staffel* comrade *Feldwebel* Gruber was posted missing. He had taken off with the *Staffel* at 18:32 to intercept an approaching enemy formation. Two days later *Feldwebel* von Podewils was forced to take to his parachute. After the *Gruppe* took off on an escort mission, over Stavanger Podewil's Focke-Wulf suddenly developed engine trouble. The pilot was ultimately forced to bale out, during which his left leg struck the tail, injuring his knee. On 8 March 3./JG 5 lost *Unteroffizier* Lieber during an escort mission southwest of Bergen. Lieber baled out after his engine failed, but unfortunately his parachute failed to open. At the end of the month, on the 23rd, *Obergefreiter* Ahlbrecht was injured in a forced landing following a combat over Haugesund.

One day earlier the *Gruppe* had received a high-ranking visitor, when *Generaloberst* Stumpff, the commander of *Luftflotte 5*, inspected the *Staffeln* in Norway. In the meantime *Hauptmann* von Wehren had turned the *I. Gruppe* over to *Hauptmann* Gerhard Wengel after being transferred to JG 3.

At the beginning of April 1943 the *Gruppe* reequipped on the new Messerschmitt Bf 109 G-2. Unfortunately the *2. Staffel* experienced two accidents during this period and two more pilots were lost. On 4 April *Feldwebel* Kaddatz took off from Stavanger on a maintenance test flight and crashed as a result of a propeller pitch problem. Then on 10 April *Feldwebel* Graupner was killed when his Bf 109 G-2 crashed about five kilometers south of Copenhagen-Vaerlöse airfield for reasons unknown. Both pilots were promising second-generation fighter pilots who had demonstrated their abilities in the big air battle on 17 May 1942.

In April there was an upswing in activity in the Norwegian coastal area. It began with an attack on a German convoy on the 12th. The *1. Staffel* was scrambled to intercept and claimed three victories. The successful pilots were *Unteroffizier* Rödig and *Leutnant* Schmidt, both of whom claimed a Handley-Page Hampden, and *Unteroffizier* Sommeregger, who shot down a Beaufighter.

The *1. Staffel* suffered a casualty on the last day of the month, when *Feldwebel* Schaub failed to return from a sortie. He was shot down and killed northeast of Aalesund. On 1 May 1943 the *Gruppe* claimed a total of twelve victories without loss when British aircraft attempted to attack another German convoy off the Norwegian coast. During the scramble from Herdla, one of the *1. Staffel*'s aircraft crashed and *Unteroffizier* Rudolf Rödig was killed. *Feldwebel* Walter Glatz was a witness to this tragic accident: "*Unteroffizier* Rödig was pushed off course and consequently lifted off too soon. One wing touched the ground and the Messerschmitt veered left and overturned in the sea. We recovered Rödig after about an hour, but all attempts to revive him were unsuccessful."

Two days later *Leutnant* Schütze of 2./JG 5 suffered a similar fate. Following an engine change, towards evening he took off on a maintenance test flight in his "Black 6", a Fw 190 A-3. Over Herdla at 2000 meters, for reasons unknown, his aircraft suddenly went into a vertical dive and then crashed straight into the sea. The same day *Oberfeldwebel* Schulte was injured when his Messerschmitt crashed while taking off from Stavanger as a result of being tail-heavy. When another of the *Gruppe*'s pilots lost his life in equally mysterious circumstances on 14 May, there was unrest among the men. There was much speculation as to what had happened and the men asked themselves if sabotage might have been behind the incidents. On that 14 May elements of the *Gruppe* took off on a typical escort mission. En route to the patrol area, for no apparent reason, the Bf 109 flown by *Unteroffizier* Koch of 3./JG 5 went into a shallow dive. The dive became ever steeper until the aircraft crashed into the sea and immediately sank with its pilot. Unfortunately, to this day it is not known if the suspicion of sabotage proved to be justified. On the other hand, it is unlikely that other units were spared such a series of accidents.

At the beginning of June there was a change in the headquarters company's personnel. The unit's commander, *Oberleutnant* Kurt Bänsch, volunteered to serve in a *Luftwaffe* assault battalion and left I./JG 5. His replacement was *Hauptmann* Taucher. Flying operations continued to be limited apart from routine missions, and there were no noteworthy events for all of June. July 1943 brought just one major operation. During this action on 7 July, *Feldwebel* Josef Sommeregger of the *1. Staffel* was shot down over the sea approximately 160 kilometers southwest of Stavanger by a Handley-Page Hampden. The native of Austria is still listed as missing in action.

Towards the end of July rumors suddenly began circulating that the *I. Gruppe* was to be transferred out of Norway. When the rumors were finally confirmed, there were few among the pilots and ground personnel who weren't pleased. It became official on 1 August 1943, when *Hauptmann* Wengel received orders for I./JG 5 to move to Denmark. The monotony of the north, the foggy weather, the cod liver oil and the diet of fish were just some of the reasons why the *Gruppe*'s departure from Norway caused little or no dismay. Poetic minds created suitable rhymes, and the one reproduced here characterized the mood of the men as follows:

"*Today there is fish meal soup,*
and we don't give a damn about the Northern Lights!
The mountains and fjords are all the same to us =
we only want one thing: home to the Reich!"

It would be months, however, before the *Gruppe* headed home to the Reich; the bitter path to the Defense of the Reich. First, however, it was sent to Denmark. After the usual back and forth of order and counter order – what unit never experienced that – I./JG 5 left its base in Stavanger and in the first days of August arrived in Frederikshaven. By then the majority of the unit's pilots had been in Norway since the spring of 1941. Only the *2. Staffel* was temporarily left behind in Lister. It flew a few more missions in September and October, losing two pilots in the process. On 7 October the *Staffel* took off on a combat mission at 10:12 hours. Precisely 23 minutes later *Unteroffizier* Hüllenkütters was forced to ditch his Messerschmitt in the sea southwest of Egersund. The pilot was picked up by the navy but died a short time later of total exhaustion. On 13 October *Leutnant* Assmy collided with a Bv 138 flying boat south of Mandal in poor visibility. From Bergen the *Staffel* flew one more mission to provide air cover for the cruiser *Lützow*.

Operationally the *I. Gruppe* did little in the weeks that followed, and its stay in Denmark was of but short duration. On 15 November 1943 transfer orders arrived ordering the *Gruppe* to Rumania to defend the Ploesti oil fields. The unit's ground personnel, some of whom departed on 29 October, travelled via Dresden, Prague, Bratislava, and Budapest to the new base in Targsorul-Nou near Ploesti, arriving 16 November. The flying elements subsequently followed.

At first the *Gruppe* waited in vain for the enemy to come, but the reason for the absence of American bombers could be found in the results of their first attempt to bomb the Rumanian oil fields. No one had forgotten 1 August 1943, when the American 9th Air Force lost no less than 54 B-24 Liberators to flak and fighters while attacking the oil refineries around Ploesti.

After just two months I./JG 5 left Targsorul-Nou, and on 9 January of the new year of 1944 moved to Wraschdebna, near the Bulgarian capital of Sofia. The very next day, the 10th of January, the *Gruppe* took off on a defensive mission which resulted in extremely fierce air battles over the Sofia area. For the first time pilots of JG 5 faced large formations of American heavy bombers of the 15th Air Force. It was an entirely new and at the same time uncomfortable feeling, for the pilots had not yet discovered the correct battle tactics and had no experience at all against the Americans. Swarms of fighters accompanying the bombers tried to prevent the Germans from getting through to the bombers. Despite this, *Feldwebel* Leitner, *Leutnant* von Thienen and *Leutnant* Senoner, leader of the *1. Staffel*, each accounted for an enemy machine. Even ramming attacks were observed during this turbulent air battle. Sadly these victories came at a heavy cost, for the *Gruppe* lost its commander, *Hauptmann* Gerhard Wengel. He sustained a head wound in combat with a P-38 Lightning east of Radomir near Sofia. Fatally wounded, he went down with his Bf 109 G-6. The aircraft of the *Staffelkapitän* of 3./JG 5, *Oberleutnant* Rudolf Müller, was hit by enemy fire and he was struck in the eye by shell splinters, while *Oberfeldwebel* Kalweit later landed in Wraschdebna with a leg wound. The third wounded pilot belonged to the *1. Staffel*. He was

Unteroffizier Holtkötter, who sustained a bruised spinal cord in an attempted forced landing. *Unteroffizier* Scherf was forced to abandon his Messerschmitt at 4000 meters, however he landed safely by parachute.

I./JG 5 had received its baptism of fire against the American enemy and at the same time had paid a high price with the loss of its *Kommandeur*. Initially *Oberleutnant* Müller continued to lead the *Gruppe* in an acting capacity until *Major* Erich Gerlitz was named the new *Gruppenkommandeur* on 25 January.

There seemed to be no end in sight to the run of bad luck, for on 29 January the *Gruppe* suffered another heavy blow when a Ju 52 carrying 18 men returning from leave went down over partisan country in Serbia. It later turned out that the transport had crashed near Jagodina, about 80 kilometers from Belgrade, on account of icing. I./JG 5 lost five men killed and three seriously injured, all members of the ground personnel.

In the Defense of the Reich

Once again the *Gruppe* was on the move. Divided into several detachments, during the first weeks of February I./JG 5 moved to Germany where it was to be incorporated into the Defense of the Reich as part of the *7. Jagddivision*. Part of the *2. Staffel* plus a cleanup detachment formed the rear guard, which stayed behind in Bulgaria. At the same time the unit reequipped on the new Bf 109 G-6/R6. Its first base was Obertraubling, south of Regensburg. The *Gruppe*'s list of command personnel was now as follows:

Gruppenkommandeur:	*Major* Gerlitz
Kapitän 1./JG 5:	*Oblt*. Senoner
Kapitän 2./JG 5:	*Hptm*. Habermann
Kapitän 3./JG 5:	*Oblt*. Müller
Adjutant:	*Lt*. von Thienen
Technical Officer:	*Lt*. Endriß
Signals Officer:	*Lt*. Dr. Ritter
Headquarters Company:	*Oblt*. Ress

It was at that time that the American 8th Air Force and RAF Bomber Command launched their combined offensive against the German aircraft industry. The operations, which lasted from 20 to 25 February 1944, were dubbed "Big Week". During this period the Americans by day and the British by night delivered heavy blows against aircraft and aero engine factories in the Reich and the occupied territories. Losses were heavy on both sides, however the Allied attacks failed to bring about a decisive drop in production.

Towards midday on 22 February elements of I./JG 5 reported contact with an American formation consisting of about 40 Boeing Fortresses. Covered by his wingman *Unteroffizier* Scharf, *Leutnant* von Podewils made three firing passes at a B-17 and finally shot it down about 15 kilometers southwest of the city at 12:15 hours. It was his second victory. Three members of the crew were seen to bale out.

Obertraubling was the target of a major bombing raid on the last day of Big Week. Bombers of the American 15th Air Force based in Italy arrived over the Messerschmitt works in Regensburg at about 13:00 with their escort of P-38 Lightnings. The air raid inflicted a number of casualties. Several pilots tried to take to the air to intercept, but they failed to get far from the airfield. One of the *Geschwader*'s veteran pilots was killed in this daring attempt. *Oberleutnant* Gerhard Senoner, an experienced fighter pilot with about 20 victories to his credit and *Staffelkapitän* of 1./JG 5, was shot down and killed by an enemy fighter.

The airfield itself and the surrounding area were turned into something resembling a lunar landscape; all of the conversion detachment's equipment, including the aircraft, lay wrecked on the ground. Remaining any longer in Obertraubling had been rendered pointless, and I./JG 5 subsequently moved to Herzogenaurach in Franconia.

From this airfield, situated west of Erlangen, the *Gruppe* took off on the morning of 16 March 1944. Twenty-four of the unit's Messerschmitts took part in this difficult and costly operation. Earlier that morning approximately 400 American heavy bombers with a powerful fighter escort had attacked the city of Augsburg, and at 12:25 hours they had set course for home. The weather on 16 March was anything but good, with eight to ten tenths cloud cover. The German air defenses were on alert, but snow showers and poor ground visibility hampered their efforts. Consequently only units of the 3. and 7. *Jagddivision* made contact with the enemy.

Led by *Major* Gerlitz, I./JG 5 and II./JG 3 "*Udet*" combined to form a large battle unit (*Gefechtsverband*), which at 12:40 hours made contact with the American bombers in the area east of Ulm. The American fighter escort immediately intervened and tried to engage the German fighters. The enemy's numerical superiority was crushing. One of the first to fall in combat with the Thunderbolts was the *Kommandeur*, *Major* Gerlitz, who had 15 victories to his credit. His Bf 109 G-6 crashed near Eybach in Württemberg. The others found themselves in dogfights in the midst of multiple cloud layers. *Unteroffizier* Kütt of the *1. Staffel* was wounded in the shoulder and forced to take to his parachute near Ulm. Soon afterwards his *Staffel* mate *Unteroffizier* Laux was hanging beneath his parachute, having been wounded in the calf. Both pilots were initially reported missing, but after several days in hospital both were able to return to their unit.

Leutnant von Podewils, who one year earlier had had the dubious pleasure of baling out, had initiated a head-on attack on a formation of heavy bombers by the *3. Staffel* when the Thunderbolts suddenly appeared. The Germans began turning and it was then that the *Leutnant*'s Bf 109 was hit: "On that day I was acting adjutant and after my first attack on a Fortress I was myself attacked by a large number of Thunderbolts. I was immediately hit in the engine and tried to put my Messerschmitt down somewhere. The weather was awful, which prevented me from seeing the ground clearly; but I didn't have much time left, as I feared that the engine might catch fire."

Leutnant von Podewils finally put his machine down in a lane in a birch forest near the village of Radelstetten. He survived with a concussion and several shell splinters in his eye.

Another of I./JG 5's fighter pilots was shot down and killed near Geislingen/Steige: *Feldwebel* Johann Veleba of the *3. Staffel*. *Unteroffizier* Kortmann of 2./JG 5 was injured and landed in Neckarhausen, while *Oberleutnant* Gerlach, the *Kapitän* of the *1. Staffel*, was also wounded and made a belly landing in Herzogenaurach. JG 3 suffered four casualties, including the leader of 7./JG 3, *Leutnant* Stahlberg, who was obliged to make a forced landing near Kirchheim/Teck.

After these operations I./JG 5 reported a total of two pilots killed, two forced to bale out and three forced landings. The *Gruppe* claimed just one victory in return: a Fortress shot down in the Ulm area by *Obergefreiter* Meyer. The BBC reported that 22 bombers and 13 fighters had fallen to the German defenses that day. A number of the heavy bombers came down in Switzerland.

The *Gruppe* was constantly in action. There was a big raid on Munich on 18 March 1944, the first daylight attack on the metropolis on the Isar, in which about 800 heavy bombers of the 8th Air Force took part. After dropping their bombs the Americans turned northwest and west on a broad front, passing over the Rhein-Main area and in some cases Switzerland once again. Once again German fighters intercepted the enemy and brought down almost 30 heavy bombers. According to English sources the enemy lost 43 bombers and 10 fighters on 18 March. I./JG 5, again part of a battle formation with the *Staffeln* of the *"Udet" Geschwader*, lost two pilots: *Gefreiter* Hubertus Hack of the *1. Staffel*, who had been badly injured in a forced landing at Targsorul-Nou in mid-December 1943, and *Unteroffizier* Kurt Schulz of the *3. Staffel*. Both were shot down in combat with enemy aircraft between Stuttgart and Crailsheim.

Not until ten days after the death of *Major* Gerlitz did the *Gruppe* receive its new commanding officer: *Major* Carganico, who had turned II./JG 5 on the Polar Sea front over to *Oberleutnant* Weißenberger. Also, the rest of the *2. Staffel* had left Bulgaria, and I./JG 5 was now completely based in Herzogenaurach.

Like March, April proved to be a very eventful month for the *Gruppe*. The incursions by the enemy became tougher, for the enemy's strength was growing steadily and his control of the air becoming more apparent. The American fighter escort often made it impossible for the German interceptors to get through to the bombers. For the time being, however, successes and losses were still about even. The large-scale defensive effort on 8 April 1944, which resulted in heavy losses to JG 1, JG 3, JG 11, JG 26, JG 27, and JG 300, also demanded its tribute from I./JG 5. Both sides suffered heavily in the ferocious air battle, and the *Gruppe* lost two pilots in the Hanover-Brunswick area, one of the focal points of the battle, *Oberfeldwebel* Glatz and Schulte were shot down and killed, while a third pilot, *Unteroffizier* Betz of the *2. Staffel*, was forced to abandon his Messerschmitt west of Celle. The certain destruction of 39 American bombers and 11 fighters and the probable destruction of another 28 heavy bombers came at a high cost. Thirty-six German fighters were destroyed and another 34 sustained more than 60% damage.

On 11 April 1944 the *Geschwader*'s Focke-Wulf *Weihe* (Harrier) was on a courier flight in the sector of the Fighter Commander Brittany. On board were *Oberleutnant* Habermann, *Gruppe* Technical Officer *Lt.* Dr. Ritter and *Obergefreiter* Burkhardt. About 40 kilometers west of Rennes near the Gael airfield, the lone Fw 58 was jumped by enemy fighters and shot down in flames. *Obergefreiter* Burkhardt and *Oberleutnant* Edgar Habermann, *Kapitän* of 2./JG 5, were killed in the crash, while *Leutnant* Dr. Ritter escaped with facial burns.

On 24 April 1944, five weeks after the first big daylight raid on Munich, the city was again the target of a large-scale attack, which also struck Ludwigshafen. The *1.* and *7. Jagddivision* achieved good results, shooting down 48 bombers and 14 fighters, however this success came at a heavy cost, for 45 German pilots were reported killed or missing. I./JG 5 lost *Unteroffizier* Kurt Glienke, who was shot down by a Mustang east of Fürstenfeldbruck. The following day the *3. Staffel* lost *Unteroffizier* Hans Meyer in tragic fashion during a mission over southern Germany. After being shot down by an American fighter, the *Unteroffizier* succeeded in making a belly landing in a field near Buchloe, west of Landsberg/Lech. Then a Mustang suddenly dove towards the pilot and opened fire. Meyer was hit in the abdomen.

The Allied air forces were extremely active in the month of May 1944. Armaments factories, refineries and Luftwaffe airfields everywhere in the Reich and the occupied western territories became targets for the American air forces based in England and Italy. Today we know that they were in preparation for the invasion. The enemy suffered heavy losses to flak and fighters, but these were not sufficient to deflect him from his purpose, and the attacks went on with undiminished ferocity. German losses were much more serious, and most fighter units experienced a rising casualty rate in May 1944. Such was the case of I./JG 5, which lost no fewer than thirteen pilots. Seven more pilots were wounded. The following is a list of the most active days on which the *Gruppe* saw action as part of *I. Jagdkorps*:

| Date | American Targets | Aircraft Losses | | Personnel Losses | I. JK |
		U.S.	German	Killed or Missing	I./JG 5
10/5/44	Wiener Neustadt	24	10	8	1
11/5/44	Saargemünd, Luxembourg	9	7	8	
12/5/44	Central Germany	81	34	44	1
13/5/44	Osnabrück, Stettin	26	16	24	
19/5/44	Berlin, Brunswick	52	42	18	1
21/5/44	Kiel	13	7	7	
24/5/44	Berlin, Vienna	73	40	27	
27/5/44	Alsace, Lorraine Southern Germany	14	16		7
28/5/44	Central Germany	47	44	18	2
30/5/44	Dessau, Halberstadt, Oschersleben	15	47	32	
Totals		**354***	**263**	**186**	**12**

*Of which at least 270 were heavy bombers.

In that month of May, when German fighter pilots were facing a severe test and achieving outstanding results in combat, while at the same time suffering grievous losses, they were accused by their supreme commander of failing in their task of defending the homeland. Too much has been written about the accusations leveled at the fighter arm and the subsequent reaction by the units for us to examine the subject in detail here. It is worth noting, however, that the OKW had failed to stay abreast of technological developments and thus failed to provide the German fighter units with the necessary aircraft. When this is taken into consideration the sacrificial actions of the German fighter pilots are all the more impressive.

On 10 May formations from I./JG 5 and III./JG 3 assembled over Passau to intercept a formation of bombers from the 15th Air Force that had taken off from

Foggia. The Americans' target was the Messerschmitt aircraft factories in Wiener Neustadt. The defending German fighters, which included aircraft from JG 27 and I./JG 53, destroyed 21 heavy bombers for the loss of 10. *Unteroffizier* Schrade of 3./JG 5 was shot down and killed south of Vienna. He was the *Gruppe*'s only casualty. One day later I./JG 5 was again in the air and assembled over Stuttgart, however the mission failed to produce contact as the enemy formations turned back prematurely.

The 8th Air Force opened its offensive against the German fuel industry with a big attack on 12 May 1944. That day the Defense of the Reich succeeded in committing all of its available day fighters for the first time, and the Americans met approximately 470 fighters and *Zerstörer*. I./JG 5 was ordered into the Rhein-Main area, where it became involved in fierce battles with the American escort fighters. The *Gruppe* suffered just one casualty. *Gefreiter* Lieberknecht of the *1. Staffel* was shot down over the Reinhard Forest near Friedrichsfeld and was still in the cockpit when his fighter hit the ground.

Another pilot was lost on 19 May near Lübtheen, west of Ludwigslust. The *Gruppe* took off from Herzogenaurach at about noon and initially headed toward the Harz Mountains to intercept a bomber force heading for the Reich capital. Combat began near Brunswick and extended northwards, during which *Feldwebel* von Ahsen's "White 6" was hit and went down with its pilot.

Then came Saturday, 27 May 1944, a black day for the *I. Gruppe* of *Jagdgeschwader 5*. Early in the morning a force of about 900 American heavy bombers with fighter escort was detected approaching Reich airspace. Their targets were transportation and industrial facilities in the south of Germany, principally in the areas of Karlsruhe, Mannheim, Ludwigshafen, Saarbrucken and Trier. There was hectic activity at all of the *I. Jagdkorps*' bases, however the weather was so poor that day that just 90 machines of the *7. Jagddivision* were able to take off to intercept.

The Messerschmitts of I./JG 5 took off from Herzogenaurach shortly after 11:00 hours, led by their *Kommandeur*, *Major* Carganico. Fierce fighting developed over Alsace and Lorraine in which the *Gruppe* shot down a number of enemy aircraft but was forced to pay a heavy death toll. *Hauptmann* Deuschle was killed over St. Dié, while *Unteroffizier* Hans Schorsch was shot down and killed over Hagenau in his "Black 4". The *1. Staffel* had four pilots wounded, including *Oberfeldwebel* Holtkötter and *Unteroffizier* Rügge, who both returned with facial injuries caused by shell splinters, while *Unteroffizier* Thomas was wounded in the leg by enemy gunfire near Ebersmünster. 3./JG 5, on the other hand, alone lost four pilots in the day's fighting: *Gefreiter* Bollinger, *Gefreiter* Glöckner, *Feldwebel* Reckendorfer, and *Leutnant* Wiesen, whose "Black 8" was shot down near Böblingen.

The *Gruppe* suffered an especially painful loss when its *Kommandeur* went down. *Major* Carganico was engaged in a fight with enemy bombers and escort fighters near Chevry, when suddenly his Bf 109 G-5 with the big Mickey Mouse on the fuselage suddenly went into a dive and seconds later crashed into the ground.

On 27 May 1944 *I. Jagdkorps* reported the destruction of eleven heavy bombers and three fighters at the cost of 16 German fighters written off. I./JG 5 paid the highest price for these successes, seven killed and five wounded.

Major Horst Carganico

From early youth, the life of Horst Carganico, born in Breslau on 27 September 1917, was influenced by aviation. His father was an airman, so it is not surprising that the son would also become active in this field. Later, when asked the question, "Say, aren't you …?", he would reply, "Yes, I'm the old man's son." Secret training in an old LVG from the First World War in Berlin-Johannisthal was followed in 1937 by entry into the new German air force. One year later Carganico was an officer in the *Jagdgruppe* commanded by *Major* Schumacher. When war broke out *Jagdgruppe Schumacher* was deployed to defend the German Bight. As the unit's technical officer, Carganico was given no opportunity to fly missions himself. The occupation of Norway and Denmark in April 1940 took the unit to Kristiansand, where he finally flew his first operational sorties, escorting Stukas to Namsos, as adjutant of the *I. Gruppe* of JG 77.

Carganico scored his first victory on 21 June 1940 during an escort mission in support of the battleship *Scharnhorst*. Victories two and three followed on 9 July over Stavanger. After a brief interlude on the Channel Front, in the spring of 1941 Carganico returned to Norway and took over 1./JG 77. On 25 September 1941, after his 27th victory, he became the second pilot in the *Geschwader* to receive the Knight's Cross. In January 1942, when the formation of JG 5 was complete, Carganico's *Staffel* became 6./JG 5, which he led until April 1942. He subsequently took command of the *II. Gruppe*, which achieved great success under his command – Carganico himself shot down his 50th enemy aircraft in June 1942.

After the death of *Major* Gerlitz, *Kommandeur* of I./JG 5, on 26 March 1944 Carganico was placed in command of the *Gruppe*, which was attached to the Defense of the Reich. By the time of his death on 27 May 1944, he had flown more than 600 combat missions and has 60 victories to his credit. Carganico, whose aircraft showed visible signs of combat damage, attempted a forced landing but flew into high-tension wires and was killed in the ensuing crash.

One day after the costly battles over Alsace, on the afternoon of 28 May, the *Staffeln* of the *I. Gruppe* took off again to intercept heavy bombers approaching over the Gardelegen-Salzwedel area. The *1.* and *3. Staffel* each lost a pilot in the ensuing action. *Feldwebel* Englert and *Unteroffizier* Doll were shot down and killed. *Oberfeldwebel* Erich Klein was wounded in the right knee over Salzwedel but was able to abandon his "Yellow 3" and parachute to safety. Unfortunately his leg later had to be amputated.

Successes and Losses – The Invasion

On 3 June 1944 *Hauptmann* Weißenberger, who by than had amassed 175 victories on the Polar Sea front, arrived in Herzogenaurach to take command of the *I. Gruppe* following the death of Carganico. He was the second *Gruppenkommandeur* of II./JG 5 to assume command of I./JG 5 in the Defense of the Reich. Weißenberger, who was promoted to *Hauptmann* on 1 June 1944, would lead the *Gruppe* during the difficult operations over France following the Allied invasion. Under his leadership the *Gruppe* would also achieve fresh successes.

It was obvious to the *Wehrmacht* operations staffs that the Allies were eager to force a decision in the west. What they did not know, however, was where and when the invasion of the mainland, the establishment of a second front, would come. Consequently, when the invasion began early on 6 June 1944, the German commanders were only able to employ a fraction of their forces to strike a counterblow.* (*The OKW did not believe information from the *Abwehr* concerning the timing and location of the Allied landings; consequently neither army nor air force units were moved into the suspected invasion area in time. Enemy activity over the Reich was limited in the first weeks of June, giving the units of the Defense of the Reich a brief rest. The unexpected respite also allowed these units to be readied for use in France.).

When the invasion came there were no *Luftwaffe* combat units stationed near the Normandy coast; therefore on the first and perhaps most important day of the Allied landing the German fighter units were taken completely by surprise and remained on the ground. Moreover, their bases were so far from the fighting that they couldn't have immediately intervened effectively. Not until a day later, with the German commanders still uncertain as to the true situation in Normandy, did the *Jagdgeschwader* begin to move. It was the start of a "*Luftwaffe* travel day."

On the afternoon of 6 June an advance party from I./JG 5 set off for France. Some of the ground personnel followed in several Ju 52s. The *Gruppe*'s

Messerschmitts also left Reich territory, taking off with the transports from Herzogenaurach. The unit's new base of operations was Montdidier, about 35 kilometers southeast of Amiens. One day later the *Gruppe* was already in action.

Unfortunately the unit suffered its first loss in the new area of operations during the transfer flight, when one of the Ju 52s was attacked by English fighters about 14 kilometers east of Montdidier and obliged to make a forced landing. Two of those on the aircraft were killed and twelve others were injured.

Hauptmann Weißenberger shot down his first enemy aircraft in the west at 09:05 hours on 7 June 1944. He and his wingman, *Unteroffizier* Ehring of the *3. Staffel*, got on the tail of a Thunderbolt southwest of Montdidier at a height of 200 meters. A short burst of fire sent the enemy machine crashing to the ground. Two other fighters, also Thunderbolts, fell to his guns about twenty minutes later. Both aircraft crashed and burned in the same area. The two pilots parachuted to safety and were captured. There was a second scramble that afternoon, which resulted in a scrap with about a dozen Thunderbolts near Beauvais. By the time Weißenberger landed back at Montdidier at 17:39, forty-four minutes after taking off, he had claimed two more enemy fighters. Five Thunderbolts on the first day of operations! The *Gruppe*'s only casualty was *Oberfähnrich* Jürgen Fricke, who was shot down and killed by enemy fighters near Amiens.

I./JG 5's cleanup detachment arrived in Montdidier on 8 June and the unit was once again complete. *Leutnant* Friedrich Bölz and *Oberfeldwebel* Reinhold were wounded during a mission over the Paris area. The same day *Hauptmann* Weißenberger recorded his 181st and 182nd victories – two more Thunderbolts. Other pilots also scored, making the *Gruppe*'s first days of operations in France very successful.

Barely a week after the landings in Normandy, American fighter-bombers attacked Montdidier. *Obergefreiter* Oelfke of the *Gruppe*'s signals platoon described the attack in his diary:

> "11 June 1944. Enemy fighters over our airfield. *Oblt.* Müller and *Uffz.* Wenninger take off. Wenninger is shot down. Müller shoots down a Lightning and barely escapes other enemy fighters that come from out of the clouds. He shoots down another Lightning from this formation."

Once the enemy had found it, Montdidier airfield was given no peace. The base was hit by a heavy attack on 12 June which inflicted severe damage. The ground personnel lost three killed and three wounded. The bulk of the *Gruppe* got airborne in the early morning and encountered a group of Thunderbolts east of Evreux. *Hauptmann* Weißenberger, who took off with *Unteroffizier* Tichy as his wingman shortly before six, brought down three more Thunderbolts within the space of twelve minutes. After Weißenberger's first victim fell, the brave *Unteroffizier* Alfred Tichy was shot down and killed by another American fighter near Evreux. Weißenberger shot down the third Thunderbolt in the Grisors area at 07:02 hours, opening fire from a range of 50 meters. His own aircraft was hit and Weißenberger was slightly wounded. He abandoned his Bf 109 G-5 over St. André and parachuted to safety. After this mission *Unteroffizier* Straube of the *2. Staffel* was initially reported missing, however he later returned to his unit safe and sound.

As Montdidier airfield had become untenable, a few days later I./JG 5 received orders to move to Peronne. The unit had no time to settle in, however, as it moved on to Chauny, a forward airfield between Noyon and Tergnier. The *Gruppe* set up its command post in a forester's house at the edge of the woods. The *Gruppe* flew several missions with *Jagdgeschwader 1* in the high cover role, however no enemy aircraft were encountered. For a short time at the end of June the *Gruppe* used three airfields simultaneously, depending on the nature of its mission: Chauny, Manancourt and Peronne. It is most likely that few of I./JG 5's men realized that they were on historic ground. Just ten kilometers to the west of Peronne was the small village of Cappy on the Somme, from where Manfred Baron von Richthofen had taken off on his final flight in his all-red Fokker Triplane on 21 April 1918.

The new month brought another move by the *Gruppe*, this time to Frieres in the Laon area. Between 12 June and 2 July, the day the *Gruppe* arrived at Frieres, Weißenberger's I./JG 5 had lost four more pilots, including three from the *3. Staffel*. On 3 July *Leutnant* Wolfgang Buth crashed in his "Yellow 7" immediately after takeoff and was killed.

The first mission from Frieres on 5 July cost the *Gruppe* one pilot killed and two wounded. *Leutnant* Eckhart Berneburg, who had taken off with the *1. Staffel* for the Caen area at 08:30, was shot down and killed between Caen and Le Havre. The next day the *Staffeln* again conducted fighter sweeps over the invasion area and shot down three Lightnings. *Hauptmann* Weißenberger claimed two Lightnings south of Cambrai at 08:48 and 08:49. The first blew up in the air, while the other crashed and exploded. The third American fighter fell to the guns of *Feldwebel* Dönch, who was wounded in the neck in this engagement. Three other Lightnings were claimed as probably shot down. The *Gruppe*'s only casualty was *Unteroffizier* Hiltwein of the *3. Staffel*, who was shot down by an enemy fighter near St. Quentin.

The next day, Friday the 7th of July 1944, was a very successful one for the *Gruppe*. The Messerschmitts took off on a fighter sweep in the late afternoon and south of Rosieres they encountered a group of 15 to 20 Thunderbolts. They almost spotted the Americans too late in the back-light. The Thunderbolts were higher and thus held the advantage, which they tried to exploit. The Bf 109 pilots reacted immediately, however, and there was a vicious dogfight.

Hauptmann Weißenberger was again able to increase his victory total, sending three Thunderbolts to the ground in the space of a few minutes. The first fell at 18:32, the third at 18:36. Victories 188 to 189! *Staffelkapitän Oberleutnant* Müller, *Leutnant* Politt, *Oberfähnrich* Mors and *Unteroffizier* Thoms each shot down a Thunderbolt in the same area, while the *Kommandeur, Unteroffizier* Ehring, *Feldwebel* Junghans and *Oberfähnrich* Lehner also claimed probable victories. This result is all the more impressive because the German pilots began the battle in a position of inferiority and suffered no fatal casualties. Just three aircraft were lost. *Feldwebel* Heimburg came away with a shoulder wound. *Fähnrich* Klaus Krebs of the *1. Staffel* had both legs broken and had to be delivered to hospital in Amiens.

Four weeks had passed since the start of the invasion. The British and Americans had greatly expanded their bridgeheads, and their air forces were flying tactical missions deep into the German rear in an effort to weaken the German defenders and interdict their supplies. I./JG 5 was in almost constant action against the numerically superior enemy fighter units in the first half of July. Four missions in one day was not unusual.

After a much-needed two days of rest, late on the afternoon of 13 July 1944 the *Gruppe* took off in search of enemy fighter-bombers in the Rouen-Bernay-Evreux area. Half an hour later the German pilots sighted a westbound formation of about ten Hawker Typhoons and immediately attacked. Attacking from out of a right-hand turn, Weißenberger shot down an enemy machine from a height of 800 meters. His wingman, *Unteroffizier* Schulz of the *3. Staffel*, saw the enemy aircraft crash and explode near Trouville at 18:24. The next Typhoon fell to Weißenberger's guns two minutes later and a third was destroyed by *Leutnant* Mors. *Unteroffizier* Binna damaged another Typhoon but was unable to determine whether the enemy aircraft survived this action or not. When the *Gruppe* landed back at Frieres shortly after 19:00, *Leutnant* Sachse's "White 6" was missing. They waited in vain for news that he had parachuted to safety, and ultimately Dieter Sachse had to be reported missing in action.

The next day the *Gruppe* flew a mission over the Caen area, claiming six victories for four losses. Its objective was to strafe American troop concentrations in the area. After completing their low-level attacks the Messerschmitts were attacked by numerous Spitfires and Thunderbolts. The aircraft of *Feldwebel* Junghans and *Unteroffizier* Geilert were hit. Both pilots baled out and were taken prisoner. Five kilometers south of Bayeux *Hauptmann* Weißenberger shot down an enemy aircraft from a height of ten meters, closing to almost ramming distance before opening fire. At 14:56 hours he also shot down a Spitfire near Lisieux. The other successful pilots that day were *Leutnant* Lehner and *Leutnant* Mors, who each shot down a Thunderbolt, and *Gefreiter* Berger and *Unteroffizier* Schröder, who each destroyed a Spitfire. *Feldwebel* Baumgart of 3./JG 5 was unfortunately also taken prisoner after his Messerschmitt was shot down. His *Staffel* mate *Gefreiter* Anton Schöppler also failed to return from this mission. Two days later, on 16 July, Schöppler contacted the unit from Paris, reporting that he had fallen victim to American anti-aircraft fire but had baled out unhurt.

That same day the 2. *Staffel* lost *Unteroffizier* Berger in the Calais-Dieppe area and *Unteroffizier* Schröder, who was shot down over Dieppe and whose fate still remains uncertain.

After the successful mission of 14 July, the next day the commanding general of the *II. Jagdkorps*, Bülowius, accompanied by *Oberstleutnant* Ihlefeld, arrived in Frieres to inspect the *Gruppe* and congratulate it on its accomplishments under extremely difficult circumstances.

A mission with the *"Richthofen" Geschwader* was planned for Monday the 17th of July 1944. I./JG 5 took off for the combat zone around Caen several times that day. Initially there was no enemy contact, and it wasn't until the final mission, which began shortly after 19:00 hours, that the *Gruppe* engaged enemy fighter-bombers in the Caen-Le Mesnil area. It must have been then that *Oberleutnant* Robert Müller was shot down. While the *Kapitän* of 3./JG 5 has been missing ever since, *Oberfähnrich* Pöllinger of the 2. *Staffel* was captured by the British near Caen and *Unteroffizier* Straube went down with his "Black 12" near Le Mesnil. This brought the *Gruppe*'s losses to three pilots against no claims.

On 18 July, however, Mors shot down three Lightnings for his 4th, 5th and 6th victories over the invasion front. That day the *Gruppe* flew high cover for units of JG 2 and JG 26 over the landing zone. Near Evreux *Unteroffizier* Wünsche claimed a Lightning probably shot down before he was himself hit and obliged to make a forced landing. Wünsche, who had taken a bullet through the calf, had to be delivered to San Sebastien hospital near Evreux. Later in the engagement the *Gruppe* added a Lightning to its victory total, shot down by *Unteroffizier* Binna.

The 19th of July 1944 was another very successful day for I./JG 5. Once again the *Gruppe* took off in the late afternoon to provide top cover for the *"Richthofen"* and *"Schlageter" Geschwader*. An hour later the Germans spotted several formations of Typhoon and Mustang fighters. Mors, the successful pilot of the previous day, claimed three more enemy aircraft, all Typhoons. Lehner, who had taken over the *3. Staffel* in place of the fallen *Oberleutnant* Müller, shot down another Typhoon. The sky over Lisieux was filled with condensation trails. The sound of gunfire mingled with the roar of aircraft engines. *Unteroffizier* Buinski's "Yellow 1" went down and none of his comrades were able to see whether he got out or was still in the aircraft. In this hectic dogfight each man had to look out for himself. Buinski was initially reported missing. His comrades' joy was all the greater when he returned to the *1. Staffel* the next day, having baled out.

This was a special day for *Hauptmann* Weißenberger, for on that 19 July he shot down four enemy aircraft. At 20:22 hours he shot down the first Typhoon north of Lisieux, the next one minute later and the third, which crashed and exploded northwest of Cormeilles, at 20:25 hours. Ten minutes later he got on the tail of a Mustang and shot it down from a distance of 50 meters. The *I. Gruppe* had shot down eight enemy fighter aircraft for the loss of one of its own aircraft, that of Alfred Buinski.

Operations were relatively uneventful until 24 July, with no enemy contact. Enemy fighter-bombers attacked the town of La Fère but their bombs failed to find the airfield just to the south.

The 25th of July, a Tuesday, was another high point in the history of I./JG 5. Once again the *Gruppe* set off for the invasion zone with JG 1 and JG 2. Its mission: *freie Jagd* in the Caen area. For days, in Frieres there had been visible excitement before each takeoff, and on this day the mechanics again showed special care in preparing the Messerschmitt with the double chevron on the fuselage. The question being asked: "Will the old man come back with his 200th today?" In fact Weißenberger's 200th victory was due. The fighter pilot who had enjoyed such success in the far north had claimed 23 victories over the invasion front – 23 enemy fighters in six weeks!

The order to take off was given at 10:30 hours. The aircraft of Weißenberger and Binnas were first to take off. The remaining Messerschmitts followed, leaving behind the waving ground crews on the dusty airfield. Then the formation climbed to combat altitude and set course for Rouen. At about 11:00 the German pilots sighted the ribbon of the Seine River. To the north was the imposing silhouette of the city's Gothic cathedral. Then a formation of Spitfires appeared and a fierce dogfight ensued. *Leutnant* Mors sent his tenth victim to the ground, while *Leutnant* Lehner inflicted severe damage on another but was unable to confirm its destruction. Then it was *Hauptmann* Weißenberger's turn. Fifteen kilometers south of Rouen, at a height of 3800 meters, he caught a Spitfire from behind and shot it down from a range of 100 meters. That was his 199th victory. The next fell two minutes later, crashing and burning southeast of Rouen at 11:02. When the German fighters landed back at Frieres the reception committee was waiting. Everyone with legs ran to the airfield to congratulate Weißenberger on his success, for the *Kommandeur*'s latest victory was also the 200th by I./JG 5.

On 26 July *Leutnant* Mors led two missions of 15 aircraft and in the afternoon *Oberleutnant* Gerlach led a third. The next day, in poor weather, the *Gruppe* flew four strafing missions in the Caen area. *Unteroffizier* Thoms was shot down on the 27th. He baled out of his "White 9" but struck his knee against the tail. It was the second time in two months that he had been wounded.

The Gruppe's Last Path

On 30 July 1944 *Hauptmann* Weißenberger left the *Gruppe* and went to Bad Wiessee on leave. That same day *Oberleutnant* Gerlach shot down a Spitfire. Then the *I. Gruppe* was ordered to take a badly-needed break from operations. The pilots were exhausted, and the stresses and exertions of the past weeks could not leave them unaffected. The struggle against a tough opponent had marked the men.

Unfortunately the rest was a short one, as the unit had to make preparations for another move, one ordered by the corps. *Leutnant* Wendlinger, the *Gruppe* signals officer, departed Frieres airfield with an advance detachment for Bretigny-Fleury. The terrain there was found to be completely unsuitable for a forward airfield and Arpajon, about 30 kilometers south of Paris, was chosen instead.

During the general decampment, however, the war in the air continued with undiminished ferocity. The situation on the Western Front looked anything but rosy, for the Allies were advancing irresistibly. American and British fighter-bombers were constantly over the battlefield. Some of their units were already operating from airfields on the French mainland, significantly increasing their range. The balance of forces in the air had long since shifted in favor of the enemy, although the German units set themselves against the enemy formations with unparalleled heroism.

I./JG 5 took off on its last mission from Frieres at 17:00 hours on 4 August. In the Alencon-Nogent area the Germans were attacked by Thunderbolts. Mors and Schöppler each downed one of the enemy fighters, however the *2. Staffel* lost its acting commander, *Leutnant* Friedrich Bölz, in this action. Bölz, who had been wounded in action on 8 June, was reported missing along with his aircraft "Black 5." The next day the flying elements also moved to Arpajon. While the Messerschmitts landed at their new base at about 12:30 hours, the main detachment under the Gruppe adjutant, *Hauptmann* Erich Mikat, had arrived two hours earlier and set about making the airfield operational. *Leutnant* Mors had assumed command of I./JG 5 in place of *Hauptmann* Weißenberger, who was in Germany. In command of the *1. Staffel* was *Oberleutnant* Gerlach, *Oberleutnant* Weyl had replaced *Leutnant* Bölz, who was missing, as commander of the *2. Staffel*, and the *3. Staffel* was led by *Leutnant* Lehner.

The very first mission from Arpajon on 6 August 1944 was unlucky. The *Gruppe* was completely war-weary and had only a few remaining serviceable aircraft. On that day the German fighters were supposed to form up into a large battle unit over Versailles, and I./JG 5 was given the task of providing top cover. But suddenly the order was changed: "Intercept incoming formation of heavy bombers!" Only three machines got airborne: *Leutnant* Mors' "White 4", *Unteroffizier* Buinski's "Black 4" and *Leutnant* Lehner's "Yellow 7". That was all that the *I. Gruppe* could put into the air. In the area of Beaumont fate ran its course. Lehner's Messerschmitt was hit and set on fire while attacking the bomber formation. The pilot attempted a forced landing but crashed. Lehner was taken to the *Luftwaffe* hospital in Clichy with facial injuries and a concussion. At about the same time *Leutnant* Mors shot down a heavy bomber for his twelfth victory in the west. But Mors' machine was also hit and he was shot through the lung. He just managed to bale out but probably lacked the strength to concentrate on the landing, for he ended up hanging from a tree. Mors, too, was taken to hospital in Clichy, where he died of his severe wounds on 8 August. Three days later he was buried in the cemetery in Ivry near Paris.

August Mors, born in Sigmaringen on 20 June 1921, had come to the Defense of the Reich with Weißenberger and achieved a total of 60 victories, the last 12 of them in the west. In recognition of his accomplishments, Mors was awarded the Knight's Cross posthumously.

The *1. Staffel* suffered another painful loss when *Unteroffizier* Binna failed to return on 7 August. Ernst Binna, whom Weißenberger often chose as his wingman, took off into the Avranches area at about 14:00 hours and did not come back.

The death of *Leutnant* Mors, which was a bitter blow to the *Gruppe*, appeared to signal an end to I./JG 5's activities in the west. There was little flying, for the Allied fighter-bombers appeared over Arpajon almost daily, bombing and strafing. At brief intervals the flying elements moved to Wunstorf in the Reich to rest and reequip, while the ground elements prepared for the long journey via Mons-en-Chaussee to Herpy near Juvincourt. With American tanks just 15 kilometers from Arpajon, the main detachment had to hurriedly abandon the base, leaving behind a team from the signals platoon whose job it was to dismantle or destroy the last communication links.

The newly-formed II./JG 6 was based in the Juvincourt area and at the time was attached to *Jagdgeschwader 27*. There retreating ground personnel of I./JG 5 were now placed at its disposal, after the main detachment arrived in Herpy on 17 August. During the night of 19 August, however, *Hauptmann* Mikat and the conversion detachment followed the flying elements to Wunstorf. There the *Gruppe* began the formation of a fourth *Staffel* on 21 August. The new unit was largely made up of personnel from the former *4./Jagdgruppe Ost*. In command of the new *Staffel* was *Leutnant* Siegfried Dönch, who left 1./JG 5.

Meanwhile II./JG 6 and the ground personnel of I./JG 5 were constantly on the retreat. These are the individual stages:

> 24-28/8/44: move to Florennes in Belgium. Everywhere the roads are covered with endless columns of *Wehrmacht* vehicles and troops, all heading east. The collapse in France can only be a matter of time.
>
> 29-31/8/44: the unit is supposed to move to Cerfontain, but on 31/8 an order arrives to depart for Marche. Two days later the *Gruppe* goes from there to Bonn-Hangelar, and more than a few of the men step on German soil again for the first time in a long while.

From Bonn it immediately moved on to Rott. After several days of rest, on 15 September 1944 the *Gruppe*'s ground personnel were finally reunited with the flying elements in Wunstorf. Waiting in Wunstorf were new Bf 109 G-14 aircraft.

After conversion training, which lasted until mid-October, Weißenberger's unit moved to Schwerin-Görries for another rest period before joining the Defense of the Reich. For the *I. Gruppe* of JG 5 the end came on 14 October 1944. On that day the unit was absorbed by the *Jagdgeschwader "Horst Wessel"* and renamed III./JG 6. *Hauptmann* Weißenberger left the unit at the end of November to take over the *I. Gruppe* of *Jagdgeschwader 7*, a new jet fighter unit being formed in Königsberg. In January 1945 he became *Kommodore* of the *Geschwader*. By the end of the war he added eight victories flying the Me 262, raising his victory total to 208.

Weißenberger's successor was *Major* Kühle. Shortly before the start of the Ardennes offensive III./JG 6 occupied a new base of operations in Bissel near Oldenburg. During the fighting during the 1944 Christmas season, the *Gruppe* achieved another big success, destroying about twenty enemy aircraft, before it, along with the other *Jagdgeschwader*, was senselessly sent to the slaughter in the notorious New Year's Day action on 1 January 1945 and suffered a serious defeat.

The ranks of the veteran fighter pilots in I./JG 5 continued to thin. In those difficult days it was truly fortunate if a fighter pilot returned safely from a mission, but the desperate heroism of the pilots could do nothing about the orders issued by the Luftwaffe's senior commanders out of ignorance of the true situation, and in the long run even the most courageous pilots could accomplish nothing against the material superiority of the Allies. Among those killed or reported missing during the final weeks of the war were many unit leaders, by then a scarce commodity, like *Oberleutnant* Gerhard Weyl on 24 December and *Leutnant* Siegfried Dönch in the Aachen-Cologne area on 25 December, and *Oberleutnant* Lothar Gerlach and *Major* Helmut Kühle on 1 January 1945 over Holland and Belgium.

Strictly speaking, the subsequent history of III./JG 6 belongs to the history of *Jagdgeschwader 6*, but for the sake of completeness a brief account of events until the end of the war is included here.

After the ill-fated New Year's Day operations in the west, a large number of fighter units, or what was left of them, were sent to the Eastern Front to give air support to the army in its struggle against the Soviets. It was much too late, however, to influence the advance by the Red Army. The end of the war was already in sight. During the first two weeks of that fateful year of 1945, III./JG 6 moved to Groß-Stein near Oppeln, from there to Ohlau on 21 January and then, because of the Red Army's advance, to Sorau. *Leutnant* Wendlinger, the former signals officer of the old I./JG 5, was posted missing at this time; his car was probably destroyed by Russian aircraft.

From Sorau the *Gruppe* flew up to four missions per day in support of the ground forces regardless of the weather. Then on 11 February it was transferred to Welzow south of Cottbus. The situation on the roads was chaotic, as all of the roads heading west were clogged with refugees and retreating *Wehrmacht* units. Because of the fuel shortage, the fighter pilots could only fly every third day.

On 11 April 1945 the signals platoon set out for Hörsching near Linz, where it was incorporated into the 11th Parachute Division and its equipment handed over to the SS. The operational activities of the *Gruppe*'s air elements finally came to an end with their transfer to Prague-Ruzyne airfield in the final days of April.

• • •

If one follows and observes the path of I./JG 5 from the time of its formation in January 1942 until it was renamed in October 1944 just briefly from a statistical angle, two things stand out. After almost two years of operations in the far north and in the Balkans, the *Gruppe* found itself in the Defense of the Reich, where it suffered its first serious losses in the struggle against the Americans: 24 pilots, including two veteran commanders in rapid succession – *Major* Gerlitz and *Major* Carganico.

I./JG 5's stiffest test, however, came during the two months following the Allied invasion of Normandy in 1944, when it paid a high toll in blood, losing eleven killed and six missing. Fourteen pilots were wounded. In return the *Gruppe* accounted for more than 50 enemy aircraft. Two men, whose names appeared in the operations reports over and over again, accounted for the bulk of these successes. They claimed two-thirds of the victories scored by the *Gruppe*:

Hptm. Weißenberger	25 fighter aircraft
Lt. Mors	11 fighters and 1 heavy bomber

The *Gruppe* operated for 33 months in the most differing theaters of war. Its losses in killed or missing during this time were: 3 *Gruppenkommandeure*, 4 *Staffelkapitäne* and 60 pilots, for a total of 67 flying personnel.

Chapter 3
JG 5 on the Polar Sea

The New Jagdgeschwader 5

During the winter months of 1941-42 the flying units under *Oberst* Holle, the *Fliegerführer Nord (Ost)*, occupied their deployment airfields on the Polar Sea Front in order to continue sustained attacks against the *Luftwaffe*'s declared target, the Murmansk railway, and interdict it through air attacks. In the meantime, however, the Soviets had been able to establish a defense front, and the Germans were soon encountering an intensive flak and fighter defense. The Russians even established temporary airfields on frozen northern lakes, from where they mounted defensive operations. These units, almost all of which were fighter units whose mission was to defend the port city of Murmansk, were under the command of the North Sea Fleet under Major General Andreyev.

In addition to the resumption of the aerial offensive, for the German fighter forces the spring of 1942 also brought with it an extensive organizational change ordered by the RLM: the formation of *Jagdgeschwader 5* under *Oberstleutnant* Handrick, the former *Kommodore* of JG 26 "Schlageter". *Jagdgruppe Stavanger* became I./JG 5 and the former *Jagdgruppe z.b.V.* became II./JG 5, while at the end of February in Trondheim III./JG 5 was created from IV./JG 1, which had previously been based in Jever.

As the *I. Gruppe*'s part in the *Geschwader*'s history was described in the previous chapter, all that remains here is to list the officers who held positions in the *Stab*, *II. Gruppe* and *III. Gruppe* of JG 5:

Geschwaderkommodore:	*Oberstlt.* Handrick
Adjutant:	*Hptm.* Brockmann
Technical Officer:	*Hptm.* Probst
Signals Officer:	*Lt.* Rutishauser
Kommandeur II./JG 5:	*Major* Strümpell
Adjutant:	*Oblt.* Glöckner
Technical Officer:	*Lt.* Hans-Dieter Hartwein

Signals Officer:	*Oblt.* Stribny
Headquarters Company:	*Hptm.* Mikat
4. *Staffel*:	*Hptm.* Schäfer (form. 4./JG 77)
5. *Staffel*:	*Oblt.* Menzel (form. 14./JG 77)
6. *Staffel*:	*Oblt.* Carganico (form. 1./JG 77)
Kommandeur III./JG 5:	*Hptm.* Scholz
Adjutant:	*Oblt.* Lüder
Technical Officer:	*Lt.* Schumann
Signals Officer:	*Lt.* Kalischeck
Headquarters Company:	*Hptm.* Hecht
7. *Staffel*: (form. 1./EJG 3)	*Hptm.* Graf von Sponeck
8. *Staffel*:	*Oblt.* Segatz (form. 11./JG 1)
9. *Staffel*:	*Oblt.* Huppertz (form. 12./JG 1)

III./JG 5 was created from the former *IV. Gruppe* of JG 1. The latter unit, formed in Brest in January 1942, had consisted of the *10., 11.* and *12. Staffel* under the command of *Kapitäne* von Eichel-Streiber, Segatz and Huppertz. At the end of February the *Gruppe* moved to Trondheim, where it was renamed III./JG 5. The other, somewhat complicated renaming of units took place as follows:

From 10./JG 1 was created 1./JG 5 under *Oberleutnant* Wolfgang Kosse, as the original 1./JG 5 under Carganico, which was created from 1./JG 77, now became part of the *II. Gruppe* as the 6. *Staffel*. 11. and 12./JG 1 were renamed 8. and 9./JG 5. There had already been a 7. *Staffel* of JG 5 in Norway since January 1942. This *Staffel*, led by *Hauptmann* Graf von Sponeck, was the former 10./JG 3. According to a telex from the OKL, 7./JG 5 existed as an independent unit under the direct command of the *Jafü Norwegen* (Fighter Commander Norway). The above-mentioned telex, dated 29/12/1941, stated that: "Aircraft complement is to be brought up to 15 Bf 109s with crews provided by the *Gruppen*. *Staffel* is to be deployed immediately. *Staffelkapitän* is to report to the Fighter Commander Norway, *Oberst* Schumacher, as soon as possible. Intended base of operations Bodö in northern Norway."

After receipt of this telex, von Sponeck hurriedly began making preparations for the transfer of his *Staffel*'s air elements. The aircraft underwent a thorough inspection in preparation for the long flight to Bodö. Personnel on leave were recalled, packed bags were unpacked. The first leg of the transfer flight, across the Skagerrak to Kristiansand-Kjevik in Norway, was scheduled for the 30th of December and at 14:00 on that day the aircraft took off from Esbjerg.

The aircraft formed up into a *Staffel* wedge formation consisting of three flights of four aircraft (*Schwärme*) and one of three (*Kette*) and set course for the Norwegian coast at high-speed cruise. Finally a broad fjord appeared before the pilots; at its end was their destination airfield, Kristiansand. The Messerschmitts flew up the fjord at a height of 500 meters. The view was magnificent, for the contrast between the somber gray-brown mountains and the white-capped emerald green of the Atlantic reflected all of the untouched nature of the Norwegian coast.

After arriving over Kristiansand the *Staffel* joined the circuit and *Hauptmann* von Sponeck was first to touch down on the concrete runway. "Nice soft landing", he thought, but no sooner had he reached this conclusion when the tail of his "White 5" slowly, and then more forcefully, begin swinging to the left. When the Messerschmitt finally came to rest it was almost at right angles to the direction of landing. The *Hauptmann* cautiously applied power and gingerly taxied to the end of the runway, from where he tensely watched the next aircraft, which was just touching down. It too began to turn, swung and completed a proper "*Ringelpiez*", or ground loop. The aircraft then dropped its right wing and ended up on its nose.

By the time the *Staffel* was on the ground, five of the fifteen Messerschmitts were littering the airfield with damaged undercarriages. The suspected reason: an ice-covered runway that had not been sanded. The chief of the base's repair facility had a completely different explanation for the crash landings, however: it wasn't the runway that was responsible, instead it was the Messerschmitts' unlocked tailwheels. A tailwheel locking mechanism had been developed for fighter units deployed in Norway on account of the high risk of ground looping on Norwegian airfields, most of which had concrete or wooden plank runways. Prior to landing, pilots were supposed to lock the tailwheel in the neutral position, while for takeoff and taxiing the tailwheel was unlocked.

Three of the five crashes resulted in serious crumpling of the fuselage, which could only be repaired at home base, while the other two Bf 109s could be made flyable again in about three days. Continuing on to Bodö was out of the question, as the Messerschmitts first had to be fitted with the tailwheel locking mechanism. And so *Hauptmann* von Sponeck and his pilots spent New Years in a barracks in Kristiansand which had previously served as quarters for a *Staffel* of KG 26.

On 2 January 1942 the 7. *Staffel* moved to Stavanger-Forus, which resulted in an interruption in the transfer to Bodö of about 14 days. The twelve Messerschmitts, two of which followed from Kristiansand several days later, were handed over to the maintenance section, which began installing the tailwheel locking systems and external fuel tanks.

Until now the former *Jagdgruppe Stavanger*, since renamed I./JG 5, had only been able to defend the Norwegian coast as far as Trondheim, leaving the northern part virtually undefended. The *7. Staffel* was now supposed to close this gap to Bodö. At that time, however, the German admiralty was planning a major operation in which battleships and heavy cruisers would attack Allied convoys bound for Murmansk. For this reason Norwegian waters would obviously gain significance as the base from which these operations would be carried out – both for German forces and those of the enemy. Against this background 7./JG 5's mission was understandable: defend the Narvik-Lofotens area against air and sea attack. Defend friendly naval forces. Defend the *Hermann-Göring-Werke*, a heavy water plant located on a fjord near the Arctic Circle.

At the end of January 1942 three Messerschmitts were received from I./JG 5 as replacements for the aircraft lost in Kristiansand and von Sponeck and his *7. Staffel* were able to set off on the next leg of their transfer to Herdla near Bergen. Almost four weeks after they began their journey, the fighters finally arrived at their final destination, Bodö.

Operations in the north by the *7. Staffel* proved extremely difficult and demanded all the skill that the pilots of von Sponeck's unit could muster, even though the "surveillance flights" themselves were nothing out of the ordinary. It was inevitable that their initial enthusiasm turned into a certain level of disappointment. The weather, in particular, made the pilots' lives difficult, and neither their training nor the air traffic control was adequate for the conditions. Thanks to the efforts of the base meteorologist, *Leutnant* Bolz, the *Staffel* was able to avoid any total losses. After about four weeks in Bodö, von Sponeck was convinced that the so-called Lofotens reconnaissance represented a complete misuse of single-engine fighter aircraft and that this kind of mission was ill-advised and therefore unjustifiable. Attempts to remedy the situation were unsuccessful, but at least he was later able to have the Lofotens flights acknowledged as combat missions.

On 6 March 1942, 7./JG 5 was finally assigned a mission that deviated from what it had become used to. The next day the *Staffel* was to provide air cover for the battleship *Tirpitz* for part of its first operational sortie. A *Schwarm* of fighters would pick up the battleship and its escorting destroyers at the Arctic Circle and remain with the warships until relieved. The rest of the *Staffel* would wait on the airfield, pilots strapped into their cockpits. The operation was uneventful, and abeam Narvik the *Staffel* left the fleet unit, whose target was a Murmansk convoy, to its fate.

7./JG 5's activities in the Lofotens area came to an end at the beginning of April. The *Staffel* moved to Finland for duty on the Murmansk front. "Shedding no tears for our time in Bodö, we embarked upon our journey and two days later, after a stop in Banak, arrived at Petsamo, our new base of operations."

Meanwhile, in mid-March the *8. Staffel* of JG 5, the former 11./JG 1, left its base in Jever on the first leg of its journey via Trondheim to Petsamo, finally arriving there in May. Unfortunately the transfer flight was overshadowed by a serious loss on 22 April, when a Ju 52 carrying some of 8./JG 5's ground personnel crashed into Breiting Mountain near Reipaa. The accident claimed the lives of 18 servicemen. They were buried with full military honors in Trondheim on 5 May.

At the urging of the Finnish army command, in the spring of 1942 there was a reorganization of the Lapland Army in the southern and central sectors of the northern front. The Finnish III Army Corps was withdrawn from the 20th Mountain Army and replaced by German units. The taking of Murmansk remained the objective of the Lapland Army. According to a postwar article in the Military Science Review by *General* Erfurth, the "German general attached to the Finnish armed forces high command", the capture of Murmansk with the two divisions then available was entirely possible. It was left to the Russians, however, to demonstrate that it was possible to commit and supply even more than just two divisions despite the difficulties imposed by the terrain. In October 1944 they launched an offensive against the positions on the Lisa front which had serious consequences for the Germans.

With Russian resistance strengthening almost everywhere on the Eastern Front, not least because of the support they were receiving from the Allies in the form of supply convoys, Murmansk and the Murmansk railway once again shifted to the center of the OKW's strategic planning. It was decided that in the spring an advance would be made from the Alakurtti area toward Kandalaksha with the objective of reaching the Murmansk railway. Dubbed "Operation *Lachsfang*" (Salmon Fishing), the operations had to be postponed indefinitely after the Soviets launched powerful attacks against the German ring around Leningrad, negating all the preparations by the German and Finnish forces. In fact, there would be no resumption of offensive movements against the Murmansk railway for the rest of the war.

This brief summary of developments in the general situation on the northern front is necessary, as *Jagdgeschwader 5* remained closely linked to the fate of the Lapland Army from the first day to the last, as they waged a common struggle in the desolate vastness of the tundra.

The city of Murmansk and the Murmansk railway and their military significance clearly impacted the war in the air over the front in Lapland, especially as the enemy had long since created a defensive strongpoint on account of the area's strategic importance. Russian activity was still largely limited to defensive operations, however, and only rarely were Russian aircraft seen on offensive missions over the front. The main Soviet fighter at this time was the British Hurricane, which replaced the famous but obsolete Rata, but the fighter pilots of JG 5 now also began meeting the MiG-3. Later they would also encounter the Bell P-39 Airacobra, Curtiss P-40 Tomahawk, LaGG-3, Yak-7 and Yak-9.

As previously related, Rovaniemi, Kemi and Petsamo, which had been taken by Dietl's 20th Mountain Army at the start of the campaign against the Soviet Union, were the first bases for attacks directed against Murmansk, and Petsamo soon became the most important base for *Luftwaffe* units in the extreme northeast. Radar monitoring of the airspace around Murmansk was initially the job of the "Reindeer" air signals position. Located on the so-called "Fischer Neck", it was equipped with a *Freya* radar. Radar stations were also set up in Petsamo and Kirkenes and these were operationally subordinate to the *Fliegerführer Nord (Ost)*. Information from these stations was evaluated by the respective staffs and then transmitted to the fighter units of JG 5 in the form of operational orders.

The air base commander in Petsamo was *Oberstleutnant* von Aaken, an Austrian, who strove to respond to the concerns and problems of the fighter units stationed at the airfield. All of those who were stationed at Petsamo have fond memories of von Aaken, the "soul of the airbase". Petsamo became an "airfield city" of more than 5,000 inhabitants, with staffs, supply units, air traffic control, kitchens, workshops, anti-aircraft units, construction companies, labor units made up of captured Russian soldiers, saunas, a movie theater and a laundry with real Lapp women (who could turn cotton batting and simple materials into wonderful Christmas decorations). Van Aaken always knew what to do, and it seemed that there were no unsolvable problems for him. The clearing of huge masses of snow to allow flight operations to go ahead or the procurement of vital replacement parts for the aircraft were just two of the many things that contributed to the base commander's universal and unreserved popularity.

The *II.* and *III. Gruppe* were quartered in barracks and Finnish tents on the east side of the base, directly in front of the steep slopes of the Petsamojoki Valley. On the opposite side was Savior Mountain, with the still-occupied remains of a famous old Russian-Orthodox monastery called Illuostari, which was the symbol of the Petsamo airfield.

After converting onto the Bf 109 F-4 at the Finnish airfield of Pori, at the end of May 1942 the *II. Gruppe* moved to Petsamo and used the Nautsi, Ivalo and Kemijärvi airfields as forward bases from which to mount operations. *Hauptmann* Scholz's new *III. Gruppe*, sent from Norway, had also been in Petsamo since the end of April. Its *7.* and *8. Staffel* were also occasionally based in Kirkenes. The concentration of two *Jagdgruppen* in Petsamo did nothing, however, to alter the numerical superiority of the Russian fighter defense. The Germans were often outnumbered ten to one in the air, and this superiority was only partially offset by better aircraft (Bf 109F) and the skill and fighting spirit of the German fighter pilots.

The difficulty of operations since the formation of JG 5 is clearly reflected in the casualties suffered by the *Geschwader* during the period up to and including May 1942: *II. Gruppe* lost nine pilots killed and the *III. Gruppe* four. Two pilots were certainly captured during the same period. The first casualties occurred in February. At that time II./JG 5 was still flying the Bf 109 E-7. On 19 February three aircraft of the *4. Staffel* took off to reconnoiter the Petri Lake area and there ran into eight Soviet I-18 fighters. *Leutnant* Ehrler, who was leading the German flight, attacked immediately. In the ensuing skirmish Ehrler shot down an I-18, however the Russians succeeded in shooting down the aircraft of *Obergefreiter* Seibt. Seibt, who is still listed as missing, was the *II. Gruppe*'s first casualty.

At this point it is perhaps appropriate to make reference to the orthographical terms. Lake in Finnish is *järvi*, consequently on Finnish maps Petri Lake appears as Petrijärvi. The Russians called their lakes *osero* and the Lapps *jawr*. When, at the start of the war in the north, the Russians began using Finnish maps, they added their own notations, and when the Germans adapted them for their own use they added theirs as well. This resulted in curious double or multiple names. Some, such as Petrijärvijawrosero-Lake may have been too much of a good thing.

Return from the Snow of the Tundra

We do not know the precise number of German pilots who baled out over or crash-landed in enemy territory and then made the difficult trek back to their own lines or were rescued by the "search Storks". Based on the extent of operational activity and the total losses suffered by the *Geschwader*, it could not have been very large, however, yet each of these harrowing experiences was an essential and typical part of the history of the Polar Sea *Geschwader*. The accounts by the fighter pilots who were tested by fate in this way all contain several common features: the struggle against the severe weather and time, the fear of discovery by the enemy and, above all, the fear of being left alone in the endless solitude.

The story of the almost three-day odyssey of *Unteroffizier* Dietrich Weinitschke of the *5. Staffel* is representative of all the other pilots who suffered similar misfortune. It began at about 14:00 on 26 February 1942, when *Unteroffizier* Weinitschke took off on a mission to reconnoiter the port of Murmansk.

When the pair of German fighters approached the Russian fighter base at Murmashi at an altitude of 3000 meters, they saw two Hurricanes closing from twelve o'clock and another on approach to land at the airfield. The Russians turned to position themselves behind the two Germans, but the latter reacted swiftly and a dogfight broke out. After the first bursts of fire the enemy aircraft broke away, one of them leaving behind a long gray smoke trail.

The Messerschmitts then turned north to complete their mission but were jumped from above by several more Russian fighters. Another dogfight broke out, in which *Oberfeldwebel* Bauer shot down one of the Russians. Then Weinitschke suddenly saw a Hurricane on his leader's tail. He radioed, "Look out! One behind you!," and at the same time hauled his Messerschmitt around to attack the enemy from the front. Although the two fighters passed close to one another, neither he nor the Russian pilot managed to register any hits. The Russian dove toward Murmashi and Weinitschke tried to follow. Below, however, snow trails revealed that more enemy aircraft were taking off.

Another Soviet fighter went down, Bauer's second victory. By the time *Unteroffizier* Weinitschke tried to climb back up, it was already too late. When he pulled up he flew straight into the fire of a Russian fighter sitting on his tail. Bullets struck his wing, the instrument panel and then the armor plate behind him. The cockpit filled with smoke. The *Unteroffizier*'s first thought was, "Get out!," but then he thought how the Russians down below in Murmashi would celebrate to have a fighter delivered to their door at the air base, and so he stayed with his machine. He pointed his aircraft in the direction of the German lines as the coolant temperature steadily rose, expecting the engine's pistons to seize at any minute. Suddenly there was a shadow beside him. "I'm here!" Bauer called to him.

"Eber, I've been hit in the radiators, I have to land immediately!"

"Viktor!"

The damaged Messerschmitt made it to a lake that Weinitschke had chosen for a forced landing. Seconds later he pulled the jettison lever and the folding canopy sailed away. The aircraft pancaked and slid across the ground, piling up the powdery snow in front of it like a bow wave. Overhead *Oberfeldwebel* Bauer circled once, saw the pilot climb out unhurt and then, waggling his wings, set course for home.

"Then I stood there, about eight kilometers northwest of Murmashi, in thirty-degree cold and knee-deep powdery snow, and thought, 'if the Hurricanes hadn't followed me, they must have landed in Murmashi to refuel.' Because of the safety interval, it took a squadron about ten minutes to land. Refuel, take off, form up, search – it would take them at least ten and no more than twenty-five minutes to get here, but if they do show up they mustn't find me here.

"Impatiently I retrieved my emergency rucksack from the baggage compartment and set off. I was about 500 meters away from the aircraft when I remembered that we had often spotted Russian patrols from the air by the shadows of their tracks, and now the same thing was going to happen to me! And so I retraced my footsteps and got my parachute from the aircraft. I opened it up, cut off the auxiliary chute and parachute lines, slung it over my shoulder and thus erased my tracks. Things went smoothly until I came to the edge of the lake, for the snow was 'only' knee-deep, but when I reached the bushes it suddenly came up to my belt. I removed my rucksack, got out my snowshoes and strapped them on. It would be a serious exaggeration if I claimed that the going became easier. I didn't sink as far as before, but as it was impossible to lift my feet onto the snow cover, the snowshoes were more hindrance than help. After a few minutes I struck one of the snowshoes against an obstacle and sprained my ankle – the snowshoe effort was over. I unbuckled them, put them away and continued wading through the snow.

"My progress was very slow, up a hill, but time was racing by. Zigzagging around the tall spruce that grew here in the warmer Kola estuary, I finally reached the top of the hill. I wasn't sure why no Russian aircraft were looking for me. It was beginning to get dark when I heard the sound of several Messerschmitt engines. They were over the lake, looking for me, but they seemed unable to see me or my tracks. The parachute must really have done its job. I waved in vain, and they were about to fly over me. I pulled out my flare pistol and fired a recognition signal. The pair immediately pulled up towards me. The footing was firmer at the top of the hill and I hurried to reach a spot where they could see me, a larger clearing. As I didn't know which way I should go, I held up the map as they roared overhead. They turned and came back. Once again I held up the map and shrugged my shoulders to indicate that I wanted them to show me which way to go. After circling one more time, they came in from the north, flew very low overhead and disappeared almost exactly in a southerly direction. And so I set a new course and ventured down the slope, southwards.

"And then they were there again, coming from the north and flying past me at a distance of 20 to 30 meters. The pair had given themselves fifteen minutes for this last circuit."

Flying the two fighters were Bauer and *Leutnant* Lesch. They had dropped a package containing equipment and woolen items for the *Unteroffizier*, however he apparently failed to see it. Now they were determined to alert him to the presence of the package. In a wide left turn Bauer wrote a note, tied it to his flare pistol and dropped it during his final pass. But Weinitschke again failed to see it.

"The descent was awful. The snow was up to my hips, so that I had to keep my elbows straight. Some snowdrifts were even deeper, and the bow wave sprayed powdery snow in my face. If I hadn't tied a silk scarf around my head my ears would already have fallen off. By then it was totally dark. I could no longer read my wristband compass and so I orientated myself using the stars. In the valley I made better progress because the snow there was only knee-deep. Then another snowdrift. The snow was literally over my head. Crawling on my parachute, it took me three-quarters of an hour to cover the 50 meters, but then I was finally through. Soon afterwards I fell for the first time. I rested for a few minutes and then went on. And again I lay in the snow. Once again I struggled to my feet and staggered southwards. How many times I lay down in the snow, stood up again and tottered onwards I do not know. By the time I could no longer stand, I had been on the move for about five hours and had covered 13 kilometers. After I removed my rucksack I was able to stand. Ahead to my left was a boulder. I got out my folding spade and shoveled away the snow beside it. I cut birch branches with my knife to create a framework and overlaid it with twigs to form a roof truss and then covered it all with blocks of snow. Finally I was finished and crawled inside the structure. For my empty stomach I allowed myself half a Schoka-Kola [caffeine-fortified chocolate], and it was absolutely clear to me that my two-day emergency rations were not going to suffice for a 100-kilometer walk. Therefore I had to portion it out so that enough would be left after four days for me to eat my fill and consume enough calories to walk.

"The air of the clear, starry night filtered through the slits in my snow house. The parachute, which I had pulled over myself, was a damned thin blanket and I slowly began freezing. I automatically pulled my legs close to my body, but no sooner had I lifted my knees when my muscles began cramping and I quickly stretched my legs out again. It was 22:00 when I first took off my boots to rub my feet warm, but unfortunately it didn't last long and soon I was shaking like an aspen leaf. Sleep was completely out of the question. After an hour I crawled out of the structure and tired to warm up by rubbing my limbs. Eight more times that night, I left the structure to rub my freezing feet and warm up by moving about. But that lasted barely fifteen minutes, and I began shivering again. Finally I pulled out my rucksack and strapped on my snowshoes again because the swelling in my injured foot had gone down and a firm layer of snow promised better progress. I put on my rucksack, draped my parachute over my shoulder and set off. I continued southwards along the hillside.

"It must have been 07:30 when from the north I heard the gentle sound of engines. A big twin-engined machine swept over the mountain like a shadow and disappeared behind the trees. Then I heard a high, singing noise that grew louder: Me 109s! I barely had time to get out my flare pistol before the first one roared over the mountain 500 meters north of me. It went into a left turn, so that all I could see were the yellow undersides of its wingtips. A bang, and my flare rose into the sky. But it only traced a shallow arc above the firs before it fell hissing into the snow. Meanwhile the second, third and fourth machines flashed past me and followed the first to the north. I fired shot after shot into the sky, but no one saw the flares for they were probably looking for me at the lake. The twin-engined aircraft I had seen was the air-sea rescue *Weihe*: it had a crew of three with snowshoes and emergency equipment, including submachine-guns, for four men. They wanted to pick me up, and if unable to take off again make their way on foot with me to Finland. Comradeship among airmen! The five circled around the lake for probably another ten minutes before flying off to the northwest through the valley where I had begun my trek. My ten flares had been expended in vain. I got replacements from my rucksack and stowed them in my pockets. Then I resumed my march northwestwards. The weather was great, my mood less so. After a night like that it was not a good feeling to have seen one's rescuers without being able to attract their attention. If I was on the right track, they would find me during the second rescue flight. I just had to be fast enough.

"I was soon warmed up again, and my sprained left foot was holding up better than I had dared hope. As I trudged through the forest I saw all sorts of tracks in the snow and tried to identify the footprints of rabbits, foxes and snow grouse. Then I came upon a deep, wide track. It must have been a big animal that broke this path for me. I followed it, especially as it was going in my direction, and after a while I suddenly saw a crouched figure moving awkwardly on the slope. I immediately took cover in the snow and tried to figure out what I was looking at. The longer I stared into the blinding brightness, the more unclear the moving shape became. All I could make out was something dark moving awkwardly on all fours in the deep snow. It couldn't be a Russian then. I wanted to know exactly what it was, so I got up and moved towards it. Sweating from exertion, I trudged along the trail as fast as I could. The forest thinned. When I emerged, there was a bear, probably 70 meters away, looking around at me. He stood still for a moment, then, contrary to my fears, he toddled off down the slope into the woods. I don't know which of us got the greater fright from our encounter, but I fear it was I.

"I moved on and soon I realized that I had to take a rest. I was also terribly hungry. I relaxed on a stone, ate half a bar of *Schoka-Kola* and gnawed on a handful of hard bread with some snow. Then I got up again. Once more I was in a seemingly endless forest. I estimated my walking pace to be two to three kilometers per hour. Before me a snow-covered ridge shimmered between the trees. I selected its peak, which I estimated to be about three kilometers away, as the goal for my noon break. Finally I came to the edge of the forest. Glimmering white in the sunshine, a kilometer-long slope stretched before me. The snow looked firm, like a board, and the wind, which often caused the powdery snow to fall in long bands from the spruce trees, was unable to dislodge even a speck from this firm surface. Just a few more steps and I would be out of the powdery snow, which was always almost up to my navel. The next moment, however, I was lying flat in the snow, a reflex to a threat which had not yet entered my consciousness. Not until I cautiously raised my head and scanned the slope, did I see two figures, one big and one small, sharply outlined against the sky. Both were standing like stones, but the more I stared the more I got the impression that they were moving a little. I dug out my sunglasses and looked up again. They were standing still. No! They were moving. What was it: a pair of sentries or two big rocks that appeared to be moving because of overwrought nerves? Pistol in hand, I began walking slowly. The walking was good on the firm snow and after 50 meters I could see clearly and plainly. Two long-legged animals turned round and fled over the peak; probably a cow moose and its calf.

"Had they been standing crosswise, they would have spared me time and palpitations.

"My rapid walking pace soon slowed to my usual jog – one foot in front of the other, about two kilometers per hour. This tempo was not exactly uplifting but I could maintain it even in changing snow conditions. I had discovered that a consistent automaton-like pace best conserved my strength. When I finally reached the peak, however, it was high time for a rest.

"I had to take stock. I had been under way for 24 hours. What had I accomplished? What lay ahead of me? Could I actually make it? So far no one had come back from the vast, snow-covered tundra. If they had still been looking for me than my prospects would have been good, but since the early morning I hadn't seen or heard any more 109s. They must think me frozen or captured. On the other hand, so far I had only eaten one bar of Schoka-Kola and some hard bread. My rations could last four or five days. I also hadn't taken any Pervitin [drug similar to Benzedrine]. I would stay awake one night without aid, perhaps two nights with Pervitin. It was possible. And so I sat down for my noon rest.

"With the help of my wristband compass and my 1:1,000,000 map I tried to fix my position. I estimated that I was about 30 kilometers from Murmashi, about an equal distance from the Russian base of Ura-Guba and about 70 kilometers from Petsamo. My march to the southwest had thus cost me about 15 kilometers and I was now on the right course. The veer I had made had very probably enabled me to avoid the Russian patrols that were surely looking for me.

"I then unpacked my rucksack in order to prepare something hot. I had potted meat, hard bread and Schoka-Kola. I decided upon hard bread with Schoka. A gasoline cooker, a bottle of gasoline and a pot were there. According to the directions, I had to fill the cooker, warm it with my hands, fill the upper rim with gasoline, turn the fuel knob and light the gasoline. I began exactly according to the instructions. I had to remove my gloves in order to warm up the cooker. My hands stuck to the cooker and became ice cold. When I pulled them away pieces of skin clung to the cooker. I lit a match and cautiously stuck it into the gasoline ring. It went out as if I had placed it in water. Further attempts also failed until I emptied the gasoline ring, filled it with storm matches and lit it. The cooker began running like a cold engine, banging and hissing. I placed it on the crust, filled the pot with snow and added the bread and Schoka. I looked away to glance at the map again and heard a hissing sound beside me. The cooker had fallen over and my attempt to make soup lay in the snow. Everything that was brown was mine. I scooped everything back in, made a new platform and put the pot back on. But before all the snow had melted, my soup was in the snow again. I was fed up with the whole thing. Once again I filled the pot with brown snow. I held the pot in one hand and the cooker in the other until I had a lukewarm brew. I fished out the softened bread and the Schoka with my spoon and drank the brown, tepid water. I had lost a great deal of time, and instead of warming myself up I was shivering from cold. While I packed my rucksack I cursed the desk jockeys responsible for giving the fighter pilots such 'perfect' survival equipment.

"When the rucksack was on my back again, I tried to pull on my gloves, however the frozen leather broke apart and I was forced to carry on without gloves in minus thirty degrees. I had soon crossed the slope and entered the tundra, which was covered with short birch trees. Once again the snow came up to my belt. It was becoming obvious that my strength was ebbing. In order to cover a specific distance, I selected a hill as my goal and walked until I reached it. If the next hill was close by, I set it as my ultimate goal for a rest break.

"For some hours a dark band of cloud had been rising from the west, and it suddenly became clear to me why I hadn't seen any more of our aircraft. The airfield must already have been socked in by bad weather. At first I hadn't given it much thought, but now I knew that a snowstorm was coming. A wind came up and slowly became stronger. The cold bit my face, and I frequently rubbed my nose and ears. At dusk I was crossing a brook when I saw two German shepherd dogs to my left. German shepherds? Russian ski patrol? No, the two animals ran off through the deep snow like shadows – wolves!

"I tried to increase my pace, but soon after my scary encounter I was staggering against a raging storm through blowing snow which stuck to my eyes, mouth and face and covered the windward side with an ice mask. I fell, got up again, staggered until the next fall and the one after that. Then it was over. I lacked the strength and energy to build another igloo. So I dug a hole in the snow and lined it with a few branches. My parachute, a pile of frozen, rumpled silk, served as a blanket. With my folding knife I opened a can of potted meat, thawed it using the tested method on the thrice-damned cooker. I wolfed down the still cold meat. Some warm water completed this meal. Now I could only freeze. Moving about in the open in the raging storm was out of the question, and I couldn't move in my hole. My feet slowly went numb, my legs became stiff, and when the storm abated I was so all in that I couldn't get back on my feet.

"When dawn came I crawled into the open in order to be on my way. When I stood up I swayed like a drunk. Surely my legs couldn't be so asleep that it felt as if I was standing on stilts! I cautiously sat down on my rucksack and tried to pull off one of my fur-lined boots. Frozen on! With a jerk I pulled off the boot, in which part of the sock and bits of skin remained hanging. I stuck the frozen sock in my pocket and massaged the foot and calf with snow until the joint could move again. The sock was warm and wet, the boot frozen. By the time I finished with the second boot, the first was like an ice block. It was time to go, the sun would be up soon, but still I was squatting there, even though I knew that I had to be stingy with the hours. I had half a Schoka-Kola for breakfast, but it was clear to me that I would have to increase my rations if I was going to hold out. I must soon reach the halfway mark, but even by the most favorable estimate I must have had more than 50 hours of walking ahead of me. In the evening I would have to break out my Pervitin ration, for the fatigue was resting in my bones like lead, and the parachute, which I was dragging behind me like a silk mountain to hide my tracks, was offering twice as much resistance. In the first hour I covered just 500 meters. Then I warmed up and my pace became faster. The sun came over the horizon, golden beams shone between the snow-covered birches, and soon afterwards the tundra was again bathed in a dazzling light."

Weinitschke did not know that a ski patrol from Murmashi had discovered his Messerschmitt and not far away the package with survival equipment. They began a kilometers-wide search for the German's tracks, but it was as if the snow had swallowed him up. What the *Unteroffizier* also did not know at that point was that 30 kilometers south of the Lisa front about twenty mountain infantrymen on skis were also searching for him, trying to find him before the Russians did. And *Feldwebel* Mendl of 5./JG 5 and his wingman were searching for him once again in a northerly direction, while farther to the south *Oberleutnant* Widowitz was airborne in his *Storch*.

"I trudged through the snow at a speed of about one kilometer per hour. I had given up hope that anyone would be looking for me after the storm. Now and then I squeezed snow in my hand and sucked on it a little. Curiously the icy snow left a very bitter taste on my tongue, so that I wasn't tempted to turn to the snow too often. Just as I stepped into a clearing, from the east I heard the familiar sound of Me 109 engines. I drew my flare pistol and a pair of fighters flew over as my red flare rose into the sky. The leader of the pair rolled to one side, thinking he was under fire, but the other saw the flare falling and turned towards me. Immediately afterwards the pair flew over me and waved before heading for home. This gift made me as happy as a child at Christmas. Nothing more could happen to me now. Soon I would have ski equipment and warm socks, gloves and a fur cap. That would mean for the remaining 50 kilometers I would be watched from the air, without the fear of falling into the hands of the Russians. My tempo increased so, that an hour later I was about two kilometers from my first meeting point, when the roar of an approaching Schwarm of Me 109s roused me from my dreams. I was in the process of crossing a large pond, where I could easily be seen. I raised my flare pistol and fired three times in succession. It was wonderful to see the four flying towards me. I began tramping the word socks, my most needed item of clothing, in the snow. I was two-thirds finished when a bottle with a red silk scarf attached came hurtling down. My comrades in the aircraft must probably have shaken their heads on seeing my efforts to pull the note from the neck of the bottle instead of simply breaking the bottle. Finally I caught a corner in my teeth and pulled the note from the bottle.

'Dear D! *Oberleutnant* Widowitz is on his way in the *Storch* to pick you up. Look for a lake where he can land. All the best, Büble.'

"Büble Artur Mendl had not considered that from my frog's perspective I could walk past the most beautiful lake and never see it, for the snow-covered birches often limited visibility to just 50 meters.

"The *Schwarm* roared over the pond again and turned south over a hill. As I watched, the formation leader's left wing grazed a tree and his aircraft crashed and exploded! I stood as if frozen. In a blur I saw the *Storch* approaching. It flew past the pillar of smoke, its skis literally sliding over the birches, so close that snow was thrown off. The *Storch* touched down gently and taxied towards me. When it halted right beside me I was still unable to move a muscle. The shock was too great.

"Mendl jumped out, led me to the door and pushed me in. We had to leave my parachute behind because it was impossible to fold the frozen lump of silk. The door was shut and off we went. *Oberleutnant* Widowitz taxied to the far corner of the pond, turned into the wind and opened the throttle. We picked up speed much too slowly. When we were almost at the other end, he lifted off, then pushed the kite's nose down so that the skis lightly touched the snow, and then lifted off for good. With the skis just over the birches, dodging the tall spruces as in a slalom, he climbed over the hill. Made it! A loop to the north and soon we saw before us the Russian strongpoint from which the patrols went into no man's land. A no man's land extending 40 to 50 kilometers to the line of German strongpoints. When we appeared a ski patrol took cover, Russians in snow smocks raced to their shelters. Tracer from a 20-mm anti-aircraft gun reached out for us, but we were already too far away, too low. Through the valleys, just above the jagged rocks, we set course for home, two fighters circling round us.

"I had regained my composure by the time we landed. The *Staffel* greeted me like the prodigal son. Moments later my comrades pulled my boots and shreds of sock from my feet and began massaging my legs with snow to bring them back to life. There was no feeling below the knees. By the time the ambulance came to get me they had done it; a red fluid began running from several open places. I was carried into the dispensary on a stretcher and there they applied the Finnish treatment, birch tar smeared on my feet and calves and then wrapped tightly. With two sleeping pills in my belly I returned to the *Staffel*, where I was greeted with a bottle of rum. They made me two-finger grog – two spoonfuls of sugar, a finger length of rum, a finger width of boiling water and a slice of lemon – until the bottle was empty. I couldn't sleep, even though the *Staffelkapitän* ordered everyone out. The room filled again after everyone went off duty, and by about 20:00 my nerves had calmed and I fell asleep."

I do not wish to conclude without mentioning the name of the unfortunate pilot who lost his life during the selfless effort to rescue *Unteroffizier* Weinitschke. He was the brave *Oberfeldwebel* Erhard Bauer who, probably blinded by the snow, crashed to his death in his "Red 6" south of Motovski Hill 338 on that 28 February 1942.

Murmansk Combat Zone – PQ Convoys

March was not without further casualties for *Oberleutnant* Menzel's 5./JG 5. On the 23rd the *Staffel* was ordered to attack a barracks camp on Titovka Bay, during which *Oberleutnant* Grobe was shot down by Russian flak. He was already on the way home when his machine took a direct hit, which forced him to make a forced landing. A *Storch* took off immediately but was only able to recover Strobe's body from the wreckage of his Messerschmitt. On the following Sunday, the 29th of March, a heavy snow shower forced *Obergefreiter* Hermann Hesse to go around while attempting to land at Parkkina. When he did not return, a search was begun, however neither he nor his aircraft "Red 1" were ever found.

On 4 April there was a dogfight over Russian territory between the 5. *Staffel* and 14 Hurricanes and three MiG-3s, in which *Oberfeldwebel* Hornig and

Unteroffizier Mendl were wounded. There was another encounter with Russian fighters on 9 April, between Ustya-Lota and Ristikent. Six Messerschmitts had taken off to escort a Henschel reconnaissance aircraft to Ristikent. Suddenly the Germans saw about 15 to 20 enemy fighters approaching and the uneven contest began. During the dogfight, which lasted about 20 minutes, pilots saw *Leutnant* Jakobi's "Red 2" hit and subsequently crash, though the pilot baled out. He was seen to land safely, but then the fighter pilots were so caught up in the action that none of them could see what became of Jakobi. The same applied to *Feldwebel* Kandziora, who was shot up by Russian fighters and obliged to make a forced landing. He made a good belly landing at the mouth of the Lutto River and Kandziora fired several flares before all trace of him was lost.

Unfortunately bad weather forced a postponement of a search effort until the following day and, sadly, it was unsuccessful. Numerous ski trails led to the spot where Jakobi landed by parachute, suggesting that the *Leutnant* had been captured. Kandziora's Messerschmitt was also found, despite efforts by the pilot to conceal it. It was also surrounded by ski tracks; consequently this pilot too must have been captured by the Russians. Of the two, *Leutnant* Jakobi was the only one to survive. He was initially placed in Camp 158 and ultimately returned to Germany.

As soon as the *7. Staffel* arrived in Petsamo, *Oberleutnant* Carganico, by then *Kommandeur* of the *II. Gruppe*, took off with *Hauptmann* von Sponeck on an orientation flight over the front. When they reached the Tuloma River, the silhouettes of two aircraft suddenly appeared against the clouds, and Carganico called a warning: "Two Indians ahead and below! We're attacking!" It was two Hurricanes, casually flying straight south. The two Messerschmitts dived immediately and soon reached the enemy's altitude. They were just 200 meters away. Von Sponeck's nervousness grew, as this was his first contact with the enemy in the new sector. His hands shook and beads of sweat covered his nose and upper lip. It made him half crazy that at that precise moment the lenses of his sunglasses fogged up; a consequence of the evaporating sweat.

"Get closer!" radioed Carganico. And then he assigned the targets: "Move up and take the element leader. I'll take the wingman!"

The *Gruppenkommandeur*'s Bf 109 dropped back and soon was behind the Hurricane. He pressed the firing buttons and pieces flew off the enemy aircraft, and suddenly its fuselage turned into a blazing torch. The Russian slowly peeled off to the left and then went straight down, a fireball trailing a long banner of black smoke. That was Carganico's victory. Then *Hauptmann* von Sponeck opened fire. Explosive rounds from his 20-mm cannon struck the Hurricane, creating the impression that its fuselage was swelling while under fire, but there was no reaction from the Russian pilot. He continued flying straight and level. The effects of the next burst were immediate. The enemy machine became shrouded in smoke and went down in a steep dive. A red parachute showed that at least one of the Russian pilots had baled out.

Hauptmann von Sponeck's first flight over the front almost ended in a crash, for in his excitement he forgot to lower his undercarriage before landing. It was not until a red flare was fired from the airfield that he realized his mistake.

In September 1941 the German troops on the Polar Sea were forced into positional warfare, while the *Luftwaffe* continued its attacks on the port and city of Murmansk. For the fighter units stationed in Kirkenes and Petsamo, this meant a continuation of their escort missions for bomber and Stuka units in the coming months. The bomber formations usually arrived over Petsamo at an altitude of 6000-7000 meters, where they picked up their fighter escort. And always the Russians were there too, for Russian lookouts reported the German intruders as soon as they crossed the front. Almost immediately, long snow or dust trails on the Russian airfields in Kola, Murmashi, Shongui and Varlamovo revealed that enemy fighters were taking off.

Carganico's 6./JG 5 was assigned such an escort mission on 23 April. He led a formation of seven aircraft flying escort for a group of Ju 87s attacking targets in Murmansk, where contact was made with a large number of Hurricanes. *Oberfeldwebel* Florian Salwender, a successful fighter pilot with 24 victories, got on the tail of an enemy fighter and shot it down for his 25th. The Russians also scored, however. It happened very quickly. Salwender's "Yellow 11" suddenly went down, and a white parachute was seen right over Murmansk. Salwender was captured but did not survive to return home.

In the same engagement *Oberfeldwebel* Rudi Müller, who would soon become the first big fighter ace in the north, shot down five Hurricanes over Kola Bay.

During the first weeks in Petsamo the *Jagdstaffeln* of the *II.* and *III. Gruppe* often flew several Stuka escort missions per day, as the dive-bombers supported the 6th Mountain Division in its defensive struggle. The Soviets had launched counterattacks all along the front in Lapland, especially in the Murmansk area and the Louhi River sector to the south. At first 7./JG 5 did not take part in these escort missions, as *Hauptmann* Scholz, *Kommandeur* of the *III. Gruppe*, had tasked the *Staffel* with flying escort for tactical reconnaissance aircraft whose job it was to take photos or direct artillery fire. For the fighter pilots it was a thankless task, because the Russians of course did everything they could to counter the bothersome flights by the fixed-gear but extremely maneuverable Henschel high-wing monoplanes.

With the increase in daylight, the bomber units expanded their activities against Murmansk and Kola Bay as well as installations associated with the Murmansk railway. The bridges in Taybola were a favorite target of the Stukas. The two *Gruppen* of *Jagdgeschwader 5* based in the north, plus the *Zerstörerstaffel*, took part in all of these operations with every available aircraft. Both *Gruppen*, except for single *Schwärme*, left behind to defend their airfields, took part in the so-called "big air raids" on Murmansk. This procedure for protecting the bomber units had developed over time from the conditions in the air over the combat zone and promised good success. The *Geschwader*'s operational strength at that time was about forty Bf 109s and as many as ten Bf 110s. This was a low figure given the great numerical superiority of the Russians, and it was only due to the superior skill of the pilots of JG 5 that losses among the fighters and bombers remained relatively low. While the Bf 109's armament and ammunition were superior to those of the Hurricane, the latter was superior in a lengthy turning fight. The MiG-3 and Curtiss P-40 began appearing in growing numbers in the summer of 1942, but this did little to alter the technical balance.

On 1 May 1942, during a maintenance test flight by four aircraft, the *5. Staffel*'s "Red 1" flew into terrain and crashed, killing *Unteroffizier* Kanbach. Some days later, on 9 May, the *8. Staffel* was escorting Stukas to Motovskiy Gulf, where about 30 Hurricanes were waiting. After the combat *Leutnant* Lechte was missing and it was uncertain whether he had been able to bale out. The same thing happened to *Unteroffizier* Bausch of 5./JG 5 over Ura Bay on 10 May.

During a morning mission, escorting Stukas to Murmansk, just beyond the front line the Messerschmitts were attacked by about ten Hurricanes and Ratas. On that 15 May *Unteroffizier* von Podewils scored his first victory. He got on the tail of a Hurricane and closed to within 50 meters before shooting it down west of Murmansk at 08:30. The enemy aircraft went down in a shallow dive and was seen to crash by *Unteroffizier* Bartels.

On 17 May 1942 the *6. Staffel* under the command of *Oberleutnant* Carganico took off for Murmansk at 08:30. Before long, approximately twenty Hurricanes appeared to intercept the German aircraft. *Oberfeldwebel* Pfränger had the misfortune to be shot down in his Bf 109 F-4 northwest of Murmansk and was subsequently taken prisoner by the Russians. One year later he had the opportunity to tell the curious story of what had happened to him, for in autumn 1943 he turned up at a German unit in the central sector of the Eastern Front. After arriving in prisoner of war camp 158 in Cherepovets, the Russians allegedly offered him a chance to take part in an anti-fascist course. Pfränger accepted and attended the course, where he received instruction in the use of radio and espionage techniques. Later the Russians provided him with the uniform of a

German *Feldwebel* or *Oberfeldwebel*, complete with decorations for bravery, and at the specified time sent him back across the lines. His mission was clear. Pfränger immediately reported to the nearest command post. He was accompanied by another German soldier who had been captured and had the same mission as Pfränger. Pfränger was immediately placed under arrest. Carganico, then a *Hauptmann* and *Kommandeur* of II./JG 5, was ordered by *Luftflotte* 5 to fly to the central sector to identify Pfränger. Later an order was received from the superior command stating that Pfränger was not to be employed in a front line unit. As far as is known, he was assigned to a flying school in the Reich as an instructor.

During another Stuka escort mission on 17 May, *Leutnant* Ehrler was again successful, shooting down a MiG-3. It is always astonishing how a vastly outnumbered handful of German aircraft often succeeded in shooting down a large number of enemy aircraft. The Russians did not employ the tactic of attacking from above as practiced by the Germans and the western Allies. Instead the Russians preferred to attack individually from all sides or come from below. Perhaps this was because, on the Murmansk front, the Russians rarely had the time to reach an advantageous higher altitude before attacking.

Despite JG 5's success in aerial combat, the *Eismeerjäger* regularly suffered casualties, as on 17 May 1942. At almost the same time as Ehrler's victory, *Unteroffizier* Schattschneider collided with an enemy fighter over Petrijärvi. The pilot crash-landed in a wood and suffered serious sprains and dislocations. After a fifteen-day walk through the tundra, on 2 June Schattschneider returned to the airbase, where his comrades of the *4. Staffel* gave him a tumultuous welcome. Unfortunately *Unteroffizier* Karl Heinz Wellner of 4./JG 5 was captured during the same mission. Ten days later *Oberfeldwebel* Sommer of 8./JG 5 parachuted over Murmashi and was reported missing.

Beginning the summer of 1942, in Trondheim-Lade the newly-formed IV./JG 5 under *Hauptmann* Kriegel assumed responsibility for defending the Norwegian coast from Trondheim to Narvik. Thus the *I.* and *IV. Gruppe* were stationed on the west coast and the *II.* and *III. Gruppe* and the *Geschwaderstab* in Petsamo, and the *Zerstörerstaffel* 10.(Z)/JG 5, which was attached to the *Geschwader* but operated independently, was based in Kirkenes. The formation of the *Geschwader* was thus complete.

The following ten points characterized JG 5's operational mission:

1. Defend the occupied airfields in Banak, Kirkenes and Petsamo. To accomplish this the *Geschwader* assigned one *Staffel* (usually two *Schwärme*) to daily operational readiness, with one *Schwarm* at 3-minute readiness from dawn till dusk (30 minutes before dawn and after dusk) except during high summer when it was all day.

2. Defend the nickel mines in Kolosjoki.
3. Defend the ports of Kirkenes and Kolosjoki.
4. Provide fighter escorts for bomber and Stuka units of the *Fliegerführer Nord (Ost)*.
5. Achieve temporary and local air superiority during the course of bombing operations against Murmansk by conducting *freie Jagd* (fighter sweeps) in the approach, target and return flight areas.
6. Provide fighter escort for supply ships and naval units in the waters between Vardö and Petsamo.
7. Provide fighter escort for tactical reconnaissance aircraft over the XIX Mountain Corps' front.
8. Defend the airspace over the XIX Mountain Corps.
9. Defend preparations and operations by the XIX Mountain Corps by mounting defensive patrols over the threatened areas.
10. Carry out low-level missions in support of local operations by the XIX Mountain Corps.
11. Preparation for fighter-bomber missions by taking the necessary steps to provide the necessary external stores racks, briefings for the crews and sufficient stocks of air-dropped weapons.

Engagement of the PQ and QP (empty convoys from Murmansk to Iceland) convoys was the task of the three air commanders (*Fliegerführer*) – North (East), Lofotens and North (West), depending in which waters the convoy was operating. The bomber units attached to *Luftflotte 5*, KG 26 and KG 30, were deployed accordingly.

Since August 1941 the western powers had been supporting their hard-pressed Soviet ally by delivering large quantities of war materiel. At first, however, this could only be delivered by sea, through the North Sea to Murmansk and Arkhangelsk on the White Sea. The first convoys reached their destination unopposed, and the German command was inexplicably slow in recognizing the threat they posed. The trigger was the appearance on the Eastern Front of large quantities of British and American guns, tanks and aircraft. A total of twelve convoys arrived at their destinations by March 1942, when convoy PQ 13 became the first to be attacked by German air and sea forces.

The dark winter months made it much more difficult to find and attack the convoys passing through the Polar Sea, and consequently they made it through to Murmansk almost unhindered. But then *Luftflotte 5* concentrated all its resources against the convoys, while at the same time the Soviets prudently stepped up their attacks on German airfields. In mid-April 1942 the total strength of the air fleet in

Norway and Finland was 165 aircraft, of which 113 were serviceable, while at the end of May it was 203, of which 141 were serviceable.

In mid-May convoy PQ 16, consisting of 35 freighters and 15 warships, left Iceland and headed for the Soviet Union. German reconnaissance aircraft first sighted the convoy on 16 May and the following day the bombers and torpedo bombers of KG 26 and KG 30 launched more than twelve missions against it. The battle lasted six days and resulted in heavy casualties among the bomber units, not just from enemy action but also because of the technical inadequacies of the aircraft used. For it turned out that the twin-engined Ju 88 and He 111 were totally unsuited to strategic, long-range anti-shipping operations. Overloaded with fuel and weapons, these aircraft could barely maintain altitude and the loss of an engine almost always resulted in the loss of the aircraft.

Despite these limitations, six ships were sunk and many more damaged. On 30 May, the last day of the convoy battle, *Jagdgeschwader 5* also joined the fray. This was in response to attempts by the Soviet air force to provide air cover for the convoy and attack and neutralize the bases used by the German bomber units. The result was one of the most successful operations by JG 5 in the year 1942. While escorting Ju 87 dive-bombers, which found and attacked the Allied convoy off the Kola Peninsula, and conducting *freie Jagd* missions, the pilots of JG 5 shot down a total of 43 fighters and 7 bombers. Among the most successful pilots were Dörr, Ehrler and Schuck. It was not until 1964, when the East German *Deutschen Militärverlag* published a history of Soviet fighter pilots, that we learned that well-known Soviet fighter pilot Lieutenant Safanov was shot down and killed over the Allied convoy. Safanov, a Hero of the Soviet Union, was credited with 25 victories and was the leading Soviet ace at the time of his death. To give a general idea of the scope of the deliveries of war materiel to the Soviet Union during the Second World War, we offer the following list of aircraft that reached the Russian Front. In addition to thousands of tanks, trucks, guns and even entire factories, the Red Army received at least 15,000 aircraft of all types, including:

2,952	Hawker Hurricanes
1,331	Supermarine Spitfires
2,091	Curtiss P-40 Kittyhawks and Warhawks
4,743	Bell P-39 Airacobras
2,901	Douglas Bostons
862	North American B-25 Mitchells

In July 1942 *Luftflotte 5* reported sinking a total of 24 ships from convoy PQ 17. In response to these losses the Allies temporarily suspended convoys to Russia.

Not until September 1942 did they dispatch another convoy, PQ 18, which was again engaged by German submarines and aircraft. Thirteen ships were sunk, but twenty-seven reached Arkhangelsk, delivering enough supplies to equip an entire army for the Eastern Front.

On 17 June *Oberleutnant* Segatz, *Staffelkapitän* of 8./JG 5, shot down his 25th enemy aircraft and *Leutnant* Bahr his 7th. Bahr was killed almost exactly one month later. On 13 July he was shot down by anti-aircraft fire over the area of Nyal Lake.

Another raid on Murmansk was scheduled for 29 June, with the 6. *Staffel* assigned to provide fighter escort for bombers of KG 30. As usual, the fighter pilots scanned the sky for Russian fighters, which usually appeared just before the bombers reached their target. They searched in vain. Nevertheless, caution was advised, for now the *Staffel* was nearing the dangerous area around Murmashi, where the Soviet fighters were based. There, too, they saw no trace of an enemy aircraft. Instead the sky was filled with countless flak bursts, small dirty black clouds which expanded rapidly. This time it was the Russian flak that rose to meet the Bf 109s.

The first to be hit was *Feldwebel* Stratmann in his "Yellow 4". Before the aircraft went down the pilot jettisoned his canopy and baled out. As he was swinging beneath his parachute about ten kilometers to the west over Murmashi, a second Messerschmitt was hit by flak. The Russian fighters appeared at about the same time and the anti-aircraft fire immediately stopped. After low fuel forced the *Staffel* to break off the engagement, it returned to Petsamo and reported two of its pilots missing. Six days later, on 7 July, 6./JG 5 received news that *Feldwebel* Emil Stratmann had avoided capture by the Russians, having made his way on foot to Field Outpost 11. Of the second pilot shot down over the Murmashi area, however, no trace had been found. *Unteroffizier* Wilhelm Kuchlingg's status remained missing in action.

Since its arrival on the Murmansk front, 7./JG 5 had not suffered any casualties, but on 8 July it lost its first pilot when *Feldwebel* Strasser was killed. That day the unit's aircraft had carried out a fighter sweep over Murmansk. Flying as von Sponeck's wingman, Strasser was on approach to land when he began having difficulties with his engine. The Messerschmitts were over Petsamojoki Valley at a height of fifty meters when the propeller of Strasser's E-7 began turning more slowly and suddenly stopped. Forced to focus his attention on a difficult forced landing, the pilot had no time to make a radio call and could only wave to the nearest aircraft before he began losing height. The narrow, isolated valley was anything but an ideal location for a forced landing, but the unfortunate pilot had no other choice, and his comrades' worst fears were realized. Although the *Feldwebel* hadn't lowered his undercarriage, the landing resulted in a serious crash. Strasser, who was pulled badly injured from the wreckage, survived only a few hours. He was later buried in the cemetery in Parkkina. The actual cause of the crash could not be determined.

Murmansk remained a target for the German bombers. On 19 July a formation of Ju 88s approached Kola Bay escorted by five Bf 109s of the *6. Staffel*. Roughly ten to fifteen Russian fighters, Curtiss P-40s, probably from Varlamovo, rose to intercept them. They were immediately intercepted by the Messerschmitts, however. A fierce dogfight developed north of Murmansk at an altitude of 3000 meters. A Curtiss got on the tail of *Feldwebel* Knier's "Yellow 3" and shot him down. The German pilot baled out.

Leopold Knier was captured but returned to his *Staffel* just eight days later. But under what circumstances! It was a curious story that he told and there were certain similarities to the case of *Oberfeldwebel* Pfränger. No one suspected this of course, because Pfränger would not appear in the German lines until autumn 1943. *Feldwebel* Knier related that the Russians had tried to "turn" him. The other side had promised him a big reward if he could steal a Bf 109 and deliver it to Murmansk, after which they sent him back. We do not know the real story behind this curious incident. We do know, however, that the Russians never acquired a Messerschmitt in this way. During the course of the war they surely had other opportunities to obtain an intact example of the type.

In July 1942 a new *9. Staffel* was formed from elements of the *7.* and *8. Staffel* and *Hauptmann* Wengel was named as its *Kapitän*. The former *9. Staffel* under *Oberleutnant* Huppertz went to Norway to become the *10. Staffel*, part of the *IV. Gruppe*. This resulted in the following organization for the north-based *Geschwader* (excluding I./JG 5 and the *Zerstörerstaffel*):

Geschwaderstab (*Obstlt.* Handrick)	Petsamo
II. Gruppe (*Hptm.* Carganico)	Petsamo-Alakurtti
4. Staffel (*Oblt.* Schäfer)	Petsamo-Alakurtti
5. Staffel (*Oblt.* Menzel)	Petsamo-Alakurtti
6. Staffel (*Oblt.* Hartwein)	Petsamo-Alakurtti
III. Gruppe (*Hptm.* Scholz)	Petsamo
7. Staffel (*Hptm.* v. Sponeck)	Petsamo-Kirkenes
8. Staffel (*Oblt.* Segatz)	Petsamo-Kirkenes
9. Staffel (*Hptm.* Wengel)	Petsamo-Kirkenes

IV. Gruppe (*Hptm.* Kriegel)   Trondheim-Lade
10. Staffel (*Oblt.* Huppertz)   Trondheim-Lade
11. Staffel (unknown)   Trondheim-Lade
12. Staffel (*Hptm.* Strakeljahn)   Bodö

This was the time when, as in the previous year, the fighting on the Murmansk front threatened to take on the character of positional warfare. The Russian White Sea Fleet had begun trying to cut the German supply line to the north, posing a serious threat to shipping to Petsamo. It was the beginning of a blockade of German supply traffic. For this purpose the enemy moved in additional sea forces, bolstered the artillery positions on the Fischer Peninsula and established a temporary airfield on the Sredniy Peninsula to accommodate a unit with the special purpose of engaging the German convoys. Before 1942 was over, shipping to Petsamo would shrink noticeably and, despite defensive efforts by the *Luftwaffe*, would almost come to a halt.

In additon to this, the Soviets all too often attempted landing operations from the Fischer Peninsula across Motovskiy Gulf in order to drive into the open flank of the mountain units on the Lisa River and Titovka Bay. In each case, however, they were halted and driven back. The *Luftwaffe* played an important role in checking these attempted landings by providing air support in the form of low-level attacks. The Stuka units based in Kirkenes had previously been responsible for ground support missions, however they left Finland in the summer of 1942 and 7./JG 5 was given this unpopular task. This was simply because, as the newest unit in the *Geschwader*, it was the last to reequip with the Messerschmitt Bf 109 F. The *7. Staffel* continued flying its older Bf 109 E-7s for some months, and as the new aircraft were much too valuable to risk in low-level attacks, *Oberstleutnant* Handrick declared the 7th to be the "*Jabo-Schlächterstaffel*" (fighter-bomber/close-support Staffel).

Black August 1942

There was a dramatic combat on 2 August, when *Leutnant* Hammel and *Unteroffizier* Tretter, both of 4./JG 5, took off on a reconnaissance flight and ran into a group of seven Hurricanes east of Verkhnye-Chornoye. Though outnumbered, the two pilots immediately joined combat. From close range Tretter shot down a Hurricane, which literally disintegrated under his hail of bullets. He was so close to the enemy machine that he was unable to avoid the many fragments and a large piece of wreckage struck his Messerschmitt. Tretter was able to abandon his E-7 at the last second, and the two fighters crashed and exploded beneath him as his parachute opened. Tretter was captured by the Russians and became a prisoner of war.

For the *III. Gruppe* as well, the month also began with a run of bad luck. On the evening of the 4th the *7. Staffel* received orders to move the next day to Pontsalenjoki, an airfield established by the Soviets in the middle of the Karelian forest on the Louhi front. There *Oberstleutnant* Handrick was supposed to temporarily take command of a battle unit (*Gefechtsverband*) consisting of a reinforced *Staffel* from *Stukagruppe 5*, a flight of three Henschel reconnaissance machines, and the *Stab* and *7. Staffel* of JG 5. The unit's assignment was to provide air support for a local operation by a unit of the *Waffen-SS*, with von Sponeck's *7. Staffel* providing fighter cover for the reconnaissance aircraft and dive-bombers. In order to conceal the transfer flight from the enemy, the *Staffel* was supposed to take off one *Schwarm* at a time, with an interval of about one hour between flights, and fly to Pontsalenjoki at low level. As there was still uncertainty as to the exact layout of the forest airfield, the pilots were ordered to stop in Rovaniemi, where air traffic control would brief them on the exact layout of the airfield.

The first to take off was the *Schwarm* consisting of Helms, Schumacher, Philipp and Scharmacher. Eleven years would have to pass before the veil of secrecy shrouding the events of 5 August 1942 was finally lifted. It began with the Bf 109 of *Obergefreiter* Scharmacher losing a tire while landing at Rovaniemi, forcing him to remain there. This was the only thing that spared him from sharing the fate of the other three members of his *Schwarm*, who became prisoners of war.

Flight leader Helms attempted to have the external fuel tanks of his aircraft refilled, however air traffic control in Rovaniemi refused his request on the grounds that fuel was in short supply and reserved for supply flights to the Polar Sea front. Helms was told, "Anyway, you can reach your destination with your normal fuel."

The fighter pilots knew that this was only possible if they flew their Messerschmitts at cruise speed and made not the slightest error in navigation. And so it was with mixed feelings that they climbed into their aircraft for the last leg of the flight. Bodo Helms, who did not return from Russian captivity until September 1953, described what happened: "In Rovaniemi all they could tell us was that we would find the landing field on the lower bend of a small stream. Before taking off, I asked Schumacher, whose abilities as a pilot no one could deny, to keep an eye on our heading, especially as we had only been able to fill our main tanks. If we flew at cruise speed and held exactly to our course, we should have had ten minute's fuel left after reaching our destination. I remember that we were exactly on course until we flew over a large lake. Then, while flying over the many islands, we must have gone off course to the south. We flew low, for the airfield had to be somewhere nearby. Suddenly we came under anti-aircraft fire. I immediately turned left in order to remain over Finnish territory. Schumacher had been badly hit and was unable to keep up. Firmly convinced that I was over Finnish territory, I picked out a place to land and made a good landing on my last drops of fuel. We had jettisoned our external tanks, which made the Russians very suspicious during the subsequent interrogation, as they were convinced that they had been bombs or mines. Schumacher made a belly landing. I pulled him from his aircraft, bandaged him, placed him on my shoulder and set off. A bullet had pierced his right thigh and another was lodged in his left thigh. All around everything was quiet, and we were certain that we would soon come across Finnish sentries. Suddenly, some distance away we saw two figures, which unfortunately turned out to be Russians armed with submachine-guns. We took cover. They didn't dare approach, even though my pistol was empty. Meanwhile we had become surrounded. Flight appeared pointless, especially as Schumacher was unable to walk. Looking back, it is pointless to think about whether I could have avoided being captured by fleeing on my own. In any case I didn't do it and stayed with Schumacher."

Meanwhile *Unteroffizier* Philipp had also landed nearby after running out of fuel. After walking for several kilometers, Kurt Philipp also fell into the hands of the Russians.

At about 08:30 on 8 August 1942, Soviet radio made the following announcement: "On 5 August three German airmen deserted and delivered their Me 109 aircraft to the Red Army. Lieutenant Bodo Helmer, Sergeant Kurt Felix and soldier Werner Funker landed on an airfield within our defense lines and surrendered." No doubt, it was the three pilots Helms, Philipp and Schumacher, who – for whatever reason – only gave their true first names. The subsequent fate of these three pilots from 7./JG 5 will be examined in detail in a special chapter dedicated to pilots of JG 5 who became prisoners of war. Werner Schumacher, who had quickly risen to become one of the 7. *Staffel*'s most successful pilots, did not recover from his wounds. He died in the Podma camp in the spring of 1943 after spending a long time in hospital.

7./JG 5's transfer flight had ended with the loss of an entire *Schwarm*. Typically, an attempt was made to place the blame for this unfortunate incident on the *Staffelkapitän*, *Hauptmann* von Sponeck. A flying field court headed by *Fliegerführer Oberst* Holle found no justification for charges against the *Staffel* command, however.

The next day Soviet close-support aircraft struck Pontsalenjoki. A warning was received from air observers in the front lines and an air-raid alarm was sounded, but by then the Il-2s were already over the airfield. Most of the

Messerschmitts were damaged and two were destroyed by fire. When the attack was over, the *Geschwaderstab* and the 7. *Staffel* had just six serviceable aircraft: a catastrophe given that the operation by the army was supposed to commence the next day. It was also unlikely that this would be the last attack by the Soviets on Pontsalenjoki.

The planned formation of a battle unit did not come to fruition and the elements of the *Geschwader* transferred to Pontsalenjoki were ordered back to Petsamo on 8 August. It is not known whether the army carried on with its attack without air support, and one can argue whether the transfer flight by the 7. *Staffel* and the loss of three experienced pilots were therefore senseless.

This was also a "black August" for the Soviets. Mass attacks by KG 30 from Banak on the west coast began. Armadas of bombers appeared over Petsamo, with the Bf 110 *Zerstörer* flying close escort and the Bf 109s of II. and III./JG 5 conducting fighter sweeps in advance of the bombers. In that late summer of 1942 the northeast part of Murmansk burned for days. That hot dry summer the old log houses, most of them two-story, fell victim to the flames. And the smoke clouds formed huge mountains of cumulus that could be seen as the pilots climbed out from Petsamo.

On 21 August 1942 seven Bf 109s of 6./JG 5 took off for Murmashi. The weather was clear and the *Staffel*'s mission was to fly escort for the *Zerstörerstaffel* as it attacked the Russian airfield. The Bf 110s dropped their bombs and were on the way home when the German formation was attacked by about 35 fighters. Though their fuel was already running low, the fighters were drawn into an extended dogfight. The result was 14 enemy aircraft shot down, including three each by *Leutnant* Ehrler, his 42nd to 44th victories, and *Feldwebel* Müller. The latter's Messerschmitt was hit in the cockpit during the dogfight, however Müller was able to regain the airfield without difficulty. The *Staffel*'s success was marred, however, by the loss of its *Kapitän*, *Oberleutnant* Hartwein. His "Yellow 6" was hit in the radiators and went down. None of his comrades were able to see him bale out and as no news of his fate was ever received, Hartwein is still listed as missing. *Leutnant* Ehrler, who also had a respectable victory total, took over command of the 6. *Staffel*. 6./JG 5, the old Carganico *Staffel*, would rise to become one of JG 5's most successful units, with pilots like Alfred Brunner, Theo Weißenberger and Rudi Müller, who received the Knight's Cross on 19 June 1942 after his 41st victory.

Murmashi, Shongui, Varlamovo

For JG 5, September 1942 was a month in which *freie Jagd* missions predominated and the *Staffeln* concentrated on the airspace above the Russian fighter bases around Murmansk. The mission by the *6. Staffel* in the early afternoon hours of 2 September culminated in a dogfight with fifteen Russian fighters directly over the enemy base in Murmashi. *Unteroffizier* Stolz's machine was hit by machine-gun fire and he was wounded in the right foot. A similar dogfight took place over Shongui airfield, south of Murmansk, on 9 September. *Obergefreiter* Günter Hoffmann was shot down and has been missing since.

During roughly the same period *Hauptmann* Scholz, the *Gruppenkommandeur* of III./JG 5, recorded his 30th victory. He had earned ten of his victories on the Channel Front.

The *5. Staffel* had temporarily moved to its forward bases near Nautsi and Ivalo in Finland so as to be able to protect the Polar Sea road, the German supply route to Petsamo. These airfields were popular targets for Russian bombers and on 11 September they attempted another attack. After a successful scramble from Nautsi, part of the *Staffel* engaged the bombers and *Feldwebel* Froböse was shot down in his F-4. He was also listed missing until his body was found in a lake near Nautsi in August 1943. *Feldwebel* Froböse was buried in the cemetery in Parkkina. Combat photos shot with his Leica camera are included in this book as a memorial to him.

At about two in the afternoon on 15 September the aircraft of 6./JG 5 taxied out again for a free chase mission over the Murmashi area. For *Leutnant* Weißenberger, who had transferred from the *Zerstörerstaffel* at the beginning of the month, this was his first mission with Ehrler's unit, having been checked out on the single-engined Messerschmitt the day before. The ten Messerschmitt fighters arrived over the enemy airfield after about half an hour. There they saw the familiar dust clouds produced by enemy fighters taking off. Twenty to thirty enemy machines, mainly Curtiss P-40s, were soon in the air and a dogfight soon developed.

Weißenberger scored his first success at 14:31. Several kilometers south of Murmashi he got on the tail of a Curtiss and opened fire. The Russian aircraft went down, trailing a long banner of smoke, and the pilot baled out before it struck the ground. After breaking away at a height of 1500 meters, the *Leutnant* saw another Curtiss flying below him. Using his superior speed in the dive, at 600 meters he positioned himself behind and to the left of the Russian. He then closed in and shot him down at 14:33.

When the fighters returned to base *Unteroffizier* Scharf was missing. His "Yellow 4" had last been seen south of Murmashi. It was later learned that the *Unteroffizier* was a POW.

That same day the *7. Staffel* lost *Unteroffizier* Braun, who was shot down by flak during a mission over the Fischer Peninsula. The 19th brought another painful loss, this time to II./JG 5. *Leutnant* Werner Kunze, the *Staffel* technical officer, took off as part of a *Schwarm* on a free chase over Murmashi. Twenty-five enemy fighters, which had taken off from Murmashi, were waiting for them. Kunze's aircraft was hit in the engine and he signaled to his comrades that he was going to attempt a forced landing. He was never seen again. At about 15:00 several Bf 109s took off to search for him, hoping to find the *Leutnant* somewhere in the wilderness, but the effort was unsuccessful. The *Gruppe* carried out another search that afternoon, but no clues as to Kunze's fate were found. The pilots flew back and forth over the tundra for more than an hour. They returned to Petsamo unsuccessful and visibly despondent.

In contrast, the 22nd of September was a successful day for 6./JG 5 and especially for *Leutnant* Weißenberger. At noon the *Staffel* received orders to conduct a fighter sweep in the Murmansk area, with special attention to be paid to Murmashi airfield. Takeoff was at 14:34 and after the usual flying time of about 25 minutes they reached the "hunting ground". This time, however, some enemy aircraft were already in the air, and the first dogfight took place west of Murmashi. All of the Russian fighter types were represented – Hurricanes, Curtisses, Airacobras and Yak-1s.

Weißenberger scored a double right away: one Hurricane at 14:59, a second one minute later. Only the second pilot baled out. The next victory was scored by the *Staffelkapitän*, *Leutnant* Ehrler, south of Murmashi, then at 15:05 it was Weißenberger's turn again. Previously *Unteroffizier* Döbrich had covered his tail, this time it was Ehrler. The Russian pilot desperately tried to shake his attacker, but his efforts were unsuccessful. Tracer suddenly reached out for him; his machine literally absorbed the deadly bursts, until it finally began to burn and went straight down, leaving behind a thick, dark smoke trail.

Hans Döbrich from Thuringia shot down two Hurricanes, victories 15 and 16: "I saw three Soviets simply bale out as soon as they came under fire and then slowly drift to earth beneath their parachutes. Black forms also emerged from the two Hurricanes I fired at and descended to the ground beneath their white parachutes. In the end we counted twelve white patches on the ground in a tight circle around the enemy airfield and sixteen burning or smoking heaps of wreckage – the remains of enemy fighters."

Weißenberger's star now began rising. Having recorded 23 victories with the *Zerstörerstaffel*, he added five victories to his tally with 6./JG 5. On 27 September, a Sunday, he would add five more in one day.

The Russian airfield at Varlamovo was also a target. Shortly after 11:00 Weißenberger and Döbrich took off to check the weather in the area, but also to try and lure the enemy into the air. Weißenberger returned from this first sortie with an Airacobra to his credit, which he had shot down north of Murmansk. According to the two pilots Varlamovo was packed with enemy aircraft, which in itself warranted another visit to the airfield.

The second mission began in the afternoon, at about 15:00, when a *Schwarm* made up of *Leutnant* Weißenberger, *Leutnant* Lesch, *Feldwebel* Bock and *Obergefreiter* Mors took off. The Russians had been warned, however. Between Varlamovo and Shongui the *Eismeerjäger* encountered a large enemy force of almost 30 machines, including twelve Curtisses and ten Hurricanes. "To hell with being outnumbered. We're attacking!" The outnumbered Messerschmitt pilots picked their targets. This was a relatively favorable tactic, as some of the Russians formed a defensive circle while the rest tried to get on the tails of the Bf 109s. The sky was filled with the rattle of machine-gun fire and the roar of powerful aero-engines. Then the first enemy aircraft burst into flames and crashed south of Shongui.

"Congratulations – victory!" *Leutnant* Resch called to Weißenberger. Another followed one minute later. Weißenberger had a third Hurricane in his sights at 2500 meters and was about to open fire when the Russian pilot hauled his aircraft into a left turn. But "Yellow 4" stayed with him and Weißenberger fired his 20-mm cannon from 50 meters. The Hurricane's tail flew off, before it slowly pitched forward and dove straight towards the ground. It crashed and exploded at 15:51, nine kilometers south of Shongui.

Five minutes later Weißenberger was able to shoot down another Hurricane. Then the Germans were forced to break off the engagement. They landed at Petsamo at about 16:30, having suffered no losses.

Two days later the 6. *Staffel* took off at noon to escort Bf 110s to Varlamovo. Twelve Curtiss fighters attempted to intercept, but the Messerschmitts were able to keep them away from the twin-engined fighters. None of the Soviet aircraft were shot down, however. Weißenberger almost came to grief on 22 October, however misfortune and luck hit at the same time. He took off from Petsamo at about ten minutes before one to fly escort for a Fw 189 tactical reconnaissance aircraft. West of Murmansk the engine of his F-4 suddenly seized. Weißenberger immediately feathered his propeller, reversed course and began gliding in the direction of the front. As soon as he reached friendly territory he baled out and his faithful "Yellow 4" crashed somewhere in the tundra. Weißenberger then spent eight difficult days walking through the wilderness until he was picked up by a long-range patrol. A message was sent to the *Geschwader* and it wasn't long before the longed-for *Storch* arrived to return the *Leutnant* to his *Staffel*.

JG 5 on the Polar Sea

Weißenberger was back in the air a little over a week later. He took part in two Stuka escort missions on the 29th, and then came the 30th of October. Once again the Bf 110 *Zerstörer* set out to attack Murmansk, and their fighter escort included 6./JG 5. At about noon, during a *freie Jagd* operation, Weißenberger had been able to shoot down two Curtisses and a LaGG-3. Now, during the second mission of the day, he destroyed two more Curtiss fighters at 15:00 and 15:06.

Otherwise October passed with no significant combat operations, however JG 5 lost four pilots at the very start of the next month. While 5./JG 5 remained in Petsamo, the *4.* and *6. Staffel* and the *Stab* of II./JG 5 moved to Alakurtti. From there, on 9 November, a pair of Messerschmitts from the *4. Staffel* took off on a weather reconnaissance flight to the Murmansk railway in the Ruchi-Chupa area. *Obergefreiter* Luther and *Unteroffizier* Zeuschel did not return from this flight. The same day, *Unteroffizier* Klaus Betz's F-4 crashed near Rovaniemi during a ferry flight, and all efforts to find him were unsuccessful. In Norway, the *11. Staffel* lost a pilot when *Unteroffizier* Burkel was killed in a flying accident at Alta airfield.

At 09:15 on 13 November a pair of fighters took off from Pudasjärvi. They subsequently encountered six Russian fighters, which shot down *Unteroffizier* Gerber-Schulz. The pilot baled out, injuring his right foot.

Meanwhile *Oberleutnant* Franz Menzel had handed the *5. Staffel* over to *Oberleutnant* Wienhusen, who would lead it until May 1944. On 13 November *Leutnant* Weißenberger was awarded the Knight's Cross after his 38th victory. *Leutnant* Ehrler, leader of the successful 6./JG 5 since the end of August, had received the same decoration on 21 October after his 41st victory and was simultaneously promoted to *Oberleutnant*. Another name that had appeared frequently in the mission reports in recent weeks must also be mentioned: *Feldwebel* Heinrich Bartels, one of the most successful pilots of the *8. Staffel*, which was under *Hauptmann* Segatz's command. Bartels, who flew his 100th combat mission on 11 September, quickly ran up 45 victories on the Polar Sea Front and on 19 November was awarded the Knight's Cross. He would increase his total to 47 before being transferred to IV./JG 27 in the Mediterranean Theater, where he continued his successful ways.

Turn of the Year 1942-1943

The Arctic winter had arrived, the first for which the German fighter pilots were adequately prepared. The *Staffeln* had long since equipped their quarters for the cold, installing chimneys and catalytic stoves. The 24th of November was roughly the last day the sun rose above the horizon north of the 70th parallel. This lasted until mid-February of the following year. Depending on the weather, it would be light for several hours, but the period between morning and evening twilight was too short to really speak of a day. Let us turn to well-known war reporter Hans R. Queiser, who wrote a graphic description of this "long night":

> "Effective immediately, as a conservation measure dawn and dusk are being combined into noon twilight – one of the many indications that the soldier's unshakable sense of humor had also dealt with the Polar night. During the bright summertime we had little need for lamps and generators, but now both were in almost constant use so as to allow life and work to go on in the quarters. But as sunlight means health as well as light, rations had to be carefully prepared to provide the missing vitamins, while doctors constantly monitored the health of the men. Increased butter rations and fresh potatoes were the main sources of vitamins. Though hardly conducive to flying, the winter weather over the Polar Sea and the darkness did not completely paralyze the activities of our unit. Crews, ground personnel and airfields in the far north were up to the challenges of bad weather and instrument flying. In addition to cold and snow, the winter brought another burden for the ground personnel. As the hours of daylight diminished, guards had to be posted on the airfield more frequently. And the most beautiful displays of the Northern Lights in a starry night, usually a sign of severe cold, could not silence the sentry's desire for a hot stove and a warm sleeping bag. While the mercury did not drop as low for those of us near the North Cape as it did for those elsewhere on the Eastern Front, this advantage was negated by the raging snowstorms that swept through the fjords with seeming regularity. Winter under the spell of the pole demanded the highest conceivable degree of physical and mental strength. At some time in his life, everyone back in Germany has surely experienced just how depressing a few consecutive days without sun can be, and can thus imagine what it means not to see the sun for months."

Before the end of the eventful year of 1942, during which *Jagdgeschwader 5* was formed and gained experience in the war on the Polar Sea Front, the unit had to face several more severe tests. On 2 December *Leutnant* Guido Erber of 9./JG 5 was forced to bale out west of Varlamovo and was captured by the Russians. In the same engagement *Leutnant* Friedrich Lüdecke of the 6. *Staffel* scored his second victory, shooting down a Yak. He had recorded his first victory over Murmashi at the end of November. On 26 December *Feldwebel* Kaiser and his aircraft "Black 10" failed to return. What subsequently happened to Kaiser was unusual. According to a report dated June 1943 he returned unhurt to the 8. *Staffel* after the Russians dropped him by parachute over the German lines. The reason for this is unclear. All that was learned was that he had been shot down by flak over Murmansk on 26 December 1942 and parachuted to safety. In any case, *Feldwebel* Kaiser did not serve again on the Eastern Front (also see Pages 206-207).

One day after Kaiser's failure to return, *Unteroffizier* Schedl of 7./JG 5 collided with a parked aircraft while taking off from Petsamo. His aircraft "Black 15" overturned and he died of his injuries later that day. The *Staffel* mourned the loss of this excellent comrade.

The Murmansk railway was again the target in the last days of December, and one of these operations resulted in the loss of *Leutnant* Rutishauser of *Stab*/JG 5, who took part in the action as radio operator in a Ju 87. On 28 December a total of seven Stukas attacked Kovda railway station on the Karelian White Sea coast. During the return flight *Obergefreiter* Fuss' machine, in which Rutishauser was flying, was hit by flak and went down. Both men were killed. The 7. *Staffel* suffered another casualty on New Year's Eve day when *Unteroffizier* Gathmann's aircraft was hit by Russian anti-aircraft fire. *Leutnant* Schumann saw the unfortunate pilot bale out. Gathmann was subsequently taken prisoner by the Soviets. *Leutnant* Rose and *Oberfeldwebel* Dörr each claimed an enemy aircraft shot down.

Despite painful losses, the year was also a successful one for the fighter pilots stationed near the Polar Sea. Murmansk, however, remained in enemy hands. And in the south of the Eastern Front, between the Don and Volga Rivers, a battle was being fought that would see the tide of war turn decisively in favor of the Allies: the Battle of Stalingrad. This huge catastrophe was caused by poor planning, not because an entire army faithfully fought a losing battle.

The turn of the year 1942-43 found the *Geschwader* split up in three different places: the *Stab* and 4. and 6./JG 5 in Alakurtti, approximately 300 kilometers south of the Polar Sea coast on the Kandalaksha front; 5./JG 5 and the entire *III. Gruppe* in Petsamo; and the 7. *Staffel*, which was temporarily based in Kirkenes. The entire *IV. Gruppe* was with I./JG 5 on the west coast of Norway, while the independent *Zerstörerstaffel* was in Kirkenes.

Frequent snowstorms blanketed the tundra with fresh snow, and enemy aircraft appeared much less frequently in the sky over the Polar Sea Front. The time of lengthy waiting began. That there was flying at all was largely due to the efforts of the mechanics. Every morning they toiled in temperatures below minus 30 degrees, de-icing aircraft, warming their engines with catalytic heaters and making them ready for operations. It may well have been in those moments that they cursed the dismal loneliness of the Polar Sea region and wished they were at a base in another theater. There were days and weeks when there was no flying activity at all. A nerve-wracking time. But sometimes the cold Polar darkness was brightened by the tumultuous glow off the Northern Lights, a fascinating display that helped lift the men's spirits. The Northern Lights were seen in different forms: as sweeping arcs, as irregular bands, as sagging folds of a moving curtain or as fan-like diverging beams. The most common color was yellow-green, with deeper atmospheric layers in red and occasionally also blue to gray-violet colors of varying intensity.

The few operations at the beginning of the new year of 1943 were extremely varied. 7./JG 5 received a new *Kapitän*, *Oberleutnant* Senoner, after *Hauptmann* von Sponeck left the *Geschwader* at his own request and was transferred to SKG 10 based in Caen, France. On 5 January a *Rotte* from the *4. Staffel* set off for the Rovye area to hunt trains. *Feldwebel* Bigalk suddenly came under machine-gun fire and was forced to bale out. He is still listed as missing. The next day, during a combat mission over Murmansk by 9./JG 5, *Unteroffizier* Rennemann's "Yellow 2" came down in enemy territory, probably because of engine failure. He was captured by Russian soldiers.

The 9th of January was another very successful day, and once again the famous pilots of the *6. Staffel* took part. At 09:35 a *Schwarm* led by *Leutnant* Ehrler took off on a fighter sweep over the White Sea coast. The Germans soon ran into about 20 to 25 Russian fighters. It was the first real air battle after a long period of waiting. And what an air battle! All four members of the *Schwarm* were successful, shooting down eight enemy aircraft over Kandalaksha. *Leutnant* Ehrler downed two LaGG-3s and a Hurricane, *Leutnant* Lüdecke and *Unteroffizier* Mors each a LaGG-3 and a Hurricane and *Unteroffizier* Rolly a Hurricane. There were no German losses and the four Messerschmitts landed back at Alakurtti at 10:30.

The year 1943 saw the rapid rise of the almost thirty-year-old *Oberfeldwebel* Franz Dörr as a fighter pilot: in August he would record his 100th victory. At the beginning of January, while flying with an unidentified *Unteroffizier*, he scattered a formation of enemy light bombers. Dörr shot down two Pe-2s and his wingman one. By the end of the month Dörr had nine victories, the last another Pe-2. *Feldwebel* Walter Schuck, a member of the *7. Staffel* who would achieve his greatest successes in 1944, also downed his 19th enemy aircraft at this time.

The Good and Ill Fortune of Leutnant Lüdecke

In mid-January 1943 it began snowing on the Kandalaksha front, and for several days the gray twilight made it almost impossible to distinguish between day and night. At that time of year there were only a few hours of daylight in the far north anyway – from nine in the morning until about noon – and this just sufficed for one or two sorties over the front. One day a Fw 189 reconnaissance aircraft returned from a sortie and reported having seen a big freight train southbound on the Murmansk railway. American war materiel offloaded in Murmansk was heading south. The Russians also sent trains the other way loaded with fuel and food. It was a single-track line, but there were a number of passing points where the trains could pass one another. One such passing point was at Polyanikrug. Evaluation of the reconnaissance reports suggested that two long freight trains would arrive at about 11:00 and carry out the passing maneuver.

A *Schwarm* of Bf 110s from 13.(Z)/JG 5 under the command of *Oberleutnant* Schloßstein had already taken off from Kemijärvi and was expected over Alakurtti. Its mission: attack and destroy the two trains near Polyanikrug. *Hauptmann* von Hahn of the *Geschwaderstab*, which had recently arrived in Alakurtti, readied a *Schwarm* from the 6. *Staffel* to escort the fighter-bombers, however *Leutnant* Ehrler argued that, given the weather conditions, a pair of fighters would be sufficient. *Hauptmann* von Hahn agreed and gave the job to *Staffelkapitän Leutnant* Lüdecke and his wingman. Lüdecke had only arrived with the 6. *Staffel* from Petsamo several days earlier, the unit having been sent to bolster 4./JG 5.

Then the twin-engined fighter-bombers were reported approaching. *Leutnant* Lüdecke and *Unteroffizier* Rolly put on their helmets and closed their canopies. Using the cold-start procedure, the engines of the two Messerschmitts roared to life. Before long the two Bf 109s were in position alongside the *Zerstörer*. In order to delay being spotted by Russian radar for as long as possible, the formation flew towards the target at low level. The terrain below them was flat, undulating and covered in snow. There was no sign of human habitation and no landmarks anywhere.

After about twenty minute's flying time the *Zerstörer* suddenly began to climb; they were almost over the target. Down below something was smoking. A dark ribbon. The Murmansk railway. Then the pilots also saw the trains and station buildings, between them moving dots. From 500 meters Schloßstein's Bf 110s dived on the target and released their bombs. "A peculiar scene played out down below", remembered Lüdecke. "As if moved by an unseen hand, rail cars leapt over one another. A locomotive reared up, fell back and lay on its side. Just like a model railroad, when one causes intentional collisions."

The fighter-bombers attacked a second time. The second-to-last Bf 110 had just dropped its bombs when several tiny dots appeared over the railroad tracks to the south.

Lüdecke radioed a warning to the *Zerstörer*: "Indians, Indians six o'clock low! Garden fence, Garden fence!" The Russian fighters were perhaps still about ten kilometers away when the Bf 110 *Schwarm* reversed course and disappeared in the direction of Alakurtti, while the two fighters flew toward the Russians at low altitude. Lüdecke suspected that the enemy had probably seen the Bf 110s but not the two Bf 109s, as their camouflage – pale blue undersides and white-gray topsides – made them difficult to spot. And in fact the Russians held course towards Polyanikrug, while the two Messerschmitts raced toward them just above the ground. There were six, eight, ten LaGG and MiG fighters altogether.

They must have come down by now if they had seen the Germans, but nothing happened. "Climbing now!" *Leutnant* Lüdecke called to his wingman. They both climbed, performed a half roll and ended up behind the enemy fighters, which continued flying straight and level in two flights. The range was still too great to be certain of getting a hit, but they were closing fast. From 100 meters the *Leutnant* opened fire on a LaGG, which was sitting large in the crosshairs. The first rounds entered the fuselage. After just a few rounds from the 20-mm cannon the LaGG rolled onto its back and headed straight down trailing black smoke.

At first the others appeared not to have noticed what was happening and they formed a big defensive circle. Lüdecke was cautiously approaching an outsider when *Unteroffizier* Rolly in his "Yellow 8" suddenly dove from above and attacked the same machine, sending it to the ground in a matter of seconds. Meanwhile Lüdecke was in the middle of the defensive circle and was on the tail of a MiG, which entered a left turn. "I was about to press the triggers, when the Russian pilot looked over at me, panicked and began a Split-S. The MiG raced towards the earth and the pilot was unable to pull out – he had insufficient altitude. The enemy crashed into the ground and disappeared in an explosion of snow."

Lüdecke gained altitude and was soon back with the Russians, who were still in their circle. Once again he got into position to fire. He tried to make a final correction with the stick, but the controls did not respond. The Messerschmitt suddenly became nose heavy and fell into a steep dive. When the *Leutnant* tried to recover he realized that there was almost no elevator pressure. Something seemed to be missing from his tail surfaces. The stick, as they used to say, had gone soft. Lüdecke didn't dare pull back on the stick for fear of losing the elevator completely. Was he about to suffer the same fate his opponent had moments earlier? Baling out at that speed and altitude was pointless. But the ground was getting closer.

The trim! Lüdecke quickly reached for the wheel and began turning it. Slowly the Messerschmitt's nose began to rise. Finally it leveled out. The pilot looked behind and saw that the Russians were all sitting behind him, waiting for him to crash. Keep trimming, thought Lüdecke. The aircraft continued to climb as he applied full power. Fortunately the engine responded, and the airspeed indicator showed 500 kph. By then the Bf 109 had reached 1000 meters and the *Leutnant* looked back again. He had left the enemy behind. They were nothing more than rapidly shrinking dots.

Lüdecke managed to nurse his battered machine back to Alakurtti. Though he had shot down two of the enemy, he dispensed with the usual waggling of wings, for he didn't want pieces of his Messerschmitt falling on the mechanics down below. He closed the throttle and switched off the ignition. The Bf 109 bounced several times and then rolled to a stop. On examination he found that his aircraft was missing its entire right elevator. The left was hanging from the mount that attached it to the fin. The variable incidence tailplane used for trimming purposes had remained intact – otherwise *Leutnant* Lüdecke would not have come back.

Several minutes later *Unteroffizier* Rolly came up beside him, clapped him on the shoulder and said dryly, "That looked bad, *Herr Leutnant*!"

Days later. On 24 January a *Feldwebel* of the *4. Staffel* flies a *Storch* into no-man's-land to pick up *Unteroffizier* Gärtner, who had put his Messerschmitt down on one of the numerous lakes. Gärtner had to hold out until the morning twilight arrived for those in Alakurtti to initiate a search. Much less fortunate was *Leutnant* Lüdecke, who failed to return the following day. He had only flown a few sorties since barely escaping death. At first, however, the 25th of January began quite normally.

At about 09:30 orders were received from the *Geschwader*: fighter sweep by the *6. Staffel* over the Russian airfields near Louhi on the Murmansk railway. Meanwhile a second *Schwarm* from the *4. Staffel* stationed in Alakurtti would be on standby to defend the airfield. Lüdecke continues: "*Freie Jagd*, that was grist to our mill. One was his own master in the air and was tied to nothing. One sought out the enemy, lured him up from his airfields if he was not in the air with a decoy pair, and then the second pair dove from above into the climbing Russians."

Shortly before takeoff at 10:00, *Staffelkapitän* Ehrler advised that he was coming along. And as no one thought of voluntarily staying behind, in the end five Messerschmitts took off from Alakurtti. They headed southeast, climbing slowly, and after about 15 minutes arrived over the lake where *Unteroffizier* Gärtner had come down the day before. While Ehrler led two machines down to strafe and destroy the Messerschmitt to prevent it falling into enemy hands, *Leutnant* Lüdecke and his wingman provided top cover. The five German fighters subsequently resumed their flight in the direction of Louhi.

Soon afterwards they overflew the first Russian airfield at an altitude of 2500 meters, encountering heavy anti-aircraft fire. They flew on, deeper into the

Russian hinterland. Then they arrived over Louhi. Below they could see well-camouflaged blast pens and in them about thirty Yak and LaGG fighters. Then the second airfield came into view. Boyanskaya! This airfield was partly laid out in a wood and to the east was bordered by a long, narrow lake. The runway was empty, likewise the gray-blue Polar sky all around. Were the Russians unwilling to risk tangling with five fighters?

Suddenly a crackle on the frequency: "Attention, we're going to strafe!" It was Ehrler's voice. Of course strafing attacks against an airfield defended by anti-aircraft and machine-guns were always risky, but the *Staffelkapitän* led his *Kette* downward. Lüdecke and his wingman followed close behind so as not to lose sight of Ehrler. The Messerschmitts leveled out and approached the airfield at low level. Then Ehrler and the two others climbed before diving on the enemy airfield and picking out their targets. Lüdecke was seconds behind. Below to his right he saw a dispersal, two aircraft and a number of figures busy with the machines.

Lüdecke turned, placed his sight on the enemy fighter and opened fire with his machine-guns. He saw tracer disappearing into the fuselage and wings of the Russian and then pressed the button for the 20-mm cannon. As he did so he felt something hit the engine in front of him. Oil and gasoline fumes immediately filled the cockpit and his windscreen became opaque. Boost pressure fell to zero, the engine was no longer pulling. The Messerschmitt was still racing towards its target at about 30 meters above the ground. Lüdecke managed to level out his "Yellow 14". At the same instant he jettisoned the canopy. The rest Lüdecke described himself:

"A jerk, the slipstream tore away the canopy. I switched on both magnetos and applied power – nothing! The engine was no longer responding. I glanced at the altimeter: 200 meters. Then the airspeed indicator: 300 kph. Get out, I thought, before the aircraft loses speed and stalls. I unfastened my belt – applied left aileron – raised my legs onto the seat – and pushed upwards! I was in the air, clear of everything, pulled the release handle and dropped. There was a jerk and my descent slowed, the parachute had opened. I looked down and saw trees rising up towards me. My feet knocked snow from the tops of several spruces, then I was hanging. I pulled hard on the lines and dropped into meter-deep snow. All was quiet – deathly quiet. But then I heard the crackle of machine-gun ammunition mixed with dull, heavy reports. The ammunition in my aircraft, which was several hundred meters away, was going off. I could see the glow of a fire and a column of smoke. Get over there quickly was my first thought. In the fuselage were skis and a winter survival kit. Perhaps I could recover these things before everything burned. Slowly I worked my way out of my hole in the snow and then sank up to my hips again. I lost one of my fur-lined boots. My progress was slow and I was leaving behind tracks like an elephant. Then I spotted figures close by amid the trees – Russians! Too late. They could have whatever was left to rescue.

"Back to my parachute. I tried to think calmly. What to do? Despite my fur-lined things I began feeling the icy cold of minus 15 degrees or less. Using my folding knife, I cut several square meters of silk from my parachute and wrapped it around my body as camouflage. I reached into my pockets: pass, photos, a letter, a box of Schoka-Kola. That wasn't much to eat for a march of 150 to 200 kilometers west through the snow-covered tundra. I buried everything I didn't need in the snow, including my parachute, and covered my tracks as best I could. Then I tramped east through the forest. Yes east, because there was a lake there. It was crusted over and would provide better footing. That would be the last place they would look for me.

"I slowly increased the distance from the crash site. I had to hang on. They would be looking for me, they would come in the Stork – but first I had to get away from that place. I heard the sound of aircraft engines overhead. They were biplanes, looking for me. The Russians had surely seen me bale out. I thought, 'had I been hit by flak without noticing it or had a 20-mm round detonated prematurely and wrecked my engine?' It was possible, for disaster struck at the same instant I fired the cannon.

"Get down! The Russians were overhead again. But then finally I reached the lake. On the firm crust I was able to pick up my pace. Wood cutters were working on the other side. I could hear the sound of chopping. An empty sleigh appeared and crossed the lake in front of me. A lone Russian was holding the reins, cracking the whip. I lay in the snow and watched. That could be my salvation. If he returned at dusk loaded with wood, I would have to get my hands on this vehicle – no matter what the cost. I checked my holster, the Walther PPK was loaded. I looked at my wristwatch: 12:00. I had taken off two hours ago and had been in the snow for an hour and a half. And in an hour it would be dark. Everything would have to be decided by then.

"I carefully crawled towards the sleigh tracks. With my hands and feet I tried to eliminate my own tracks. When I got to the trail I began digging myself into the snow beside it. Suddenly I heard voices. I looked from my snow hole: figures on skis were searching the lake. They were coming towards me, 50 to 100 meters apart. I wriggled deeper into the snow. With my hands I threw crusty snow over my head and body. Then I waited. My heart was pounding. The voices grew louder, shouting something I did not understand. And then, behind me, more voices. I hadn't heard them coming on their skis. There was no point in trying to hide any longer. I felt along my body, grasped my pistol, sprang from my hole and turned around. A blow from a rifle butt – my pistol flew away. A second blow – I was lying on the ground. Three Russians were standing over me and five more were approaching. It was all over, but no, they suddenly stopped. Another blow in the back meant stand up. I struggled to my feet. Before me in the snow lay my fur-lined jacket, mesh helmet, boots, gloves and other things that had been taken from me. They tossed me the jacket, helmet and boots, then they brought me – carefully escorted – to the airfield. It probably took half an hour before we arrived at some barracks. A door opened, revealing a room filled with men. Pilots, as I soon found out. They stared at me with hostility in their eyes, touching everything, my headset helmet, my fur-lined jacket. My wrist compass and watch and my folding knife were passed around – was I a man from Mars? '*Ersatz, Ersatz*', was all I could understand. They smoked so much that you could cut the air, but none thought to offer me a cigarette. I thought of how we entertained shot-down enemy pilots in the mess. I immediately realized that there was no comradeship among airmen here. The door opened again and more soldiers came in with pieces of my Messerschmitt. The annealed bush knife from my survival kit was held up in front of me while they made the motion of cutting off my head. Lying in front of me on the table was the aircraft's long mast compass, crushed like a faded rose.

"Then, in broken German, they made the first attempt to interrogate me: 'You partisan?' They didn't believe that I was a pilot and had baled out of the Messerschmitt. 'Pilot kaput!' They probably thought the Messerschmitt was a two-seater, which could complicate things. 'You partisan!' Perhaps my identity papers could have helped me, but I had buried them. They didn't believe me. They grabbed me and dragged me outside. Standing there were the soldiers who had captured me. On command, they raised their rifles and pointed them at me. They gestured for me to go to a post that was sticking out of the snow next to the barrack. I stumbled towards it. Would I reach it? Finish it, this is the end, I thought. Then I turned around and looked into the muzzles of the rifles. Go ahead, shoot! I had resigned myself; what a miserable end.

"A new command! The Russians came up to me, struck me in the back with a rifle butt and shoved me in front of them. We followed a path in the snow around several barracks and finally stopped. Then they began looking for something in the snow. They scratched and shoveled with rifle butts and hands, moving away the snow. Something wooden became visible. A door! They tugged and worked away and soon a dark opening gaped. A jab, a step, and, crouched low, I passed through the dark hole and landed in an icy cell under the ground, the first of many on my long path through POW camps from the Polar Sea to the Urals.

"An unanticipated odyssey lay before me, which only ended in Friedland on 22 May 1949."

The Jabostaffel

As the reader has learned, in the summer of the previous year it became necessary to form special units to provide air support for ground combat operations, as the Stuka units previously responsible for this task had gradually left the northern theater of operations, for use in the central sector for example. *Hauptmann* von Sponeck's 7./JG 5 took on the role of *Jabostaffel*, however this was only a temporary measure as it, too, soon reequipped on more modern versions of the Bf 109 and again became a conventional fighter unit. Experience soon showed, however, that the lack of a dedicated fighter-bomber unit was a serious disadvantage, and at the beginning of 1943 it was decided to form a unit that could support land forces but which could also effectively attack shipping, gun positions and other Soviet installations.

In about mid-February *Hauptmann* Strakeljahn, previously the commander of 12./JG 5 in Norway, formed a *Jabostaffel* in Petsamo which was designated 14.(J)/JG 5. The *Staffel*, which was equipped with Fw 190 A-2 and A-3 fighters, would achieve great success, especially against shipping along the Polar Sea coast. Unfortunately few records exist concerning 14.(J)/JG 5.

Hauptmann Strakeljahn brought some of his pilots from the west coast with him to the *Jabostaffel*, including *Feldwebel* Hammesfahr. He was wounded during one of the first operations by the new unit on 20 March. Almost every mission flown by the *Staffel* in the coming months was carried out at low level, and losses were unavoidable. On 5 April *Unteroffizier* Dobner went missing in the Murmashi area after his "Black 14" was shot down by anti-aircraft fire. *Unteroffizier* Wendler was also shot down by anti-aircraft fire northeast of Petsamo on 13 April while returning from a sortie. His Focke-Wulf went down in an almost vertical dive. Wendler baled out but was too low for his parachute to open.

On 11 May a Russian transport escorted by motor torpedo boats was sighted in Pummanki Bay. It was assumed that this was a supply convoy bound for somewhere on the Fischer Peninsula and a pair of Fw 190s was sent to attack the freighter. *Leutnant* Busse was shot down on the very first pass. He dove on the enemy ships and was shot down by anti-aircraft fire from one of the torpedo boats. The *Leutnant* failed to pull out and his A-3 crashed and sank immediately.

On Saturday, the 22nd of May, *Leutnant* Klaus Biwer, an outstanding pilot, was unfortunately lost. That day the entire *Staffel* took off for the northeast corner of the Fischer Peninsula to attack an enemy convoy. Biwer had only joined 14.(J)/JG 5 from *Ergänzungsjagdgruppe West* in Cazaux in the spring, but he soon became one of the *Staffel*'s most experienced pilots. The *Leutnant*'s bomb-laden Focke-Wulf was last seen diving towards one of the targets near Zyp Navolok. Biwer did not return and to this day there is still uncertainty as to how he came to crash. None of his fellow pilots was able to say with certainty that he had been shot down by flak.

The 18th of June was another bad day, as two of the *Staffel*'s pilots were lost. *Feldwebel* Luy and *Feldwebel* Hünlein took off on the first mission of the day, an armed reconnaissance sortie over the mouth of Kola Bay in search of enemy shipping. They only found a single freighter, steaming along the coast abeam Cape Pogan, and decided to attack. The attack on the freighter proved to be *Feldwebel* Hünlein's undoing, for he flew too low over the ship and struck its mast. The pilot was killed in the ensuing crash. The pair of *Oberleutnant* Koch and *Unteroffizier* Pohl took off for the same area at 14:10. Pohl was shot down by Russian anti-aircraft fire and his Focke-Wulf crashed into the sea two kilometers west of Cape Pogan with its pilot still aboard.

Meanwhile the total tonnage of Russian shipping sunk by the *Jabostaffel* rose steadily. By the turn of the year 1943-44 it stood at almost 39,000 gross registered tons, including several torpedo boats of the Soviet White Sea Fleet. 14.(J)/JG 5 logged its 1,000th fighter-bomber sortie at about the same time. *Hauptmann* Friedrich-Wilhelm Strakeljahn, born in Lübeck in 1914, received the Knight's Cross from *Fliegerführer Oberst* Kühl on 19 August 1943 in recognition of his success as a *Staffelkapitän*. By then he had also shot down nine enemy aircraft.

The unit suffered no more casualties until the end of the year. On 28 December the pair of *Feldwebel* Türk and *Feldwebel* Culemann was ordered to make a surprise attack against a Russian artillery position on the Small Fischer Peninsula. The *Rotte* successfully dive-bombed the enemy positions, however Culemann, who was flying behind his element leader, was shot down by anti-aircraft fire.

At the beginning of April 1944 the entire *Jabostaffel* left the *Geschwader* unit for transfer to Italy, where it became the *4. Staffel* of *Schlachtgeschwader 4*. While part of JG 5, the unit had achieved outstanding success while keeping losses within limits. During its operations in the north the *Staffel* lost six pilots killed and two were listed missing in action. It suffered its last casualty on 14 February when *Leutnant* Froschek failed to return from a sortie over the Louhi front.

That same summer the *Schlachtgeschwader* found itself back in Russia, and *Hauptmann* Strakeljahn, who had built up and left his mark on the former *Jabostaffel* and thus earned a solid place in the history of JG 5, had by then been named *Kommandeur* of II./SG 4. Strakeljahn, or "Straks" as he was called by many, was killed on the Eastern Front on 6 July 1944.

1943: An Eventful Year

February brought a series of missions, almost all of which resulted in fierce combats, especially escort missions to Kandalaksha for the *Zerstörerstaffel* and to Murmansk for the *Jabostaffel* with subsequent fighter sweeps. While the *III. Gruppe* was still flying the Bf 109 F-4, II./JG 5 had already reequipped on the new Bf 109 G-2. The conversion process was not without difficulties, and on 6 January *Feldwebel* Wirtz was killed in a crash apparently caused by pilot error.

The early days of the month were quiet, but then the action picked up with an unusual incident. During an operation on 9 February the *Zerstörer* lost an aircraft, which was forced to come down somewhere south of Alakurtti while on its way home, still in enemy territory. When Theo Weißenberger learned the next day that was the aircraft of his brother, *Unteroffizier* Otto Weißenberger, he did not hesitate for a moment to search for him in the tundra. He and *Unteroffizier* Krischkovski took off in the *Gruppe*'s Storch just after ten o'clock. Their search was in vain, and after an hour and forty minutes they landed in Kemijärvi, refueled and took off again. This time they returned with the pilot and radio operator from the downed Bf 110. Weißenberger arrived back in Alakurtti at 15:42. The fear he had felt for his younger brother had been a visceral experience for Theo. He regretted having brought the younger Weißenberger to join him in the far north: "Never again will I serve in the same *Geschwader* as a relative."* (*Uffz.* Otto Weißenberger was killed in action over Germany on 23/3/44 while serving with the *1. Sturmstaffel.*).

One of the first missions with the new Gustav involved a *Schwarm* from the *6. Staffel*. The four fighters flown by Weißenberger, Müller, Fenten and Krischkovski headed into the Kandalaksha area on a fighter sweep. It was 19 February 1943. There were no Russian fighters to be found anywhere, but there was plenty of anti-aircraft fire. Suddenly *Unteroffizier* Fenten's "Yellow 6" was swallowed up by a dirty-brown smoke cloud. Moments later, after the smoke had cleared, Rudi Müller was able to see the Messerschmitt going down over the northern outskirts of the city. The *Staffel* mounted a search that same morning, which unfortunately was unsuccessful. Not until much later was it learned that Fenten had survived unhurt and was a POW.

Operations continued, with fighter sweeps near Kovda on the 17th and over Kandalaksha from the 18th to the 21st. Meanwhile at the end of the month the *III. Gruppe* flew several missions over the Fischer Peninsula. *Feldwebel* Schwippert of the *9. Staffel* failed to return from one such operation on 21 February.

Four days later the *Jabostaffel*, escorted by a *Kette* from 7./JG 5 under *Oberleutnant* Senoner, attacked the airfield at Varlamovo. An engagement broke out over the airfield with eight Hurricanes and MiGs, which attacked the Germans in two flights of four. *Unteroffizier* Beth immediately got on the tail of the trailing Hurricane on the right. He fired a long burst from short range and saw strikes flashing on the engine and cockpit of the enemy fighter. The aircraft immediately caught fire and at a height of about 2000 meters it rolled to the left and went down trailing black smoke. It was 13:05 when Beth saw the aircraft crash and explode three kilometers northeast of the airfield – his first victory.

The following months of March and April 1943 were much more eventful and, though clouded by painful losses, represented a high point in the history of the *Geschwader*.

In the morning hours of 5 March the young *Feldwebel* Jakob Norz piloted one of the aircraft of the *III. Gruppe* which scrambled to intercept an incoming formation of IL-2 close-support aircraft. At that time Norz had five victories to his credit and was just beginning his successful career as a fighter pilot. On this day he quickly shot down one of the IL-2s over friendly territory before turning towards another. The Soviet pilot took evasive action, but Norz closed in and pressed the firing buttons. To his dismay only one of his machine-guns responded. He then closed to point-blank range and kept firing. The second Il-2 went down, but pieces of the aircraft's tail section struck Norz's Messerschmitt. His engine faltering, Norz began losing altitude. His only option was a forced landing on a lake in no-man's-land. There is no need to describe here the exertions of a trek through hip-deep snow in the isolation of the tundra, perhaps hoping in vain for the help of his comrades and in constant danger of being discovered by the enemy. After eight hours Norz came upon a strongpoint manned by German mountain troops, who initially thought him a deserter. The troops had also captured the pilot of a downed Il-2, so that Norz was able to return to his unit with two victories, a forced landing and a prisoner.

Early on the morning of the following day, the 6th of March, the *II. Gruppe* temporarily moved to Pontsalenjoki. While landing there the aircraft of the technical officer, *Oberleutnant* Lorenz Bauer, left the runway, ran onto soft ground and overturned. Bauer was injured in the crash and was unable to take part in the mission scheduled for 09:40. Elements of the *Gruppe* set out for the Kyem area, far to the south on Onega Bay on the White Sea. Over Uzhmana they spotted two SB-2 bombers escorted by eight LaGG fighters. The Germans attacked immediately and at least one of the enemy aircraft, Weißenberger's 39th, went down before the Messerschmitts returned about an hour after taking off. The *Gruppe* flew a second mission into the same area at about noon and this time it was attacked by ten Soviet fighters. Another fierce dogfight broke out. At about 13:11 Weißenberger got on the tail of a Curtiss and opened fire. The Soviet fighter blew up. He fired at a second, which went into a left turn and continued

Jagdgeschwader 5

in a shallow dive until it struck the earth. Once again the *Gruppe* returned to Pontsalenjoki without loss. Weißenberger was the top scorer on that 6 March with four victories.

The 10th of March 1943 followed the same pattern. The 6. *Staffel*, having arrived in Salmijärvi, made a sortie over Murmansk, where about thirty Airacobras, Hurricanes and Curtisses were waiting. The *Eismeerjäger* flew into the mass of enemy aircraft like hornets. They split up the Soviet formations and in pairs attacked the Russians, who seemed unable to come up with the right defensive response. It was just before ten in the morning. Six minutes later Weißenberger had already sent two Kittyhawks and an Airacobra to the ground, *Unteroffizier* Gärtner covering his tail. The *Leutnant* repeatedly selected an enemy aircraft, got on its tail and shot it down in a single firing pass. Only his final victim, his sixth in that engagement, required three passes. The Curtiss went down in flames and crashed about 45 kilometers southeast of Murmansk.

Let us turn briefly to the west coast of Norway, where there was much less operational activity that spring. The *IV. Gruppe* in Trondheim had to deal exclusively with the British, who overflew the coast frequently, usually on reconnaissance flights but also to attack the ports of Trondheim, Bergen and Stavanger. The big victory totals of the Polar Sea Front were not to be found there. There were casualties, however, while ferrying new machines or during escort missions over water. On 16 January 1943 *Unteroffizier* Heinz Schmitz was supposed to deliver a Bf 109 G to the *Staffel* but failed to arrive. He was reported missing until his body was discovered in the wreck of the machine southwest of Grindel in July 1943. On 21 January the *12. Staffel* carried out a routine patrol, during which the Focke-Wulf flown by *Feldwebel* Koch crashed near Vaernes from a height of 1000 meters, cause unknown. Three more losses were suffered during similar missions in March and one pilot was reported missing. On 11 March *Unteroffizier* Jasbec, also of 12./JG 5, took off with *Feldwebel* Dombacher on an escort mission. A bad weather front moved in and it is believed he became disoriented.

In contrast, on the Polar Sea Front the 12 of March 1943 was a very busy day. At about 13:45 seven aircraft of 5. and 6./JG 5 took off to escort the *Zerstörerstaffel* into the Murmashi area. It was to be another very successful mission for *Oberleutnant* Weißenberger. Thirty minutes after takeoff the Germans ran into four Kittyhawks and about twelve Airacobras east of Shongui and a fierce dogfight erupted.

Unteroffizier Krischkovski watched as Weißenberger, in his aircraft "White 4", initiated his first attack on a Kittyhawk and opened fire from behind out of a left turn. The Russian's tail flew off and the aircraft went down out of control, before crashing about 20 kilometers southeast of Murmashi at 14:17. Then, with *Oberfeldwebel* Brunner watching his element leader's tail, Weißenberger shot down a second Kittyhawk at 14:18. One minute later he closed on an Airacobra from left and behind. He opened fire from 80 meters and the aircraft blew up in the air.

Feldwebel Weinitschke of the *5. Staffel* had also just shot down a Curtiss. He broke away but suddenly there was a Russian on his tail. Weinitschke, who on that day happed to be flying the aircraft of the *Gruppenkommandeur*, *Hauptmann* Carganico, was climbing at a height of about 700 meters when the Russian pilot began spraying him with bullets. There was an explosion in the fuselage and the controls jammed. The pilot's only choice was to bale out before the aircraft stalled. Weinitschke let himself fall from the spinning fighter and by the time he pulled the ripcord he was only 100 meters above the ground. It was almost too late, for there was just enough time for his parachute to swing once before he struck the snow. The *Feldwebel*, who almost exactly a year earlier had survived the indescribable ordeal of returning from the snow desert, was captured by the Russians the next day. His experiences in a variety of camps will be described later.

Meanwhile the air battle continued to rage over Murmashi. Twice more *Oberleutnant* Weißenberger emerged victorious from engagements with Airacobras. One, which Weißenberger shot down from behind in a dive, was seen to go down by *Unteroffizier* Rolly, while Krischkovski observed the second three minutes later. By the time Weißenberger landed at Petsamo, he had added five more victories to his total and had surpassed the fifty mark.

Worried about the *Staffel*'s missing pilot, six minutes after returning to base Weißenberger led a *Schwarm* into the air to search the combat area in the hope of finding a trace of *Feldwebel* Weinitschke. The search was unsuccessful. That same Friday the *5. Staffel* suffered another casualty during a Stuka escort mission to the Murmansk railway by eight Bf 109s. *Feldwebel* Stratmann's engine failed and he was obliged to make a forced landing. The wing of his F-4 grazed a tree and the aircraft flipped over. Emil Stratmann's body was later recovered from the wreckage.

The *Geschwader*, and especially the *III. Gruppe*, was constantly on the move. In March it operated from Pontsalenjoki, Alakurtti, Salmijärvi and Petsamo. From the middle of the month the *6. Staffel* spent a period of time in Salmijärvi on the Finnish-Norwegian border, 4./JG 5 and the *Geschwaderstab* remained in Alakurtti and 5./JG 5 in Petsamo. The pilots were rarely out of their flight suits, for they were in the air every day, sometimes three or four times.

The 13th of March began with a mission in the direction of Motovski Bay. At 09:27 *Leutnant* Weißenberger and *Feldwebel* Rolly took off to intercept a formation of Pe-2s reported to be heading for Petsamo. The two pilots attacked the Russian formation from above. Weißenberger shot down the first at 09:35 after two passes, the second one minute later, and Rolly brought down a third Pe-2. The three Soviet bombers were shot down just 25 kilometers from the unit's base in Petsamo. It was probably from one of these aircraft that 9./JG 5 recovered the tail fin that was subsequently hung on the wall of "Cloud Cottage", the *Staffel* home, and used as a scoreboard. The tail gunner in the Pe-2 shot down by Rolly put up a brave fight, however. Return fire hit his Messerschmitt's engine and he was forced to bale out. Rolly landed hard on rocky ground. A strong wing caught his parachute and dragged him across the ground, resulting in a wrenched leg. Rolly was an outstanding wingman, and Weißenberger did everything in his power to find him and bring him home safely. It was the first time Rolly had been injured; it would happen twice more in the coming year.

Towards noon the *Zerstörerstaffel* flew from Kirkenes to Varlamovo, the Russians' most dangerous fighter base located north of Murmansk. A pair of Bf 109s provided the fighter escort. Over Ura Bay a flight of Curtisses tried to get to the twin-engined fighters. Weißenberger and his wingman, *Oberfeldwebel* Brunner, dove on one of the P-40s and shot it down as it tried to escape. As they regained altitude a second enemy aircraft appeared before them and, after a slight correction, Weißenberger shot it down too. The left wing of the Curtiss came off and the pilot baled out. One other significant event occurred on 13 March 1943: 6./JG 5 commanded by *Oberleutnant* Ehrler scored its 500th victory.

The next day *Unteroffizier* Alfred Kern failed to return. The *7. Staffel* flew a mission into the Murmansk area. Kern's aircraft was probably hit by flak, and during the return flight he was obliged to make a forced landing in the area of Urd Lake. The pilot made a desperate attempt to reach the German lines but was caught by Russian troops. Kern fought back but was finally captured. His comrades knew nothing of this, and there was initial uncertainty as to Kern's fate. That day at 14:00 Weißenberger took off with Krischkovski and Brunner to escort a *Storch* to Urd Lake. The search effort was interrupted when four to six Airacobras suddenly appeared. The Russians very probably expected to find German aircraft there and thought that they could take them by surprise while in the act of searching for their missing pilot. The outcome was very different, however. A lengthy dogfight developed over the lake. The Messerschmitt pilots did their best to keep the enemy away from the defenseless *Storch*, and the Russians paid for their attack with the loss of three of their aircraft. They were Weißenberger's 58th to 60th victories.

Saturday, the 27th of March 1943: another big day. The *Zerstörerstaffel* was airborne for an attack on Murmashi and Shongui. At about 13:30 elements of the *II.* and *III. Gruppe* of JG 5 took off to rendezvous with the Bf 110s and escort them to the target area. Typically, after completing their escort duties, the fighters conducted a fighter sweep in the same area. While they usually had to go looking for the enemy over his own airfields, on this day the German fighters had a rare stroke of luck. Over Shongui they ran into a group of Airacobras, Kittyhawks and Il-2s, about thirty aircraft in all, which had probably taken off to attack JG 5's air bases.

The enemy formation was flying low over the tundra, heading west, when the Messerschmitts dived in fours on the main body. A fierce battle broke out, with the Russian fighter pilots doing their best to make things difficult for the attackers. They obviously failed in this, for within a matter of minutes Weißenberger sent down two Airacobras. They crashed and exploded in the snow-covered forests between Murmashi and Shongui. Then Weißenberger downed two Kittyhawks in quick succession. By then the Russian formation had lost all semblance of order. Previously pairs of fighters had clung to the main formation of about fifteen aircraft, but now there was total confusion in the Russian ranks. Fighters bearing the black cross mingled with aircraft wearing the red star. *Staffelkapitän Oberleutnant* Ehrler shot down five enemy aircraft within the space of four minutes before getting into trouble himself. The following is from the account he gave to waiting war reporters on his return: "Two of my kills went down in quick succession east of the Tuloma, the third on the west bank of the river, while I shot down the fourth and fifth in a shallow right turn. The next candidate was flying ahead and to my left. I was then at a height of 150 meters, and three Kittyhawks and an Airacobra were still circling below me to the left. Just as I was about to open fire on the enemy in front of me, there was a bang in the cockpit, which immediately filled with black smoke. What had happened? A heavy machine-gun bullet had entered just behind the engine, striking the cannon ammunition feed and setting off one of my own 20-mm rounds. After breaking away I tried to determine the extent of the damage. The engine was still running normally. I had taken a few tiny splinters in my left leg and hand, but as yet I felt little pain. In the left wing, however, there gaped a huge hole, while on the right the wingtip had been torn away. After minutes of vacillation as to whether I should rejoin the battle, with a heavy heart I decided to head home." Ehrler had made a wise choice, for after he landed it was discovered that the throttle linkage of his Gustav had been hit and was hanging by a thread. Had he rejoined combat it would undoubtedly have broken and caused the pilot to come to grief. And so Ehrler's tally for the day remained at five.

The *Staffel* waited in vain for the return of *Unteroffizier* Krischkovski. He had been shot down by a Russian fighter and was now a prisoner of war. It was therefore not surprising that the ensuing search effort was unsuccessful. 7./JG 5 lost another pilot on this day: *Unteroffizier* Riess, who is still listed as missing.

The month ended with an attack on Salmijärvi airfield by twenty Il-2s, Airacobras and P-40s on 28 March. Weißenberger shot down three Airacobras but was hit by Russian ground fire and had to make a belly landing on his way back to base. The *Storch* picked him up and he was back in the air three hours later.

By now the Arctic sun was rising higher in the sky. Its reddish-yellow rays still cast long shadows over the frozen tundra, but their splendor was like a new beginning after such a long period of dark isolation. The snowstorms had not yet ended completely, and fat gray clouds frequently obscured the brilliant disc of the sun. Soon, however, it would bring a new awakening, replenishing spirits and causing the men to slowly forget their depression.

One day at about this time two unusual aircraft landed in Petsamo. At first glance they resembled the familiar Bf 110s of the *Zerstörerstaffel* – twin tails, twin engines. But the cockpit appeared to have been pushed forward and the engines looked different, being housed in nacelles beneath the wings. They also wore different codes than the *Zerstörer*: GL+QA and GL+QB. As it turned out, the aircraft were two prototypes of the new Arado Ar 240 A-0 series. They were there to undergo operational trials with JG 5, and other aircraft of this type were sent to units in other sectors of the Eastern Front. Initially conceived as a high-speed heavy fighter, the Ar 240 A could also be used as a fast reconnaissance aircraft, high-speed bomber or night-fighter. Only a few were built, however, as development and production were halted in favor of other projects, even though the Ar 240 had excellent handling characteristics and a good performance. The *Geschwader* emblem was applied on the noses of the aircraft and cameras were installed in their engine nacelles, and they soon began operations, their principal role being to photograph the Murmansk railway. In the summer of 1943 one of the Arados was sent to *Fernaufklärungsstaffel 122* in Italy, however there is no information as to how long the second Ar 240 remained with JG 5, who its pilots were, or where the machine finally ended up. It would be interesting to learn further details on this topic.

The "Hunter of Murmansk"

Aerial activity in the north dropped off somewhat until mid-April 1943. There was little happening in the entire northern area of operations, as it received scant mention in the situation reports. After the fall of Stalingrad the tide of the war had slowly begun to turn in favor of the Allies. Since the spring of 1943 the Axis powers had been irretrievably forced onto the defensive, however Germany was still able to defend "Fortress Europe" on all sides. The question was, how long would the available forces and reserves be sufficient to continue doing so? On 27

January American bombers carried out the first raid against a German city by day: Wilhelmshaven. Toward the end of March the RAF began its strategic bombing offensive, which was initially directed against the Ruhr. Later, in combination with the Americans, it would extend to the entire Reich. Axis forces were also on the retreat in North Africa, where at the beginning of May the legendary Africa Corps was forced to lay down its arms. And on the Eastern Front the Red Army was now on the advance. Leningrad had been relieved and hopes of yet taking Murmansk with the 20th Mountain Army in Lapland had to be abandoned.

In the first weeks of the month the *Eismeerjäger* flew the usual escort missions, as may be seen from the following data:

4 April 1943: Escort for Bf 110s, combat with ten Curtisses. In the Petsamo area, an engagement with about ten Il-2s attempting to attack the airfield. *Uffz.* Bela Preiser (7./JG 5) made a forced landing due to engine trouble. The next day the pilots of the search aircraft twice saw him about 15 kilometers behind the lines, before he was captured by the Russians.

8 April 1943: Escort.

11 April 1943: Fighter sweep after escort mission, no enemy contact.

13 April 1943: Fighter sweep in the Murmansk area with air combat.

Of these missions, the one on the 13th of Aril proved to be another extraordinary success for the *Geschwader*. That day 6./JG 5, the "*Staffel* of Experts", shot down no less than 18 Soviet aircraft. Just five Messerschmitts took off from Salmijärvi at 16:48. Northeast of Murmansk they encountered a group of enemy aircraft, ten Hurricanes and P-40s plus twelve Airacobras, and at 17:00 one of the biggest dogfights to take place in the Murmansk area to date began. The young *Feldwebel* Erwin Fahldieck was on just his fifth combat sortie, and he crowned it by shooting down an Airacobra. The experienced *Unteroffizier* Mors also scored. But it was Weißenberger, Ehrler and Brunner who did most of the damage, sending down one enemy aircraft after another. All of these aircraft ended up crashing and exploding, and only a few of the Soviet pilots were able to escape by parachute, as in the case of the Airacobra pilot shot down by Weißenberger at 17:16. The *Staffelkapitän* blasted pieces off the enemy fighter before it went down in flames, while *Oberfeldwebel* Brunner recorded his 46th victory.

When the Messerschmitts returned to Salmijärvi after 58 minutes in the air, there was indescribable jubilation, for five of the *Staffel*'s pilots had virtually wiped out an entire enemy fighter unit in about half an hour. Ehrler and Weißenberger each claimed six victories, Brunner four, and Fahldieck and Mors one each. An outstanding result! The following is a list of JG 5's most successful pilots at that time:

Ofw. Müller	6./JG 5	91 victories
Oblt. Ehrler	6./JG 5	83 victories
Lt. Weißenberger	6./JG 5	77 victories
Hptm. Carganico	II./JG 5	52 victories
Fw. Döbrich	6./JG 5	52 victories
Ofw. Brunner	6./JG 5	46 victories
Fw. Bartels	8./JG 5	46 victories

There was no doubt that the air battles on the northern front had become much more difficult, as evidenced by German casualties. And newcomers to the *Geschwader* were not the only victims, as experienced, battle-tested and successful pilots were also lost. The high spirits from the successful mission of the 13th of April had scarcely faded away when the 6. *Staffel* suffered a serious loss. One week later, on Monday the 19th of April 1943, *Oberfeldwebel* Müller, the *Geschwader*'s most successful pilot, met his match over Bolshoye Lake. Six aircraft of 6./JG 5 took off from Salmijärvi shortly before 10:00 to conduct a fighter sweep in the Murmansk area, with special attention to be paid to the Vayenga (Varlamovo) airfield on the eastern shore of Kola Bay.

A total of approximately 40 Russian fighters rose to intercept this incursion and the opposing fighters made contact at about 11:20. Four minutes later *Leutnant* Weißenberger shot down an Airacobra, which hit the ground in a cloud of snow. It was his 78th victory, confirmed by *Leutnant* Schmidt.

A fierce dogfight then developed and, according to one of the few accounts by a Soviet veteran to reach the west, Flying Officer Skibnev shot down two German aircraft while Bokiy, Sorokin and Titov each accounted for one. The surviving *Geschwader* records of JG 5 do not support these claims, as they show that just one pilot was lost on 19 April 1943, and that was *Oberfeldwebel* Rudolf Müller. There is uncertainty as to who shot Müller down, as both Bokiy and regimental commander Captain Skibnev claimed the honors. According to Skibnev's version of events, he climbed above the German machine and scored hits with his machine-guns, whereupon the Bf 109 went down in a steep spiral. Müller's comrades saw him land on Bolshoye Lake but then lost track of him. Soviet victory and loss reports were often falsified for political-ideological purposes and are often contradictory. There are numerous examples of this.

Skibnev landed next to the Messerschmitt while the air battle was still raging, however tracks in the snow showed that its pilot had already set off on snowshoes and disappeared into the tundra. The search for the *Oberfeldwebel* would last several days, before Russian soldiers captured him near the front. There is a clear report from the enemy side that Müller was captured in April 1943. To date, however, all inquiries in Moscow have been fruitless, event though there are statements that he was still in a Russian POW camp in 1947. But then his trail vanished forever. This uncertainty resulted in the most imaginative stories about Rudi Müller among the fighter pilots in the POW camps, including one that he had been "a fighter instructor for the Ivans."* (*Meanwhile, in 1968 the family allegedly received notification from the Red Cross or Red Crescent that *Fw*. Müller "died in Russian captivity in October 1943.").

The *Staffel* grieved over the loss of this brave comrade for a long time. Born in Frankfurt/Main on 21 November 1920, Rudi Müller was supposed to have become a gardener, but the pull of flying was stronger. He joined up and initially served in an army signals battalion, but then in the spring of 1940 he received a transfer to a flight training school. From there he went to Rumania and then to the Polar Sea Front. He scored his first victory on his very first operational sortie on 12 September 1941 and within six weeks he raised his victory total to thirty. One of his greatest successes came on 23 April 1942, when he shot down five Hurricanes over Kola Bay. On 19 June of the same year, after registering his 41st victory, he was awarded the Knight's Cross with a simultaneous promotion to *Feldwebel*. Müller was the first great fighter ace in the far north – until he was captured after 94 victories and then disappeared. What happened to him will remain a secret forever. In any event, it is very likely that the Russians knew who they were dealing with when they captured him. At that time Müller was our most successful fighter pilot on the entire Polar Sea Front and the most dangerous to the Russians.

Colonel Kursenkov was a pilot in the Russian air force. He had ten victories and was one of the most successful pilots in Major Safanov's celebrated squadron, which was deployed on the northern front. In his book *Fighter Pilot* (Deutscher Militärverlag, Berlin), he wrote the following about operations in the spring of 1942: "In those days the fascists had a Messerschmitt with a special camouflage scheme. This striped machine and its companion always stayed grandly above the other patrolling fighters. This pair never took part in group combats. They only ambushed pilots who were daydreaming and thus became separated. We began hunting him, but that fascist ace was not so easy to get." It is not difficult to figure out that the subject was then *Unteroffizier* Müller. Once again the account is in the typical ideologically tainted Soviet style used to disseminate "authentic" information to the world.

Erwin Fahldieck failed to return on 29 April. The *6. Staffel* fought Soviet fighters over Murmansk, and it cannot be confirmed that he was captured.

The successes achieved to date by *Jagdgeschwader 5* could in no way belie the fact that the air war on the Polar Sea Front had entered another phase. Operations in the spring of 1943 demonstrated the growing strength of the Soviet aviation regiments. The vast industrial capacity of the Soviet Union enabled the enemy to make huge strides in aircraft production, mobilizing all available industries and increasing output of new aircraft immensely. As a result, deliveries of new aircraft to the northern front allowed the Soviets to make good their losses and also form new units. The White Sea Fleet was bolstered by the 46th Close-Support Regiment plus one torpedo-bomber, one dive-bomber and one fighter regiment. Soon the ratio of forces on both sides was about equal, which from about the middle of the year meant the beginning of a struggle for air superiority. The commander of the Soviet 6th Fighter Division was Major Petrushkin, one of the most successful enemy fighter pilots.

It also cannot be overlooked that the Russian pilots had improved their tactics and understood how to exploit the capabilities of the aircraft types sent them by the western allies. Adding their numerical superiority in most engagements, they had become an opponent who could no longer be underestimated. For the German fighter pilots, victories became more difficult to come by and depended in large part on the total exploitation of their flying skills.

Nevertheless, Soviet fighter losses must have been grim in the summer of 1943. Many times entire units were decimated. Feigned "transfers" were used to cover up these losses. It must have taken much effort to maintain the fighting spirit of the pilots, for the additional burden of having to fight deep over enemy territory now fell to the Russians as well. The political officers spread hate, true to Stalin's words: "He who cannot hate also cannot fight!" This political indoctrination naturally led to tensions, whereby the Soviets inevitably remained inferior to the sporting-casual lone warrior spirit of the Germans. Free aerial combat could not be regulated – one had to master the rules of the game. *Hptm.* Schmidt, *Kapitän* of 9./JG 5, found this confirmed when, at the beginning of 1944, he found himself "over there" in Varlamovo, the most dangerous Russian hornet's nest. He was put on display, probably to demonstrate to the Russian pilots that the Germans also lost unit leaders. He found himself sitting opposite the commanders of Boston, Pe-2, Il-2, Airacobra and Yak units that he had met in the convoy battles off Vardö. They simply couldn't believe it when he told them that of the two to three dozen crashes that could be counted in the water, 95% were Soviet losses, and that the German *Staffeln* were still intact in the evening, apart from one or two losses. He could only tell them that he couldn't understand it either, and that he often landed back at Petsamo fearing that he would be met by numerous casualty reports, which never happened. Whenever their political officers weren't present the Russians spoke candidly and openly, as the British or Americans would have done, and asked Schmidt about German tactics. He told them the formula of his *Kommandeur*, *Major* Ehrler: "Close in from behind unnoticed to 30 meters; a short burst and he must blow up!" The Russians weren't sure if he was telling the truth or not. In the evening he met all of the Soviet flying personnel. The Russian commanders presented their best people and he was amazed: all outstanding human stock. Many of them, especially those from guards or naval units, were almost western in their uniforms, haircuts and manners. It became obvious to him that tough times lay ahead for the men of JG 5 if the Russians, despite all their losses, despite the reorganization of their industry, their training centers and supply sources, could mobilize such potential in men and materiel – he was even shown a Yak fighter – in the far north. In the evening he and his escorting officer went to a navy mess to eat. There was an American destroyer in Vayenga Bay, and the American officers were obviously undergoing a course of vodka treatment. Schmidt was kept far away from the Americans, of course,

This visit to Varlamovo was the "highlight" of his eight-week interrogation period in Murmansk, which by the way was tough and grueling. The next day he met the senior interrogator, who had undoubtedly dealt with many German prisoners. He spoke several languages, was familiar with the west coast of Norway, and knew about hotels in Denmark, France, Aalborg and Berlin. One could have gotten the impression that he had been there. He probably wanted to check the results of the brainwashing himself, after the subject had behaved so openly. But when it came to the tough key question, whether Schmidt was prepared to actively work for the Soviets, the answer was no. The interrogation ended abruptly. The interrogating captain, who had put in so much hard work for weeks, cast him a hard look and disappeared. *Hauptmann* Schmidt had become uninteresting and was thrown into the big pot. Before him lay the usual road to Kildinstroy, about 20 km south of Murmansk, where apparently all the trains were assembled. Several days later he and several other German prisoners, including mountain infantrymen, were put in a wire cage in the usual prisoner car, in which many dozens of civilian prisoners were also transported, and sent south. He was transported from Arkhangelsk to Cherepovets, a trip that lasted thirteen long days.

• • •

At the beginning of May 1943 the two *Gruppen* of JG 5 stationed on the Polar Sea had just over 60 serviceable aircraft. This number remained largely unchanged throughout the summer, but towards the end of the year it would fall to 30 machines.

The reduction in JG 5's aircraft complement was not just due to losses in combat, for dawn to dusk operations on the airfields also demanded their tribute. Forced landings, crashes and accidents were routine occurrences. Occasionally a returning pilot would put his Gustav down on its belly because battle damage prevented his undercarriage from lowering. Others, like *Unteroffizier* Lorenz, veered off the wooden plank runway and crashed, while others overturned on landing. Another regrettable accident occurred at Alakurtti on 2 May, when a Messerschmitt collided with the *II. Gruppe*'s ambulance while landing. The collision touched off a cannon round, which exploded inside the vehicle. *Gefreiter* Georg Kästner, the driver of the ambulance, was severely wounded when struck in the head by shell fragments.

The *Geschwader* lost another of its best pilots when *Oberfeldwebel* Alfred Brunner was shot down on 7 May. After Rudi Müller he was the second rising ace from the 6. *Staffel* to be lost. Brunner was returning from a sortie over Murmansk and was over the German lines when he was suddenly attacked by an Airacobra. His aircraft was hit and he was forced to bale out. Brunner was too low, however, and his parachute had no time to open. German infantry later recovered the body of the 25-year-old *Oberfeldwebel*. Alfred Brunner, who had served from the beginning with 6./JG 5, victor over 53 Russian aircraft, was awarded the Knight's Cross posthumously on 3 July 1943.

Late in the afternoon on the same day, Walter Schuck shot down his 36th enemy aircraft. Schuck was a born lone warrior. Toughness, willpower and a touch of recklessness, paired with outstanding eyesight, would help him score 200 victories and join Weißenberger and Ehrler as top scorers in the far north. Schuck must also have possessed one other quality that distinguished the outstanding fighter pilot: the sangfroid that enabled him to react a fraction of a second sooner than his opponent. Let us take a closer look at his victory of 7 May.

The mission order was received at about 17:00: escort for Strakeljahn's *Jabostaffel* to Motovski Bay. A *Schwarm* from 9./JG 5 took off ten minutes later, soon caught up with the fighter-bombers and positioned itself above the formation. Because of the 250-kilo bombs slung beneath their bellies, the Focke-Wulfs were somewhat slower, and the escorting Messerschmitts had to turn constantly to stay with them. On this day Schuck's wingman was Heinfried Wiegand.

Suddenly a warning call: "Enemy fighters at eighty degrees!" The German machines still had not reached their target, so for the time being the Focke-Wulfs could not engage in aerial combat. The fighter *Schwarm* had no other choice, therefore, but to attack alone – four Bf 109s against two groups of enemy fighters, more than 20 Hurricanes and Airacobras altogether.

The *Schwarm* immediately split up. Schuck and Wiegand went after the Airacobra formation. A tight right turn, and they were beside the enemy aircraft, which were in the process of turning towards the fighter-bombers. The two Messerschmitts roared through the enemy formation. Schuck blazed away with no hope of hitting anything, but in doing so he caused confusion among the Airacobra pilots. Several broke away and the Russian formation disintegrated. As the *Jabos* had dropped their bombs, the escort mission was completed and the Messerschmitt pilots could concentrate fully on their métier, hunting the enemy.

It was Schuck's first encounter with the heavily-armed Airacobra (37-mm engine-mounted cannon). It was slightly slower than the Messerschmitt but more maneuverable. The Russians had already formed a defensive circle which was difficult to penetrate. Schuck dropped a wing and, at full throttle, flew into the defensive circle. Just a few meters in front of him was an enemy fighter. He turned left and moved in even closer, but his Messerschmitt was carried out of the circle again. "Don't get discouraged!" the *Feldwebel* thought to himself, and at that same instant he saw another Airacobra appear before him. He entered the turn about 50 meters lower in order to attack the enemy from behind and below, as he had practiced countless times. The Russian pilot seemed unaware of the approaching danger, for he continued flying straight and level. The Messerschmitt was now less than 60 meters away. Flashes danced from Schuck's guns and shells struck home. At 19:42 the Airacobra went down like a stone and crashed.

The next day fate caught up with *Leutnant* Rolf-Viktor Sadewasser, the adjutant of III./JG 5. *Major* Scholz and his *Gruppe* took off at about 12:00 to escort a group of bombers to Murmansk. Sadewasser was flying in the *Stabsschwarm* as wingman to *Leutnant* Schumann, the *Gruppe* technical officer. The *Kommandeur* himself later described what happened: "Over Murmansk we encountered eight to ten Airacobras and Kittyhawks. In the course of a fierce dogfight *Leutnant* Sadewasser was attacked by an enemy fighter. His aircraft immediately began trailing thick black smoke. Escorted by *Leutnant* Schumann, he tried to head for home, but apparently his aircraft caught fire. Schumann saw Sadewasser bale out. Unfortunately we could not see whether he got down safely, as we were again attacked by the enemy. As soon as we landed, several flights were dispatched to the bale-out area to look for the pilot. The terrain was extremely difficult, and they were unable to find him. From there it was about eighty kilometers to our lines and the chances of a return were slim."

In *Leutnant* Sadewasser the G*eschwader* lost an excellent officer and adjutant. To this day his fate remains a mystery.

In the spring of 1943, fresh Russian divisions took the offensive on the northern front, probably in an attempt to weaken or divert German attacks on the Murmansk railway, which by then was heavily defended by anti-aircraft guns and air forces. The offensive was focused in the Murmansk area, for it was there that the railway was most threatened by German ground forces. Much farther south, on the other hand, there were areas where military operations were impossible and where activities were limited to small offensive patrols. Dense forests, countless lakes and swamps made the movement and supply of larger units impossible. The only remaining option was attack from the air and, considering the fact that throughout the month the Russians had strengthened their air defenses, making attacks against the Murmansk railway were ever more dangerous.

Leutnant Steinmann was shot down over Kovda Lake during one such operation on 11 May, when the *4. Staffel* escorted Ju 87s to Kandalaksha Bay. "White 3" was hit by anti-aircraft fire and Steinmann baled out. He is still listed as missing.

On 13 May the Stukas again appeared over the Murmansk railway, this time escorted by seven Messerschmitts of the *II. Gruppe*. The period of twenty-four-hour daylight was finally beginning after the long Polar night, and on this day the *Gruppe* had taken off very early. Once again the Germans were greeted by heavy anti-aircraft fire. Long glowing strands rose up from the ground and became heavier, forcing the Messerschmitts to take evasive action. *Leutnant* Günther Zeuch's G-2 was hit while climbing. It was precisely 06:56 when he jumped from the blazing aircraft. Zeuch's parachute failed to open, however, and he fell to his death. Perhaps Zeuch had been wounded and was unable to pull the ripcord, or perhaps he had been killed by the anti-aircraft fire.

On the afternoon of 23 May a German convoy was off Vardö where, as usual, the ships turned south towards the port of Petsamo. Then the *III. Gruppe* received a report that Russian bombers were approaching the convoy from the Fischer Peninsula. The *7. Staffel* was scrambled. At 15:32 a *Schwarm* lifted off and headed towards the Russians. Senoner was leading. Northwest of the peninsula the Germans came upon four DB-3 bombers escorted by six Airacobras. One of the bombers was shot down into the sea on the first pass. The Russian fighter escort must have failed to spot the approaching Germans; in any case they reacted too late. Now they had been alerted, however, and tried to prevent the German fighters from getting to the bombers again. The battle raged for ten minutes, with neither side able to gain an advantage. But then *Unteroffizier* Beth saw his chance. He approached an Airacobra from below in a right-hand turn, opened fire and saw his bursts striking the cockpit of the enemy machine. Out of control, the Russian fighter spun down vertically and crashed north of Subovka Bay. The time was 16:05. It was Beth's second victory.

The *Geschwader* suffered further grievous losses in the first half of June, when two pilots were killed, two posted missing and another captured. It began on 3 June with an escort mission in support of the *Jabostaffel*, which had taken off to attack enemy shipping in Kola Bay. 6./JG 5 provided four aircraft for the escort. Just short of the target the Germans encountered ten Russian fighters, to which *Leutnant* Harder fell victim. Early on 5 June *Leutnant* Steinle's "Yellow 9" was hit by the dorsal gunner of a Russian bomber over Motovski Bay and the Messerschmitt was forced to come down on a lake north of Ura Bay. Both Harder and Steinle are still missing.

Feldwebel Gaehne failed to return on 12 June, on the 14th *Unteroffizier* Kimmeskamp was killed, and a day later the courageous Mors was shot down. On that 15 June 6./JG 5 fought a pitched battle against twenty Russian fighters northwest of Murmansk. Mors was shot down and parachuted to safety. On 18 June a search aircraft found him and flew him back to base unharmed.

On 16 June the *4. Staffel* escorted a *Gruppe* of Ju 87s to the Murmansk railway. When the unit returned, *Unteroffizier* Seedorf's "White 3" was missing. A search was initiated at once but was unsuccessful. Later a Russian radio transmission was intercepted by chance, and it provided clear evidence that Seedorf was in the hands of the enemy.

Weißenberger and 7./JG 5

The transfer of *Oberstleutnant* Handrick to the *8. Jagddivision* in Austria resulted in a personnel shuffle. *Major* Günter Scholz became the new *Geschwaderkommodore* and *Major* Ehrler took over as *Kommandeur* of the *III. Gruppe*. Weißenberger briefly took over the *7. Staffel* and then on 14 September was named *Kapitän* of the *6. Staffel*. *Oberleutnant* Segatz was transferred to JG 1 on the Western Front and *Oberleutnant* Horst Berger took over his 8./JG 5.

Whenever the "far north" is spoken of, one probably imagines a snow-covered landscape of perpetual ice and cold. Summer in the far north is much different, however. In June a pitiless sun shone down on the dried-out airfields, and engine run-ups and takeoffs produced clouds of dust that shrouded the fields and made it almost impossible to breathe. And even the twilight period brought little relief from the heat. The barracks and Finnish tents became incubators. The tundra burned in many places, for the dry caribou moss could self-ignite in the terrific heat. Swaths of smoke, up to 300 meters high, could almost blind a pilot flying at low level and prevent him from seeing the ground.

The 22nd of June 1943 was one such day and it would witness large-scale battles in the air over the Karelia Front. 7./JG 5's mission order that day: "Fighter sweep over the Murmansk-Murmashi area. Takeoff at 09:10!" Half an hour prior to takeoff *Staffelführer Leutnant* Weißenberger assembled his pilots for final instructions. Everyone realized that there would be aerial combat.

Major Scholz, the *Kommandeur* of III./JG 5, took off punctually at 09:10 with his wingman *Feldwebel* von Hermann of 8./JG 5 and six Bf 109s of 7./JG 5. They immediately turned on course. Soon after takeoff *Major* Scholz's aircraft developed engine trouble and had to return to the airfield, while *Feldwebel* von Hermann joined the *Rotte* led by *Oberfeldwebel* Beulich. The Messerschmitts climbed out over the burning tundra and leveled off at 4000 meters. After about fifteen minutes they reached Kola, a few kilometers south of Murmansk.

The Messerschmitt pilots saw large dust clouds rising from Kola-South airfield. Russian fighters were taking off. "We immediately descended to low level and positioned ourselves in the sun for a surprise attack," wrote *Unteroffizier* Beth, describing the start of the action. "A flight of Hurricanes formed up right over the airfield without noticing us. More and more aircraft took off. Our first *Schwarm* moved into a favorable position to attack the Russians. Then the dogfight began, for by then their other aircraft had appeared and tried to attack us. This they were unable to do, however, as we were faster. We split up into pairs and attacked the various formations. By then there were 25 to 30 Russians in the air."

The first enemy aircraft fell to Beulich's guns at 09:25. Two minutes later *Leutnant* Weißenberger caught another Hurricane from behind. It went down trailing dark smoke and crashed into a wood about three kilometers northeast of Kola Station. At 09:28 *Oberfeldwebel* Beulich sent a third Hurricane crashing to the ground.

A fierce battle then developed right over the Russian airfield. Now and then the Russian anti-aircraft guns fired a few rounds without effect. Weißenberger's "White 4" was soon on the tail of another turning Soviet fighter. The Russian straightened out just as the *Leutnant* reached firing range. Weißenberger opened fire from almost ramming distance at the Hurricane's seven o'clock position. It burst into flames and went down almost vertically from 600 meters. The Hurricane crashed and burned at 09:30.

Beulich and his wingman, *Unteroffizier* Beth, were at 800 meters when they approached two Russian fighters from below. Beth attacked the last of the two enemy machines, which blew up after the first burst. There was no witness for the victory however. The second Hurricane tried to escape by making a Split-S. Beth scored a few hits but was unable to observe their effect, for at the same moment he was himself fired upon and had to take evasive action.

Leutnant Eichhorn and *Feldwebel* von Hermann each shot down an enemy fighter, and at 09:24 *Leutnant* Geisen also brought down one of the enemy. Another followed at 09:38, but then Geisen's comrades saw his "White 10" suddenly go down. *Leutnant* Walter Geisen has been missing since.

At 09:40 Weißenberger shot down his third enemy aircraft, having crept up on a Hurricane unnoticed. It went down in a shallow dive and crashed east of Kola Station. Weißenberger had recorded his 92nd, 93rd and 94th victories.

It was probably *Oberfeldwebel* Beulich who scored the *7. Staffel*'s 100th victory sometime between 09:40 and 09:45, shooting down an Airacobra.

Far below the Hurricanes circled, apparently waiting for the Germans to come down. In no time they were there and attacked again. At first the Russians evaded skillfully and split up, but that gave the attackers the advantage of each being able to select a target. When one of the Hurricanes tried to get behind Beulich's "White 8", *Unteroffizier* Beth closed to 30 meters and scored hits on the Russian's engine and cockpit. Enveloped in flames, the Hurricane spun straight down and at 09:46 crashed ten kilometers south of Kola, at the same time as a Hurricane shot down by *Feldwebel* von Hermann hit the ground. One of these last two machines was also the 350th victory by III./JG 5.

The battle went on for half an hour until low fuel brought the dogfight to an end. Fifteen minutes later, after 10:00, the Messerschmitts landed at Petsamo. The day had been a total success. Thirteen enemy fighters had been shot down, almost over their own base, and the *Staffel* had suffered just one casualty. The balance for 22 June 1943 was:

Confirmed victories
Uffz. Beth	1 Hawker Hurricane
Ofw. Beulich	2 Hawker Hurricanes
	1 Bell P-39 Airacobra
Fw. Drößler	1 Hawker Hurricane
Lt. Eichhorn	1 Hawker Hurricane
Lt. Geisen	2 Hawker Hurricanes
Fw. v. Hermann	2 Hawker Hurricanes
Lt. Weißenberger	3 Hawker Hurricanes

Own losses
Lt. Geisen	missing

While the mission of 22 June had resulted in a high victory total, the 4th of July saw a repetition of this success – this time 7./JG 5 would come home with sixteen victories. Toward evening the *Staffel* received orders to provide air cover for a German convoy that had already sailed. A *Schwarm* under Weißenberger's command subsequently took off at 20:26 and headed for the specified area to protect the ships. Then radar spotted a target north of the Fischer Peninsula. It turned out to be a Pe-2 reconnaissance aircraft and the *Schwarm* was immediately diverted to intercept. The Messerschmitts spotted the enemy aircraft about 18 kilometers north of Vayda-Guba. Weißenberger positioned himself on its tail and a short burst was enough to cause the Pe-2 to burst into flames. The dorsal gunner jumped without a parachute and moments later the blazing machine fell into the Polar Sea. It was 21:07.

The *Schwarm* then returned to patrol over the convoy. About a half hour passed before ground control reported: "Enemy formation over the north tip of the Fischer Peninsula!"

At ten minutes before ten in the evening the fighter pilots sighted an enemy formation of about 25 to 30 bombers and torpedo aircraft in the area indicated by the ground controller. Its target was undoubtedly the German convoy. Leading the formation were antiquated Handley-Page Hampdens, which the Germans also called the "tadpole Hampden" on account of its bulbous fuselage, followed by several pairs of Il-2s, then a formation of Pe-2s and several Bostons. There was no fighter escort.

Four more Messerschmitts of the *7. Staffel* had taken off at 21:12 to join the first *Schwarm*. The entire group of fighters was sent to attack the Soviets, who were flying in several waves. The first combats took place abeam the north tip of the Fischer Peninsula. Most of the Russians jettisoned their bombs and torpedoes and their formations disintegrated. The *Staffelführer* of the 7th shot down three Il-2s in the first three minutes, recording his 100th victory at 21:54. At 21:55 *Oberfeldwebel* Beulich shot down a fourth Il-2, which was followed one minute later by a fifth, which fell to the guns of *Unteroffizier* Beth, his fourth victory.

The Russians desperately tried to fight off the persistent Germans, but their formations had fallen into disorder and all they could do was take evasive action. Their defensive fire was not to be underestimated, however. Streams of tracer reached out towards the attacking Messerschmitts. Inexplicably, none found their targets. Experience had shown that the men behind the machine-guns were certainly not bad shots, but this time they must have been taken by surprise. The nimble Messerschmitts, suddenly appearing and then diving or climbing away, presented the Russians with the most fleeting of targets. Weißenberger positioned himself behind the Hampden formation, which seemed not to have noticed the combat going on behind it. The Hampdens were still flying in tight formation. Then "White 4" rushed in and, guns blazing, climbed through the enemy formation. The first Hampden began to burn. Weißenberger scored hits on its starboard engine. The fires spread quickly to the wing and fuselage and the torpedo-bomber dropped its starboard wing and crashed into the sea about 15 kilometers northwest of Pummanki Bay. Just prior to this Beulich, who was flying somewhat higher on the *Staffelführer*'s right, had brought down another Hampden, and one minute after Weißenberger's victory he also destroyed a Pe-2.

Meanwhile other bombers were trying to escape at wave-top height, but they were unable to shake their attackers. Weißenberger closed in from behind, adjusted his aim and fired – a Hampden went down into the glittering sea, followed seconds later by another. The last, his seventh victory in this action, exploded 100 meters above Pummanki Bay and pieces of wreckage burned on the surface of the water for some time.

Oberfeldwebel Dörr and *Feldwebel* Drößler scored victories almost simultaneously, Dörr claiming a Boston, Drößler a Pe-2. The last victory of the day, another Hampden, went to *Leutnant* Eichhorn at 22:12.

The *Staffel* had carried out its mission. The bombers had been scattered, they failed to reach the German ships, and the convoy went on its way unmolested. More than half of the Russian aircraft – five Il-2s, seven Hampdens, three Pe-2s and a Boston – were at the bottom of the Polar Sea. The victorious 7./JG 5 landed back at its base at 22:19. The distribution of victories on 4 July is shown in a chronological table on the following page.

At this point it is appropriate to say a few words about Weißenberger's person. How did he achieve his successes, what distinguished his career as a fighter pilot? Weißenberger was characterized by a coarse naturalness in manner and appearance. He would surely have become a gardener like his father had he not been gripped by flying, which lifted him into the higher sphere that magically appeared during his youth. At that time – Weißenberger was born in Mühlheim/Main on 21 December 1914 – aviation was still naturally comprehensible and manually achievable; his age class built its own airplanes. The freedom of flying had seized every fiber of Weißenberger's being, but this passion was paired with the voluntary subordination to the discipline of the natural rules of flying, which at that time were not yet fully understood.

Jagdgeschwader 5

Time	Type	Victor	Victory for Pilot	7./JG 5	III./JG 5
21:07	Pe-2	*Lt.* Weißenberger	98	107	363
21:53	Il-2	*Lt.* Weißenberger	99	108	364
21:54	Il-2	*Lt.* Weißenberger	100	109	365
21:55	Il-2	*Lt.* Weißenberger	101	110	366
21:55	Il-2	*Ofw.* Beulich		111	367
21:56	Il-2	*Uffz.* Beth	4	112	368
21:57	Hampden	*Ofw.* Beulich		113	369
21:59	Hampden	*Lt.* Weißenberger	102	114	370
22:00	Pe-2	*Ofw.* Beulich		115	371
22:01	Hampden	*Uffz.* Beth	5	116	372
22:04	Hampden	*Lt.* Weißenberger	103	117	373
22:06	Hampden	*Lt.* Weißenberger	104	118	374
22:08	Hampden	*Ofw.* Beulich		119	375
22:09	Boston	*Ofw.* Dörr		120	376
22:09	Pe-2	*Fw.* Drößler		121	377
22:12	Hampden	*Lt.* Eichhorn		122	378

Weißenberger made his first flight in a glider on 16 November 1935 with the *Deutschen Luftsportverband* and his 645th on 20 July 1941. By then he had logged 196 hours and 46 minutes of unpowered flight – in the Rhön, in Silesia, in Bavaria, and most as an instructor. It was not until 1939 that he began flying powered aircraft. His 1,654th powered flight took place on 30 October 1944, by which time he had flown more than 700 000 kilometers. And that was far from everything. He had flown more than 400 combat missions, scored 208 victories, flown missions in the Me 262, baled out several times, been wounded once, risen from the rank of *Gefreiter* to become a *Geschwaderkommodore* (of JG 7) and awarded the Knight's Cross with Oak Leaves. Weißenberger's military career was marked by long waits for promotion, for he was a reservist. He, the older and mature flight instructor, frequently clashed with "higher ranks", who criticized his easygoing ways. Several times he got out of trouble because of good friends putting in a good word with the *Kommandeur*.

Weißenberger never had much time for uniforms and formalities; his success was the result of a passion for flying and his skill. Weißenberger was neither ambitious nor politically involved. In an uncomplicated way he served his country and his people, and because there was a war on shooting down enemy aircraft was part of his duty. His duels in the air show that his motivation lay in a manly naturalness, which drove him to do what was necessary. This he did without compromise and with ruthlessness. He was implacable in combat, while mastering the complicated technology of his aircraft, armament and navigation. Anyone who flew with him became aware of the technical perfection with which he flew. He was usually able to get a little more out of his machine – whether more speed, a tighter turn or greater endurance – such as the time over Murmansk when his Bf 109 F developed a supercharger problem. He nursed his machine 70 kilometers back to Lisa with a sputtering engine, throttling his engine back to the exact point where the supercharger still functioned, and lowering the flaps to the precise angle where the drag coefficient, combined with the lift coefficient, gave the best glide ratio. He also took advantage of the thermals among the billowing cumulus clouds. Like a youth, he was capable of rejoicing whenever he pulled off one of these masterstrokes of flying. "I went gliding in a 110!" declared a beaming Weißenberger after a ferry flight in the heavy twin-engined Messerschmitt heavy fighter. After encountering one of these "bomb thermals" over northern Finland he had throttled back both engines and flown the machine like a glider. This also typified Theo Weißenberger, for whom flying was always full of new conquests. He also studied the performance figures and characteristics of enemy aircraft and their pilots. This also contributed to his success. His victories speak for themselves.

It only remains to be said that after the war Weißenberger sought a replacement for flying, from which he was banned, and found it in auto racing. On 10 June 1950 he crashed at the Nürburgring. Weißenberger would certainly have made a career for himself in peacetime. But whether his unspoiled naturalness, which made the military corset so difficult for him to bear, would have been at home and happy in the convention and perfection of the present-day world – including aviation – something we'll never know for sure.

The Russian Air Force Becomes More Active

In the summer of 1943 the focus of operations shifted to attacks by *Kampfgeschwader 30* against big Allied convoys, which consisted mainly of so-called Liberty Ships – armed freighters developed especially for convoy operations. After changes in the military situation forced the transfer of parts of the *Geschwader* to the Mediterranean Theater, Russian bomber and torpedo-bomber units in turn began attacking the German supply convoys to Petsamo. Usually the *Jagdstaffeln* of JG 5 were able to fend off or at least hamper these attacks, due in large part to excellent cooperation with the well-developed early warning and control system. Radar played a major role in the defensive success on 4 July.

Of course these defense and escort operations were not always so effective, as the casualty figures attest, even though casualties, though bitter enough, were kept within limits. *Feldwebel* Hans Döbrich had the ill fortune to be shot down for the third time on 16 July, this time over Petsamo Fjord, where there was an encounter with Russian fighters. He himself shot down two enemy aircraft before he was hit. He was pulled from the water by the crew of a German ship, having suffered serious facial injuries. In September Döbrich would be awarded the Knight's Cross after 52 victories.

Jagdgeschwader 5 lost nine pilots during convoy defense missions in the period until October 1943, including several experienced pilots. *Unteroffizier* Oberländer of 6./JG 5 was killed on 20 July when his aircraft struck the water during combat. He had nine victories to his credit when he died. *Unteroffizier* Leibersperger of 9./JG 5 was killed on 10 August and *Oberfeldwebel* Beulich of 7./JG 5 on 14 September. On the 28th the 9. *Staffel* lost its *Kapitän*, *Oberleutnant* Wulf Dietrich Widowitz, who was killed in the crash of a Go 145 communications aircraft northwest of Petsamo. The *Geschwader* mourned his loss in particular, as he had been the last hope of more than a few fighter pilots shot down over enemy territory. His search and rescue flights in the Fieseler *Storch* had earned him an almost legendary reputation, and often enough he succeeded in plucking a pilot from hostile areas, rescuing them from the murderous tundra and saving them from certain death or the clutches of the Russians. Now *Oberleutnant* Widowitz found his final resting place in the military cemetery in Parkkina. His successor as *Staffelkapitän* of 9./JG 5 was *Hauptmann* Hans Hermann Schmidt. He had transferred from the *Zerstörerstaffel* in October 1942 and in November-December 1942 he briefly commanded 7./JG 5, relieving *Hauptmann* von Sponeck. He was subsequently transferred to the *4. Staffel* of *Ergänzungsgruppe West* in Cazeaux, south of Bordeaux, to allow his wounds to heal. He commanded the replacement training *Staffel* until July 1943. 4./EJG West prepared graduates from fighter schools for the special operational conditions faced by JG 5 whose flying standards were very high. As many as 120 young fighter pilots passed through the replacement training unit each month. Each *Geschwader* provided instructors, usually for a period of six months. An assignment to the replacement training *Geschwader* was regarded as being akin to a stay in a convalescent home.

On 2 August 1943 two fighter pilots stationed on the Polar Sea Front were awarded the Oak Leaves: *Major* Ehrler after his 112th and *Oberleutnant* Weißenberger after his 104th victory. At the time they were the most successful pilots in the *Geschwader*.

Although its units were physically separated – I. and IV./JG 5 in Norway, II. and III./JG 5 on the Polar Sea – there was constant contact between them and the *Geschwader*, as the entire unit was attached to *Luftflotte 5*. These links were strengthened by the frequent transfer of pilots between units. In October, for example, *Leutnant* Scheufele, who had spent "18 months on the west coast desperately searching for something to shoot down", was transferred to II./JG 5. His first stop was Petsamo, where he received a warm welcome from the men of the *III. Gruppe*. Scheufele found this all the more pleasant, as the mere mention of the names of the successful Polar Sea fighter pilots was enough to cause shivers of awe among the "west coasters." But now they were trying to help him achieve the status symbol of a skilled fighter pilot, his first victory, on his very first combat mission. Then he flew in the unit Storch to Salmijärvi, where the *II. Gruppe* was based. Scheufele described his reception there:

"When I asked where I could find Herr Carganico and company, I was told: 'They're in the Kolosjoki nickel mine, but they should be back soon.' And they came! And how!

"An hour later, in a cloud of alcohol fumes, the "high society" of the *II. Gruppe* came through the door to the mess. My attempt to present myself as militarily as possible failed several times. I finally succeeded in taking up a position in front of Carganico and shouted, so as to be heard over the background noise: '*Leutnant* Scheufele reporting for duty with II./JG 5!'

"The facial expression of my future commanding officer was first apathetic, then disbelieving and finally turned into an enraptured smile: 'Victories?'

"Sheepishly I informed him that despite my 60 combat missions I had never laid eyes on an enemy aircraft, to say nothing of having put my sights on one.

"So there I was in my first hour with my new unit – ostracized, a second-class person, and I felt ever smaller despite my six feet four inches; I was the only plain one, no crosses on my chest or throat. It was thanks to Mikat and Glöckner that I even dared sit on a chair that had supported so many prominent rear ends.

"Within an hour, however, my self-confidence had risen tremendously, for I had noticed that my general knowledge with respect to the concept of percentages was significantly more comprehensive than that of the *Kommandeur*. True, the initiated fighter pilot and reader may argue that this was no real compensation, but for my psychological situation it was decisive. It happened like this: I somehow found myself sitting next to Carganico. Disregarding rank and decorations, he began a friendly conversation, just as if we were old chums. As he did so he tapped me on the left knee with his lump of nickel ore – a gift from the famous nickel mine in Kolosjoki – and asked in his most beautiful, inimitable Berlinese: 'Scheufele, can you understand that this stone is supposed to be 40 percent? It seems much too light for that.'

"Speechless, I stared at him and tried to gain time for my answer. As I did so I had to comprehend the thought process that had led him to ask such a question. Finally I answered diplomatically, meaning even though I knew better: '*Herr Hauptmann*, I can't explain it either.' This admission seemed to satisfy him, for he was very cordial to me for the rest of the evening and the time that followed. I had been accepted. It didn't even bother me much that, after I went to bed, I repeatedly had to lie flat on the ground because *Leutnant* Vetter kept shouting 'Take cover!' while testing the strength of the walls or the penetrative power of his new Walther PPK."

One would be very wrong to assume that fighter pilots took every opportunity to take part in extended and merry binges. Long winter nights, no organized entertainment, youth, celebration of "birthdays", problems – of course they knew how to celebrate – but they also knew how to fight. There is probably no one who would argue this, and it is obvious from the narrative so far – and it would be proved again on 13 October 1943. On that day the waters of the Polar Sea provided the setting for a large-scale air battle. A German convoy was fighting its way through the sea with the goal of reaching Kirkenes. When it was between Kiberg and Ekkerö, a Russian attack force consisting of about 70 bombers, close-support aircraft and fighters closed in. The first wave of Bostons and Hampdens with fighter escort was followed by a second of Il-2s.

The *Staffeln* of III./JG 5 took to the air shortly before 13:00 to intercept the attackers. There were 22 fighters altogether. The *Schwarm* led by *Oberfeldwebel* Schuck intercepted the Bostons, which were flying at 2500 meters, and picked its targets. Some of the twin-engined bombers jettisoned their torpedoes so that they could take evasive action, but Schuck was already on the tail of the first. He fired several brief bursts, causing pieces of the tail to fly off, and seconds later the port engine began to smoke, but the Russian flew on. Then the *Oberfeldwebel* scored hits on the starboard engine. There was a tremendous explosion and the torpedo-bomber crashed in flames into the sea. Schuck's speed carried him past his victim and he moved right and positioned himself behind the next. It too went down.

Schuck heard someone screaming into the radio, "Look out, Curtisses!," but he had already spotted the four enemy fighters behind him. He glanced quickly to the side. Two Bf 109s from the *Schwarm* were there, but the fourth was missing. Schuck put his aircraft into a steep climb. The Russians immediately broke away and the other Messerschmitts gave chase. They raced away just above the water's surface. There – an enemy aircraft struck the wave tops with one of its wingtips. The machine reared up and disappeared in a cloud of spray. At the same instant Schuck got his sights on another Curtiss. From 200 meters he opened fire and sent it crashing into the sea. Victory number three.

Meanwhile, not far away, the *7. Staffel* had also made contact with the Russian fighters over the convoy. *Unteroffizier* Beth fired at an Airacobra from close range and at 13:07 it crashed vertically into the water. Another Airacobra followed three minutes later, shot down by *Leutnant* Dörr. Prevented from dropping their bombs, the Soviets turned away. The German fighters gave chase and there were further combats with Il-2s and Airacobras north of the Fischer Peninsula. Beth, who was flying in Dörr's *Schwarm*, attacked the last Il-2, which went into a shallow climb. The *Unteroffizier* followed, scoring further hits, which silenced the dorsal gunner. It was the second attack that sealed the Il-2's fate, however. The Russian aircraft snapped left into a spin, went down vertically and struck the water about nine kilometers north of Cape Navolok. Beth shot down his next victim, an Airacobra, at 13:30 east of the Cape. It was his twelfth victory.

By about 14:00 all of the *III. Gruppe*'s aircraft were back on the ground. They had achieved a major success and the convoy had been able to continue on its way undamaged. The unit had scored at least twelve victories, including two Bostons and a P-40 by *Oberfeldwebel* Schuck, two Airacobras and an Il-2 by *Unteroffizier* Beth, a Hampden and an Airacobra by *Leutnant* Dörr, a Hampden by *Oberfähnrich* Vogel and an Il-2 by *Oberleutnant* Glöckner. Four more Soviet aircraft had been shot down by *Kriegsmarine* escort vessels.

At the beginning of November 1943 the *II. Gruppe*, whose subsequent history will be described in the following chapter, was transferred to the Leningrad front, leaving III./JG 5 alone on the northern front. Most of its actions took place in the broad area around the Fischer Peninsula, as the Russians were very active there that fall. There were numerous gun positions on the peninsula, and from the same area Soviet bomber units made frequent attacks against German convoys in the Polar Sea. The *Gruppe* suffered a series of casualties in the months until the end of the year, including such experienced pilots as *Unteroffizier* Link, *Leutnant* Schumann and *Feldwebel* Thomann. The latter was shot down by German light anti-aircraft guns over the port of Kirkenes while flying beneath low cloud. He was buried in the military cemetery in Parkkina. The *Gruppe* continued to score steadily, however. On 3 November German supply ships were again en route to Kirkenes and radar detected a group of about 15 Curtisses approaching the convoy. At 13:20 south of Vardö these fighters ran into the *7. Staffel*, which had taken off from Petsamo about ten minutes earlier. The first attack by *Leutnant* Dörr scattered the enemy formation. *Feldwebel* Beth picked out a lone P-40 and after a three-minute chase sent it crashing into the sea. Abandoning their plans to attack the convoy, the Russians tried to flee in all directions, but the Messerschmitts clung to their heels. *Oberfeldwebel* Klante scored at 13:35, two minutes later another was shot down by Beth, and finally Dörr destroyed an enemy fighter at

13:40. The surviving Russians disappeared to the east and the *7. Staffel* returned to Petsamo with four victories.

On the morning of 25 November a large formation of Russian close-support aircraft with a powerful fighter escort approached the Petsamo area at low level to strike the base of III./JG 5. The last of the *Gruppe*'s Messerschmitts had just taken to the air when the Russians swept over the airfield. The radio monitoring service post on Savior Mountain had provided timely warning of the enemy raid and this time the *Eismeerjäger* had an easy time of it. Soon after taking off, *Feldwebel* Beth shot down two Il-2s in quick succession, however the anti-aircraft guns defending the airfield were also blazing away and unfortunately hit his machine. Beth was forced to make a belly landing on his own airfield, but survived unharmed. Before he was shot down, Beth witnessed the destruction of an Il-2 by *Leutnant* Vogel. Dörr guided his wingman, *Leutnant* Gayko, onto the tail of a Curtiss and then instructed him by the book until he shot it down. It was Gayko's first victory. At 12:30, after beating off the Soviet attack, the aircraft landed again, having suffered no losses.

And yet there was a very noteworthy casualty among the ground personnel. While the Bf 109s of the *9. Staffel* were taking off among the attacking enemy fighter, several mechanics joined the battle against the low-level attackers with their carbines. They were led by *Obergefreiter* Johann Kigler who, standing in front of his blast pen, blazed away at one of the Kittyhawks. He was hit by a burst of machine-gun fire and fell dead. The joy felt by the pilots of 9./JG 5 over their success was overshadowed by the death of this brave mechanic. The total: 36 enemy aircraft destroyed, including those brought down by anti-aircraft fire. Vogel had three, Dörr, Schmidt, Rost and Beth two each, and Drößler, Eichhorn and Gayko one each, to say nothing of those claimed by the *Experten*.

Meanwhile *Luftflotte 5* had received a new commanding officer. *Generaloberst* Stumpff left to take over *Luftflotte Reich* and on 28 November 1943 was succeeded by *General* Kammhuber. Kammhuber, who since 1940 had systematically built up Germany's night defenses, had been the Inspector of Night-Fighters, however his new plans and ideas had encountered considerable resistance from the supreme command. As a result he was relieved of his post and essentially pushed aside.

Leutnant Günter Eichhorn was captured on 2 December. During the mission on 25 November Eichhorn had shot down his seventh enemy aircraft and then rammed another P-40, which was then probably finished off by *Unteroffizier* Amend. War reporter Kurt Marek, who was stationed in Petsamo for some time and later became an author under the pseudonym C.W. Ceram, then commented on the incident as follows:

"The men of the ground personnel stood below. They shouted out numbers, the code numbers of the individual fighters that had already come back. As there were aircraft still in the air, they wanted to determine if one of theirs had scored a victory. And if one of them had, the man who serviced the aircraft's weapons justifiably felt as if he had played a part in downing the enemy machine.

"A Messerschmitt roared low over the airfield. Would it waggle its wings? They waited. Yes, it rocked its wings. 'Who is that?' shouted a voice. 'It's *Leutnant* Eichhorn!' came the answer. One of the men danced, prancing around on the bunker – *Leutnant* Eichhorn's first mechanic. This aircraft had scored a victory. 'Go!' shouted the *Hauptfeldwebel*, 'To the command post!'

"The motorcycle skidded in the curves and almost landed in the ditch. Who cares about such trifles at such moments? The Messerschmitt taxied in as the *Feldwebel* sprang from the motorcycle. *Leutnant* Eichhorn jumped out, pulling off his helmet as he did. His hair was matted with sweat. The excitement of the air battle was reflected in his face, in his movements. He dangled his headset back and forth meaninglessly.

"'Children, did you see it? I rammed one!' There was nothing in his manner to suggest the risk involved in such a ramming, closing with the enemy until collision; he merely asked: 'Children, did you see it?' He then showed how it happened, how he had dived at the enemy 'nose to nose', how at the last moment had had laid his Messerschmitt on its side, how the enemy's wing had been torn off into a thousand pieces,"

The year 1943 came to an end. It had been an eventful year that had brought the *Geschwader* great success but had also sealed the fate of many comrades, friends and brothers in arms. The polar darkness, snow and bitter cold had long since reclaimed the landscape. Whenever operations permitted, the men crawled into their warm, weatherproof quarters and sometimes even found time to shake off the experience of war. Armaments minister Speer was the *III. Gruppe*'s Christmas guest. He brought with him Dr. Schreiber, who later became famous under the name "Kalanag". Schreiber enthralled the men with his magic tricks, and the 1943 Christmas holiday in Petsamo provided unforgettable hours to many members of the *Geschwader*. It was a well-deserved break after long dark weeks on the Polar Sea.

Two administrative inspectors of the Petsamo *Staffel*, *Oberzahlmeister* Schultz and Gustel Berkefeld, are deserving of special mention. Their example typified many who did their duty without regard to their own safety. Despite the threat of partisans, they hitchhiked 600 kilometers in the dead of winter up the Polar Sea road to Rovaniemi, received their allotments, requisitioned a repaired truck belonging to some Petsamo unit, which otherwise would have been driven back half empty, and returned with delicacies which normally rarely found their way to the far north. The *Staffeln* thanked them in aviator style, taking the two along on anti-partisan patrols or searches over the tundra, and after 20 flights over the front they were eligible for the Operational Flying Clasp. More than that and there was the Iron Cross, Second Class. Paymaster officials with combat decorations naturally carried a lot more weight in the rear – when it came time for the next allotments.

At the end of 1943 it was not difficult to see that air superiority in the area of the northern front had passed to the Russians. The battles in the air were becoming larger and more difficult, and the Russian fighter pilots had become much more experienced, while their supply of aircraft seemed inexhaustible. It was from this standpoint that *Jagdgeschwader 5* entered the new year 1944. The *III. Gruppe*, the only element left on the Polar Sea, lost seven pilots in January alone, and the *7. Staffel* lost two of its pilots at the very start of the month. At 11:34 on 3 January, Arthur Beth, who had been promoted to *Feldwebel*, and *Gefreiter* Oskar Amann took off from Petsamo on a terrain orientation flight in the direction of Murmansk. West of Murmansk they encountered several Yak-7s and then came under fire from anti-aircraft guns defending the air base. Both Messerschmitts were shot down. Beth became a prisoner of war and did not return to Germany until 1949. Until then he was the only one who knew that his wingman Amann had been killed on his final mission.

Odyssey on the Polar Sea

At the beginning of January 1944 the staff of the *Fliegerführer* tasked the *III. Gruppe* with a reconnaissance mission upon which depended a combined operation by the army and navy. Conventional reconnaissance aircraft were unable to provide suitable results because of the polar twilight; consequently orders were issued for a visual reconnaissance by the fighter pilots. They were received by the *Kapitän* of the *9. Staffel*, who was filling in while the *Kommandeur*, Major Ehrler, was away on leave. As the mission was secret and very important and *Hauptmann* Schmidt had known the Fischer Peninsula for three years, he flew the mission himself. His objective was to determine what condition the roads were in and look for troop movements. As he would have to fly right through the Soviet flak concentrations, he made careful preparations for the mission using good maps and aerial photos.

The Fischer Peninsula, Rybachiy in Russian, is approximately 55 by 40 kilometers in size and consists of two parts, the western "small" and the eastern "big" Fischer Peninsula, which are only connected by a two-kilometer-wide bridge. The only link to the mainland is the six-kilometer-wide "Fischer Neck", which had been a static front since 1941. Rybachiy had two airfields, Pummanki and Subovka, a torpedo boat base and a commanding general with winter-tested Siberian troops. Since 1941 the Soviets, who could only be supplied by sea, had been holding onto this barren slab of rock projecting into the Polar Sea. There were hills up to 280 meters high, where no trees and very few bushes grew.

After four days of heavy snow the weather improved. Around noon on 11 January *Hauptmann* Schmidt took off with his wingman, *Unteroffizier* Amend. Leaving behind a large cloud of snow, the two Bf 109s lifted off Petsamo airfield, climbed away and disappeared to the north. The wingman held position as if pinned there. All he knew about the mission was that abeam Pummanki Bay the *Hauptmann* would descend and conduct reconnaissance and that he, *Unteroffizier* Amend, was supposed to fly to the northwestern tip of the island to wait for him out of range of the anti-aircraft guns.

All that he said to his wingman before takeoff was: "If I haven't joined you after twenty minutes, fly back home and give them my best regards!"

Then the wait was over. Schmidt waved, waggled his wings and then dove through several clouds. In a shallow dive he soon reached a speed in excess of 700 kph and then leveled out low above the ground. The Messerschmitt raced over the naked, snow-covered lines of hills. To his right was Pummanki Bay. The notorious torpedo base must have been on the other side and before the hill the tiny fighter airfield. Then his objective, the road he was supposed to reconnoiter, appeared beneath him. It was completely snow-covered. There were no tracks, thus not much traffic. A small hill appeared before him. From the left Russians ran towards their light anti-aircraft gun position with their circular protective walls. Schmidt loosed off a burst of machine-gun fire and they disappeared into cover. At high speed the Messerschmitt swept over their heads. The *Hauptmann* noted positions, quarters and changes in the road. He had to have been approaching the valley basin, where ravines and roads from several directions merged. The Soviet headquarters were there, guarded by several flak batteries. They must have been alerted by now. His best chance was to fly under them. There was just one large hill he had to cross, as low as possible. Bad luck – a snow shower was suspended just there. The contours of the hill were invisible against the gray twilight. For safety's sake he was forced to climb a few dozen meters higher. It was at that moment that the light and medium anti-aircraft guns opened up. Glowing multicolored streams of tracer converged on him from all sides. It was a fascinating sight in the twilight of the frosty polar day. The deadly show lasted just a few seconds, then he dived back into the valley below the anti-aircraft fire. He had been lucky. Apart from several minor hits in the wings everything appeared to be OK. The Bf 109 was flying normally, the instruments read normal and he again concentrated on the road beneath him. It was just 20 kilometers to the northwest tip of the peninsula, where Amend was waiting. To his right: several barracks. Then there were just the crooked posts of a telephone line to show him the way in the gray wasteland.

Schmidt glanced at the instrument panel. The coolant temperature gauge showed 100 degrees! The *Hauptmann* now realized that the several dull thumps he had felt must have damaged the coolant lines. He had only a few minutes of flying time remaining. He pulled the throttle lever back to the economical cruise setting. He abandoned his mission – he certainly wasn't going to make it to the northwest cape and then fly home over the sea. But if he reversed course to the right through no-man's-land and flew across the six-kilometer-wide fjord to the south in the direction of the Finnish border, he just might make it if the damage wasn't too severe. And so he turned to the south, avoiding the anti-aircraft positions. The terrain rose. Coolant temperature 100 degrees. He flew on at low altitude, but the temperature was rising too rapidly. And whilst he was still debating whether he could still risk a crossing of the fjord, the engine began running more roughly. At that time of year the fighter pilots flew with winter equipment. They had folding skis but no life vest. In the icy Polar Sea a man would succumb to hypothermia in a few minutes. Not to mention the seas were rough; white strips of foam formed on the wave peaks. One could not ditch a Bf 109 at 200 kph in such conditions without going under immediately. And while he was still struggling with the realization that he was going to have to come down in enemy territory, the engine took the decision away from him. There was a dull grinding sound. A sophisticated 1,700-hp engine was dying of overheating. There was a heavy jolt. The broad propeller blades looked at him over the engine cowling. His speed immediately dropped. Schmidt was forced to push the nose down to avoid a stall. Oil boiled over and sprayed the windscreen. He could no longer see. He opened the side window and, gently side-slipping, scanned the dark gray, shapeless terrain just beneath him. It was snow-covered but littered with crags and rocks. Just don't overturn, he thought. Then he was out of time. Powerless, but still travelling at 230 kph, the three-ton machine touched down softly in the snow and slid uncontrolled into the white nothingness. It struck obstacles and Schmidt felt the straps tearing at his body. Then the aircraft stood on its nose, hesitated briefly in that position and finally fell back again.

An eerie silence followed, interrupted only by the crackling of the overheated engine and the bubbling of the boiling coolant. After several attempts the *Hauptmann* finally succeeded in forcing open the jammed canopy. He jumped out into the knee-deep snow. It took some time for his nerves to settle down. His eyes, in particular, kept moving. After the intense concentration of the long low-altitude flight they couldn't focus on a fixed point. Everything was moving, and everywhere he looked he thought he saw Russians rushing down the slopes towards him.

Many years after the war, H.H. Schmidt wrote about his last flight. Here is his account of what followed:

"Keeping a lookout to all sides, I hastily unpacked the most necessary items – the thick white Arctic clothing, the flare pistol, rations. Then my first priority was to get away from the aircraft. I struggled through the deep powdery snow. Because of the heat in the aircraft, my exertions and the excitement, I was dripping with sweat. While the winter clothing isolated me on the outside, the inside didn't dry and I suffered constant chills. The thought of freezing from the severe cold was demoralizing. With difficulty I made it to the top of one of the surrounding hills, from where I had a good view and could descend on any side. I looked for a cleft in which to find shelter from the wind, hung up several strips of parachute, got out my map and located my position. In the morning, when it got light, they would come for me in the *Storch*. Then I waited for total darkness. It became night at about 15:00. It was unlikely there would be any Soviet patrols, and so I headed back to my machine to collect the rest of my equipment, especially the folding skis, which were strapped in the rear fuselage and not that easy to reach. As I climbed down a howling snowstorm began.

"The air was filled with sharp ice crystals, which seriously reduced visibility. Orientation was no longer possible, even with the compass. Unable to reach the Messerschmitt, I cowered in a hollow and sheltered myself from the storm. After a long time it was finally quiet again. The blowing snow became lighter and I could see a few stars blinking between the clouds. The northern lights allowed me to see a little. I was only a few meters from my Messerschmitt. I unpacked my things, rendered a few items unserviceable, adjusted the folding skis to fit and set off up my hill again. When I reached the top I dug out my watch, hoping that the night would soon be over. It was just 17:00. I tried to eat but was unable to. As soon as I removed my damp fur mittens and exposed my hands to the icy wind, they froze so that I couldn't hold anything. And so I just nibbled on the lightly-packed raisins and some grape sugar. What good were the best emergency supplies if one couldn't get at the ingeniously-packed rations? I couldn't even manage the *Schoka-Kola* in tin boxes. When I placed one on a ski and tried to break it open with a stone it slipped into the deep snow. My fingers were incapable of opening even the smallest foil cover. The cold was bearable. It was between minus 15 and 25 degrees. But the constant sharp wind was wearing, blowing snow everywhere, especially into my eyes, and made it almost impossible to rest or think clearly. But the hope that the *Storch* would come in the morning made everything easier."

Suddenly the *Hauptmann* heard foreign voices. He peered out. A full moon had emerged. Below in the valley dark forms were approaching the wreck. Five Russians were fiddling about with the machine after having fired several bursts from their submachine-guns. Then they began looking for tracks. Schmidt had meanwhile strapped on his skis. As he watched from atop the hill he saw a fresh snowstorm approaching. Relieved, he slid down the back slope; the storm would obliterate his tracks. The storm at his back, he slowly moved away towards the south.

After several hours he came to another chain of hills, from which he could see the small port on Eina Bay – to the left of his course. His hopes of stealing a boat there were dashed, because there was too much activity despite the time of night. A bright full moon shone down most of the time. Once he had to take cover when several soldiers on skis crossed his path only a hundred meters in front of him. To the south he could now see the bay on the Polar Sea, which separated him from the Finnish coast. Far to the south gleamed a mountain range, beyond which lay Petsamo. An irrepressible will rose up in him; he had to get to the other shore – which was about 6 kilometers away; he had to find a boat. Soon there would be another snowstorm. More and more frequently the *Hauptmann* had to brace himself with his ski poles to prevent being blown away by the icy gale. It became pitch black. A gale-force wind seized him and forced him to his knees. The cold penetrated to his skin. The wind howled. It was a hurricane, stronger than all the previous storms. Schmidt realized that he was freezing. Hurriedly he pulled his feet from the ski bindings, burrowed lengthwise into the soft snow and was soon drifted over. Now the deadly cold couldn't penetrate to his skin. He moved his hands and feet. Just don't fall asleep! He felt as if he was lying in cold water. Outside the storm was deafening. For the first time the *Hauptmann* thought he understood what panicky primal fear was.

"At first I didn't know how long I had been lying there. The cold in my back had become a regular radiating pain that went to the marrow, but which gradually dissolved into numbness. I moved more vigorously to avoid freezing. The horrific roar finally weakened noticeably. With stiff limbs I crawled out of the snow, located my skis, laboriously put them on and tried to warm up by cross-country skiing across the ice surface. After the storm had passed the moon, which had been in the east before the storm, came out again precisely in the south. I had thus spent six hours walled up and shivering in my hole in the snow. Constantly fearful of running into the Russians and aggravated by the continuous unnerving wind and the constant, sometimes knee-deep snowdrifts, I glided forwards. The hills became steeper. Then I saw the Polar Sea. I leaned against a rock – sitting down was out of the question because of the powdery snow close to the ground –

and thought: do I stay here on the plateau and leave open the possibility that the *Storch* might find me or climb down to the coast, where I should be able to find boats? A long, extremely dangerous time drifting in moderate seas or a flight in the *Storch* lasting a few minutes? The weather situation with coastal fog made the latter possibility an illusion, however. It could have taken days for them to find and rescue me there.

"So I climbed down. I don't exactly know anymore how I negotiated the approximately 200 meters height difference to the sea – near Motka Mountain, at almost 290 meters probably the highest point on the Fischer Peninsula. Sometimes my skis ran off on me, often I only just managed to work my way out of deep holes in the snow, and ultimately I left my snowshoes behind and kept just one ski pole. Finally I was at the bottom. There, in the shelter of the hill, it wasn't so terribly windy. Exhausted and hungry, I stopped. I dug a hole in the snow cornice of a hill face, pushed a piece of parachute in front of me, because the fresh snow was much too powdery to support me. I succeeded in undoing the ties on my rucksack and warmed my fingers enough to allow me to use them. In the last 36 hours I had only eaten some grape sugar and a small packet of raisins with nuts. After many attempts, using my storm matches and Hindenburg candles, I managed to get my cooking pot lukewarm. But I only half melted the snow. The candles went out with a hiss when blowing snow touched the melted wax on the wick. Into the mixture of ice and water I added some instant coffee and sugar and thought: physically exactly zero degrees. Then the candles went out again. The struggle was hopeless. And so I slowly drank the cold brew. It sapped the last of the warmth from my viscera. I felt very full. But the wind continued to lash me. It isn't easy to die in the snow. Somewhere or other conscious action stopped. The athletic attitude towards physical feats, the joy of bearing up, lapsed. My will was becoming tired. Two nights of heavy exertion with no sleep and too little food led to hallucinations. Another storm came up and I immediately went under the snow. I scarcely felt the cold and chills any more. I started and got up just before I fell asleep. Falling asleep was deadly. I continued trudging along the coast, direction west. It was half tide. Walking on wet gravel was easier than in deep snow, but where it was frozen over I fell heavily. My wet fur-lined flying boots wore down.

"Dawn rose on my third morning on the peninsula. And then the hallucinations came. I saw things that couldn't be there. I had expected it, for I remember stories told by comrades who had been lost in the tundra. In their exhaustion – like the *fata morgana* – they had seen cities, houses and people and heard bells ringing, things that did not exist anywhere in the desolate wilderness of the far north. The first time I saw a group of men pointing wildly at me, I still thought it was real.

Jagdgeschwader 5

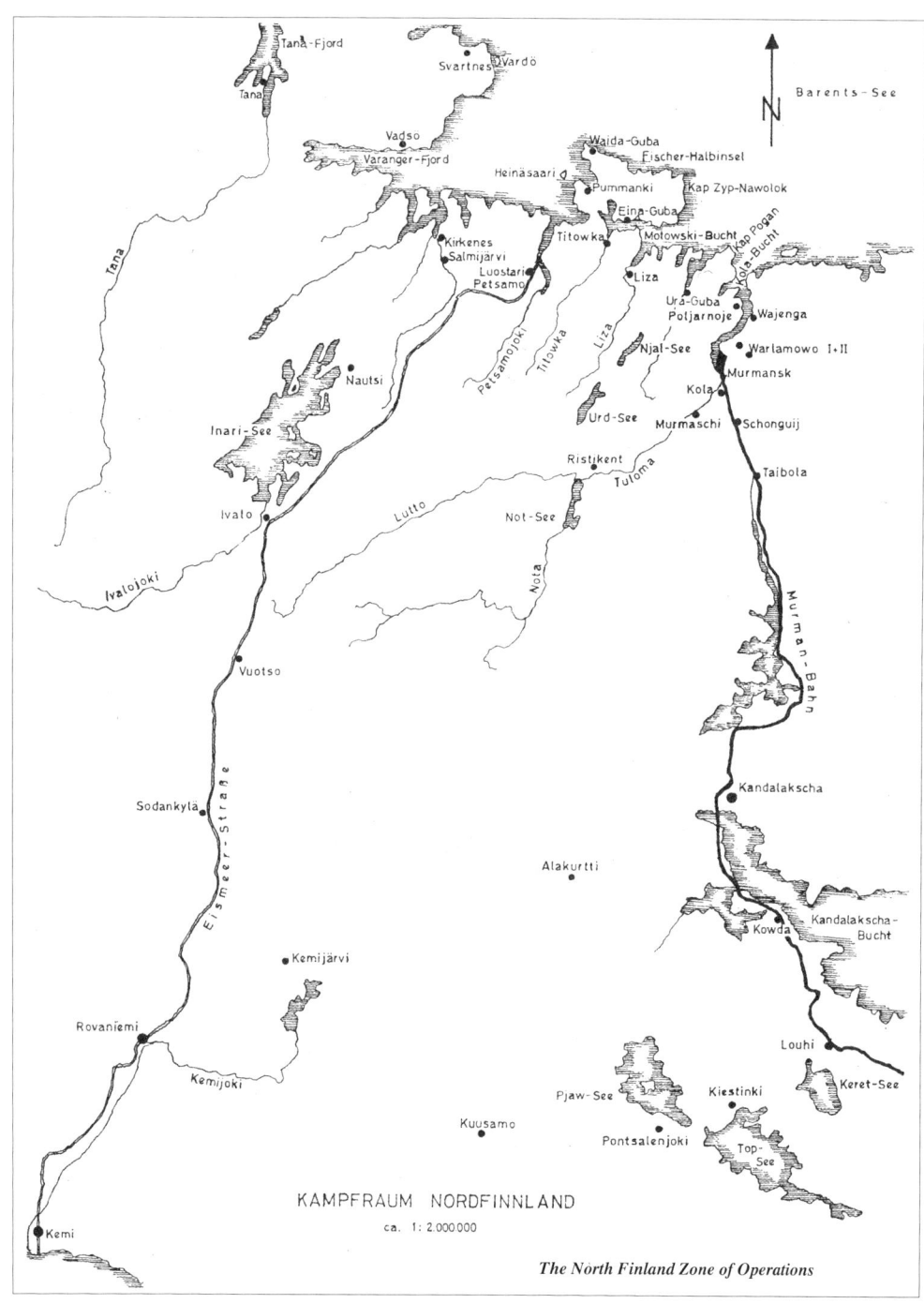

The North Finland Zone of Operations

I hid behind a rock for a long time. Later I went to the spot but found no trace. Then I was joined now and then by a dog. Like a ghost, sometimes it was there and sometimes it was gone. Much later, in the weak light of midday, I stumbled onto something smooth in a snowdrift. It sounded hollow. They were boats. Reinvigorated, I began to dig. But it was going to be a tiring job, dragging an ice-covered boat from high up the beach down to the water. Then the hallucinations returned. I thought I saw uniformed men on the small ridge in front of some rocky cliffs. They had rifles and were pointing at me.

"Angrily I tried to chase away the hallucinations. I had to get my nerves under control. I couldn't waste time on mirages when I had to dig out the boat. But they were real. They came nearer and turned into a reality that decided my subsequent fate. There I was, an exhausted man, standing with the help of my ski pole. I stared at them, too tired to raise my hands. One of them stepped towards me, pointing his submachine-gun. Smiling, proud of his knowledge, he said: "You Messerschmitt!" and "*davai*" (come on), a word that would accompany me for the next five and a half years."

Successful Summer 1944 – Schuck, Norz

During this period 9./JG 5 had little luck with its *Staffel* commanders. Following the loss of *Hauptmann* Schmidt, on 29 February his successor, the 12 victory ace *Leutnant* Wolfgang Rost, became a prisoner of war. One month earlier it had been the *Staffel* officer, *Leutnant* Klaus Walter, who was lost – the two men saw one another again in captivity. During a mission by the *Staffel* southwest of Murmansk, Rost's wingman collided with his aircraft "Yellow 2". The *Leutnant* baled out but had no chance of escape. He was picked up by the Soviets and flown by U 2 communications aircraft to Murmansk for interrogation. But Rost stubbornly kept his silence. Under heavy guard he was driven to a valley about four kilometers south of Murmansk. There they let him out of the car and pointed towards a narrow path in the snow, which climbed through a rocky quarry-like landscape. The interrogating officer waved his pistol about. Rost was convinced that he was about to be shot. Farther up he was directed into a dark passageway that led into the snow-covered rock face. He came to a small room with a brick cooking stove, three beds and two sentries and – to his total surprise – found himself standing face to face with *Hauptmann* Schmidt. It was a type of shock therapy employed by the Soviets to shake prisoners from their mental equilibrium. The treatment failed to shake Rost, however. He remained composed and calm. The two were allowed to talk for several minutes, but they only spoke about things that the Soviets might – possibly – learn about.

The spring of 1944 did not have a promising beginning for the *III. Gruppe*. By the end of April it lost nine pilots killed or missing, while another six were captured. The *8. Staffel* bore the brunt of the casualties with six, not counting the wounded.

In mid-February *Oberleutnant* Rudolf Lüder, who had previously commanded 12./JG 5 on the west coast, was named *Geschwader* adjutant and arrived in Petsamo. One month later the *Geschwaderstab* was in Alakurtti, where it remained until May before moving to Stavanger on the west coast. At that time Alakurtti was a frequent target of Soviet bombing raids, while formations of Il-2 close-support aircraft frequently attacked the airfield.

On Good Friday, the 7th of April 1944, *Oberleutnant* Scholz and Lüder flew to Pontsalenjoki to lead a Stuka attack against an assembly of motorized sleighs on Top Lake. *Hauptmann* Dickwisch, the acting commander of the Stuka unit, was less than enthusiastic about the operations, however, as the ceiling was too low. So Scholz decided to go to Alakurtti in order to attack enemy artillery positions from there. Prior to landing, Lüder struck one of the radio towers that were difficult to make out against Lusmavara Mountain. He tried to land his damaged machine but was unable to keep it on course and it ended up heading straight for a blast pen. The Messerschmitt tried to drop its left wing but, using all his energy, the *Oberleutnant* returned it to the horizontal. With the brakes locked, the aircraft's wheels slid like skis on the packed snow. In order to avoid colliding with a parked Fieseler *Storch*, Lüder had to allow the Bf 109 to veer left and it immediately flipped over in the deep snow. It wasn't long before many helping hands raised the machine to get the pilot out of the cockpit. Fortunately he suffered only minor head injuries.

On 26 March 1944 *Oberfeldwebel* Jakob Norz was awarded the Knight's Cross after 74 victories, and on 8 April *Oberfeldwebel* Walter Schuck was similarly decorated after his 84th victory. That was cause for a celebration. The next day, when the *Gruppe* unexpectedly had to move to Pontsalenjoki, there were difficulties. The approach to land at Pontsalenjoki could be made from a left or right turn, and sometimes there were as many as three aircraft on the runway at a time. Fortunately there were no incidents. *Leutnant* Gayko recalled other details of that day: "In lousy cold Finnish tents, with smoking stoves and frozen water, we all got miserable colds and sore throats. We then turned out for the official Knight's Cross presentation by the commanding general looking frightfully scruffy – unshaven, unwashed and with cardboard Easter eggs (??) instead of decorations. When there were not enough seats at the following banquet, the last to arrive, including me, had to squat at chair level for a long time and thus feigned that everything was alright. The muscle cramps were free."

The Russians immediately got wind of the move to Pontsalenjoki and the vulnerability of the Petsamo area and immediately sank two ships in Kirkenes harbor. Ehrler's *Gruppe* subsequently returned to Petsamo as quickly as possible. On 12 April a Soviet fighter aircraft was shot down there and its pilot captured. He was 26-year-old Lieutenant Turganov of the 20th Naval Aviation Regiment based at Varlamovo II. While under interrogation he confirmed that *Leutnant* Eichhorn, *Hauptmann* Schmidt, *Leutnant* Walter and *Leutnant* Rost were in fact in Soviet hands.

In May the Polar winter began yielding to the first signs of spring. The meter-high piles of snow collapsed, and the packed snow runways became soft, causing the wheels of aircraft to sink into the wet, soft subsurface. These conditions required extreme concentration and a fine touch by the pilots during every takeoff.

After the *Geschwaderstab* moved to the west coast on about 10 May, the *III. Gruppe* was left alone in the north. Because of the spring thaw it temporarily moved to Salmijärvi, but it soon returned to Petsamo and from there bore the brunt of the Soviet attacks on German supply convoys and Kirkenes in the summer of 1944. It was not unusual for thirty Messerschmitts to encounter hundreds of Soviet bombers, close-support aircraft and fighters. Despite their numerical inferiority, German losses remained low, while the aces of the *Gruppe* again began racking up victories. Thanks to the radar station on Savior Mountain near Petsamo, the fighters could always be guided onto the enemy in good time, while an efficient ground organization stood ready to quickly refuel and rearm the fighters that landed at the satellite airfields.

On 15 May air fleet chief Kammhuber decided to take the long way round instead of making a direct flight, and Gayko was assigned to escort the general's aircraft on the Pontsalenjoki to Alakurtti leg. Low fuel forced him to leave the general's aircraft. Kammhuber assigned a harsh punishment without bothering to learn the reason, which of course resulted in a confrontation with the *Kommodore*. Feeling that he had been sentenced unjustly, Gayko allowed himself a stiff drink before returning to III./JG 5's base in Salmijärvi at low level. The next day, when the *Leutnant* took off from Svartnes and shot down one of the few Spitfires operating in the north, all was forgotten. "The dream target of every *Eismeerjäger*! Through dumb luck I, a beginner, brought it down in a picture book victory. There was a big celebration and Ehrler generously forgave me my previous 'crimes.'"

In May *Oberstleutnant* Scholz was named Commander of Fighters Norway and handed the *Geschwader* over to *Major* Ehrler. At the same time *Oberleutnant* Dörr took over the *III. Gruppe*. The resulting *Gruppe* command structure was as follows:

Commander III./JG 5:	*Oblt.* Dörr
Adjutant:	*Lt.* Neumann
Headquarters Company:	*Hptm.* Hecht
7. *Staffel*:	*Lt.* Schuck
8. *Staffel*:	*Oblt.* Glöckner
9. *Staffel*:	*Oblt.* Andresen

Schuck was now leading Dörr's *Staffel* and Glöckner succeeded *Oberleutnant* Horst Berger, who had been shot down over the Fischer Peninsula on 8 May and posted missing. The "big" summer of 1944 overtook the *Eismeerjäger*, compensating many of them with copious victories that had not been seen for months, indeed years. The main reason was probably that the Soviets were coming in huge numbers and that the combats were taking place over German territory. What pressure was taken off the *Eismeerjäger*, who for three years had been forced to fight on the enemy's side of the lines, where every hit, every case of engine trouble, every bale-out meant becoming a prisoner, which for many was worse than death. Good people, outstanding pilots, who for two or three years could count their victories on the fingers of one hand, rose like comets as this conscious or unconscious burden was lifted from them, scoring 10, 20, 30 and more victories in this last great summer of the *Eismeerjäger*.

The 25th of May 1944 provides a good example of this. In the evening, about 80 enemy aircraft tried to attack a German convoy northeast of Berlevaag. Nineteen Bf 109s of 9./JG 5 took off from Svartnes and fierce dogfights broke out above the convoy, with the other *Staffeln* of III./JG 5 joining in. *Major* Ehrler and his wingman, *Unteroffizier* Rudolf Artner, attacked the fighter escort east of the convoy, and Ehrler shot down the first Airacobra at 21:43. The second fell to Artner one minute later, and the third was shot down at 21:45, also by Ehrler. At 21:48 the *Kommodore* shot down a P-40 for his 150th victory. The *Staffeln* of JG 5 returned from this action without loss while claiming a total of 33 victories, including twenty Bostons plus eight P-40s and Airacobras.

The Soviets returned in the early morning of 26 May and there was a large air battle, probably over the same convoy. At 04:22 the *Gruppe* again put 19 aircraft into the air, but this time they encountered a force of 80 to 100 Soviet machines. Russian losses that morning were ten Bostons, ten P-40s, nine Il-2s and eight Airacobras. Ehrler returned with his 151st to 155th victories and his wingman Rudi Artner scored his fourth and fifth. Once again the *Eismeerjäger* suffered no losses. At about 11:30 Ehrler and Artner took off again, this time to search for a P-40 which Artner claimed to have shot down at 05:08. Ehrler: "I located what was clearly the wreckage of a downed P-40 in the reported location, ten kilometers southwest of Navningsberg in quadrant 37 East PA 33d. The ground was still covered in snow and it was easy to see the impact site. All indications were that the crash had taken place just a short time ago. Artner's victory number five was thus confirmed. We subsequently flew back to Petsamo and landed there at 12:00."

Rudi Artner, a native of Upper Austria and a master tanner by trade, very soon became a remarkable figure in the *9. Staffel*. His capabilities as a fighter pilot and his reliability were why Ehrler and Schuck liked to have him as their wingman. And when the "lions" of the *Geschwader* came home with five, six or seven victories, the young second-generation pilot usually returned with one of his own. Within nine months Artner was promoted from *Gefreiter* to *Feldwebel*, scored a total of twenty victories, received the Operational Flying Clasp in Gold, the Iron Cross, First Class and the Honor Goblet. No wonder then that he was still flying gliders and powered aircraft in the 1970s.

• • •

The Russians, most of them junior pilots, preferred to combine their units during attacks. Flying at wave-top height, formations of torpedo-bombers with strong fighter escort attacked the German convoys, while formations of Bostons at heights of 1000 to 4000 meters dropped their bombs or parachute torpedoes simultaneously or shortly afterwards. And above the bombers flew Yak-9s. That's how it was on 17 June 1944. German supply ships were off the Varanger Peninsula when a large force of Russian torpedo-bombers and close-support aircraft with fighter cover was reported approaching from the Murmansk area. The *III. Gruppe* was immediately ordered to take off. The last aircraft were still taking off when the first intercepted enemy aircraft sent to attack the airfield. Schuck got on the tail of a Russian who turned and dove away. He shot him down and then climbed fifty meters to position himself on the tail of the next. Schuck opened fire and the Soviet aircraft went down vertically in flames. Three more followed.

A formation of Bostons was reported beyond the northwest coast of the Fischer Peninsula. "Torpedo aircraft at 320 degrees!"

The twin-engined bombers were surrounded by fighters, but the German pilots were undeterred. They burst through to the bombers. Schuck scored his sixth victory of the day and the blast wave from the explosion tossed his Bf 109 upwards. Then he moved on to another. Flying at high speed, Schuck turned, descended beneath the Boston and moved closer. Soon the Boston was enveloped in smoke, its starboard engine fell away and the gunner baled out. A blazing wreck, the Boston crashed into the sea.

Jagdgeschwader 5

Here is an extract from 9./JG 5's account of the battle:

At 07:33 on 17/6/1944 six Bf 109 G-6s scrambled to intercept an enemy formation attacking one of our convoys. Soon after takeoff contact was made with the first wave. The victories achieved in combat were distributed as follows:

Lt. Gayko	1 Curtiss P-40	08:12	(6th victory)
Fj.-Ofw. Schuck	1 Curtiss P-40	07:43	(102nd victory)
	1 Curtiss P-40	07:44	(103rd victory)
	1 Il-2	07:50	(104th victory)
	1 Il-2	07:52	(105th victory)
	1 Curtiss P-40	07:59	(106th victory)
	1 Boston	08:02	(107th victory)
	1 Boston	08:04	(108th victory)
Fw. Lübking	1 Il-2	07:53	(12th victory)
	1 Curtiss P-40	07:55	(13th victory)
	1 Curtiss P-40	07:58	(14th victory)
Uffz. Artner	1 Curtiss P-40	07:45	(7th victory)
Uffz. Grams	1 Curtiss P-40	07:44	(2nd victory)

The pilots landed to rearm and twenty minutes later they were back in the air. Schuck returned from this second mission with three more P-40s to his credit. On the way home the Germans ran into a formation that had bombed Kirkenes – Il-2s, Pe-2s and about 18 Airacobras. Schuck shot down one of the latter then ran out of ammunition. Norz shot down five enemy aircraft, while Ehrler and Glöckner each claimed three. The *Gruppe*'s only casualties in this big action were *Oberfähnrich* Vollet and *Gefreiter* Suske, both of the 7. Staffel, who were wounded.

But that 17th of June 1944 was not yet over. Two hours after the mission over the Polar Sea a lone reconnaissance aircraft appeared over the airfield. This of course could not go unchallenged and so Schuck and Gayko took off into the night. The enemy machine was flying very high and therefore there was little chance of an interception, but Schuck wanted to try. Both Messerschmitts gained altitude, climbing east to cut off the Russian's retreat. And in fact they caught up with the enemy machine. It was a Spitfire. The first burst missed, but the second hit the enemy aircraft's wing and fuselage. Suddenly there was a white jet from the Spitfire's radiator. The aircraft began to smoke, stalled and went into a spin. The pilot baled out. It was Schuck's twelfth victory on that 17th of June and his 113th overall.

The 27th of June was another big day for III./JG 5, with Dörr and Norz each shooting down twelve Russian aircraft. Twenty-six victories were scored on 4

July and 37 on 17 July, including seven each by Schuck and Glöckner. The climax came on 17 August, when a total of 40 enemy aircraft were shot down, and on 23 August, when 29 Soviet aircraft fell to the pilots of III./JG 5. The strain on the pilots and ground personnel was enormous, and the men often went days without sleep. In good weather six to eight scrambles a day were not unusual. Nevertheless casualties remained low. In the five days of major combat described above the *Gruppe* lost five pilots, a very low rate of loss measured against the number of victories. Among the fallen were *Gefreiter* Elken, *Unteroffizier* Hinz and *Leutnant* Schneider. *Feldwebel* Schlammer and *Gefreiter* Wien were reported missing. July also saw a number of personnel and organizational changes in the *III. Gruppe*. Schuck's *7. Staffel* became 10./JG 5, and the *8. Staffel* led by Glöckner became 11./JG 5. The bulk of the *9. Staffel* went with *Oberleutnant* Andresen to II./JG 5 in the Defense of the Reich, while the rest formed the foundation for a new 9./JG 5: the *"Eismeerstaffel"* under the command of *Leutnant* Werner Gayko. Expansion of the *Gruppe* into four *Staffeln* resulted in the formation of 12./JG 5, of which *Leutnant* Linz was named commander.

At that time Schuck's wingman was *Leutnant* David "Fritz" Wollmann. Even after the renaming of units, Schuck retained the number "10" on his aircraft, although it was now black. It was more by chance that Wollmann flew as the *Staffelkapitän*'s wingman; he had previously had no fixed position and was forced to fly with different pilots. One day Schuck's wingman had to turn back and Wollmann immediately joined the formation leader and nothing in the world could shake him off. The mission was a big success and from then on Schuck had a new wingman. The only difficulties came during takeoff, for Wollmann's "Black 15" was parked at the far end of the dispersal in Petsamo, and the *Leutnant* always had to sprint to his machine in order to take off at the same time as Schuck. Incidentally Schuck recorded his 150th victory on 28 August 1944.

After the hugely successful missions of the past weeks, it gradually became apparent that the fortunes of war in the far north were turning. Like Rumania and Bulgaria, Finland had separated itself from the Reich and concluded a ceasefire with the enemy, and the loss of this former ally had unavoidable consequences for the overall situation. The Russians gradually gained the upper hand, which would lead to more bitter air battles over the Polar Sea Front. While the fighter units rarely came home empty handed, they did suffer tragic losses, especially in September. On the third *Leutnant* Linz shot down a Pe-2. Pontsalenjoki, where Lüder had been sent to collect one of the last Focke-Wulfs, was already burning from end to end. On the 8th, during one of the many transfer flights, *Unteroffizier* Hirschfeld was killed in the crash of his machine. On 15 September 10./JG 5 engaged about 20 Airacobras over Pummanki Bay; *Unteroffizier* Lork was shot down. He baled out with fragments in his heel and was picked up by an air-sea rescue machine. *Leutnant* Fuhrmann was reported missing in the same area.

16 September. Two *Schwärme* from the *11. Staffel*, including Schuck, Norz and Glöckner, took off to intercept enemy aircraft heading for Kirkenes. The formation consisted of Bostons, Il-2s and numerous escort fighters. Glöckner claimed two victories, a Boston and an Airacobra, and Schuck had just sent down his second Il-2 when a voice was heard on the frequency: "Yellow 8 here. Have been hit in the engine. It's smoking!"

Then the others spotted the Messerschmitt, which was smoking heavily. It was Norz. "Bale out!" radioed an agitated Schuck.

'I'm going to try to reach the airfield."

It was about twenty kilometers to Kirkenes, no distance for a fighter aircraft. Ten kilometers to go. The ground station was advised and preparations were made on the airfield.

From "Yellow 8" came the message: "Controls no longer functioning!" The other three Messerschmitts of the *Schwarm* were alongside, shepherding the crippled machine back to the airfield. The elevators were jammed. At that moment Norz was 80 meters above the ground, but down below there was nowhere suitable for a forced landing, for the terrain surrounding Kirkenes is littered with boulders and rocks. The smoking Bf 109 went ever lower. It touched down, slid over the ground, shedding pieces as it went, and then struck a boulder. One could literally sense the metal being crushed. The fuselage buckled, then the aircraft overturned and the engine broke away.

The other three pilots, witnesses to this terrible event and still feeling the effects of the drama they had just experienced, were distraught when they landed on the airfield. A recovery team was dispatched immediately. The men found the wreck but "Jockel" Norz was dead, killed after 117 victories.

The 26th of September was another eventful day in the north. The Russians attacked Vardö and almost all of the *Staffeln* were scrambled. *Kommodore* Ehrler and Lüder flew with 10./JG 5 out over the Polar Sea to intercept the enemy on his way home. They first ran into a large number of Yak-9s. Ehrler reacted immediately, diving on the three lowest machines. As soon as they were in range he opened fire. His target immediately burst into flames and the Yak dove into the sea from a height of 20 meters. Lüder picked out a second Yak. He fired a short burst across its nose, and the Yak pilot immediately turned left, offering the adjutant a perfect target. He saw three small explosions in and around the cockpit. Flames spurted from the left side of the aircraft, which then rolled over and crashed into the water.

Meanwhile the groups of Russians and the pursuing JG 5 fighters had disappeared into the haze in the direction of Pummanki. Lüder and the *Kommodore* returned together to Petsamo, where they both made victory passes over the airfield. The ground crews were no doubt amazed that "old Lüder" had come home with another victory.

Even though fourteen Russian aircraft were claimed destroyed, the day was not entirely satisfactory, for three Focke-Wulfs and two Messerschmitts, all flown by new pilots, also failed to return. *Unteroffizier* Heinrich Pflaum went down near Eckerö. A search pair ultimately spotted him in his life raft, but darkness prevented a Do 24 from picking him up. The aircraft had previously rescued a downed Russian pilot who had been spotted by the pair of Messerschmitts escorting the flying boat. Pflaum was blown ashore near Kiberg early in the morning on 28 September. He lived and showed no ill effects from his two days adrift in the Polar Sea.

Unteroffizier Zeuner lost his orientation after the air battle and made a wheels-down landing in the area of the Tanja Fjord. He subsequently made his way home, reducing pilot losses to three. *Oberfähnrich* Haschke of 10./JG 5, and *Unteroffizier* Hagemeyer and *Unteroffizier* Thonemann, both of 13./JG 5, remain missing.

By that time Schuck had raised his victory total to 171 and on 30 September he was awarded the Knight's Cross with Oak Leaves.

Captivity

No history of the *Eismeerjäger* would be complete without mentioning the chapter of Russian captivity. Hardly any other *Geschwader* on the Eastern Front had such a high percentage of missing. An analysis of the various *Geschwader* records and the official casualty reports reveals that the units of *Jagdgeschwader 5* engaged on the Eastern Front had a total of 78 missing pilots. Of these 41 are still registered as tracing cases by the German Red Cross. As to the remaining 37 pilots, it is not known with certainty whether they were killed, captured, missing or even returned. For this reason it would be most welcome if readers – especially former *Eismeerjäger* – could provide additional information so that the *Geschwader*'s losses could be corrected.

There is evidence to prove that 33 pilots were captured by the Russians. The *Eismeerjäger* possessed certain survival skills, and the meager, often primitive quartering and living conditions in the far north may have served to some degree to prepare them for life as prisoners of war. About two-thirds of the prisoners, probably the most resilient among them, later returned to their homes.

On closer examination of the casualties, the *III. Gruppe* leads the way with 39 pilots missing and 16 captured, followed by II./JG 5 with 25 missing and 14 prisoners of war. There are still 38 open tracing cases from these two *Gruppen* alone.

The following facts account for the large number of the pilots who landed in or baled out over enemy territory. For one thing the front from Petsamo to southern Finland was static for about 3½ years; consequently II. and III./JG 5 were deployed in the same sector of the front from June 1941 to about October 1944. In no other theater of war was this the case. For another, until the beginning of 1944 the Soviets fought a purely defensive war. As a result, except for escort missions over the Polar Sea, the German fighter pilots had to seek out the enemy more than 120 kilometers beyond the lines, to the area around Murmansk area and farther south, along the Murmansk railway, as far as Louhi. Consequently, in the overwhelming majority of cases, every mechanical problem, every forced landing and every bale-out resulted in a total loss and a captured pilot.

A series of other factors had a significant influence on this issue. The Germans had to fly and fight over an area almost completely devoid of landmarks. The terrain consisted of forest, tundra and rock, and there were almost no roads, towns or railways, making visual navigation extremely difficult. Compasses failed over large areas with large ore deposits, which are not uncommon in the far north, further complicating the task of navigation. And then there were the climatic conditions. All too often extreme variations in temperature, polar darkness, storms and sudden onset of fog helped place pilots in hopeless situations, much more often than was seen on other fronts.

From 1941 until about May 1943 the Soviets employed tough, often cruel methods against their prisoners. An OKL order, according to which the attitude of prisoners toward their Russian captors was supposed to reflect the National-Socialist ideology, may have been largely responsible for this treatment. The Soviets understandably regarded the order as symptomatic of the Germans' belief in their racial superiority. For propaganda reasons, treatment of prisoners improved significantly in 1943-44, although overall it always remained below the norm by western standards. The German side erred by giving its soldiers unrealistic information about the Russians and their mentality. This was confirmed by *Hauptmann* Schmidt. A secret report concerning *Feldwebel* Kaiser, which Schmidt had an opportunity to read in January 1944, shortly before he was captured, helped him greatly. He remembered the following: Sepp Kaiser of 8./JG 5, who was captured on 26 December 1942, identified himself as an Austrian communist using his brother's Austrian Communist Party card. The Soviets trained him as a radio operator and the following summer he and a mountain infantryman, equipped with parachutes and radio equipment, were dropped from the bomb bay of a Boston bomber south of Petsamo. The mountain infantryman's parachute failed to deploy fully. He fell into a swamp and suffered a fractured pelvis. Sepp Kaiser turned himself in to the Germans and reported that the Soviets had ordered him to transmit radio reports regarding traffic on the Polar Sea road, where they wished to expand their partisan activities. They had already blown up a number of trucks, forcing the Germans to resort to travelling in escorted convoys. Sepp Kaiser characterized the OKL order concerning behavior in captivity as provocative to the Russians: it only provoked mistreatment, because it only confirmed the propagandistic concept of German arrogance. Kaiser recommended that prisoners indicate a clear willingness to talk to the Russians. If someone wanted to keep something secret, it was recommended that he declare: "That was kept secret from me too, only generals could know that!" That argument was accepted by every Russian.

Hauptmann Schmidt had good experiences with this recipe, all the more so because he had no difficulty telling the most fantastic stories for hours. To good friends Sepp Kaiser never made a secret of his experiences in Russian captivity. He never served in the east again.

In commenting on the experiences of German pilots held as prisoners by the Russians and evaluating the stories told by returning pilots of the *Geschwader*, I have sought to avoid any political bias regardless of which side is involved. This was done for historical reasons, not least to complete the history of the *Geschwader*.

The first pilot of the *Geschwader* to be captured by the Soviets was *Hauptmann* Alfred von Lojewski. A member of 14./JG 77, on 29 June 1941, after shooting down an enemy aircraft, he was hit by Russian anti-aircraft fire and obliged to make a forced landing. He attempted to make his way back to the German lines, but three days later he was picked up by Russian troops. During his early days in the camp he heard little about events at the front, and it was not until he was interrogated in Lubyanka prison in Moscow in 1942 that a commissar told him that the German fighter pilots on the northern front were giving the Russians plenty of trouble. At the beginning of the year in Saratov, von Lojewski heard from a new prisoner that the *Jagdgruppen* of JG 5 were still engaged in attacks on Murmansk and that Carganico had become an ace. Later, in another camp – during his nine years of captivity von Lojewski passed through no fewer than 13 prisons and 17 different camps – he met *Leutnant* Jakobi, who had been captured on 9 April 1942. "He was wide-eyed when he saw me, for they thought I had been killed," reported von Lojewski. "He also explained why no effort had been made to rescue me. After I failed to return, Russian radio in Murmansk had claimed that

I was alive and a prisoner, however this information was thought to be unreliable and it was believed that the Russians had just found my body."

The sporting fairness and chivalrous comradeship shown a defeated aerial opponent, practiced in the west as fruits of the First World War, were foreign to the Soviets, where even today personal and political hatred of every good soldier is still a prerequisite for good fighting morale. In general the physical and psychological pressures endured by the prisoners of war were beyond tolerable. The sense of abandonment and inner loneliness felt by captured fighter pilots, who were always held in solitary confinement, was great, while their knowledge of what awaited them was zero. This made it impossible for them to realistically assess their situation, their prospects, their rights and their possibilities. On the contrary, one-sided negative reports, which were circulated for propaganda reasons, reinforced their helplessness and diminished their hopes for survival. Von Lojewski added: "That the German soldier was sent to war with so little knowledge about Russia, about the Geneva Convention and about the conditions to be expected in enemy hands, was a mistake and a disaster for the individual. This was a serious burden that few prisoners were able to overcome. Another point, and this applies in particular to prisoners captured at the beginning, concerns the stress caused by systematic gentle persuasion. Despite all the physical hardships such as interrogations of all shades, hunger and cold, the psychological mistreatment by the Russian *politruks* bothered me more. One had to bravely take one's courage in both hands. The Soviets were already waging 'psychological warfare' against us. Reconciliation with our fate of being experimental subjects can give us hope that the soldiers of today, if not protected against this tool of war, may at least be better prepared for it."

The second pilot of the *Geschwader* to become a prisoner of war, even before *Leutnant* Jakobi, was *Hauptmann* Gerhard Schaschke of the *Zerstörerstaffel*. He was definitely seen in one of the known camps (Camp 158), but then he disappeared without a trace. On the other hand *Oberfeldwebel* Florian Salwender, who fell into the hands of the Russians on 23 April 1943, is known to have died later in the camp.

Three pilots of the *7. Staffel* became prisoners of war on the same day, 5 August 1942: *Leutnant* Bodo Helms, *Unteroffizier* Kurt Philipp and *Unteroffizier* Werner Schumacher. As we know, these three pilots ran out of fuel during a transfer flight to Pontsalenjoki and were picked up by the Russians. After interrogation by officers of a Soviet regiment, they were taken blindfolded through the lines. Bodo Helms: "After a long drive we arrived at an airfield, on which a three-seat biplane was sitting. A wildly-gesticulating mob led us to suspect the worst. Our hands and legs were tied and we were placed in the machine, where there were no harnesses of any kind. Using hand signals, a major made it clear to us that we were going to be thrown out during a loop. But they then kindly lashed us in. We were flown to Belomorsk (Sorokna), where I was interrogated by two generals. Afterwards Philipp and I were taken to a prison that was unfit for human beings. Our three-week stay there was interrupted by interrogations, mainly at night. Then we made a two-week trip to Krasnogorsk near Moscow. Schumacher was given medical treatment. There were many airmen in the camp and they helped lighten my fate, especially as there were old friends and acquaintances among them. Pieck and Ulbricht regularly visited the camp and tried to start an anti-fascist movement amongst us. Their efforts were not exactly crowned with success, however, and only a few succumbed to the propaganda or rather the porridge pot, for hunger became the worst hostage of captivity."

The wounded *Unteroffizier* Schumacher had to spend a long time in hospital. *Unteroffizier* Philipp stayed in Camp 74, while *Leutnant* Helms was taken to Murmansk at the end of November 1942. He later learned that Schumacher had died in the Podma camp in the spring of 1943, probably on account of his wounds and his sensitive nature.

Dietrich Weinitschke gave a particularly detailed account of his experiences in Russian captivity. *Feldwebel* Weinitschke was shot down on 12 March 1943. In his experience they used five main methods in dealing with the prisoners. These characteristic points are apparent in the following account, which can stand for others:

1. Taking prisoners by surprise by correcting false statements made while under interrogation.
2. Softening resistance by constant repetition of interrogations and apparently pointless questions.
3. Extortion of statements from wounded by denying medical aid or benefits (tobacco, straw mattresses, blankets or clothing, favorable workplace, etc.).
4. Setting up a spying system.
5. Arrest with infiltrated spies.

"On 12/3/43 I took off with *Oblt.* Weißenberger for Shongui. After a scrap with enemy aircraft I was attacked by an Airacobra at low level. Warned by the high cover unit, I climbed to about 700 meters, whereupon the fuselage exploded. My radio was out, controls jammed, aircraft stalled and rolled over. I baled out and allowed myself to fall through the Russian formation before pulling the ripcord at about 100 meters. After one swing beneath my parachute I landed in the snow. I set off on foot, as I had the year before, but this time I had no emergency supplies as they burned up in the luggage compartment. At dusk I was spotted by a U-2. In the morning four Bf 109s strafed the Russian patrol following me, however they failed to see me as I was walking among tall trees. Afterwards I saw only Russian aircraft, which constantly patrolled the airspace above me, looking for my tracks. At noon I was discovered by a lieutenant accompanied by an NCO. In the ensuing fight I was shot, resulting in a broken bone and nerve damage. My right hand was paralyzed. I was marched to a Russian strongpoint with my hands tied behind my back. A female medic cut off the right sleeve of my Channel jacket and sweater – which were blood-soaked and frozen – with scissors. She twisted the arm and put the broken radius back into place with a blow from her fist. Fifty centimeters of gauze bandage completed the treatment. They removed the laces from my mountain boots as a precaution, and I was transported to the railroad by five men. During the night I was taken to Shongui in a logging truck. There I was interrogated for four hours until I passed out. They gave me a glass of water, a stool to sit on and then questioned me for another four hours until they gave up. There I was told that a Stork that had been searching for me had been shot down. The crew had been killed.

"Before I was transported to Murmansk I was given a bowl of soup. The guard during transport was strict but professional. An NKVD captain interrogated me and after a shot while declared that I was lying. He confidently stated that I would be telling the truth in ten minutes. When asked about my *Staffel* comrades I had given him the names from the roll of honor. It took him less than five minutes to ask me how long Oblt. Menzel had had an officer school in Luostari. (Allegedly I had not yet been to the front, only in Munich.) Then he gave me the exact date on which each had been shot down. He declared that I would see Lt. Jakobi and *Ofw*. Pfränger again in the airmen's camp if I gave him useful information. I made a sketch of the airfield, which he looked at then pushed aside with a laugh. He then showed me a 50x50 cm aerial photo bearing precise information. 'You say that the ammunition dump is here, but it's the light anti-aircraft guns. You say here is the fuel dump, but it is the heavy anti-aircraft guns. You say …' And so it went on for half an hour. When I asked why he was questioning me when he already knew the answers to everything, he said: 'We want to determine your attitude. You have surrendered but you haven't laid down your weapons! If you give us useful information you will be sent to a camp with good food: black bread, white bread, soup and kascha three times a day, and tea and dessert.' He also told me that he had met *Oblt*. Menzel and *Lt*. Lesch in Stavanger and gave good descriptions of both.

"My first meal there, fish soup and 200 grams of soggy bread, was more like an appetizer. It was a clear broth with a few fish bones, from which a few fish eyes stared at me sadly. My accommodation was a five by seven meter room, about four meters high, with a window that was nailed shut except for an opening at a height of 3.5 meters. Furnishings consisted of a field cot with boards and a huge stove with no fire. They gave me a sheepskin, but with my suit, skivvies, trousers, Channel pants, sweater and Channel jacket – less its right sleeve – it was definitely too little. Once in twelve days there were a few sticks of wood, but it wasn't enough to heat the stove.

"I was interrogated every day and night, for five minutes to four hours. Sometimes I was roused during the night to tell how old my father was or how many windows and doors we had in our house. From then on, however, most of the interrogations were carried out by a German and an Austrian or Bavarian. The German asked the questions, wrote down the topic, stated what the Russians knew of it, and when I answered yes or no wrote down an entire novel on his form. He also told me that they had an airman with a wounded leg there, and that things weren't going well for him because he refused to say anything. I later heard that he lost his leg. (It may have been *Uffz.* Wassermann from Magdeburg. He had been attached to an air-sea rescue unit. Wassermann crashed in a Dornier Wal during a rescue attempt and was captured injured by the Russians. By 1945 he was exercising on the high bar in Cherepovets with one leg.)

"Found to be an unsuitable candidate, after 14 days I found myself in a tiny camp. There I met Rudi Fenten, who had a head injury, and Dietrich Gathmann, who had a crookedly-healed fractured femur. The rations were such that we stole oats from the Russian horses, which we roasted at first, then after discovery boiled and finally chewed raw. We discussed escape plans, together with the Finns drew a map and secretly dried bread. But it was too late. The barber came, our heads were shaved and we were shipped out. In the cell of a prison car we were transported south. The first day we were given 200 grams of bread, three small salted fish, a little bigger than sprats, and soup. On the second day we had bread and fish again; on the third day the small fish and hot water. Then there was only hot water. After eight days we had to get off and received new guards. The *starchi* sergeant observed that we had eaten too much and that the rations bag was empty. When we told him we hadn't eaten in five days, he shook what was left in the sack into a pot, resulting in a mixed soup: pea flour, millet, vermicelli and jute fiber. Hunger drove us to eat it, and in our condition it even tasted good, and soon we were full.

"After arriving in Cherepovets, we hobbled to Camp 158 in Makarino under heavy guard, I believe ten men and a dog handler. There we were first sent to the *banya* to wash and delouse our clothing and it was there we met Freidel Rennemann, who was serving 21 days arrest for making fascist statements. After we had handed over all our clothes we went into the bathroom. Waiting for us was a barber for the most uncomfortable procedure of captivity. In the presence of a nurse, who was supervising, and the examining female doctor, our armpit hair, heavy body hair and pubic hair were shaved off. Then we were given 10 grams of soap, two liters of warm water and several liters of cold water to rinse with. Shivering from cold, we then stood in front of the doctor, whom we called 'Auntie Ju' on account of her clumsiness. It was embarrassing, but after she had made sufficient fuss over my stinking feet, from which the black frozen skin was hanging in shreds, I was given two gauze bandages. After our clothes were returned we were once again put behind barbed wire, in quarantine. By our standards the food was good: 400 grams of bread, even though it was as soft as pudding and often contained pieces of potato and potato skins, 400 grams of vegetables, namely gherkins, and the liquid in the container counted as part of the weight, 70 grams of fish in the soup and 70 grams as a meat substitute, 10 grams of millet and 3 grams of fats and 7 grams of sugar in the hand. After quarantine and many interrogations by the NKVD we entered the camp and were assigned work. Workers were given an extra 200 grams of bread, and for completing 101% of normal work outside the camp one received another 100 grams of bread and *kascha* (millet gruel).

"At the end of April we met *Lt*. Fritz Lüdecke, who was passing himself off as an *Obergefreiter*, *Fw*. Rudi Braun of the reconnaissance *Staffel* (Hauschild), *Uffz*. Bela Preisler, and in the summer *Uffz*. Krischkovski. Also at the end of April, guards took about 100 men who were sick or unable to work to a camp in a small wood about seven kilometers away to dig out 200 small spruces and 50 birches and bring them to the camp. Ornamental flower beds were laid out to mark the 1st of May. Made of crushed brick and chlorinated lime, they resembled layer cakes decorated with Soviet stars, red flags and May Day slogans. The 1st of May was a holiday and it began with a giant search on the 'sports field'. At the same time, groups of guards scoured the barracks, searching in beds, coats and bags as well as under the floorboards for knives, pencils and drawings of all kinds. Afterwards we exchanged our winter clothing for linen underwear and dungarees. In the afternoon there was a big May Day meeting, during which a Dane, a Dutchman and two Germans declared themselves to be anti-fascists.

"One day in the middle of May all of the 'work brigades' returned to camp at noon. From that day on everyone was given hospital food and, apart from work in the camp and for the camp, no work was done. Instead the units were herded into the barracks and clubroom, where the anti-fascists gave us daily lectures. Conversations with the Russians were restricted to talk of peace and returning home. At that time as well, the airmen could only see and speak to each other secretly. Often enough, minutes after a conversation between two airmen, both would be summoned individually to the commandant's office for interrogation. We immediately caught on and came up with a separate story for the Russians. During the next 'meat inspection' (inspection of the work groups) all of the airmen were assigned to different barracks, making closer contacts impossible.

"One reason for this was probably the nearby airfield, from which Il-2 units were still flying night missions in the spring of 1944. Spaniards were used as ground personnel. *Leutnant* Eichhorn soon learned to speak Spanish and became familiar with the Il-2's technology, hoping one day to be able to pass himself off as a 'Spaniard' and 'march out' with them.

"A few times in May there were still air raid alarms – probably Ju 88s on weather reconnaissance flights. Words cannot express the longing to fly felt by the airmen. It was worse than thirst and homesickness.

"Ultimately all of the labor groups had to return to their construction sites and we returned to our old rations. I later learned that exactly the same thing had happened in the other camps. Another account reads as follows: a still unexplained incident took place on Cherepovets in May-June 1943. Suddenly there was better food, '*Skora Domoy*' slogans, breaks in the city and the work brigades no longer had to leave the camp. A hospital ship was tied up in Lake Rybinsk to evacuate the sick. Money was paid out and a few stalwarts are said to have sewn swastika flags. In June, however, all of the perks disappeared again. It became more difficult than before with respect to treatment, work and food. At that time, after Stalingrad, there was conjecture that peace feelers had been extended by way of Sweden. Hopelessness spread. An epidemic broke out that was survived by only a few hundred *plennies*. Those who did survive were forbidden to speak about this period, as were the Soviets. We never learned any more about this, even in the postwar accounts.

"When I ended up in hospital with malaria, Rennemann was gathering bread and butter for a group that wanted to escape. In July 1943 a group of Latvians was ordered to replace the canvas roof of one of the camp barracks. They discovered a compass, maps, clarified butter, salt fish and dried bread. Twelve men, who were suspected, were placed under arrest for 21 days and subsequently transported to the Urals. At the time the camp held about 1,000 men, of which about 300 were Spaniards of the Blue Division, 400 Germans and 300 Bessarabians, Poles, Lithuanians, Finns, Dutch, Danes, one Frenchman and even an American who had been drafted into service as the son of German parents.

"Hopes for an end to captivity, stirred up by the incomprehensibly good time, were dashed. The number of men unable to work and deaths rose. A hospital for prisoners of war was set up in the city. The number of newcomers increased steadily. In autumn a trainload of prisoners came from the south, and about 800 men were quartered with us. They told us that, after their arrival, 400 men who had died during the three-week trip in sealed cars were carried off. The *Antifa* received the newcomers in the barracks. Decorations and medals were torn off and trod upon, rank badges were cut from their uniforms, and they were threatened with imprisonment for making fascist remarks. Before long 95% of the Germans had signed up for the National Committee to escape the daily pressure, which, for those who could not be convinced, culminated in nightly punishment expeditions, or more accurately beatings outside the barracks. A fascist barracks was set up which became an off-limits zone within the camp. In addition to airmen, the handful of holdouts included several ranks from the tanks, artillery and a few infantrymen. At that time Rennemann and others from the above group looked into an evening of entertainment to give the men a few hours of relaxation without political indoctrination. Though approved by the camp commander, the evening was forbidden by the anti-fascists, who refused to make the clubroom available to the fascists. After a long and serious discussion, during which each member of the group expressed his personal feelings about the *Antifa*, seven men marched into the clubroom and demanded the refusal in writing. The first non-political play in the camp took place three days later. Violins and cellos were soldered together from sheet metal and guts and horse hairs were stolen for the strings. The evening was a complete success and was repeated several times. Under the direction of and with participation by *Eismeerjäger*, the group operated until the camp was disbanded. The number of prisoners grew steadily. Camp 437 (Bokorovski) was opened north of Cherepovets in 1944. The number of satellite camps grew to ten. The toughest were Vitogra, Chaika Chagoda-Torf and Sokol. Prisoners of Work Group 1 were sent to these camps. From these camps came prisoners unfit to work. The number of prisoners in the camp was estimated to be 10,000 in the summer of 1944. The great dying began in the autumn of 1944. Camp 158 (Makarino, 3,000 men) had as many as 30 dead per night; the city camp with 700 men about 30 dead; Camp 437 (Bokorovski, 4,500 men) about 20 dead per day in the worst days.

"In the camp at that time were: Arthur Beth, Günter Eichhorn, Rudi Fenten, Bodo Helms, Hans Link, Bela Preisler, Wolfgang Rost, Hans H. Schmidt, Klaus Walter, Dietrich Weinitschke. *Uffz.* Krischkovski and Alfred Kern died. As far as I remember, Friedel Rennemann was taken to Moscow. The food had been improved several times since the beginning of 1943. Instead of 3 grams of oil we received 7 grams of fats. There was also 20 grams of flour products and 7 grams of *machorka* (tobacco). Nevertheless, this level of rations was insufficient to enable one to bear up under the physical and mental stress, even though conditions had eased greatly since the early days in the camp. In 1943 there were daily sick parades, during which the camp commandant checked the sick chits and made many of the sick well by tearing off the pass and sending the healed back to work. In the evening everyone had to form up in front of the barracks for roll call, no matter what the weather. At that time there were often misunderstandings caused by mispronunciations. Once, for example, the entire camp stood in the rain for a solid hour because the prisoner *Ra-uchga-use-gans* failed to answer. How was Hans Rauchhaus supposed to recognize his name? In 1944 the prisoners were counted in their quarters when the weather was bad, and the sick were permitted to remain on their beds.

"In the summer *Fw.* Braun and I went to Chaika, where *Hptm.* Müller (student decathlon champion in 1936) was able to obtain numerous privileges for the prisoners, such as berry and mushroom picking after work quotas had been filled, permission to fish near the camp (two kilometer radius), group outings on Sundays to villages within a radius of ten kilometers, and baking of German-style bread.

"In 1948 I met another fighter pilot, whose name I have forgotten, in the kitchen of Camp 437. The yearly interrogations about our flying activities also continued there.

"I had been on the transport list five times and each time I was struck off just prior to departure. The sixth time they pulled me out of the returnee column just twenty meters from the gate. On my seventh attempt, on 20 March 1949, I passed through the camp gate on my way home."

After *Feldwebel* Weinitschke, on 14 March 1943 *Unteroffizier* Alfred Kern was shot down west of Murmansk. He made a forced landing and tried to reach the German lines, however he was discovered by Russian soldiers: Kern resisted but was overpowered and taken prisoner. He was first taken to Murmansk for interrogation and soon afterwards was transferred to a forest camp in Kildinstroy, about 30 kilometers south of Murmansk. Kern was then sent by train to Cherepovets, where he arrived on 8 June 1943.

Cherepovets is on the Leningrad-Vologda rail line on the Sheksna River, about 400 kilometers from Leningrad and 100 kilometers from Vologda. It was a large camp with a capacity of 3,000 prisoners. At that time they worked exclusively on the port at the north end of the vast Rybinsk reservoir project (140x100 km). Today the reservoir is used as a shipping link from the Volga to the north and northwest. It was an old camp: the date 1890 was supposedly present in the *kalabossa*, or jail. Alfred Kern initially worked as a metalworker in the forge. In the following winter he was hospitalized on account of lung complaints and sore throat. At that time it was the fashion to diagnose all throat illnesses as diphtheria, but in reality few of the prisoners actually contracted the disease – it was a specialty of the female doctor and everyone profited from having a throat complaint as they didn't have to work while she had them under quarantine.

In the summer of 1944 Kern returned to work in the forge. He was also suspected of having tuberculosis at that time. He was probably unaware of it himself. In roughly January 1945 he suddenly developed pneumonia and was sent back to the hospital, a barracks in which he joined about 100 other German military personnel. German doctors and medics and Russian female doctors and nurses cared for the patients, however most of the malnourished prisoners died on account of a shortage of medicines and sometimes inadequate rations. The officers and enlisted men received exactly the same treatment. Kern's nutritional condition was initially very good, but the tuberculosis must have been more advanced than originally recognizable.

His friends visited him regularly. H.H. Schmidt saw him for the last time on at about ten in the evening on 5 February 1945. Kern had already been lying unconscious for a long time and did not recognize his nurses. That evening he regained consciousness. He must have learned about the seriousness of his condition, for he told Schmidt that he didn't have much time left. Schmidt tried to encourage him, but Alfred scarcely heard his words and closed his eyes. After midnight he was given another injection. He did not regain consciousness again, and according to a medic Alfred Kern died at 4:30 in the morning on 6 February. He was buried in the camp cemetery in Cherepovets. In 1950 Schmidt was able to give several carvings made by Kern to his relatives.

According to estimates by prisoners of war, this cemetery contained about 15,000 graves; that was in 1946, after the camp had been in existence for only three years! Kern's early death spared him a long, difficult period of suffering, for with his illness there is no way he could have survived the long years until 1947 or 1948. As an airman and a German, who could not change his attitude at will, he would not have been granted an early release.

Unteroffizier Krischkovski of 6./JG 5, who was captured on 27 March 1943, was also unable to endure the demands of prison life. He died in Camp Makarino.

Oberfeldwebel Rudi Müller of Frankfurt/Main suffered a similar fate to that of *Hauptmann* Schaschke. When he was shot down on 19 April 1943, Müller was the top ace on the Polar Sea Front with 94 victories. It cannot be ruled out that the Russians singled him out for special treatment on account of this. According to reliable statements, Müller was later seen in Lubyanka and as late as 1947 there were signs that he was still alive. After that, however, *Oberfeldwebel* Müller vanished.

For every German soldier, service on the Eastern Front came with the additional considerable burden of potentially becoming a prisoner of war. This was especially true of fighter pilots, who flew their missions far beyond the front lines. It is understandable, therefore, that a number of fighter pilots who were shot down or crash-landed in enemy territory chose to fight to the death or in the end even turn their weapons on themselves, convinced that they had chosen the better fate. It is known, for example, that after being shot down on 16 January 1944, *Leutnant* Karl Heinz Vogel of the 7. *Staffel* resisted capture until his pistol ran out of ammunition and was then shot. A Russian captain told *Hauptmann* Schmidt, who had been captured a few days earlier, that two German fighters had run out of fuel and crash-landed near the Motovski camp. He must have been referring to *Leutnant* Vogel and *Gefreiter* Horst Bergmann. The two airmen were on their way towards the German lines but were intercepted by a Russian patrol. Schmidt waited in vain for the arrival of the two pilots. Several days later he learned that they had defended themselves to the end and had fallen in the exchange of fire.

It is also known that *Oberleutnant* Oskar Maertins of the *Zerstörerstaffel* took his life to prevent capture by the Russians. On 28 February 1943 his aircraft was shot up by Russian fighters near the Murmansk railway and Maertins and his gunner Steinbeck were obliged to make a forced landing. While *Unteroffizier* Steinbeck was captured by the Russians unhurt, Maertins put a bullet in his head.

H.H. Schmidt, whose last flight over the Fischer Peninsula has already been described in detail, was the second pilot to fall into Russian hands in January 1944, after *Feldwebel* Arthur Beth. The first *Kapitän* to be captured since *Hauptmann* Schaschke in 1941, he was something of a show piece and was passed around accordingly. First he was interrogated by the senior general on the Fischer Peninsula. After three days with almost nothing to eat and two nights without sleep, constantly exposed to the severe cold and wind, he was placed into an overheated bunker, was given one *stakan* (100 grams) of vodka, some gruel and bread and then allowed to sleep. No sooner had he fallen into a deep sleep, when he was roused and brought to the general. He wanted to know which sentries he had slipped past or bribed on the Fischer Peninsula. Schmidt could hardly believe his ears. After harsh threats, using a map he outlined his route in detail. The general became angry and said that, as no man could have survived the fierce storm and cold temperatures in the open, he must have found shelter in one of the outposts. Schmidt related how he survived. Nods of approval. The interpreter told him that the general had ordered an evaluation of Schmidt's experiences. "Some *njemetz* (German) has to come and tell us how to behave in a storm!" Schmidt's treatment became significantly better. The three anti-aircraft gunners who brought him down were brought before him, proudly wearing the Red Star and Red Banner medals they had been awarded for the feat. Later he was allowed to sleep and the next night was taken by coastal cutter to the military port of Polyarnoye. The tub rocked so that he had to cling to the top bunk and was unable to sleep. When one of the guards became terribly seasick, Schmidt was able to open a small porthole, but then he became very cold again.

Polyarnoye was the largest Soviet naval base on the Soviet Polar Sea. It was a bustling port with big stone buildings and tall towers. In true navy style, even among the Russians the mariners were the "lords." Schmidt was interrogated by the commander of Fortress Murmansk, General Andreyev, who made a great impression on him.

There was plenty of information about the fate of other prisoners but very little about missing cases. Each story had to be treated with great caution, as wild rumors often circulated. One day in March 1944, while under interrogation, *Hauptmann* Schmidt was suddenly asked about a *Leutnant* Gieren of the *8. Staffel*. They described to him a tall, youthful-looking man with blonde hair who had been captured injured after his Messerschmitt flew into the ground near an anti-aircraft position on the Fischer Peninsula. Schmidt denied knowing a *Leutnant* Gieren, and under the usual threats and abuse he was told that he must know him, as he had been stationed in Petsamo for some time and had several victories to his credit.

Not until later did it occur to the *Hauptmann* that in Russian script the Latin capital D reads like G and the small p like r. They must therefore have been talking about *Leutnant* Hans-Bodo Diepen, who had been shot down on 8 March 1944. After the misunderstanding was cleared up, Schmidt was able to deduce from the interrogating officer's answers that *Leutnant* Diepen's condition must be very serious and that he had not yet been interrogated. Three days later Schmidt received news that Diepen had died.

It should not go unmentioned that, from about mid-1943, the Soviets issued strict orders to immediately transfer every prisoner to the most senior Russian headquarters without harming them or stealing their personal effects. No Russian would have dared disobey this order. At the same time care of the wounded was also surprisingly good. In any case there are noticeable differences in the statements made by prisoners in 1941 and 1942 and those who were captured in 1943 or 1944. And in 1944 the many stories of inhumanity on the part of the Russian could no longer, as a rule, be verified, at least from the Murmansk area. It must therefore be assumed that *Leutnant* Diepen received treatment for his injuries.

JG 5 on the Polar Sea

In concluding this topic it must be emphasized that comparisons with the well-known problems encountered by prisoners held in the east during the Korean and Viet Nam wars are not applicable here. Refined Asiatic methods may have been employed there to make prisoners submissive. However the American prisoners drew strength from the knowledge that the eyes of the world were upon them and that they were backed by the most powerful nation in the world. The eastern mentality in these matters is now generally known. The soldiers who fight against the east have been provided with strict rules of conduct, and their training prepares them mentally and physically for the possibility of capture. This is especially true of American pilots. If, nevertheless, the USA has failed to find ways and means to effectively help the POWs, this only proves – and that is why it is mentioned here at all – that the fate of captivity, as experienced by the members of JG 5, should not be measured subsequently, no matter which path they took on the other side.

Frank and open discussions at the *Eismeerjäger* reunions, which have been held almost yearly since 1947, have fostered various harsh accusations or misunderstandings that separated JG 5 returnees from other members of the *Geschwader* to be explained and cleared up.

Chapter 4
Other Fronts

II. Gruppe Leaves the Polar Sea Front

Toward the end of 1943 there was a change in the *Geschwader* structure resulting from the progress to date in the war on the Eastern Front. II./JG 5 was ordered to move to the front area encompassing Nevel, Leningrad and Lake Ilmen. To bring relief to the hard-pressed army in the area of *Luftflotte 1* under *General der Flieger* Pflugbeil, on 3 November 1943 the *Gruppe* left the north and flew to its new bases via Kemi, Pori and Reval. Its initial mission was to provide fighter escort for the close-support units. While the *Gruppe* headquarters and the headquarters company settled into Pskov-South, the flying units operated as required from frontline airfields such as Idritsa, Dno, Goshkina-Guba and Dorpat. With the move, II./JG left the command of *Luftflotte 5*.

Just an hour before 6./JG 5 began its transfer flight on 3 November, Weißenberger shot down two Bostons, an Il-2 and a Hurricane over the Fischer Peninsula northwest of Vayda-Guba. On 11 November the *Staffel* left Pskov and flew to its new airfield at Idritsa, arriving at about 09:00. First contact with the enemy took place on the 17th. The unit's pilots encountered new aircraft types, as the Russians mainly operated the LaGG-5 and Yak-9 in this sector. Encounters with American types were very rare.

In this particular sector the pilots also soon felt the effects of the enemy's determination and numerical superiority, for the Russians had steadily increased their pressure on the German front, and the missions that the *Jagdstaffeln* flew there, though very successful in terms of enemy aircraft destroyed, inevitably resulted in casualties. The 5. *Staffel* suffered the first loss on 8 December, when *Unteroffizier* Weiser failed to return from a sortie near Lyutkova. On the 11th *Leutnant* Schmidt (6./JG 5) was brought down by Russian small arms fire. At 08:25 on 17 December, 4./JG 5 took off on a mission over the Nevel front, where it ran into Il-2 close-support aircraft. *Staffelführer Leutnant* Lamprecht was initially reported missing after this engagement.

Temporarily transferred into the area of *Luftflotte 2* (*Gen.Oberst* Ritter von Greim), in January 1944 the Gruppe took part in the defensive battle of Vitebsk, operating from Orsha-South or Polotsk in the central sector. On 24 January

Gefreiter Schnelling and *Unteroffizier* Kindler were lost in the Pustoshka area. While Kindler's Messerschmitt was shot down in flames by anti-aircraft fire, Schnelling's aircraft was observed trailing coolant and he was seen making a forced landing. On 31 January southeast of Zlotsiy, Weißenberger scored his first victory after leaving the northern front, shooting down a LaGG-5. At that time the 6. *Staffel* was based in Dno.

February was another busy month. On the first day of the month the 5. *Staffel* ran into a group of LaGG-5 fighters in the Zlotsiy area. A dogfight broke out in which *Gefreiter* Ludewig was shot down. At about the same time 6./JG 5 was ordered to escort a formation of Ju 87s to the front. Northeast of Dno, just after takeoff, *Unteroffizier* Schad's aircraft developed engine trouble. Schad was killed in the ensuing crash. That was not the end, however. The next day the *Gruppe* had to report one of its pilots missing when *Unteroffizier* Zimmermann failed to return after a skirmish with Russian fighters over Pustoshka.

At noon on 11 February the *4. Staffel* was given another escort assignment. It subsequently strafed Russian troops on frozen Lake Peipus, destroying two artillery sledges. After this the pace of operations slowed somewhat for two weeks. The entire *Gruppe* moved back to Pskov and, after it was abandoned before the Soviet advance, to Jakobstadt in Latvia. On the 24th 5./JG 5 fought another tough battle with Yak-9s over Pustoshka. *Unteroffizier* Karl Schrag failed to return. A search flight from Dorpat had to be aborted and Schrag was never seen again.

Shortly after 10:30 on 28 February, *Oberleutnant* Schwanecke shot down a Yak 9 in the Idritsa area. It was his tenth victory and the 96th by the *Staffel*.

The *Geschwaderstab* remained in Petsamo until the end of February and in March moved to Alakurtti. The *II. Gruppe* arrived there from Latvia at the same time, however its stay in Alakurtti – 4./JG 5 in Pontsalenjoki – was but a short one. The purpose of the move was to provide air support to the army, which was fighting off a major attack aimed at Lapland. *Feldwebel* August Mors remained the undisputed victory king, claiming the highest single day victory total achieved to date in the far north. He claimed a total of eight victories that day, and seven of his victims were Il-2s.

Unteroffizier Erlinger of the *4. Staffel* shot down his first enemy aircraft near Pontsalenjoki – another Il-2. On that same 22 March Schwanecke also shot down an Il-2 and on 2 April he destroyed another enemy aircraft. In the morning 4./JG 5 flew escort for Stukas, then at about 16:00 it was ordered to escort *Generaloberst* Dietl's Ju 52 to Pontsalenjoki. In doing so the German fighters encountered a formation of Il-2s about to attack the airfield. The *4. Staffel* destroyed a total of six Russian aircraft. Three of these fell to Schwanecke's guns, at 17:16, 17:20 and 17:25. They were victories thirteen to fifteen (10 with JG 5).

At the end of April the *Gruppe* returned to Jakobstadt, and with this move it left the Polar Sea front for good. In March Carganico left for the Reich to take over I./JG 5 following the death of *Major* Gerlitz on 16 March. There was another personnel change. Weißenberger was named the new *Kommandeur* of II./JG 5, after which the *Gruppe*'s roster of staff positions looked like this:

C.O. II./JG 5:	*Hptm.* Weißenberger
Adjutant and Operations Officer:	*Oblt.* Glöckner
Technical Officer:	*Oblt.* Bölz
Signals Officer:	*Oblt.* Hedergott
Headquarters Company:	*Hptm.* Mikat
4. *Staffel*:	*Oblt.* Tetzner
5. *Staffel*:	*Hptm.* Wienhusen
6. *Staffel*:	*Lt.* Scheufele

The *Gruppe* also did not remain long in Jakobstadt, even though it carried out a number of extremely successful operations from there. On 18 May Weißenberger claimed his 173rd to 175th victories west of Ostrov. Unfortunately *Unteroffizier* Werner Erlinger was posted missing on 9 May. It is not known if he fell victim to enemy fighters or anti-aircraft fire. As well, *Gefreiter* Ziersch of the 5. *Staffel* was killed on 15 May. He was shot down by a Russian fighter southeast of Pustoshka. His Messerschmitt entered a spin and the pilot had no chance to escape.

At the end of the month the entire *Gruppe* was transferred to the Defense of the Reich. After the *Geschwaderstab* moved to Stavanger on 10 May, only III./JG 5 was left on the Polar Sea front. The *Zerstörerstaffel* had been in Herdla since February, the *Jabostaffel* was on its way to Italy, and in June *Hauptmann* Andresen and his 9./JG 5, part of the *II. Gruppe*, left for the Reich, where I./JG 5 had been since February 1944. In the north *Jagdgeschwader 5* had been reduced to two *Gruppen*.

The *II. Gruppe* arrived at Gardelegen, its new base of operations, in the final days of May and came under the command of the *1. Jagddivision*. The pilots had to become accustomed to an entirely new combat situation with significantly different conditions and requirements than those on the Eastern Front. How difficult this task would be, they would be able to gauge from the missions flown by the *I. Gruppe*, which had been in action over the Reich for some weeks. And as the unit had just lost its second *Kommandeur* on 27 May, with the death of *Major* Carganico, Theo Weißenberger, who had been promoted to *Hauptmann* on 1 June, was transferred to I./JG 5 to become its new commanding officer. Simultaneously *Oberleutnant* Hans Tetzner took over the *II. Gruppe*.

The long-planned Allied invasion of Normandy began early in the month of June. The American air forces based in southern England concentrated their operations almost exclusively against targets in France, and raids against targets inside the Reich came to a virtual standstill. The German day fighter units were not transferred to France until Allied troops had set foot on the mainland, and precious time was lost as a result. There is no need to delve any further into why these transfers to the front were not carried out much sooner, but shortsightedness on the part of the highest levels of command was largely responsible for the almost complete absence of German fighter aircraft over the beachhead on 6 June 1944.

Meanwhile the *II. Gruppe*'s ground personnel had covered a lot of ground. One part was still in Großstein, Upper Silesia, while a small element was in Pilsen. There was a serious accident there on 6 June, during the transfer to the Reich, when, for unexplained reasons, a Ju 52 went down about 30 kilometers north of Pilsen and exploded just prior to impact. Thirteen members of the *5. Staffel* were killed.

In Germany the *Gruppe* reequipped on the more heavily-armed Bf 109 G-6. Two 13-mm MG 131 machine-guns replaced the rifle-caliber MG 17s mounted over the engine. Beginning with the G-5 variant, bulged fairings appeared on both sides of the engine cowling in front of the cockpit to cover the heavier-caliber weapons' ammunition feeds and breeches. These resulted in the aircraft being nicknamed the "*Beule*" (bump). Thus equipped, II./JG 5 set out for Evreux in France. During the transfer, on 20 June *Unteroffizier* Scharf crashed while attempting a forced landing in the Verneuil area, while *Feldwebel* Eichelmann went down southwest of Paris after running out of fuel. Both pilots were killed. Two days later eleven of the *Gruppe*'s aircraft attacked a group of American heavy bombers in the Paris area and *Unteroffizier* Demmig of 4./JG 5 was killed in the ensuing combat.

On 23 June a group of eight to ten aircraft of 6./JG 5 ran into a large force of Thunderbolts immediately after takeoff. *Unteroffizier* Giese wrote: "Everything was quite hectic. For me as a beginner it was very difficult to keep track of what was happening. As I later learned, *Fw.* Mecke of our *Staffel* shot an enemy fighter off my tail.

"Suddenly I no longer saw any of our aircraft – just American stars. I tried to escape the Thunderbolts by diving away to the east – which I saw as my only way out. It turned out to be less than an ideal decision, for the much heavier Thunderbolts soon overtook my 'Yellow 14'. A shell struck the armor glass plate behind me and I felt a blow on the back of my head. Half conscious, I pulled back on the stick with both hands and in no time I was back at 1000 meters. I must have been very near to the ground when I pulled up. Still semi-conscious and with blood in my eyes (probably from the head wound) I tried feverishly to get out, but the shell that struck my head armor had jammed the canopy and it refused to budge. Now I was wide awake and pushed against the canopy with both hands. In vain!

"The Americans were now busy using my 109, which was dangling before their noses like a ripe plum, for target practice. Small holes appeared in the wings and with increasing frequency I heard the unpleasant sound of bullets striking. In those seconds I was at least able to make the correct decision to immediately put the nose down and attempt a belly landing. Then a terrible thought went through me that the Americans had shot a hole in my head, for I still had a burning sensation in the back of my head and warm blood was running down my neck. I reached back and felt the back of my head and was happy that I didn't find the suspected hole. Only my hands were covered with blood. All of this happened in a few seconds, and at the same time I rolled over and dove towards the earth at quite high speed, spurred on by fear that my aircraft might be hit and rendered uncontrollable.

"As I dove I pulled the straps as tight as I could, to prevent striking anything during a possible rough crash-landing. Then there was a jerk, and I immediately realized that one undercarriage leg must have come down. The undercarriage position indicator immediately confirmed this. The Thunderbolts had probably shot away the locking mechanism. Nevertheless, I swooped over several fruit trees and put the aircraft down. While still in the air there was a crack and a jerk, as if the undercarriage had been ripped off. The noise was terrific as the aircraft bounced and slid over the ground, before it finally came to rest in a huge cloud of dust. Once I was able to think clearly again, the ensuing silence seemed to me unusual and eerie. Not until I had felt myself was I certain that I had gotten away once again.

"In the distance I heard the roar of aircraft engines and the sound of gunfire. Then I was seized by fear that escaping gasoline might ignite on hot engine parts and set the aircraft on fire, but there was no danger as the engine had been separated from the airframe by the rough belly landing.

"As I was still unable to open the canopy, I began smashing a large cockpit side panel with the shattered pieces of the armored windscreen. While this was going on two Frenchmen came running towards my machine. Given the situation in which I found myself, I had doubts as to whether the approaching pair's intentions were peaceful. From reports, I knew that members of the Gaullist movement were 'liquidating' every 'German' they laid their hands on behind the front. I was lucky, however, and the Frenchmen helped me from the cockpit and even carried me to a country road. Soon afterwards I was picked up by two *SS-Scharführer* in a truck and was later driven to hospital in Bernay."

These were the first serious encounters with the Americans. The fighter pilots had had little time to familiarize themselves with their new opponent and the experience they gained came at a high cost. On 24 June the former *Eismeerjäger* were over the invasion zone. Near Caen the *5. Staffel* was bounced by about 12 to 14 Thunderbolts and the ensuing skirmish resulted in the loss of two officers. *Leutnant* Meyer and *Leutnant* von Thienen were shot down, and it is not known if they were subsequently captured. Three more pilots were lost by the end of the month, two of them from Andresen's *9. Staffel*. *Unteroffizier* Gerhard Siegmund of 4./JG 5 was posted missing after an engagement with about 30 enemy aircraft in the Dreux area.

Because of heavy losses over the invasion front, Headquarters *I. Jagdkorps* ordered a number of day fighter units back to the Reich. There they were initially held at various fighter airfields to rest and reequip. One of them was II./JG 5, even though the *Gruppe* was less battle-weary than other units. In the first month in the west the *Gruppe* had lost nine pilots killed, wounded or missing in just five operations. The following month would see this figure double, and in August losses would triple.

Defensive Struggle over the Homeland

Since 1 July the *II. Gruppe* and attached *9. Staffel* had been in Salzwedel. From there the units took part in defensive operations above the Reich, together with units of JG 3 and JG 300, for after the Allies solidified their front in the west the enemy bomber fleets again turned their attention to strategic targets in Germany. On 6 July the Americans bombed Kiel, then on the 7th more than 1,000 heavy bombers of the 8th Air Force attacked the hydrogenation (synthetic oil) plants in Leuna, Böhlen and Lützkendorf and aircraft factories in the Leipzig area. Simultaneously, the American 15th Air Force based in Italy dispatched an equally-strong bomber force to attack the hydrogenation plants in Blechhammer and Odertal. On this day II./JG 5 would take part in its first major air battle over German soil.

Fierce battles with large formations of Fortresses and Liberators raged over Thuringia and the Harz Mountains. This was also the day when the newly-formed *Sturmgruppe* under *Major* Dahl would achieve its greatest success. The victories achieved came at a high cost, however. 4./JG 5 made contact with the combat boxes of heavy bombers over the Erfurt area. The fighters met fierce defensive fire and almost every attempt to break into the combat formations failed. *Unteroffizier* Heines' "White 12" was hit by return fire from one of the B-17s and he was wounded in the chest. Heines managed to abandon his blazing machine over

Heldrungen but did not survive the bale-out. Fellow *Staffel* member *Oberfähnrich* Dettmann was killed over Keula a short time later.

Four of the *II. Gruppe*'s pilots were wounded in the same engagement. *Gefreiter* Anderweit broke his right arm while baling out, while *Fähnrich* Karl Junker was delivered to the reserve hospital in Aschersleben with a bullet in his calf. He had been shot down by one of the many enemy fighters. *Unteroffizier* Obermeier made an emergency landing near Herzberg in his "Yellow 5", and *Unteroffizier* Gonschorek baled out of his Bf 109 G-6 in the same area.

According to *I. Jagdkorps* records, a total of 62 bombers and six fighters were shot down over Reich territory that Friday. German losses were 13 pilots killed and 16 wounded from IV./JG 3, II./JG 5 and JG 300.* (*According to the official history of the American 8th Air Force, losses on this day were thirty-seven bombers and six fighters. The 15th Air Force undoubtedly suffered additional losses.).

II./JG 5 suffered a grievous loss during the big air battle over western and southwestern Germany on 19 July: its *Kommandeur*, the young *Oberleutnant* Hans Tetzner from Königsberg, was killed over Holzkirchen. An experienced fighter pilot and one of the original *Eismeerjäger*, he had 20 victories to his credit when he died. That day the Americans attacked the Dornier works in Unterpfaffenhofen near Munich, while a secondary group struck the city of Augsburg and the airbase at Lechfeld. Widespread fighting developed over the Munich area and a large number of enemy aircraft were shot down. The defending *II. Gruppe* also lost a number of its aircraft.

After Tetzner's death *Oberstleutnant* Kurt Kettner took over the *Gruppe*, but the very next day another unit leader was lost. In the morning the *Staffeln* took off to intercept four waves of bombers over Saxony. The powerful fighter escort prevented the German fighters from closing with the bombers, resulting in fierce fighter-versus-fighter duels. The Germans were outnumbered, and one of the first to fall was the *Kapitän* of 9./JG 5, *Oberleutnant* Andresen, who was shot down over Neukirchen. *Unteroffizier* Baumann of the same *Staffel* also failed to return. The 5. *Staffel* lost *Unteroffizier* Steinke, who was shot down and killed by a Mustang near Wittenberg.

As part of the expansion of almost every *Gruppe* in the fighter arm to four *Staffeln*, 9./JG 5 was now permanently integrated into the *II. Gruppe*, and at the beginning of August it was renamed 8./JG 5, while the *4. Staffel* became 7./JG 5. After this reorganization, the *Gruppe* flew its next defensive mission on 4 August. On that day the 8th Air Force dispatched a record 1,417 heavy bombers and 750 escorting fighters in several large formations to attack the rocket experimental station in Peenemünde, the port of Kiel, the city of Bremen and the refineries in the Hamburg area. II./JG 5 intercepted the enemy over Altmark and lost three

Other Fronts

pilots. *Unteroffizier* Heitmann of the *6. Staffel* was shot down by a Mustang east of Salzwedel. He baled out successfully but his wounds proved so severe that his left arm had to be amputated.

Losses on 5 August were much worse. Once again the fighters took off to intercept American aircraft in the Hanover-Brunswick-Magdeburg area. On that day the *I. Jagdkorps* put about 100 aircraft into the air and there was bitter fighting, mainly between Bremen and Hanover. Together with the units of JG 3 and JG 300, the fighter pilots scored one victory after another, however losses would exceed successes. II./JG 5 suffered its worse one-day casualties, with four pilots killed, two missing and two wounded. The *8. Staffel* bore the brunt: *Unteroffizier* Amend, *Oberfeldwebel* Sels and *Oberfähnrich* Tengler all fell prey to enemy fighters. Twenty enemy aircraft were shot down on 5 August 1944 for the loss of 29 German fighters.

Given the published production figures, the question constantly arises as to the whereabouts of the German fighter aircraft. A comparison of victories and losses reveals that, in the months of July and August 1944 for example, a total of 550 enemy aircraft were brought down over the Reich by air defense units for the loss of about 630 fighter aircraft. We now know that American losses were only about one percent of total sorties flown, whereas German losses were thirteen times greater. Seen in this way, in the defensive struggle over the Reich the German fighter arm's strength was being steadily eroded despite rising fighter production. The subsequent relentless air raids against the aircraft industry also contributed to this weakening of the fighter arm, and in the weeks and months that followed production figures took a definite downward turn.

Much more serious was the shortage of replacement pilots, for the number of experienced and battle-tested pilots was dropping daily. II./JG 5's situation was no different, and it lost 17 of its pilots in August alone. To name but a few of the unlucky airmen: there was *Gefreiter* Ernst Liebe of 6./JG 5, who was killed in action west of Kirchheim/Teck on 9 August. He was shot down by enemy fighters protecting bombers attacking airfields in southwest Germany. Then there was *Unteroffizier* Thomas, also of the *6. Staffel*, who on the 15th baled out of his "Yellow 12" over Havelte, Holland at a height of just 60 meters. He suffered serious injuries on impact and died the same day. *Unteroffizier* Kortmann of 7./JG 5 baled out over Helmstedt on the 16th. His parachute became caught on the tailplane of his G-6 and he was dragged to his death. *Oberfähnrich* Jusa was shot down during the same mission. Badly wounded, he was delivered to hospital in Einbeck however the doctors were unable to save him. Then there was 21-year-old *Unteroffizier* Weidner, who went missing in the Hamburg area on the 24th. His body was discovered near Uelzen four days later.

On the 25th of August the American air forces carried out another major raid against targets in northern Germany. *Oberstleutnant* Kettner was shot down and killed over Mecklenburg, becoming the second *Kommandeur* lost by the *II. Gruppe* in a short period. Also shot down were *Gefreiter* Heubel of the 7. *Staffel* and *Oberfähnrich* Papenschütz of the 6. *Staffel*. Papenschütz also sustained severe wounds and died three hours after being shot down.

The *Gruppe* subsequently remained on the ground for an entire month and received a well-deserved rest break. The mechanics and repair teams finally found time to work on the damaged aircraft and return them to some degree of operational readiness. On 31 August 1944 the *I. Jagdkorps* reported approximately 470 day fighters on strength, of which about 310 were combat ready. One third of all fighters were thus unavailable for operations due to various reasons (serious battle damage, mechanical trouble, etc.).

During October there were growing rumors that the *II. Gruppe* was going to be reassigned to JG 4 as that unit's *IV. Gruppe*. I./JG 5 had already been renamed III./JG 6 on 14 October. The *Gruppe*, under the command of *Hauptmann* Wienhusen after the death of Kettner, had to take part in one more tough mission on the 16th of October, however. On that day heavy bombers of the American 15th Air Force launched mass attacks against refineries near Brüx and targets in Austria, especially the tank works in St. Valentin and the engine factory in Graz. With bad weather preventing the Allies from conducting strategic operations in the west, the defenses concentrated their efforts over Austria. The action resulted in the loss of 16 German aircraft. The 8. *Staffel* of II./JG 5 fought a running battle with the Americans from over the Sudetenland to the area north of Prague. As far as is known, the powerful fighter escort prevented the unit's pilots from getting to the bombers, and the *Staffel* lost three of its Messerschmitts. *Unteroffizier* Steiner was killed over Willitschin, while *Unteroffizier* Mahnke was shot down in his G-14 over Jeschnitz. *Fähnrich* Ehrhardt ran out of fuel and was obliged to make a forced landing. He put his "Blue 8" down on its belly north of Prague near Postelberg.

These were the last casualties suffered by the *Gruppe* before it moved to Finsterwalde, from where it would take part in the final battles as IV./JG 4. What follows is a brief description of its martyrdom. Wienhusen remained as *Gruppenkommandeur* and at the end of October the unit was organized as follows:

IV./JG 4 (formerly II./JG 5)   *Hptm*. Wienhusen
13./JG 4 (formerly 5./JG 5)   *Lt*. Kunz
14./JG 4 (formerly 6./JG 5)   *Lt*. Scheufele

15./JG 4 (formerly 7./JG 5)	unknown
16./JG 4 (formerly 8./JG 5)	*Oblt.* Schleef

The *Gruppe*'s very first mission from Finsterwalde was a costly one. It was 2 November 1944, a day that saw one of the most extensive air battles of the entire war play out over central Germany. American bombers attacked the synthetic oil plants around Merseburg. They were accompanied by an unusually powerful fighter escort which wrought carnage on the *Jagdgruppen* that took off to intercept the raid. The only units to achieve any success that day were the *Sturmgruppen* of JG 3 and JG 4, which destroyed thirty heavy bombers for the loss of a roughly equal number of their own machines. The other units, however, were barely able to defend themselves against the Mustang escort fighters and suffered heavy losses. It was simply impossible to get through to the bombers, as the enemy fighters were everywhere and demonstrated their air superiority over the Reich. JG 4 alone lost at least 21 aircraft over Saxony. Fourteen pilots were lost, including five from the former *Eismeergruppe*.

Almost all of the German day fighter units were concentrated in northern and western Germany in preparation for the major counterattack planned by the *Wehrmacht*. The so-called "Operation Bodenplatte" would be the central focus of the fighter arm at the end of 1944, however this major operation was kept secret until the last moment. In November JG 4 transferred to airfields in the Frankfurt area. The *IV. Gruppe* was based at the Frankfurt-Main airfield and its pilots and ground personnel were quartered in Sprendlingen.

The unit's next mission on 25 November was also less than successful. The order called for the *Gruppe* to intercept enemy fighter-bombers approaching the Strasbourg area. Between Iffezheim and Rastatt the unit encountered numerous Thunderbolts, which immediately jettisoned their drop tanks and attacked. The result: the *13.*, *14.* and *16. Staffel* each lost a pilot. Three others were wounded, and two of these baled out.

Then came Sunday, the 3rd of December 1944, a fateful day for the *Gruppe*. It was ordered to fly tactical missions in support of the army in the area of front around Aachen, from where the Americans were attempting to advance eastwards. The entire *Gruppe* took off and joined up with I./JG 4. As the aircraft approached the American assembly areas at low level, they encountered a fierce anti-aircraft barrage. Light, medium and heavy guns, including mobile anti-aircraft weapons in short everything the enemy had turned on the approaching Messerschmitts. The result was anything but encouraging. *Gruppenkommandeur Hauptmann* Franz Wienhusen was killed, while *Leutnant* Scheufele, *Kapitän* of 14./JG 4, was shot down and captured. The *15. Staffel* lost three pilots. Altogether, sixteen of JG

4's pilots, including eight from the *IV. Gruppe*, failed to return. Some of these survived and were captured by the Americans.

But even worse was to come. Taking advantage of poor weather, on 16 December the Germans launched the Ardennes offensive. At first they advanced rapidly. The enemy was taken completely by surprise, but just two weeks later the attack ground to a halt. The German forces had no reserves and an improvement in the weather permitted the Allied air forces to intervene again tactically, which ultimately led to the complete disruption of the supply lines in the rear. By that time IV./JG 4 had lost another 13 pilots in its missions over the Reich and attacks in the area of the front. Among those lost was the *Kapitän* of 16./JG 4, *Oberleutnant* Hans Schleef, who went down near Bad Dürkheim on 31 December.

The fighter arm was forced to endure further serious bloodletting on the morning of 1 January 1945 during "Operation Bodenplatte". This was to be its final deathblow. With a few exceptions, the plan, which called for German units to knock out Allied airfields in Holland, Belgium and France in a surprise attack, was a failure. The New Year's action has been described in detail in other publications. A brief summary: JG 4's target was Le Culot airfield in Belgium, where Thunderbolt units were based. The *Gruppen* missed their actual target, causing the attack to lack cohesion. The *Geschwader* lost a total of 23 pilots killed, missing or captured, including eight from IV./JG 4.

On 14 January the battered and exhausted *Gruppe* had to take part in another big air battle over southern Hesse. *Leutnant* Josef Kunz, who at that time was leading the *13. Staffel*, was shot down near Neustadt a.d. Weinstraße. Severely wounded, he was forced to abandon his blazing "White 1". Not until many months later was he able to leave the hospital.

It was becoming ever clearer that the war was almost over. In the final days of January IV./JG 4 and other day fighter units moved to the Eastern Front, which was the source of great danger at that time. The *Gruppe* operated from airfields in Reinsdorf, Welzow, Solpke and Sachau. Then in April it was stationed in Mark-Zwischen near Jüterbog. Together with *Ergänzungsjagdgruppe Ost* it took part in the fighting in the Berlin area.

Oberleutnant Schwanecke, who had been attached to the latter unit for some time, was able to shoot down a Yak-3 on 12 April and an Il-2 on the 17th. Early in the afternoon on 20 April 1945 Schwanecke claimed what was probably the last victory over the Reich by a former member of the *Eismeergeschwader*, a Spitfire. He subsequently took part in fighter-bomber missions against Russian tank and infantry concentrations within the city limits of Berlin.

In Jüterbog IV./JG 5 gradually disintegrated. Elements of the ground personnel were drawn into the final battle for Berlin, while most of the aircrew were able to escape to the north. Then on 2 May the German surrender ended the bloody struggle.

"Westside Story" – Standing Guard over Norway's Fjords

The last time we turned our attention to the *IV. Gruppe* of JG 5 it was the summer of 1943. It had meanwhile relieved I./JG 5, which had gone to Rumania and then to the Defense of the Reich. At that time the *Gruppenstab* and the *10. Staffel* (*Oberleutnant* Schneider) were in Trondheim, the *11. Staffel* (*Staffel* commander not known) in Stavanger and the *12. Staffel* (*Oberleutnant* Lüder) in Herdla. Compared to the big actions on the Polar Sea, operational activity on the west coast was much quieter. Victories were few and casualties were also modest. Most losses were the result of accidents or other non-operational causes. On 24 August, for example, *Unteroffizier* Kauper flew into the ground near Kirkehustadt and was killed. Then, during a scramble from Stavanger on 30 August, the aircraft flown by *Unteroffizier* Neugebauer stalled at a height of 30 meters and crashed, killing the pilot. *Unteroffizier* Homann crashed into the sea during an escort mission on 4 September.

Until then the *Staffeln* had primarily been employed to escort warships and merchant vessels, intercept high-flying Mosquito reconnaissance aircraft, and conduct fighter patrols. Contact with enemy aircraft was quite rare. The focal point of the enemy's incursions shifted increasingly to the area of Cape Stadlandet, where north- or southbound German convoys had to leave the protection of the fjords and sail round the cape. The area between the bases in Trondheim and Herdla was too great for German fighters to effectively intervene against attacks on the convoys, and it was decided to use the island of Gossen as a base of operations. A *Schwarm* from 10./JG 5 moved there towards the end of September and the rest of the *Staffel* followed in late autumn. The transfer did not go entirely smoothly, however, for on 10 October *Unteroffizier* Nieke collided with another Focke-Wulf and crashed into the sea.

The unit's fighters occasionally encountered Beaufighter reconnaissance aircraft, but as the flying time from Gossen to the Cape was still about 15 minutes, including time to scramble, the fighters usually arrived after the enemy had flown away.

On 24 September *General* Harmjanz, the commanding officer of the Air District Command Norway, paid the *12. Staffel* a visit in Herdla. The purpose of his visit was to advise that the battle-cruiser *Lützow* was going to be sailing south and that the *Staffel* would be responsible for providing air cover. For this purpose 11./JG 5 and the *Zerstörerstaffel* were moved to Herdla.

Jagdgeschwader 5

On 10 October 1943 there was hectic activity in Herdla. The *Lützow* had slipped through safely, however there had been difficulties, as bad weather delayed the *10. Staffel*'s arrival from Gossen. It did not arrive completely in Herdla until noon. The escort mission was completed without incident, although the battle-cruiser and its escorting warships were spotted by British reconnaissance aircraft. That same evening two Blenheims appeared over Sognefjord. After scrambling to intercept the intruders, *Oberleutnant* Lüder spotted an aircraft at a height of 200 meters, however the suspected enemy aircraft turned out to be a Ju 52. A regretful Lüder subsequently declared, "So much for my victory!"

A *Rotte* from the *10. Staffel* had better luck four days later. On 14 October *Leutnant* Prenzler and *Unteroffizier* Halstrick took off to patrol the Stadlandet area, where they shot down a lone Beaufighter. On 8 December the *Rotte* of *Unteroffizier* Becker and *Unteroffizier* Halstrick sent another Beaufighter into the sea in the same area.

Shortly after 08:00 on 25 October, Lüder, who had been acting *Gruppenkommandeur* since the beginning of the month, filling in for *Hauptmann* Kriegel who was on leave, received a telephone call informing him that two British motor torpedo boats had been sighted north of Trondheim. An alert *Rotte* immediately took off, but something went wrong. From a height of just a few meters, the aircraft flown by *Feldwebel* Wawrzin suddenly crashed and exploded. His wingman, *Unteroffizier* Felser, continued the flight alone, but he soon returned after failing to locate the British vessels. Meanwhile *Oberleutnant* Schneider had also taken off with three Fw 190s. Fifteen minutes later Lüder led three more Fw 190s into the air. A fourth, piloted by *Leutnant* Hoffmann, had to stay behind because of a blown tire.

The estimated position of the enemy ships was about 70 kilometers north of the Halten lighthouse. On arriving there Lüder spotted two white wakes. As the aircraft were flying spaced far apart, he first had to summon his wingmen, *Oberleutnant* Beyer and *Unteroffizier* Sepharim, but the element of surprise was lost. After joining up into a loose formation, the three fighters, coming from out of the sun, descended to three meters above the wave tops. The British opened fire while with tracing ammunition while they were still far off. The first firing pass left the trailing vessel smoking. Two more attacks followed, with the fighters attacking from different directions simultaneously.

Later another five aircraft of 10./JG 5 took off. They located the first boat adrift in its previous position, strafed it and left it in flames. A search for the second boat was unsuccessful. One week later the *12. Staffel* was also involved in an action with an enemy torpedo boat. *Feldwebel* Schalk spotted it first, then three pairs of fighters attacked one after the other. On the first pass *Leutnant* Metz's aircraft was hit by 40-mm anti-aircraft fire and he was forced to break off the attack. The pilots subsequently lost sight of the boat and were unable to find it again. *Feldwebel* Reitmeier took off in the air-sea rescue *Weihe*, but he too was unable to locate the torpedo boat. The last *Rotte* lost its way and by the time it returned to base it was completely dark. Schalk landed without incident, however *Unteroffizier* Suth ended up putting his aircraft down on its belly.

Over time Norway became of increasing importance to the German armaments industry. Located about 125 kilometers west of Oslo, the Norsk Hydro plant, which produced heavy water, of vital importance in nuclear research, became Defense Objective No.1, while the industrial area with the molybdenum mines in Knaben, about 90 kilometers southeast of Stavanger, became Defense Objective No.2. The British had already attacked both targets in December 1942 and March 1943. On 16 November two formations of USAAF B-17s entered Norwegian airspace, one headed for Rjukan, the other Knaben. It appears that only a part of 11./JG 5 intercepted the enemy over the coast. *Gefreiter* Schmiletzky's *Gustav* was hit and caught fire and the wounded pilot was forced to take to his parachute near Egesund. It is uncertain whether any of the bombers were shot down, however two Fortresses failed to make it back to England.

Until the end of the year IV./JG 5's losses remained within limits. In November the *Gruppe* reported just four pilots wounded. *Feldwebel* Paul Schalk and *Unteroffizier* Sepharim both made forced landings on 7 November. In both cases the cause was mechanical trouble, as neither was due to enemy action. Five days earlier *Gefreiter* Ziersch had been forced to ditch near Stavanger.

Unteroffizier Willi Sürth, the pleasant native of Cologne, was killed during a scramble from Gossen on 16 December. He had just taken off when a Mosquito suddenly emerged from the clouds and shot him down from a height of 50 meters. The Focke-Wulf *Weihe* search and rescue aircraft that had also taken off suffered the same fate. Two days later *Unteroffizier* Fleischhauer went missing near Stadlandet. The last casualty of 1943 was due to an unfortunate accident which claimed the life of *Oberfeldwebel* Lindinger. On 27 December he crashed from a height of 400 meters while performing aerobatics, which was contrary to orders, over Stavanger-Sola airfield.

Unteroffizier Brenner of 12./JG 5 was lost on 4 January 1944. He must either have flown into a rocky outcropping or crashed into the sea somewhere. All that wingman *Feldwebel* Simme could say was that Brenner was suddenly no longer there.

At the beginning of February the headquarters and 12./JG 5 moved to Stavanger. At the same time *Oberleutnant* Lüder was named *Geschwader* adjutant and handed his *12. Staffel* over to *Oberleutnant* Beyer, but first he had to take part in one more mission. On 6 February the *Kriegsmarine* carried out a small operation near Stadlandet, for which the *IV. Gruppe* was supposed to provide air cover. On that day *Unteroffiziere* Hornberger, Merkl and Reber picked up three Fw 190s for the *10. Staffel* in Gossen, but they never arrived there. It began when *Oberleutnant* Schneider reported the three Fw 190s overdue. There was radio contact with one of them, however the aircraft's position was not known. Later it was learned that, after losing the other two, Hornberger had made a safe belly landing in Hoyanger in the Sognefjord. In the evening word was received that another pilot was safe on the island of Fjell. It was *Unteroffizier* Reber. Merkl, however, who was never found. After he was picked up, Reber related that, while the pair was descending through a hole in the cloud, he suddenly got the feeling that Merkl's machine had stalled. A subsequent investigation turned up nothing, and it was not until 13 September 1944 that the *Unteroffizier*'s body was discovered near Förde, about 100 kilometers northeast of Bergen.

In the spring the British resumed their attacks on German convoys along the entire west coast of Norway, and it was not until May, probably because of preparations for the invasion, that the sector became quieter again. On 30 March the *IV. Gruppe* encountered a formation of Beaufighters, seven of which were shot down. *Hauptmann* Kriegel was one of the successful pilots. *Leutnant* Hoffmann, IV./JG 5's technical officer, was forced to ditch in the sea northwest of Koparvik and was reported missing. One day later *Oberfähnrich* Kümpfel of the *12. Staffel* crashed into the sea as a result of engine failure.

British aircraft carriers now began operating off the Norwegian coast, as on 8 May, when the *10. Staffel* took off to intercept carrier-based Hellcat and Corsair fighters. *Leutnant* Prenzler, *Unteroffizier* Halstrick, *Oberfähnrich* Otto and *Unteroffizier* Brettin caught up with the enemy aircraft as they were on their way back to their carrier. One was shot down by Prenzler and Halstrick claimed two more. The other *Rotte* failed to return to Gossen, however. Both pilots went missing in the Kristiansund area.

In about mid-May 1944 all of the *Staffeln* of the *IV. Gruppe* were renamed. The *10. Staffel* became 13./JG 5, the *11. Staffel* 14./JG 5 and the *12. Staffel* 15./JG 5. Later, in November, the *Gruppe* was to receive a fourth *Staffel*, the newly-established 16./JG 5 under *Leutnant* Hans Vollet, which was formed in Stavanger. In the meantime *Hauptmann* Kriegl had handed command of the *Gruppe* over to *Hauptmann* Fritz Stendel, who would lead it until the end of the war.

10./JG 5, now equipped with Fw 190s, had meanwhile moved to Lister, in order to intercept the larger enemy incursions together with the *Staffeln* in Stavanger and Herdla. On the second to last day of the month there was a lengthy air battle with about 20 Beaufighters and 20 Mustangs off the south coast of

Norway. *Leutnant* Salz was killed and two other pilots of the *11. Staffel* were reported missing: *Unteroffizier* Kreikemeier and *Unteroffizier* Kwiotkowski. *Leutnant* Horst Mülling of 12./JG 5 also went missing.

Most operations failed to result in contact with the enemy, even though large incursions were frequently reported. Each time the *Staffeln* scrambled and then assembled over the Rjukan area to defend the Norsk Hydro plant. On 28 August the *12. Staffel* lost its *Kapitän* in a tragic accident. Over the Saltenfjord he collided with the Messerschmitt of *Unteroffizier* Fuchs and subsequently crashed. It is not known who took over the *Staffel* after Beyer's death.

In the autumn the situation on the Polar Sea front began to come to a head. It appeared to be just a matter of time before the Russians launched a major offensive there. To bolster the *Jagdstaffeln* based in the Finland, IV./JG again moved to the far north for a brief period. At the end of August-beginning of September the *Gruppe* found itself in Salmijärvi, Petsamo, Nautsi and Berlevaag, but in October it was forced to fall back before the advancing Russians and moved to airfields in Kaamanen, Bardufoss and Kjevik. As the *IV. Gruppe* operated together with III./JG 5, these combined operations, which represented the *Geschwader*'s final battles, will be described in the following chapter.

Chapter 5
Back on the West Coast

Retreat from Finland

When, on the night of 3 September 1944, the Finnish government unexpectedly presented the Germans with an ultimatum to leave the country by 15 September, the German divisions were almost 400 kilometers from the ports on the Gulf of Bothnia and more than 600 kilometers from the north Finnish-Norwegian border. On 19 September Finland signed a ceasefire agreement in Moscow and thus officially ended the war against the Soviet Union.

Suddenly the erstwhile comrades in arms – Germans and Finns – faced each other as enemies. Relations with the Finns had always been characterized by an almost legendary mutual respect, and so it was more than a tragedy when the *Eismeerjäger* now encountered Finnish "enemies", as on 6 October 1944. Shortly before noon a *Schwarm* from 9./JG 5 took off from Rovaniemi to fly escort for seven Ju 87s whose mission was to bomb ground targets and troop concentrations near Tornio. Just short of the target the fighters engaged three Ju 88s with Finnish markings and two SB-2s. The following is from the victory witness report filed by *Feldwebel* Bößenecker:

"At 11:45 we made contact with five Finnish bombers. In the course of the action I saw *Uffz.* Artner attack an enemy Ju 88 from behind. After an effective burst of fire the Ju 88 showed a dark smoke trail and crashed vertically into the water. The crash occurred about 12 kilometers south of Kemi at 11:50."

On 7 October the enemy launched a major offensive in the north. The first and decisive blow struck the thin, strongpoint-style front held by the German mountain troops southeast of Petsamo, an attack that such a front was unable to withstand. The Russians bypassed the German strongpoints and left them, at least those that had not been pulverized by artillery fire, to be surrounded and mopped up by the following reserves. One day later the Red Army, supported by powerful bombers, close-support and fighter units, also launched an offensive at the Titovka River. The German positions, thought to be impregnable, were overrun.

Petsamo was now threatened and in places the Soviet spearheads were little more then ten kilometers from the airfield. There was great commotion among the fighter *Staffeln*, especially as there was total uncertainty as to the situation to the south of the base. One scramble followed another and the *Staffeln* were tasked to the limit. The last aircraft were barely off the ground when the first aircraft began landing again. Then it happened – *Oberleutnant* Kirchmeier, who had just returned to JG 5 from night-fighter training and who had scored two victories on the morning of that 8 October, set up for a landing with two anti-personnel bombs still beneath the wings of his Fw 190. For reasons unexplained the undercarriage failed to lower, and when the aircraft touched the ground it was literally torn to pieces by the exploding bombs. Any help was too late for the *Oberleutnant*.

One day later, on 9 October, *Jagdgeschwader 5* achieved another great success. Once again the Russian formations appeared in unprecedented strength. The final total that day was 85 victories, including the *Geschwader*'s 3,000th. It was an extraordinary result. Lüder contributed a Pe-2, while *Oberfeldwebel* Birk of 12./JG 5 added an Il-2 and two Airacobras.

Petsamo was abandoned. The *Staffeln* were supposed to fall back in stages to Bardufoss, while the bulk of the ground personnel was already on its way to Kirkenes. Already on 10 October the Russians began laying mortar fire upon the fighter units' bases and, after much back and forth, the flying elements took off for Kirkenes in the afternoon. *Unteroffizier* Suske of 10./JG 5, one of the *Staffel*'s rising stars, was hit by flak during the transfer flight. He attempted to bale out of his shot-up "Black 7", however he struck the ground near the airfield before his parachute could fully deploy. A small party went back across the Petsamo River to erect a simple wooden cross at the crash site. That was all that they could do for their fallen comrade.

Soon after the fighters took off, a Russian reindeer brigade appeared on the grounds of the airfield. The last fighter pilot to depart was *Leutnant* von Podewils, who took off from Petsamo, which had been home to the *Eismeerjäger* for just under three years, in the Fieseler *Storch* PP+QU at 10:10 on 11 October. With signals *Unteroffizier* Obermüller on board, von Podewils evaded the enemy ground fire without difficulty, but just short of Kirkenes five Airacobra fighters suddenly appeared. Through a skillful turning maneuver he finally shook off the enemy fighters on the dark side of the fjord and at 11:20 landed safely in Kirkenes.

The Soviets began large-scale attacks on Kirkenes on the 11th. They came with Bostons, Il-2s and large formations of fighters, leaving the port ablaze. The pilots of JG 5 shot down 25 enemy machines. *Unteroffizier* Schmiletzky was initially posted missing after a fight with six Airacobras, however three days later he returned wounded to the *14. Staffel*. At that time IV./JG 5 was still in Salmijärvi.

Each day brought a series of tough combats, such as on 12 October when the *III. Gruppe* lost *Unteroffizier* Heinelt and *Unteroffizier* Hornberger. The Russians finally took Petsamo on 15 October. The 19th Mountain Army Corps was forced to give up Parkkina and withdraw in the direction of Kirkenes. The big military cemetery in Parkkina, where so many of the *Geschwader*'s fighter pilots were buried, was rolled flat by Russian tanks. The same day *Leutnant* Fritz Simme was lost. He shot down four enemy aircraft over Petsamo, including a LaGG-5, but was hit by anti-aircraft fire. He was probably unable to escape from his burning Messerschmitt. Simme was one of the last surviving pilots of the old *12. Staffel* and had been selected to command the new *16. Staffel*.

On 16 October enemy torpedo-bombers appeared over a German convoy off Kiberg. There was a scramble from Kirkenes: Ehrler, Lüder and a pilot of the *11. Staffel*, plus Dörr and the adjutant. Visibility over the Polar Sea was extremely poor. When the five aircraft reached the convoy the Soviet formation was at their ten o'clock position, with a large number of Airacobras slightly higher at about 600 meters. The roughly 17 Bostons were just approaching the convoy, making them top priority. Ehrler had already shot down one Boston, when Lüder opened fire, however his first burst, fired from a left-hand turn, was short of the target. The second was more accurate and the bomber's port engine burst into flames. Lüder passed beneath the Boston and found himself alongside another. Suddenly a wave of Il-2 appeared over the ships. Lüder got one in his sights and pressed the firing buttons. Pieces flew off the Russian aircraft. He just avoided the doomed Russian before setting course for Petsamo, where he landed with a dented engine cowling and spinner. Both of his victories were confirmed by Dörr.

In the evening the Soviets returned to the convoy and torpedoed and sank the mine-sweeper R 301.

On 17 October Russian aircraft were reported nearing another convoy off Eckerö. The German fighters were scrambled, and in hazy conditions they came upon a group of Il-2s and Bostons, above which hung Airacobra and Yak-9 fighters. The close-support aircraft were already sweeping over the German ships, but, ignoring the threat posed by their ship's anti-aircraft guns, the Messerschmitts closed in and attacked. They succeeded in shooting down a total of 17 Il-2s. *Unteroffizier* Fuchs was shot down by a Yak-9. *Leutnant* Wollmann shot down one enemy aircraft, but then he was hit in the left wing and undercarriage by the rear gunner of an Il-2. Despite a shot-up tire, he landed safely in Kirkenes. Luckily for him his aircraft did not overturn. Behind the cockpit of his "Black 12" there was a hole so large that a man could easily have passed through it, and the pilots of 7./JG 5 were amazed that he got back to Kirkenes at all.

Back on the West Coast

Finally the *IV. Gruppe* moved from Salmijärvi to Nautsi, while the *Stab* and III./JG 5 transferred to Kaamanen. First, however, the installations in Kirkenes were supposed to be destroyed to prevent a repetition of what had happened in Petsamo. More than a million liters of fuel plus materiel, quarters and camp allegedly fell into Russian hands intact, enabling them to continue flight operations without interruption.

On 22 October the enemy appeared to be executing a major operation. The alert *Rotten* were scrambled, and east of Salmijärvi they came upon two huge gaggles of Il-2s and fighters heading in the opposite direction, 40 to 50 aircraft altogether. While the Germans stayed just beneath the clouds so as to approach the enemy unseen, ground control reported multi-engine bombers approaching Kirkenes. The fighters had to turn round and head for Kirkenes. In the distance the pilots could see flak bursts. Near the harbor they saw swarms of Il-2s with fighter escort. Lüder closed in from below, but then he was spotted by the Russian fighters. He rolled left and dove, then latched onto several Il-2s flying low over the fjord. "I made three attacks and observed hits each time," he recalls. The Il-2 in front of me turned like mad, the rear gunner fired, the Russians behind me also fired, plus there was anti-aircraft fire. I suddenly felt a powerful draft on the left side of my face. Fortunately it wasn't a hit – the cockpit window had just blown out. When I was again able to turn my attention to the Il-2, I saw it and several Airacobras flying away to the left and right. Finally I turned away too. I returned to Kirkenes exhausted, soaked in sweat and with a bullet hole in my tail."

Kommodore Ehrler shot down his 199th enemy aircraft that day. The *9. Staffel* lost one of its pilots, however. The day before *Fähnrich* von Lilienhoff had been shot down by a Yak-9. On this day 18-year-old *Fähnrich* Dellbrück was killed when his "White 15" overturned while taking off and went up in flames.

A mood of defeatism prevailed in Kirkenes and the city lay in soot and ashes. Now, on Reich Party Day, the Russians flew overhead almost unhindered. *Hauptmann* Malottki, a long-range reconnaissance pilot, who always knew how to lift spirits with his humorous sayings, ended up on his back while landing. Pilots and ground personnel of 9./JG 5 tried to rescue him from his burning aircraft, but before they could get to him the machine's fuel tanks and ammunition exploded. There was nothing left to save, and the next day he and *Fähnrich* Dellbrück were buried near the airfield. *Feldwebel* Mondschein, a member of the reconnaissance unit, took several photos of the gravesite, which was probably leveled by the Soviets soon afterwards. Mondschein, who had recently shot down an Il-2, subsequently took off on a transfer flight but was attacked by enemy fighters. He tried to return to the airfield, his aircraft trailing smoke, but he was forced to come down in the bay. He was seen swimming in the icy water and he was finally rescued, but the pilot did not survive the night.

By then Ehrler, whose aircraft was undergoing an engine change, Lüder, Gayko and *Oberfeldwebel* Villing, who was temporarily leading Schuck's *Staffel*, were the last of the *Geschwader*'s pilots on the airfield. Given the few available aircraft and the enemy's numerical superiority, there was no point in attempting another mission. On 23 October 1944 Gayko left Kirkenes with the last pair of fighters and headed for Kaamanen. From there he flew on to Banak, arriving there at 14:10. The *Luftwaffe*'s presence in Finland had come to an end.

Meanwhile in Kirkenes the Russians had begun repairing the airfield, which the Germans had rendered unusable when they left. The Red Army's front line was now near Neiden. At the front things had quieted down somewhat, and on the 7th of November German troops crossed the Tana River, losing contact with the Russians in places. There were perhaps political reasons why the Soviet pursuit was slow, for they were now on Norwegian territory. On the other hand, overextended supply lines may also have been to blame. A mountain army corps was still near Kaamanen, but there too the Russians and their new Finnish ally followed tentatively. The entire German withdrawal was made in the direction of Kautokeino.

Following the evacuation and destruction of Kirkenes, Banak was the temporary base of operations for the *Stab* and remnants of III./JG 5, which had just seven serviceable aircraft. There was still combat in the air, however. *Feldwebel* Scharwächter of 13./JG 5, which by then was in Berlevaag, was killed on 24 October. There was a scramble and he was shot down in combat with a large number of P-40s and Il-2s over the Varanger Peninsula in northern Norway. In Banak, almost 200 kilometers from the front, the fighter pilots finally got a well-deserved rest. None were unaffected by the hectic events of recent days, particularly in Kirkenes. New aircraft arrived, 56 Messerschmitts altogether. And that at the end of 1944! The men had not seen deliveries of new aircraft on such a scale for a long time.

On 6 November the *IV. Gruppe* moved without aircraft to Stavanger, where it was issued new Bf 109 G-6s, while the *9. Staffel* took over the remaining Focke-Wulfs. Two days later III./JG 5 went to Bardufoss. There the *Gruppe* immediately began converting onto the Fw 190. The 12th of November fell during these preparations. That momentous day was to be one of the most unfortunate in the history of *Jagdgeschwader 5*: the day that British bombers sank the battleship *Tirpitz*.

The Tirpitz Affair

With the statement on 25 March 1942 that the elimination of the battleship *Tirpitz* would completely change the situation of the war at sea, the British war cabinet began the hunt for the biggest battleship to operate in European waters during the Second World War. It was to last more than two years. Enemy intelligence had followed every move made by the *Tirpitz* since its launching in April 1939, and even as the huge vessel was undergoing sea trials in the Baltic the British succeeded in estimating its speed – 27 to 31 knots – based on aerial photos. Such a battleship would tie up defensive forces wherever it went. A direct attack on the *Tirpitz* would be extremely costly, and there was no certainty that the ship could even be sunk in this manner. It was a colossus 242 meters long with a displacement of 52,600 tons, armed with twenty 150-mm and 380-mm guns, thirty-two 37-mm and 105-mm anti-aircraft guns, more than fifty 20-mm guns and eight quadruple torpedo tubes.

Since the spring of 1942 the *Tirpitz* had been in Faetten Fjord near Trondheim, where it posed a constant threat to the Allied convoys sailing to Murmansk. A double anti-submarine net barrier, which was also supposed to block aerial torpedoes, surrounded the well-camouflaged ship. The British also found the warship there, but their air attacks in 1942 were unsuccessful. Minor damage was quickly repaired and the *Tirpitz* remained seaworthy and dangerous. At the end of the year the battleship moved to Alta Fjord and anchored in its southernmost part, the Kaa Fjord. Once again the ship was heavily defended.

The British then tried a new weapon. On 22 September 1943 they attacked with miniature submarines. Despite heavy casualties, they managed to penetrate the numerous nets and barricades and inflicted heavy damage on the *Tirpitz*. Not until the beginning of March 1944 was the battleship again combat ready.

On 3 April British bombers struck again, scoring a number of hits. Another raid on 17 July was unsuccessful. But meanwhile in England they had developed the 12,000-pound Tallboy bomb, which was now to be used against the *Tirpitz*. As the Lancaster bombers could not reach Alta Fjord in a direct flight – the bases in Scotland were almost 2000 kilometers away – an agreement was reached with the Russians that enabled the RAF to briefly station its bombers in Yakolnik near Arkhangelsk on the White Sea. On 15 September 1944 twenty-eight aircraft took off from there and crossed northern Finland at low altitude. The attack inflicted heavy damage on the *Tirpitz* and the battleship was later towed to Tromsö Fjord where it was thought it would be safer.

Two further air attacks, on 22 and 29 October, missed the battleship. But then came 12 November 1944. Wing Commander Tait led thirty-one Lancasters of Nos.9 and 617 Squadrons into the air from Lossiemouth in northern Scotland. The latter unit had gained fame for its attack on the German dams in May 1943. To deceive the German air defenses, the Lancasters flew at low level to Sweden and then turned over Torneträsk Lake. The battleship, anchored in the Sandnessund, was taken completely by surprise and was struck by several Tallboy bombs. In less than half an hour the *Tirpitz* capsized and *Kapitän zur See* Weber and almost 1,000 members of his crew were killed.

The destruction of the *Tirpitz* had disastrous consequences for the German air defense service and *Jagdgeschwader 5*. Much has been written about the loss of this ship, but what really happened and why did the *Staffeln* of JG 5 not intervene in time? *Kommodore* Ehrler, one of the most successful fighter pilots on the Polar Sea front and a wearer of the Oak Leaves, was brought before a court martial. It was obvious that adequate measures had not been taken to defend the battleship, but were they now seeking a scapegoat to take the blame for the catastrophe in Tromsö Fjord?

We will try to reconstruct the events of 12 November 1944. That morning the Mosjoen radar station on the island of Doenna picked up the Lancaster formation. Far to the south, the enemy aircraft were heading towards Sweden. More than an hour later, observers suddenly spotted four-engined bombers north of Torneträsk Lake heading north. That was when air defense center in Bardufoss ordered the fighters of JG 5 to the Swedish-Norwegian border, anticipating an attack on the *Tirpitz*.

Since completing its withdrawal from Finland, the 9. *Staffel* under *Oberleutnant* Gayko had been stationed in Bardufoss and was in the process of reequipping on the Fw 190. It received 22 aircraft of various subtypes, which were also equipped with different radio equipment. Consequently radio communication was only possible between aircraft of the same series. Gayko himself wrote of that 12 November:

"Our orders read: reequip and defend the airfield. Nothing was said about defending the *Tirpitz*. We only knew from reports that it was anchored near Tromsö. That was a restricted area. There was a chain of hills at one end of the runway in Bardufoss; consequently we could only scramble in the other direction, towards Sweden. The *Staffel* command post and the blast pens were at the opposite end; consequently there were delays in taking off on account of the lengthy taxi times. On the morning of 12 November I was in the officer's quarters when a general air raid alert was sounded. I saw a number of four-engined aircraft in loose formation over the airfield at a height of about 1000 to 2000 meters. *Hauptmann* Dörr and I immediately drove to the runway, where he left me the vehicle so that I could get to the *Staffel* command post more quickly. He went on foot to the fighter control station. The *Staffel*, about 18 aircraft strong, had meanwhile taken off, except for one Focke-Wulf whose engine would not start. In that aircraft was the *Staffel* officer. I ordered him out and was able to get the engine running. I then took off at 09:30, about ten minutes after the rest of the *Staffel*.

After takeoff, while climbing out I saw anti-aircraft fire on the horizon and set course for it. Several minutes before I got there the anti-aircraft fire ceased. Arriving off Tromsö, I saw a large ship lying keel-up – there was no sign of the enemy or my *Staffel*. I changed altitude several times but was unable to find anyone. There was no radio contact and after a long unsuccessful search I returned to Bardufoss.

In my opinion the failure to intercept the British was due to the late and also too lengthy takeoff time. Instead of the prescribed three minutes, which was achieved at other airfields, the *Staffel* required nine minutes to get airborne because of the unusual layout of Bardufoss airfield.

Just before I landed I came upon a four-engined aircraft, which I twice attacked from the front. Each time my guns jammed after firing a few rounds. Suddenly a Messerschmitt also appeared nearby, however it did not take part in the attack. I was forced to break off my attacks as I had reached the Swedish border. I subsequently landed in Bardufoss at 10:38."

Major Ehrler, the *Kommodore*, was also in the air. He had just arrived in Bardufoss from Banak in his Bf 109 and was about to take off for Alta when the British bombers appeared. He and *Leutnant* Schuck immediately took off at the head of the *Staffeln* stationed in Bardufoss. He later pursued a lone Lancaster and it must have been – his aircraft which *Oberleutnant* Gayko had seen during his two attacks on the Lancaster. Ehrler also abandoned his pursuit of the enemy aircraft, as they were already over Swedish territory. Recently, near Kemi in Finland, Gayko's wingman had shot down a Swedish aircraft that had tried to attack him. This resulted in a great deal of anger and diplomatic entanglements and explains why the pilots tried at all costs to avoid infringing upon Swedish airspace. On the other hand, the violation of Swedish airspace by the British bombers must be seen as much more serious.

At the time of the incident the *Stab* and III./JG 5 were the only fighter units based in northern Norway: the *Geschwaderstab* and the *11. Staffel* (Glöckner) in Alta, and, apart from the previously mentioned 9./JG 5, the *10. Staffel* (Schuck) and *12. Staffel* (Linz), since 8 November in Bardufoss, about ten minutes flying time from Tromsö. On that 12 November, a Sunday, the *Staffeln* were holding ten-minute readiness. After the air-raid sirens went off, at about 09:10, *Oberleutnant* Kurt Schulze, adjutant of the *III. Gruppe*, rushed to the command post where he met Dörr. The air situation map revealed that, because of an extra number added by mistake, the enemy aircraft were initially reported to be farther south near

Alta instead of near Bodö. This may have been why the *Staffeln* in Bardusfoss were not informed sooner. After the situation map was corrected, it was revealed that the heavy bombers had come in south of Bodö heading east and had now left Norwegian territory in the direction of Sweden. The purpose of the enemy incursion was therefore unclear, and it was surmised that the British were flying on to Russia.

Kurt Schulze still remembers exactly what followed: "The situation map analysts then received an unpleasant surprise when, suddenly, a formation of enemy bombers was reported over the Norway-Sweden-Finland border triangle, about five minutes flying time away. The reaction: air raid alarm and scramble for the fighters based in Bardufoss. As soon as we had been briefed on the enemy's course, Dörr and I immediately took off. Takeoff was about eleven minutes after the air raid alarm. Once airborne I heard a report over the radio: 'Anti-aircraft fire over Tromsö!' This must have been at the time of the attack on the *Tirpitz*. When we reached Tromsö there was nothing to be seen of the enemy aircraft, for it had taken us 15 minutes to get their on a direct course, including time to climb. We received no more reports on the position of the enemy formation, and so I headed straight for home and was one of the first to land. I assumed that *Major* Ehrler, who had been the first to take off, had made contact with the enemy, and, as he never returned without a victory, my comrades and I began making preparations to congratulate him on his 200th victory. During this time a four-engined bomber flew right over the airbase at 3000 to 4000 meters. The aircraft still in the air were immediately advised by radio, however they were unable to shoot it down as the Lancaster very quickly ducked into Swedish airspace."

Several accounts of the "Tirpitz affair" published after the war claim that the German fighter pilots failed to find Tromsö. Now the pilots of JG 5 had flown over Lapland, over the tundra and over the primeval forests of Karelia – why then would they have failed to find their way to Tromsö in an area with such distinctive fjords and roads? Furthermore Tromsö could be seen from a height of about 1500 meters over the airbase. The claim that the captain of the *Tirpitz* was in contact with the *Jagdgruppe* by telephone prior to the attack is also false, as only a very few even knew of the battleship's presence in Tromsö Fjord.

Be that as it may, immediately after the sinking of the *Tirpitz* all participants from the *Luftwaffe*, flak and the signals corps as well as from the navy were brought before a court martial in Oslo. As the naval personnel were tried separately, there is no information as to the outcome. *Geschwaderkommodore* Ehrler, however, was sentenced to three years imprisonment and about ten officers of the signals corps and the flak received lengthy jail terms. In Gayko's opinion the verdict against Ehrler was fabricated. He was not found guilty of the sinking of the *Tirpitz*, rather because as fighter control officer he had left a senior non-commissioned officer in his place, which was contrary to orders. "At that time we couldn't leave any officer on the ground, because the few who were still there had to fly. Our mistakes and our handicaps were probably as follows:

1. Insufficient warning of the approaching enemy formation
2. Absence of an operational order to defend the *Tirpitz*
3. Impairment of the *Staffel*'s operational capability as a result of the just-completed conversion [onto the Fw 190] and poor airfield conditions"

Oberleutnant Schulze reached a similar conclusion: "Despondently we trudged to the command post, where the first alarming reports were coming in. The officers of the staff of the general of the German air force in Norway and of the Air Commander Lofoten had suddenly awakened from their hibernation and for the first time told us that the *Tirpitz* was in Tromsö and had been 'overturned' by the attack. What to do now? Whom could they shift the blame onto? As it soon turned out, the *Eismeerjäger* would be the whipping boys. One thunderstorm after another came down the already visibly heated lines: cowardice in the face of the enemy, a breach of the *Reichsmarschall*'s orders, trial before the Reich court martial by order of the *Führer*, immediate investigation. The first interrogations took place that night. Our first written statements were put to paper that same afternoon. *Major* Ehrler, two officers of the staff and I added sentence after sentence. After an hour the fighter pilots, known opponents of the paper war, were tired of debating and reproached me for attaching far too much importance to clarifying the question of guilt. 'If they make too much trouble for us, then in the future they can go up themselves' – with these and similar words they expressed their indignation. They were confident that they had no one to fear in the air, for *Major* Ehrler and *Hauptmann* Dörr had claimed about 320 victories between them.

"They tried to place the entire blame on Ehrler and Dörr. How convinced the two were of their innocence was shown by the fact that *Hauptmann* Dörr fell asleep during the trial. The charge of 'cowardice in the face of the enemy' of course could not be proved, but then they turned the game around and convicted *Major* Ehrler because he had, allegedly out of personal ambition to gain his 200th victory, taken off himself instead of directing operations from the ground as prescribed by Göring's general order. He was convicted, even though it was clearly shown during the trial that the air raid on the *Tirpitz* could not have been prevented even under his personal direction. Four weeks later he was pardoned and had to begin a probationary period as cannon fodder in the Defense of the Reich."

Together with Weißenberger and Schuck, *Major* Heinrich Ehrler was one of the outstanding figures in the war in the far north. He succeeded in amassing a total of about 200 victories – before the sinking of the *Tirpitz* tarnished his spotless career. It is perhaps not uninteresting to hear the opinions of former enemies, the renowned authors Constable and Toliver: "It is strange that a single fighter pilot and unit leader was found guilty in such a complex case."

At 28 years of age *Major* Ehrler was a broken man and he flew his final missions with no will to fight. He was finally transferred to JG 7, where he achieved four more victories flying the Me 262. *Leutnant* Schuck also joined the jet fighter unit and the three great aces from the far north were reunited in JG 7: Ehrler, Schuck and Weißenberger. On 4 April 1945 Heinrich Ehrler was shot down and killed in combat with American bombers over the Berlin area.

The real reason why the battleship *Tirpitz* met such an inglorious end on 12 November 1944 probably lies elsewhere. The supreme command should have known what was in store for the *Tirpitz* after the first attacks by the British. Unfortunately it failed to take steps to provide a comprehensive, adequate and coordinated defense of the ship, whose mere presence in Norwegian waters was sufficient to keep the enemy at bay at sea and which in fact represented a threat to the British.

Towards the End

At the beginning of December 1944 the fighter *Staffeln* in northern Norway faced another transfer, this time to the south of Norway, where the *IV. Gruppe* had been stationed for some time. The *III. Gruppe*, under the temporary command of *Oberleutnant* Glöckner in Dörr's absence, was split up. Two *Staffeln*, 10. and 11./JG 5, plus the *Geschwaderstab*, flew via Bodö and Örlandet to Gossen, while the 9. and 12. *Staffel*, both now equipped with the Fw 190 A-8, went to Herdla.

On 7 December, several hours after the units' arrival in Gossen, there was a large air battle with a group of British bombers. More than 30 Beaufighters plus numerous Mosquitoes, escorted by several flights of Mustangs of No.315 Squadron were headed for Trondheim. The Messerschmitt *Staffeln* of III./JG 5 took off and intercepted the enemy over the sea off Gossen.

At 14:15 *Leutnant* von Podewils attacked a Beaufighter from above and behind at an altitude of 500 meters and set its starboard engine alight. One minute later the aircraft dove vertically into the sea about 13 kilometers off Gossen. The victory was witnessed by *Leutnant* Linz. That day von Podewils was flying "Yellow 12A", a very unusual aircraft code. As there was already a "Yellow

12" in the *Staffel*, a letter "A" was simply added to the aircraft number on the *Leutnant*'s Messerschmitt to differentiate the two machines.

Glöckner shot down two more Beaufighters, his 31st and 32nd victories. Soon after taking off, *Gefreiter* Dieter Baasch of the *10. Staffel* lost the other members of his *Schwarm* and therefore joined up with a Bf 109 wearing the number "Yellow 12". That was Glöckner's machine. Glöckner recalls, "After about 20 minutes we engaged three British Beaufighter torpedo aircraft. I saw 'Yellow 12' shoot down one of the enemy aircraft, whereupon the others turned west. Approaching from above and behind, I positioned myself behind the trailing Beaufighter and fired from about 100 to 50 meters. I saw shells striking the starboard engine and it began leaving a thin white smoke trail. The enemy aircraft descended, probably intending to ditch in the sea. Before it touched down, I saw flames shoot from the starboard engine and the machine crashed into the sea." 14:27, about 15-20 kilometers northeast of Altmestad: it was *Gefreiter* Baasch's very first victory. That day the two *Staffel* succeeded in shooting down no fewer than 13 twin-engined aircraft and at least two P-51s. One of the Mustang pilots baled out and was taken prisoner. III./JG 5 reported two pilots missing: the aircraft flown by *Unteroffizier* Bernhardt of the *10. Staffel* was damaged and he made an unsuccessful attempt to ditch in the sea. *Unteroffizier* Bruscagin of 11./JG 5 was also shot down.

This was the opening act in southern Norway. There were more casualties in the days that followed, all for reasons other than enemy action. On 12 December, while taking off from Bardufoss to fly to Herdla, *Leutnant* Peters of the *9. Staffel* crashed and was killed. One day later 16./JG 5 also moved to Herdla, with two *Schwärme* flying escort for a Ju 52 carrying the *Gruppe*'s technicians. Unfortunately the transport flew over a German ship, which mistook it for an enemy aircraft, and was shot down. On 14 December *Oberfähnrich* Hans Albert of *Stab* IV./JG 5 crashed in flames into Hjelte Fjord as a result of engine trouble.

On 26 December the *16. Staffel* recorded the first victory since its formation, when *Feldwebel* Halstrick shot down a Mosquito in the Haugesund area. Several days later *Unteroffizier* Schmejkal recorded the *Staffel*'s second victory when he shot down a Mustang.

This brought the year 1944 to an end. The number of German aircraft on Norwegian airfields had dropped significantly, to less than 150, half of them fighters. *Luftflotte 5* had been disbanded at the end of September 1944 and the units were attached to the Commanding General of the *Luftwaffe* in Norway or the *General* of the *Luftwaffe* in Finland while at the same time a new *Feldluftgau Norwegen* was formed. All of the *Staffeln* of the *III.* and *IV. Gruppe* of *Jagdgeschwader 5* were now concentrated in southern Norway. On 1 January 1945 its command structure and bases were as follows:

Stab/JG 5	*Major* Ehrler	Trondheim
Adjutant	*Hptm.* Lüder	Trondheim
Technical Officer	*Hptm.* Probst	Trondheim
Signals Officer	*Oblt.* Kalischeck	Trondheim
Aide-de-Camp	*Lt.* Naps	Trondheim
III./JG 5	*Hptm.* Dörr	
	Oblt. Glöckner (acting)	Gossen
Adjutant	*Lt.* von Podewils	Gossen
9. Staffel	*Oblt.* Gayko	Herdla
10. Staffel	*Oblt.* Schuck	Gossen
11. Staffel	*Oblt.* Glöckner	Gossen
12. Staffel	*Lt.* Linz	Herdla
IV./JG 5	*Hptm.* Stendal	Stavanger
13. Staffel	*Oblt.* Schneider	Lister
14. Staffel	*Lt.* Neumann	Kjevik
15. Staffel	*Lt.* Keppler?	Lister
16. Staffel	*Lt.* Vollet	Stavanger

As an allied nation, Norway was spared the type of major daylight and night raids the Allies conducted against the Reich. Their attacks were therefore directed exclusively against strategic targets. In autumn 1944 the British tried unsuccessfully to convince the Americans to join in attacks on the submarine pens in Trondheim and Bergen, and at the turn of the year the RAF attacked these targets alone. Did the Americans fear that the inevitable near misses would inflict casualties on the Norwegians, or were they deterred by the powerful flak and fighter defenses surrounding the naval bases? As it turned out, the RAF would pay a heavy price for its attacks against these targets.

Operationally, January was a busy month, as British bombers appeared over the coast of southern Norway almost every day. On the 11th *Unteroffizier* Köhler and *Unteroffizier* Nieft, both of the *14. Staffel*, were killed in an engagement over the sea about 30 kilometers west of Lister, however the next day saw the two *Staffeln* based in Herdla achieve a major success when they intercepted a formation of Lancasters on their way to bomb the submarine pens in Bergen. Alerted in time, the Focke-Wulfs raced from the airfield to intercept the high-flying bombers. Approximately 16 heavy bombers were shot down, several of them by flak, while III./JG 5 suffered two casualties: *Unteroffizier* Kirchner and *Feldwebel* Lieber, who was seen to ditch, failed to return.

Leutnant Rudi Linz, leader of the *12. Staffel*, was killed in action against enemy aircraft near Horstad on 9 February. The exact circumstances of his loss are unknown, but soon after shooting down a twin-engined machine – it was his 70th victory – he was most probably shot down by another British aircraft. His "Blue 4" crashed on a small island, not far from where his last victim had gone down. Linz, a 28-year-old from Thuringia, was awarded the Knight's Cross posthumously. His successor as *Staffelkapitän* was *Oberleutnant* Koch.

On 9 February Artner scored his 18th and 19th victories. At about 16:08 nine Fw 190s of 9./JG 5 encountered thirty Beaufighters and ten Mustangs and a fierce battle developed 50 kilometers north of Sogne Fjord. The *Staffel* claimed nine victories, including two by *Unteroffizier* Orlowski, who was then forced to bale out after his engine was damaged. *Unteroffiziere* Eisermann, Hellwig and Opitz all recorded their first victories, but *Feldwebel* Otto Leibfried was missing after the action.

By then *Major* Ehrler had left *Jagdgeschwader 5*. In the end his sentence of three years imprisonment and loss of rank imposed as a result of the *Tirpitz* affair could not be upheld, but it did result in his transfer to the Defense of the Reich. Schuck and Glöckner also ended up in JG 7. The position of *Geschwaderkommodore* was not filled and consequently JG 5 came under the *Jagdfliegerführer* (commander of fighters), *Oberstleutnant* Scholz. *Hauptmann* Treppe, *Kommandeur* of IV./ZG 26, took over the position of Fighter Sector Commander Trondheim. He subsequently exercised command over that *Gruppe* as well as III./JG 5 and some of the signals units in operational and disciplinary matters. Following the tragic outcome of the court martial against *Major* Ehrler, *Major i.G.* Wilhelm was named Fighter Sector Commander Trondheim, and pending his arrival and takeover of the position, *Hauptmann* Lüder was held responsible for his duties.

In February in Herdla, preparations were made for the formation of a new II./JG 5, which was essentially made up of the old *Zerstörerstaffel*. The *III. Gruppe* gave the *9.* and *12. Staffel* to *Hauptmann* Treppe, the *Kommandeur* of the new II./JG 5, and simultaneously received the *13. Staffel* of the *IV. Gruppe* as the new 9./JG 5. As a result, all three *Gruppen* of the *Geschwader* now had three *Staffeln*.

Because of persistent bad weather, the size of the operational area and the associated difficulty in providing accurate air situation reports, encounters with the enemy now became extremely rare, although what engagements there were ended more or less successfully. Combat with the enemy was noticeably tougher, however, and this was reflected in higher loss rates, especially among the younger, less-experienced pilots. Nevertheless, intensified operations by the former *Eismeerjäger* did cause the British to limit their attacks to targets that were far from JG 5's bases, and they turned for home as soon as their bombs were dropped. During one such attack on 16 February, *Feldwebel* Kindt was shot down over the sea near Aaleslund, while *Unteroffizier* Jäger was wounded and baled out. Schuck claimed one victory and the recently promoted *Unteroffizier* Baasch two more. At that time *Leutnant* Wollmann reported a reconnaissance flight undertaken from Gossen by a *Schwarm* from the *10. Staffel*. Equipped with external fuel tanks, the four aircraft took off and headed west. The weather deteriorated noticeably and finally the cloud base dropped to just 50 meters above the water. When they reached the turning point they suddenly encountered British carrier aircraft, probably Avengers, one of which Wollmann shot down in a frontal attack.

Toward the end of March *Oberleutnant* Gayko had another, less heroic experience, which he described: "The 25th of March 1943 was the day that I opened the bathing season off the Norwegian coast with a Fw 190. After ditching successfully following engine failure – or was I shot down by a Mustang? – with subsequent submersion test, I made it back to the surface and tried to climb into the inflatable dinghy attached to my parachute. When I first climbed in, the dinghy filled with water which I could not bail out of because of numb fingers. For the next hour I kept myself awake by singing pop songs, and then a Norwegian cutter fished me out. When I gratefully passed around my full cigarette case, they probably thought I wanted to warm myself with a cigarette, even though I was on my last legs. As all of mine were wet, one of the two fishermen rolled me one from wrapping paper filled with a kind of seaweed. Out of courtesy I smoked it and of course became violently ill.

"They then transported me to a small island and tucked me into a bed, which was in a post office. Wrapped in a comforter I felt much better. To eat there was boiled dried cod in groats. Brrr.

"The next day they collected me in a Do 24, which soon after takeoff managed to find itself near several Mosquitoes. Fearing the worst, my crew ducked into a fog bank and landed on the water, only to discover that the seas were too heavy to take off again.

"After dramatic hops between Skylla and Charybdis we climbed onto a small island where, for lack of anything better to do, we ate our emergency rations, which we had of course brought with us. After several hours of fireworks, some Norwegians found us and took us straight through minefields home to our airfield in Herdla. Never again did I have such a fear of these big mines, which were plainly visible in the clear water. Once home, our good doctor stuck me in a hot bath and gave me mulled wine to drink. Apart from a kidney infection I was no worse for wear."

On 12 March *Leutnant* Neumann, the *Kapitän* of 14./JG 5, was awarded the Knight's Cross after his 62nd victory. He shot down his first enemy aircraft on 22 July 1943 while flying with the *7. Staffel* and he later raised his total to 49 victories on the Polar Sea Front. Unfortunately the action on 12 March resulted in serious casualties. 13./JG 5 lost its *Kapitän*, *Oberleutnant* Hans Schneider, and *Oberfeldwebel* Stebner, both of whom were shot down. *Feldwebel* Hermann Jäger, who had escaped by parachute in a battle the previous month, was also killed in March.

The *Staffelkapitän* of 15./JG 5 lost his life in tragic fashion on 5 April 1945. Jakob Gern recalled that *Leutnant* Keppler's aircraft swung on takeoff. Its undercarriage got caught on the rocks and the aircraft overturned, trapping Keppler in the cockpit.

At the beginning of April the *16. Staffel*, newly formed in late autumn 1944, moved to Rygge in Oslo Fjord. At the same time *Leutnant* Vollet was ordered to the Reich to retrain on the Me 262, and *Leutnant* Adolf Gillet assumed command of the *Staffel*. The very first mission from Rygge on 11 April resulted in several Mosquitoes and Mustangs shot down, but the engagement also cost Gillet his life. A Mustang shot him down over the fishing port of Porsgrun. *Fähnrich* Schüler was also shot down but parachuted to safety.

On 14 April *Leutnant* Höhn took over the *Staffel* in an acting capacity. That same day *Unteroffizier* Schoppert and *Unteroffizier* Voltmer failed to return after a scramble. The pair must have encountered Beaufighters, which were on an anti-shipping strike, and their escorting Mustangs.

According to a description from the other side, that Saturday five Mustangs spotted a lone Bf 109 flying low near Lister airfield. The aircraft, probably on approach to land, climbed back up to engage the Englishmen. Although it was five against one, the pilot of the Messerschmitt put on an admirable display of flying, frequently opening fire and from time to time shaking off the pursuing Mustangs. But then the inevitable happened. The lone Messerschmitt fell to the guns of the British leader and sank in the sea. As JG 5 reported three casualties on 14 April 1945; this courageous pilot could only have been *Gefreiter* Bahlmann.* (*According to Jakob Gern of 15./JG 5, the action in question took place on 20/3/45.).

The *Geschwader*'s days in Norway were now numbered. When the war ended, *Jagdfliegerführer* Scholz, also *Kommodore* of JG 5, had under his command three *Gruppen* of day fighters with nine Staffeln (II., III. and IV./JG 5), plus a night-fighter *Staffel* (4./NJG 3) and a *Zerstörerstaffel* (11./ZG 26). The *Staffeln*, all of which were below authorized strength, were distributed all over southern Norway. 13./JG 5, led by *Oberleutnant* Kurt Schulze, was renamed 6./JG 5 at the beginning of May 1945, however there is no mention of this in the official records. On the day of the German surrender the following units were in Norway:

Fighter Commander Norway

also *Kommodore* JG 5	Stavanger-Forus
Stab II./JG 5	Herdla
5. *Staffel*	Herdla
6. *Staffel*	Rygge
7. *Staffel*	Stavanger-Sola
Stab III./JG 5	Gossen
9. *Staffel*	Herdla
10. *Staffel*	Gossen
11. *Staffel*	Gossen
Stab IV./JG 5	Kjevik
13. *Staffel*	Lister
14. *Staffel*	Kjevik
15. *Staffel*	Lister

Attached units:

4./NJG 3	Kjevik
1 *Kette* of 4./NJG 3	Gardermoen
2 *Schwärme* NJG 100	Gardermoen
11./ZG 26	Örlandet

There was no inexorable retreat or a collapse such as occurred at the fronts in the Reich for example. There was no great chaos. In Norway the Germans were essentially isolated and waited for what was to come. There were no enemy troops anywhere. After the signing of the *Wehrmacht*'s unconditional surrender on 8 May 1945, the unit commanders received the order from the *Luftwaffe* commanding general in Norway to make their way with their units to certain "reservations" to wait for further orders. For the units stationed in the Oslo area this was Camp Höhnefoss, northwest of Oslo, while the units on the west coast had to set out for Boemoon near Bergen. At that time *Hauptmann* Treppe functioned as liaison officer to the Norwegian military authorities, who were now responsible for the camp. At the direction of the Allies they were also responsible for executing and maintaining the conditions of the internment process.

For the *Geschwader* the war came to an end with no significant incidents. It must have been with heavy hearts that the fighter pilots left their remaining aircraft for the British air forces. There they stood, modern warhorses, on whom the scars of the most recent battles could still be seen. They were no longer needed, their powerful engines fell silent forever. The men took one last wistful look at the few Messerschmitts and Focke-Wulfs formed up for one last parade before heading off for temporary internment and captivity. The process was completely orderly. To close out the *Geschwader* history, however, there remains one bloodless "battle" with the victorious powers to report on, which took place in the Boemoon camp in the days after the surrender.

Treppe still had his "*Staffelkapitän*'s reserve" – wine, spirits, tobacco products – which, as described elsewhere, were issued to the members of the *Staffel* on special occasions. Later, after Treppe took over II./JG 5, this stash was upgraded to "*Kommandeur*'s reserve". It and other supplies not expressly forbidden by the hastily-issued Allied order were of course taken along to Boemoon.

The men were transported by steamer from Herdla up the Hardanger Fjord. At the gangway at their destination, the still heavily-armed garrison of the base in Herdla went ashore, watched by a lone, hastily-called-up Norwegian home defense man wearing an armband and carrying a submachine-gun. One of the first *Gefreiten* to go ashore struck up a conversation with the man. To the general relief of the passing soldiers, he so disassembled the Norwegian's submachine-gun that the man couldn't reassemble it again. Finally Treppe was forced to intervene and ordered a soldier to help reassemble the weapon.

Boemoon, an unoccupied operational airfield, which bordered on a Norwegian training camp, consisted of many small wooden houses, where the men initially assumed quarters. New orders arrived daily, calling for the Germans to surrender the supplies, trucks, live cattle and food they had brought from Herdla. For this reason *Hauptmann* Treppe decided to distribute his "*Kommandeur*'s reserve" to the members of his *Gruppe* as quickly as possible, so that they could administer and safeguard their shares. Treppe:

"Under the strictest secrecy my operations officer, my adjutant and the paymaster prepared for the distribution, setting up the stocks in a barn in the farmyard: champagne, red wine, cognac, schnapps, many kinds of white and black cigarettes in packets. As there had already been thefts of food and luxury items in the reservation, which now held about 1,500 members of the air force and army, our operations officer posted a sentry armed with a rifle in front of the barn. He was relieved at regular intervals so that the 'reserve' could not be stolen during pauses when there was no one standing guard. This precautionary measure was to be the undoing of the '*Kommandeur*'s reserve' however."

Until then, apart from the lone guard at the landing bridge, no Allied soldier had looked into the reservation. But at the very moment that the precious supplies were arranged for distribution, a Jeep filled with British paratroopers suddenly roared into the camp. These men were undoubtedly looking for booty, and being frontline soldiers they had a nose for hidden alcohol. Immediately one of them noticed the sentry standing in front of the barn. The Jeep stopped, the British jumped out and threw open the barn door – and there were the bottles they were seeking, neatly lined up and ready to be taken away.

The British cordoned off the area and Treppe was summoned.

A lieutenant informed him that he was confiscating these supplies as per order number X, sector Y. If just one cigarette was removed, all participants would be brought before an Allied court-martial. Then the paratroopers took inventory. They told Treppe that they would soon return with a truck and were making him responsible for ensuring that everything that was on the list they had made was still there when they returned. Then the British troops disappeared again.

"Now we hadn't been born yesterday and weren't easy to bluff," related Treppe. "But what was I going to do? We could only change the quality, not the quantity, of what was going to be stolen. We later learned that not only did they rob us, but the Allied zone commander as well.

"We quickly set up lookouts to report the return of the paratroopers. Meanwhile we exchanged all of the cigarette packages with light tobacco for ones with black tobacco. Just as we were in the process of emptying the red wine bottles and filling them with coffee, a report came that the English were coming. Some of the red wine bottles contained the noble fluid that we so begrudged the British. The pain over the loss of the hoard was only slightly mitigated by the knowledge that most of the bottles contained coffee.

"By the way this was only an unplanned part of our actual stores, which we, having learned the hard way, had so skillfully hidden that no British or Norwegian ever found it."

A short time later a Norwegian battalion moved into the training camp next door. The German prisoners were squeezed into a much smaller area and from then on were guarded by that battalion, which was in loose contact with the Allied commander.

The first men were released to go home in about mid-August 1945. It was a fallacy, however, for it soon turned out that all of the soldiers living in the American zone, including more than a few members of *Jagdgeschwader 5*, were soon handed over to the French and subsequently found themselves back behind the wire for a long time. *Leutnant* von Podewils was one of them. In mid-January 1947 his escape made headlines in the Alsatian press:

15 January 1947: Despite bad weather, German escape attempts have increased recently. In the course of the past week no fewer than six such prisoners escaped from a local camp. The number of recaptured escapees since 1 January of this year is twelve. Two former officers of the German military, who escaped from a camp in Baccarat with four other prisoners, were caught on Sunday. Among them was the Bavarian landowner Baron von Podewils.

Chapter 6
Dachshund Staffel - the Zerstörer

First Operational Experiences on the Polar Sea Front

Throughout its operational history, from the occupation of Norway in April 1940 until the formation of the new *II. Gruppe* of JG 5 in February 1945, the *Geschwader*'s *Zerstörerstaffel* was attached to various units under various designations, but on the whole it led an independent life. That is why a separate chapter has been dedicated to the history of this *Staffel* within the *Geschwader* history. Its operational career is also described separately because its equipment – the *Zerstörerstaffel* flew the twin-engined Messerschmitt Bf 110 – distinguishes it from a pure fighter unit. Correspondingly its functions were completely different from those of the *Geschwader*'s fighter units.

2./ZG 76 was attached to the *X. Fliegerkorps* and had been stationed in the north since the occupation of Norway, its mission to defend Norwegian airfields. In the spring of 1940 the *Staffel* was in Stavanger, from where it carried out its first successful operations. One year later 2./ZG 76, led by *Leutnant* Felix Maria Brandis, moved to Herdla.

In April 1941 the heavy fighters, operating with *Hauptmann* Reinicke's I./ZG 76, scored a number of additional victories while defending the port city of Stavanger against frequent air raids by the RAF. ZG 76 left Norway shortly before the attack on the Soviet Union; the only *Zerstörer* units left behind were *Stab*/ZG 76 and 2./ZG 76. The latter was attached to the new *I. Gruppe* of *Jagdgeschwader 77* and in the summer was given the designation 1.(Z)/JG 77. When the Russian campaign began the *Staffel* moved to its operational base in Kirkenes.

Kirkenes! This small town is situated on the Varangerfjord in the north-easternmost corner of Norway. Across the Polar Sea there is only pack ice and then the North Pole. Kirkenes is the same distance from the Pole as it is from Berlin – 2000 kilometers. The tree line lies farther south, and all that grows there is scrub birch and blueberry bushes, marsh grass and moose and caribou moss. Elsewhere stone and boulders rule: barren rock as far as the eye can see, interspersed with bogs, ponds and lakes, dominated by the Polar Sea fjords that extend deep inland.

That is Kirkenes, which was to be home to the *Zerstörer* crews for a long time. It was not without reason that they came to the conclusion: "This is where Europe ends!" – The German Academy of Science.

The early warning company set up its lonely position on the Holmengrafiel Peninsula, approximately 20 kilometers northeast of Kirkenes. The station, codenamed "Puma", was one of the few German air defense radar stations in the far north. Equipped with a *Freya* early-warning radar, once active it provided early warning service for the aviation units based in Kirkenes.

Like every other flying unit of the *Luftwaffe*, *Jagdgeschwader 5*'s *Zerstörerstaffel* had a special identifying code on its Bf 110s. Unlike those of day fighter units, however, this consisted of four letters. The first two letters of the code, LN, identified the *Geschwader*, while the last letter, R, identified the *Staffel*. The third letter varied and identified the individual aircraft. *Leutnant* Brandis often flew aircraft "Anton", LN+AR, and *Leutnant* Weißenberger "Paula", LN+PR. Towards the end of the war this code changed in some cases to 1B+?X, with the third letter again identifying the individual aircraft.

But the *Staffel*'s most distinctive characteristic was its affection for the dachshund. Dachshunds accompanied the *Zerstörer* crews throughout the war; they became the *Staffel* animal and from August 1941 images of these dogs appeared on the noses of the unit's aircraft as the *Staffel* emblem. Some dachshunds even went along on operations. Brandis, Schloßstein and Franzisket got their first dachshunds in May 1941, naming them "Herdla" after their base and "Lockheed" after Brandis' first victory [a Lockheed Hudson]. At some point they were joined by "Bamse", which is Norwegian for bear. Before long everyone was calling the *Zerstörer* unit the "Dachshund *Staffel*". Thus named, the *Zerstörer* unit soon gained a reputation in the far north, where it flew its most difficult missions and achieved its successes.

The heavy fighters' most important mission was flying escort for the Ju 88 units of KG 30 based in Banak and the *I. Gruppe* of *Stukageschwader 5* during missions against Murmansk, the important supply base and seaport. While German land operations soon settled into positional warfare, the *Luftwaffe* did all it could to interrupt the flow of Allied supplies to the Soviet Union. The city and port of Murmansk were attacked regularly. Other popular targets for the *Zerstörer* were the fighter airfields around the city. The airfields that were the targets of repeated German air raids were called Kola South and North, Murmashi, Shongui and Varlamovo. These names appeared in the mission orders day after day, and they soon became a nightmare to German airmen, for most were 100 kilometers beyond the front lines. Flying over the Soviet Union created a great deal of additional stress. "Loading sacks in Murmansk until you drop", was the fate of the shot-down airman. And a member of KG 30 later said: "Better three times to London than once to Murmansk". Murmansk was one of the four targets most heavily defended by flak during the Second World War – the two Ls (London and Leningrad) and the two Ms (Murmansk and Malta).

On the very first day of the new campaign *Luftflotte 5* struck a major blow against the airfields around Murmansk and bombed targets and shipping in Kola Bay.

On 28 June 1941 there was a regrettable accident at Kirkenes caused by a ground collision. *Oberleutnant* Kriegel of *Stab*/ZG 76, who was then acting as Fighter Commander Northern Norway and later became the first *Kommandeur* of the new IV./JG 5, was taking off on a scramble in his Bf 110. A Bf 109 taking off from the crossing runway collided with Kriegel's Bf 110, which overturned. The *Oberleutnant* escaped with head injuries, however his radio operator, *Unteroffizier* Kurt Kühn, and the pilot of the fighter, a *Fähnrich*, were killed.

The *Zerstörerstaffel* suffered its first combat casualty on 5 July during a mission in the Titovka area. The crew of *Leutnant* Weyergang and *Unteroffizier* Tigges was shot down by flak and obliged to make a forced landing, after which they were reported missing. Their fate was cleared up two weeks later, on 14 July, when a Finnish patrol came upon the shattered remains of the Bf 110 (LN+ER) at the north tip of Lisa Bay. The bodies of the pilot and radio operator were recovered from the wreck. On 17 July, during an escort mission over the Fischer Peninsula, *Leutnant* Brandis' Bf 110 was hit by anti-aircraft fire. He immediately headed west over the sea in the direction of the flat, barren island of Heinsässari, where the dependency of a monastery had once stood. (Those sent there must have been serious penitents. Anyone who flew over it knew – this is the end of the line.)

The damage was such that Brandis was forced to ditch in the sea before reaching the mainland. While the pilot got out quickly, his radio operator, *Gefreiter* Matthias Gans, failed to escape from the machine and drowned. It was assumed that the cable of his helmet had become tangled. *Leutnant* Brandis drifted around in the waters of the Polar Sea for four hours before the crew of a steamer – more by chance – spotted him in the dense fog and rescued him. After a meal of fried eggs and several stiff drinks, he slept a little on the ship. As soon as he arrived back in Kirkenes he took off again and reduced "his" light flak battery to matchwood.

Two days later the *Staffel* was given another escort mission that took it to Kola, southwest of Murmansk. Over the target the Germans were greeted by heavy anti-aircraft fire and *Leutnant* Schloßstein saw LN+DR, flown by the crew of *Leutnant* Klappenbach and *Gefreiter* Methke, go down after being hit by flak and make a forced landing west of Kola. It is not known if Klappenbach and his radio operator were captured by the Russians or were killed.

Success always comes at a cost, as our first descriptions show. The missions flown by the *Zerstörer* crews that summer demanded all their skill and were certainly not pleasant flights over the front.

Meanwhile the German mountain troops, after expanding their bridgehead on the east side of the Lisa River, successfully blocked access to the Small Fischer Peninsula. As the corps was unable to advance any farther, however, the Russians were able to deliver troops to the peninsula by sea, resulting in tough, costly fighting. Despite heavy casualties, in mid-July 1941 the Germans renewed their offensive against Murmansk, with all available air resources taking part. The attackers came close to forcing a breakthrough in the direction of Murmansk, but then the attack was repulsed by Soviet troops. At about the same time the British caused an unexpected interruption in the operations against Murmansk through an event that in the history of *Jagdgeschwader 5* came to be known as the "Air Battle of Kirkenes."

In the early summer of 1941, due to the attack on the Soviet Union, a not inconsiderable part of the *Kriegsmarine*'s resources was shifted into the Baltic to support German troop movements. This inevitably affected British naval strategy. The British Fleet, which had previously maintained a defensive posture, saw an opportunity to take offensive action against shipping movements along the North-European coasts. The Russians also pressed their western Allies to attempt to block German supply routes to their supply ports in Kirkenes in northern Norway and Petsamo in northern Finland.

At the end of July 1941 aerial reconnaissance spotted a British task force sailing from Iceland, including the aircraft carriers *Victorious* and *Furious* plus two cruisers and four destroyers. By 30 July the unit was in the Polar Sea for a surprise attack on Kirkenes, which at that time was as important to the Germans as the ice-free port of Murmansk was to the Russians. Though detected by aerial reconnaissance, the attack by about 30 Albacore torpedo aircraft and nine Fairey Fulmar fighters took the Germans by surprise. All of the aircraft had taken off from the carrier *Victorious*.

As chance would have it, the fighters and *Zerstörer* of I./JG 77 were just forming up in the same area in order to escort a Stuka unit to Murmansk. This mission was immediately abandoned so that the German aircraft could intercept the attackers approaching from the sea. A total of 13 British aircraft were shot down in the course of a lengthy engagement. Two more aircraft were destroyed from another group of 18 Albacores, Hurricanes and six Fulmars that attacked Petsamo at the same time.

The following description of the events of 30 July 1941 was made by one of the enemy airmen, British Lieutenant Turnbull:

"That day I was flying an Albacore of No.827 Squadron, which was on the *Victorious*. Our orders were to attack ships in the Polar Sea port of kilometers with Duplex torpedoes. As I recall, the mission was just as sketchy as our knowledge of what was actually in the port at that time. The Fulmars of No.809 Squadron were supposed to provide fighter cover. My crew consisted of Lieutenant Sergeant as observer and Leading Airman James as radio operator. The entire attack was led by Lt. Commander Moore, who flew in Lieutenant Read's aircraft. We took off and formed up under a completely clear sky and set course for Kirkenes without incident.

"Probably by accident, we flew into a fjord east of Kirkenes, with the result that we had to turn west and climb over the approaching line of hills. We therefore flew over the crest of the hill, then the port and the piers. There were just two merchant ships and a cruiser in the harbor. As I later learned, the cruiser was the flak ship *Bremsa**, which then opened fire on us. I stayed on course towards the ship, but my approach was poor and took me too far from the target but close to a merchant vessel armed with anti-aircraft guns. Shells struck the wings, canopy and cockpit. Despite the damage we continued buzzing around the harbor until I suddenly heard Serjeant shout 'Fighters!'. But apart from a Ju 87, which passed by from right to left, I saw nothing. (*The vessel was in fact the gunnery training ship *Bremse*.).

"After an unsuccessful torpedo attack on the *Bremsa* I dove away. My heading took me over a very long fjord, which appeared to be full of friendly and hostile aircraft. Hugh screamed again: 'Fighters!' A Bf 109 attacked us but missed. I believe we had a Fulmar (probably flown by Alistair Eaton, who was later shot down), which turned into the enemy, to thank for that. But we came under fire from somewhere, for I saw parts of my wingtip shot off. Another hit appeared to knock out both valves and my altimeter. I noticed that the needle of the oil temperature gauge was hanging out above the clock.

"Together with another Albacore we were leaving the fjord in the area of Vardö or Vadsö when a Bf 110 appeared behind us. It made several passes and suddenly the other aircraft went down in a steep right turn. All I heard was a terrible crash and was therefore more than a little surprised when I later learned that the crew of the Albacore had survived. The Messerschmitt then turned its attention to us. We were hit in the wings, and especially in the engine, which soon began to run roughly. The men behind me reported that the Bf 110 was coming in again. At that precise moment the engine quit.

"I remember very little about the crash itself, except that when I reached for the canopy lever it was no longer there. The next thing I saw was the sea, on which the sunlight was harshly reflected. A German boat picked us up soon afterwards – and thus for us the war was over."

Escort to Murmansk

The British continued their efforts to assist their new ally by sending supply convoys by sea. The Russian aviation units were soon bolstered by deliveries of Hawker Hurricane fighters, also delivered by sea. While sailing around northern Norway to Murmansk, most of the British convoys passed within range of the bomber, fighter and *Zerstörer* units of *Luftflotte* 5. The convoys were beyond the range of RAF aircraft, and for this reason on 12 September 1941 twenty-four Hurricanes of Nos.81 and 143 Squadrons flew from the aircraft carrier *Argus* to Vayenga airfield near Murmansk. As a result, the *Luftwaffe* units had to be more alert.

In August the *Zerstörerstaffel* moved to Rovaniemi in Lapland for a short time to support the army, which had launched an operation from Alakurtti in an attempt to reach the strategically-vital Murmansk railway near Louhi. During one of the subsequent missions by 1.(Z)/JG 77, *Leutnant* Brandis became disoriented over confusing terrain around Rovaniemi and had to make a forced landing in Swedish territory.

One of the most successful pilots in recent weeks was the leader of ZG 76's *Stabsschwarm*, *Hauptmann* Gerhard Schaschke, who shot down a number of enemy fighter aircraft during the course of *Zerstörer* missions. In doing so he developed his own tactic. Covered by a Bf 109, he took off for the Russian airfields and engaged the enemy's alert pair as it rose to intercept. He used this tactic with success until he too met his fate, on 4 August 1941. His aircraft was hit by anti-aircraft fire and crashed. Schaschke, who by then had achieved 20 victories, was posted missing along with his radio operator Michael Widtmann.

The independent *Zerstörerstaffel* in Kirkenes was in fact an unusual formation. In the proper sense it had no *Staffelkapitän*, no *Kommandeur* and no *Kommodore*. When remnants of the west coast *Zerstörer* moved to Kirkenes in the summer of 1941, *Staffel* officers, whose first priority was flying operational sorties, took over the running of the unit. *Hauptmann* Schaschke was considered particularly well-suited to lead, but he failed to return from a combat mission.

The *Zerstörerstaffel*'s run of bad luck continued, for its next commander never arrived. On 12 August 1941 *Major* Erich Groth of ZG 76 was airborne in his Bf 110, en route to Kirkenes to take over the *Staffel*, but he never arrived. No trace of the crew or their aircraft was found and Groth and his radio operator, *Unteroffizier* Herbert Muche, were reported missing. The only memorial to this unfortunate transfer flight was a stone in Haavenga cemetery – until more than two years later, when the remains of a Bf 110 were discovered near Fodalsnaase, about 160 kilometers northeast of Bergen. Bits of Groth's uniform and shoulder boards and Muche's identity disc were found in the wreckage. There was no longer any doubt that Groth and Muche had been killed in the crash.

Oberstleutnant Schumacher, the successful commander in the "Air Battle over the German Bight", was supposed to take the reins of the units in the north, however he had the tragic misfortune of forcing down a Finnish DeHavilland D.H. 89 ambulance aircraft while on one of his first orientation flights in the Alakurtti area. For this reason his stay in Finland was a short one.

While the fighter *Staffeln* were soon combined into a *Gruppe*, the *Zerstörerstaffel* remained orphaned, which in no way hampered it operationally. Because of their greater range and payload, the special operational roles of the *Zerstörer* were those of bomber, long-range fighter and escort aircraft for ships and bombers. It therefore goes without saying that the crews received their mission orders either from the air commander (*Fliegerführer*) or even directly from the air fleet.

Because of his large number of victories and not least because of his superior ability, command of the *Staffel* remained entrusted to *Leutnant* Brandis. An old cannibalized bus served as command post, but its seats still provided a very cozy atmosphere. And a small, low cabinet, which stood in for a desk when a signature was needed or operational reports had to be written, contained a jumble of life vests, helmets, flare pistols, oxygen masks, mission orders and flight rations. A truly grotesque picture! But a start had been made.

Operations against British and Soviet naval forces increased steadily in the summer of 1941, with the *Zerstörer* flying escort for the German bombers. There was also an unbroken series of attacks against enemy air bases in northern Karelia, the Murmansk area and the Polar Sea coast as well as lines of communication in the Soviet rear.

On 14 September 1941 five new crews arrived from the *Zerstörer* school in Neubiberg: *Oberleutnant* H.H. Schmidt and *Gefreiter* Friedrich, *Leutnant* Dahn and *Gefreiter* Pfeiffer, *Leutnant* Reichel and *Gefreiter* Boehmer, *Feldwebel* Weißenberger and *Obergefreiter* Geißhart, and *Unteroffizier* Fiedler and *Obergefreiter* Brüggenthies. During their transfer flight there was an unusual encounter while on a stopover in Stockholm. It turned out that sitting in another corner of the restaurant in the Swedish airport, which the men were allowed to enter without weapons, was the crew of a British Blenheim. The British airmen casually sipped their tea while trying to take no notice of the Germans.

While the *Staffel* had received some fresh crews, ground personnel were still in short supply. Around the turn of the year 1940-41 *Hauptmann* Mikat took over as company commander of the 5th Airfield Operations Company of ZG 76, which had been transferred from France to Stavanger-Forus. When the *Zerstörerstaffel* moved to Finland six to eight weeks later, 5. FBK ZG 76 stayed behind. Transferred to Stavanger-Sola in June 1941, it was there that it looked after *Jagdkommando 77* and *Jagdgruppe Stavanger*. The technical personnel were later removed from the airfield operations company and distributed among the various *Staffeln* of II./JG 5, while the rest were absorbed by the *II. Gruppe*'s headquarters company.

The number of available aircraft also left something to be desired, as there were now more crews than serviceable Messerschmitts. And so initially the pilots took regular turns flying tactical reconnaissance sorties over the front and Stuka escort missions. Aerial combat was rare, although combats took place during escort missions, as on 15 September and 17 and 21 October.

Leutnant Hoffmann and his radio operator Boehm failed to return from a mission on 15 September 1941. Hoffmann, one of the original group of *Zerstörer* pilots with three victories to his credit, peeled off from his *Schwarm* to attack a low-flying Rata. As he did so, he was attacked from behind by another Rata. The Bf 110 suddenly went into a roll, probably because of a frozen propeller. It crashed from low altitude and struck the ground about five kilometers east of Zapad Lisa in a tremendous explosion.

At 12:10 on 24 October 1941 the *Staffel* took off on its first fighter sweep in a long time. *Leutnant* Brandis led the small formation over the lakes west of the Lisa River, where Russian fighter aircraft had been reported. The *Zerstörer* soon spotted the enemy and attacked at once. The enemy aircraft were mainly older I-153 fighters. At 12:35 *Feldwebel* Weißenberger destroyed one of the fighters in an attack from above and behind. This victory was the start of Weißenberger's extremely successful career as a fighter pilot. The name Theo Weißenberger would remain closely linked to the operational history of the *Zerstörerstaffel* and later with that of II. and I./JG 5.

Locomotive Hunt on the Murmansk Railway

November 1941. The first Arctic winter broke over the units on the Polar Sea with darkness, snow and storms, to say nothing of the cold. For the flying units there was no longer any point in using the few hours of daylight for operations, especially from Kirkenes airfield, which was exposed to storms on a high plateau and had no hangars. Only in Petsamo close to the front was the experiment attempted of leaving 14./JG 77, the "*Menzel Staffel*", to ride out the winter.

The Stukas and *Zerstörer* moved to the "sunny south", to Rovaniemi, 600 kilometers away, about 70 minutes flying time in the Bf 110, close to the Arctic Circle. It was on the 67th degree of latitude, where on 21 December the sun briefly peeked over the horizon before disappearing again.

The *Zerstörer* crews moved into their new barracks on 4 November 1941. They were dispersed among the thin clusters of pine trees to reduce their vulnerability to air attack, about ten minutes away from the airfield, right next to the Stuka camp. Herds of reindeer roamed the area. From Rovaniemi the objective was the Murmansk railway, the only overland lifeline to Murmansk.

Disrupting this rail link for any period of time proved difficult, however. What was destroyed today was repaired tomorrow – after a twenty-hour polar night. The crews therefore specialized in attacking trains, especially the locomotives – which had to be a very special bottleneck for the Russians.

Orientation in winter was particularly difficult. Everything looked much different when covered in snow. Even the normally prominent lakes changed their appearance when they and the bordering swamps became shrouded in white. There were no railroads, no major roads. The maps contained no compass deviations, which made a difference on long segments – such as the 300 kilometers to the Murmansk railway.

While it was possible to fly round the clock in summer, now, in the brief hours of twilight, there was scarcely time for a single proper mission. Even in clear conditions, it was almost impossible to take off before 10:00 and by 14:00 the airfield lighting was required for landings.

The *Staffel* flew a number of operations before the end of the year, the most important of which are summarized here:

25/10	fighter sweep
26/10	escort for Ju 87s to the Fischer Peninsula
27/10	escort for Ju 87s to Taibola (Murmansk railway)
31/10	escort for Ju 87s to the Fischer Peninsula
1/11	escort for Ju 87s to Taibola
10/11	bombing of the Murmansk railway
12/11	bombing of the Louhi-Kestenga rail line
13/11	bombing of the Louhi fighter airfield
14/11	escort for Ju 87s to Louhi
29/11	escort for Ju 87s
16/12	train hunting
23/12	fighter sweep in the Louhi area
26/12	escort for Ju 87s, Hauralanka power station

These missions were not flown without casualties. There was a terrible accident on 15 December, a bitterly cold winter day, in which *Leutnant* Reichel from Silesia and his radio operator, *Gefreiter* Boehmer, would lose their lives. Shortly after ten o'clock the aircraft flown by the crews Schmidt/Friedrich and Reichel/Boehmer took off on an escort mission to Kestenga. This was not to be, however, for shortly after takeoff Reichel's aircraft flew into the ground five kilometers southeast of the airfield. *Oberleutnant* H.H. Schmidt later recalled that, "The Messerschmitt flew into the tall forest in a shallow dive with its engines running and cut a long swath. The aircraft probably crashed because the pilot's view was impaired, as at more than 20 degrees below zero the space in the armored windscreen had become opaque."

Winter begins early in the northern latitudes and it gets dark early, which limited operational activities to a few hours each day. The frigid cold also helped restrict or completely paralyze flying operations, and the prevailing winter conditions made regular operations almost impossible. Often it was difficult to put more than a single *Schwarm* into the air. Dangerous single-engined flights caused by the loss of an engine were nothing out of the ordinary, as Weißenberger learned on his second mission on 13 November. The number of available aircraft was so low that every loss could affect the outcome of an entire mission. For it was not just on account of their low speed that the Stukas of I./SG 5 under *Hauptmann* Blasig relied on the *Zerstörer* for fighter cover.

The difficulties faced by the *Zerstörerstaffel* are reflected in the notes of Gerhard Friedrichs, *Oberleutnant* Schmidt's radio operator. Near the end of 1941 the *Staffel* received the following mission order: "Soviet division advancing towards Lake Tollwand on skis and with sleighs. Take off immediately and engage the enemy with guns."

Friedrichs wrote: "A beautiful sunny Sunday! The first aircraft was running an hour after the mission order was received. Then, at last, after another hour, three more aircraft, but their engines kept cutting out. Finally at 13:00, by the skin of their teeth the engines of two Bf 110s were running. As darkness fell at 14:00, however, takeoff was no longer possible."

Another time, when four Bf 110s were supposed to fly escort for a He 111 transporting air fleet chief *Generaloberst* Stumpff to Kiestinki (Kestenga), the temperature plunged from minus 20 to minus 40 degrees overnight. The next morning half the aircraft had a "flat", as their tires had become porous. Once again, despite feverish changing of tires, just four aircraft could be made serviceable. Then another Bf 110 went unserviceable because the technicians could not screw in a small screw for the radio equipment in the fuselage. The task required bare hands, which immediately froze despite warm rags, regardless of whether they belonged to a radio technician or someone from the higher echelons.

Schmidt was forced to interrupt his operational activities for more than half a year. On 21 December he took off in LN+OR to hunt trains in the Kovda area. His aircraft was hit by Russian anti-aircraft fire and he was wounded. He nursed his machine back to Kiestinki, where he made a smooth landing. After a lengthy hospital stay, he returned to the *Staffel* in mid-June 1942. The following account may be seen as typical of the experiences of many pilots who were wounded and tried to get back to their own lines:

"A second pass, this time from the other side, two long bursts, a few meters above the pines. Suddenly there was a bang, and smoke and white flakes filled my cockpit. A heavy blow. Hit! Everything went black. I pulled up. When I came to, my Bf 110 was wallowing and on the verge of a stall at 600 meters. I advanced the throttles and put the nose down. A cold shock: there was a large exit wound in my right wrist. Blood everywhere. I wanted to say something but had to cough. Had I been shot through the lung? There was a gurgling in my throat, I swallowed and coughed blood. From behind 'Fritz' Friedrich called, 'What's happening?' 'I've been hit. Guide me home and keep an eye open for Indians. I can barely speak.' Fritz tried to pass me dressings but the armor plate was in the way.

"Several instruments were no longer functioning. The oxygen bottles had exploded. Bits of fur from my boots and jacket were whirling around before my eyes. I headed southwest, towards Kiestinki. Hopefully no Russian fighters would find us. It was just 30 minutes to Kiestinki. Just beyond the front lay our snow-covered emergency landing lake. I had to make it that far. I was having difficulty breathing. Blood in the trachea. I couldn't breathe deeply because I was strapped in tight. We didn't have adjustable belts, and because of our thick fur clothing we sat with our heads so close to the gunsight that we had to be strapped in especially tight to avoid banging our heads in the event of a belly landing. 'Fritz' gave course corrections. I was lucky to have someone with me I could rely on. The exit wound in my arm looked so big that I doubted that my hand was still attached. The artery, at least, must have been hit. But there was no spurting blood Nevertheless, I would soon lose so much blood that I wouldn't be able to make a belly landing. I had to get down before I became too weak. Outside barren tundra, covered in deep snow. About minus twenty degrees. The Soviet outposts were thinly spread, it was possible to slip through, but we had no skis and one needed to be healthy. But 'Fritz' was a bear of a man, 19 years old. He could do plenty. But keep flying! Every second of flight meant one less hour of walking.

"The Bf 110 was well-trimmed. I flew it with my left hand, my right lay on my knees. It was a big effort to pull off my glove. The hand was still there and I could even move my fingers a little. I placed the glove over the wound, as it was also cold inside. My Bf 110 droned faithfully and flew despite having been hit. I felt nauseous and my throat tickled. The urge to loosen my straps became more powerful. But I mustn't, as the effort would tire me out. I was becoming so tired. Should I land now? No, too cold outside. Flying is better than walking – hang on! I had ducked my head and pressed the throat microphone firmly against my neck to reduce the bleeding. I became drowsy. Time passed. To the right it was dark.

To the left, toward the south, there were reddish streaks between the cloud layers. The sun was shining there somewhere. And in two days it would be Christmas.

"The rays of light served as indicators for my attitude and heading. All of a sudden the horizon began floating to the left. I felt lighter. Suddenly 'Fritze' shouted, 'Hey! Left wing up! Pull up!' I jumped. Had I nodded off? Good! He was flying for me. I could close my eyes without worrying. He would watch out. 'Fritze' became angry a second time. From far away he gave course corrections. I had to stay more alert. The thirty minutes seemed never-ending.

"'Fritze' later told me that he had twice stood in the rear by the machine-gun hatch with his parachute attached, ready to jump, and watched as the Bf 110 slowly dropped its left wing. The he had shouted and given corrections and the aircraft reacted. At 400 meters, he would have baled out otherwise.

"Then suddenly he screamed, 'There, at eleven o'clock, the positions, we've made it! We're almost to the airfield!' But not down yet. Now it's my turn. My will to live reawakened. I had to make the landing. But he should bale out. 'Get out!' – 'No!' – 'That's an order.' – No further response.

"Landing the twin-engined Bf 110, which had no automatic pitch control, on the lake – barred to air traffic because of heavy snowdrifts – with one hand, was not simple. But everything happened automatically. I even lowered the undercarriage. The lights showed green; the undercarriage had not been hit. Landing flaps? Not necessary. The lake was huge and I wouldn't have to go around. Throttles back. Trim. Gliding. Flare. I seemed to float forever, but eventually the 110 plopped down into the snow. But then it acted up again, ran into a snowdrift and tried to stand on its nose. That was dangerous. The predetermined breaking point was directly above my knees. I rammed the throttle levers forward and pulled the stick into my stomach. The elevators reacted and the nose came back up. I cut power and pulled. All this with one hand. Somewhere, perhaps after two kilometers, the machine came to a stop. We had made it!

"Then 'Fritze' was banging on the cockpit. Of course he hadn't baled out and was standing on the wing. I got out of my harness. He had a ready-to-use dressing and bandaged my arm. Then we taxied back to where several old blockhouses stood at the edge of the forest on the shore. It was called Kiestinki. I was tired and satisfied. Later, in a tent in the field hospital, under the glare of a Petrix lamp, after giving my personal data, I slowly slipped under the anesthesia: 'But doctor, I have to fly again in eight days.'

"'But of course!'"

It would be eight months.

Meanwhile the opposing side had also done something. On the northern front the Russians had inexorably built up their air defenses, which had become formidable. The Germans realized this in December 1941, when for the first time there were no longer Rata fighters in the air. Instead they began meeting the sleeker MiG-3 and LaGG-3.

These were the aspects under which the year 1941 came to an end in the north. Christmastime finally gave the men of the *Staffel* something to be happy about, for there was a change from the monotonous daily rations of dried potatoes, hardtack and cheese in a tube: ptarmigan in wine sauce! No one knows who actually shot them, but there is probably no need to waste any words about the joy with which this holiday meal was received.

"But the frozen sweet potatoes with it were an atrocity!"

With the start of the new year the escort missions went on as before, but now the *Staffel* began to take form. Technical personnel arrived, making it possible for the unit's aircraft to be properly maintained, in an orderly manner. In the coming weeks the *Staffel* would also receive new aircraft and crews.

On 24 January 1942 it was *Oberfeldwebel* Theo Weißenberger's turn again. At noon he took off with *Oberleutnant* Franzisket to hunt trains on the Murmansk railway. Fifteen minutes later Weißenberger shot down an enemy fighter northeast of Boyaskoye railway station and was in the process of attacking another, a Hurricane. At 13:40 Franzisket and *Unteroffizier* Pfeiffer, radio operator in Weißenberger's LN+IR, observed the enemy aircraft crash near Toporny station, thus confirming Weißenberger's second and third victories. He provided a brief description of the action in a letter to H. H. Schmidt, who had been a friend since their gliding days together and was now lying in hospital: "On 24 January two Bf 110s hunting trains with cover from three Bf 109s. Sudden attack by four I-18s and three Hurricanes. In the course of the air battle I shot down an I-18 from a range of 50 meters at a height of 300 meters. I then shot down a Hurricane at low altitude from point-blank range (20-30 meters). The Bf 109s shot down two more, making four victories altogether."

Meanwhile the new *Jagdgeschwader 5* had been created from the existing fighter units and initially the *Zerstörer* unit was administratively attached to II./JG 5, the former *Jagdgruppe z.b.V.* under *Major* Strümpell, although it retained its own distinct character.

At the end of January snow and fog dominated the operational area and the *Staffel* was forced to remain on the ground. Any flying that was done involved extraordinary risks. The 2nd of February 1942 was a black day in the history of the *Zerstörerstaffel*. That Monday Brandis, who had been promoted to *Oberleutnant*, took off with a dozen Messerschmitts shortly after 11:00 to hunt trains. As the mission produced no results, during the return flight he ordered a landing in Kiestinki. As they approached Kiestinki the aircraft suddenly flew into a bad weather front, and in minutes the pilots lost sight of the horizon. Over the radio came the message, "Kiestinki airfield socked in!", whereupon the pilots tried to divert to Rovaniemi, flying low over the numerous and now invisible lakes. A cacophony of voices filled the airwaves. No one knew exactly where they were. Schloßstein went off on his own and flew through a snow shower to Kiestinki. The crews of Brandis/Baus and Franzisket/Pittack followed. But then both aircraft crashed as they made 180-degree turns. While Franzisket was able to make a belly landing, Brandis' Bf 110 struck the ice of Pyav Lake. The *Staffelkapitän* was killed and his radio operator Herbert Baus was thrown from the aircraft and suffered serious injuries. Franzisket, whose machine came down not far from Brandis', finally managed to locate the injured Baus. Together they made an exhausting nine-hour trek to a Finnish outpost. Schloßstein later sent a *Storch* to collect the two men.

What happened to the rest of the *Staffel* in the meantime? When the wall of snow reached the *Zerstörer* formation returning from the front, Weißenberger and Munding flew through the weather front on instruments and landed safely in Rovaniemi. *Oberleutnant* Hans Kirchmeier flew into the ground southeast of Kiestinki and his aircraft overturned. When he regained his senses he found himself under the BF 110 between one of the engines and the cockpit. He would have suffocated there if his radio operator hadn't pulled him free after several tries.

At 25 years of age, *Oberleutnant* Brandis, who lost his life so tragically, had become one of the *Zerstörerstaffel*'s most capable and exemplary personalities, respected and revered by the entire *Staffel*. By the time of his death he had shot down 14 enemy aircraft. On 11 February Brandis was buried with military honors in the military cemetery in Rovaniemi. Leadership of his *Staffel* passed to *Oberleutnant* Karl Fritz Schloßstein.

Throughout February 1942 the *Staffel* flew escort missions for Ju 87s and Ju 88s to Ferosero, the military port of Polyarny and Murmansk. On 25 February *Oberfeldwebel* Weißenberger shot down two Hurricanes between 11:15 and 11:22. One day later the *Staffel* returned to Kirkenes, where the crews moved back into their former quarters on the road to Neiden. The dispersal was at the western edge of the base. On 16 March the *Staffel* was renamed 10.(Z)/JG 5 and placed under the direct command of the *Geschwader*, whose headquarters was still in Oslo and would remain there until June, when it moved to Petsamo.

The German bombers now shifted their main effort to Murmansk. Escorted by Messerschmitt heavy fighters, KG 30 and I./St.G. 5 were constantly over the area of the Tuloma River and Kolskiy Bay. Special attention was paid to the two Russian airfields at Murmashi and Varlamovo, from where enemy fighters took off to intercept the German attacks. The obsolete I-153 and especially the Rata had by then disappeared from the northern front, their places taken by the more maneuverable Hurricane and Airacobra. While these types were faster than the *Zerstörer*, the victories achieved demonstrated that the *Staffel* was capable of holding its own against them. *Oberfeldwebel* Weißenberger alone recorded eight victories in April 1942, including three in two sorties west of Murmansk on 15 April.

While covering the return of Stukas on 8 April, a *Schwarm* of Bf 110s fought a fierce battle against 12 to 15 Russian fighters north of Ristikent. "We pulled away in steep turns until the Russians were low on fuel", wrote Gerhard Friedrich, *Oberleutnant* Franzisket's radio operator on this mission, "then we tried to join up with the Stukas again. Things had become very hot for us." At about 15:20 Weißenberger shot down a MiG. *Leutnant* Kirchmeier and *Leutnant* Koch had to make forced landings but were uninjured.

The *Staffel* flew its last mission of the month on the 25th. At 07:20 it was scrambled against a group of about 20 Pe-2 bombers. The enemy aircraft were sighted south of Motovskiy Bay. Weißenberger shot two bombers down in flames on his first pass after silencing their rear gunners. As he closed in on the next bomber, three other Pe-2s suddenly turned to cut off the German fighter. Weißenberger shot the tail off the aircraft in front of him before enemy fire struck his Bf 110's starboard fuel tank. Weißenberger immediately broke away, but his starboard engine was in flames. He managed to nurse the crippled fighter back to the German lines, where he made a smooth belly landing. Weißenberger and his radio operator *Unteroffizier* Pfeiffer were picked up a short time later by *Oberleutnant* Widowitz in the Fieseler *Storch*. He later wrote: "That day I was flying LN+BR, *Oberleutnant* Koch's beautiful new machine. It was consumed by flames and exploded."

It should not go unmentioned that Widowitz's rescue efforts had become famous, not unlike those carried out, for example, by *Hauptmann* Kroseberg and his "Stork *Staffel*" with JG 27 in the North Africa theater. In the far north there were more than a few pilots who probably owed their lives to the tireless and self-sacrificing search missions by *Oberleutnant* Widowitz.

At the beginning of May 1941 the *Zerstörerstaffel*'s victories were distributed as follows: *Oberfeldwebel* Weißenberger 13, *Oberleutnant* Franzisket 4, *Unteroffizier* Fiedler and *Oberleutnant* Schloßstein 3 each, *Leutnant* Krippahl, *Leutnant* Maul and *Oberfeldwebel* Munding 2 each. On the 10th of May, a Sunday, the *Luftwaffe* recorded a major success on the northern front. In the morning a *Staffel* of Bf 109s engaged three times their own number of Russian fighters over Ura Bay northwest of Murmansk, and the result was six victories for one loss. The *Zerstörer* then joined the battle and shot down three more enemy aircraft. In the afternoon the *Zerstörerstaffel* flew escort for dive-bombers and engaged a group of about 30 Russian aircraft, the majority of them Hurricanes. Fierce battles developed over the coast of Motovskiy Bay in which no fewer than 13 Soviet aircraft were destroyed. In the area between Eina-Guba and the Lisa, Weißenberger alone shot down three MiGs and a Hurricane in a matter of minutes. Bf 109s then attacked and destroyed three more Hurricanes. The day ended with two Hurricanes shot down during an evening escort mission in the direction of Murmansk. The enemy's losses for 10 May 1942 totaled 37 aircraft, 22 of them Hurricanes. During a midday mission on 15 May Weißenberger shot down his twentieth enemy aircraft, a Hurricane, 20 kilometers west of Murmansk.

At that time the Russian air force was still maintaining an essentially defensive posture and its offensive efforts were largely limited to nuisance raids against *Luftflotte 5*'s airfields. At night they sent U-2 biplanes, the so-called "sewing machines" that were known all across the Eastern Front, over the German bases to drop fragmentation bombs or simply to disturb the night rest. The *Zerstörerstaffel* was often sent up to try to intercept the nuisance raiders, usually without success, such as on the bright night of 1 June 1942, when the Bf 110s were scrambled from Kirkenes at 00:03 and again at 01:31. That same day, during an afternoon mission to Murmansk, the first Curtiss P-40 fighter fell to the *Zerstörerstaffel*. Once again the victorious pilot was Weißenberger. Five kilometers southwest of Murmansk he shot down the enemy machine from a distance of 30 meters from out of a left turn.

On the afternoon of 18 June ten of the *Staffel*'s BF 110s again escorted the Stuka *Gruppe* to Murmansk, and this time they were attacked by ten Airacobras. In the ensuing scrap west of the port city *Leutnant* Krippahl's LN+LR was lost. The aircraft went down at about 15:20. *Leutnant* Harry Krippahl, who had been married just four weeks earlier, and his radio operator, *Oberfeldwebel* Erich Kulik, failed to return and were reported missing.

In June a fourth *Gruppe* was added to *Jagdgeschwader 5*, resulting in the renumbering of many *Staffeln*. On 26 June 1942 10.(Z)/JG 5 received its ultimate designation, 13.(Z)/JG 5, but remained directly attached to the *Geschwader*. The nature and execution of the unit's missions also remained unchanged. On or about 15 June the *Staffel* flew its 1,500th mission since the start of the eastern campaign. It is noteworthy that in the summer of 1942 there was a steady flow of equipment and personnel to the unit; at times the *Zerstörerstaffel* had more than 18 crews and was overstaffed with officers. As a result, many of them – especially older men with no hopes of achieving a command position within the *Zerstörer* unit – accepted transfers to the day fighter units in Petsamo. These included such successful pilots as Dahn, Kirchmeier, Koch, Maul, H.H. Schmidt and Weißenberger. In the fighter units there was a constant demand for *Staffel* leaders and the *Zerstörer* pilots were experienced and instrument qualified, which proved extremely useful in the extended darkness of winter and periods of bad weather.

An extensive air park was established in Pori in southern Finland, where engine and airframe checks could be carried out. For this purpose, until the end of 1942 the *Staffel* seconded pilots to Pori for maintenance test flights on a rotating basis. Whereas the unit's activities were limited in June 1942, the following month saw a significant resurgence. A number of these missions are associated with a very special incident – no one could suspect the repercussions this mission would have. It was the last flight by *Leutnant* Hans-Bodo von Rabenau.

The Rescue of the Sonderführer

In the second week of August 1942 a very special vehicle appeared at the Dachshund *Staffel*'s dispersal in Kirkenes. It turned out to be an antiquated radio vehicle carrying two army war reporters. They had come from the Dietl Mountain Corps to report on cooperation between the airmen and the mountain infantry. Someone observed that the vehicle must surely have been captured in Spain, and the *Zerstörer* crews wondered how the long-legged automobile had made it all the way to the far north. In any case, the unusual guests from the army were given a warm welcome, because for the *Staffel* it meant a change from the daily routine of tough missions. The two propaganda company men hardly made a lasting impression on the men in Kirkenes, but this did not appear to bother the two print reporters, who looked rather intentionally formal. By mentioning Keitel's "Red Pass", they slyly revealed that they were persons cleared for access to secret information, which authorized them to set foot on any military installation, even those considered top secret.

At first the units hosted the men and told them about their combat experiences, and it soon became obvious that the two reporters were eager to go along on an operational flight. Franzisket's immediate reaction was, "Certainly not with us!," as he considered it a matter of safety. Taking along a third man in a Bf 110 would have been a problem on account of the extensive sea survival and tundra emergency equipment carried in the aircraft, especially if enemy aircraft were encountered.

The two propaganda company men were eager to go up, however, and they weren't carrying their famous passes for nothing. And so Franzisket finally contacted his superiors and expressed his willingness to take the two radio people along, certain that the idea would be firmly rejected. And at first it was. "What kind of boys are these, thinking they can make Strength through Joy excursions to the front with us?" came the reply. "We're going to consult with corps immediately."

The return call came quickly, however: "It's on. These reports are considered especially important here. Within the realm of possibility you are to give these PK people the opportunity to take part in operational sorties, of course only if it does not affect the *Staffel*'s operational readiness and if men and materiel are not placed at risk."

There were long faces among the *Zerstörer* airmen. "Well, if that's the way it is, then why not? We can do it on a Sunday when Ivan's in church!"

The moment came just three days later, on 13 August 1942, a "risk-free" mission. The *Staffel* was to escort Ju 88s to Murmashi, a Sunday outing. Franzisket decided, however, that only one of the two officers could go. Then he held the mission briefing.

"*Leutnant* von Rabenau will take the man in his machine, *Leutnant* Weißenberger will fly as wingman and provide cover. And please ... be very careful."

The choice fell upon *Sonderführer* Kuhnke, who was kitted out with a life vest, helmet, aviation sunglasses and parachute by the ground personnel, who also gave him all the necessary instructions. Then he took his position in the gunner's cockpit. *Unteroffizier* Schröder, von Rabenau's radio operator, who usually operated the machine-guns, squeezed himself into the middle of the cramped cockpit. Ten Bf 110s taxied out for takeoff. The "Sunday mission," on which nothing was supposed to happen, got under way.

But something did happen. At first the escort mission was uneventful, until all of a sudden several Russian fighters showed up and attacked the *Zerstörer* formation. They concentrated their attacks on one machine – the Bf 110 of *Leutnant* von Rabenau with the war reporter on board – almost as if they knew that the rear gun was manned by someone with no experience. *Leutnant* Weißenberger was able to chase away the first and then the second enemy fighter and prevent further attacks on the Bf 110 he had been ordered to protect.

But then the last attacking Russian scored a lucky hit, such as frequently had a great impact tragic or not. The enemy bullet hit the Messerschmitt's port engine and set it on fire. Many pilots had returned with dozens of hits in the engine, but now of all times it had to catch fire.

The Russian fighters disappeared again as quickly as they had appeared, allowing Weißenberger and his covering *Rotte* to turn their attention to von Rabenau's smoking aircraft. He safely escorted it west over the forests and lakes of the tundra. "Raven 7 from Raven 9! Don't worry, Indians have broken off."

"Viktor, Viktor!" replied von Rabenau calmly. "Everything is OK here!" No one knows what the PK man was thinking. He probably thought that nothing else could go wrong. Urd Lake was already in front of them and from there it was just 40 kilometers to the first friendly outposts.

"Raven 9 from 7. The engine's losing power – losing altitude!" It seemed that the hit hadn't been as harmless as originally thought, for now the excess weight of the third crewman and his equipment was preventing the Bf 110 from maintaining height on one engine. *Leutnant* von Rabenau wouldn't be able to stay airborne much longer. For this reason he gave the order to bale out. For the veteran radio operator Schröder this was the signal to push the well-packed *Sonderführer* Kühnke rather roughly and quickly out of the aircraft, after once again going over how to operate the parachute. Then *Unteroffizier* Schröder advised his pilot that he was going and jumped too.

Leutnant von Rabenau felt the lightening of his machine and was more or less able to maintain altitude. Flying beside him was Weißenberger, who advised him to bale out immediately in case the engine fire got worse. But who can predict if and when a fuel tank is going to explode? On the other hand, every flying minute towards home was about three kilometers less of enemy territory. It was something that every pilot in that situation took into consideration, for in the event of a forced landing one wanted to be as close to one's own lines as possible.

Similar thoughts were probably on von Rabenau's mind and he kept flying his burning Bf 110. Then he spotted a small level marshy area where he could make a belly landing. Scarcely had the machine touched the ground, however, when there was a huge flash. The port fuel tank had exploded, shattering the forward part of the machine. *Leutnant* Bodo von Rabenau found his grave in the vastness of the tundra. The fire at the crash site smoldered for three days, while the remains of the Messerschmitt slowly sank into the swamp.

The *Staffel* had meanwhile returned to its base in order to organize an immediate rescue effort. Of course there was great unrest on the Kirkenes airfield, as by then headquarters had learned of the incident. The main concern was for *Sonderführer* Kuhnke. "Don't you know," *Oberleutnant* Franzisket was told, "that this man carries the red pass? And you take him with your *Staffel* to Murmashi and then plonk him down at Ivan's feet! The corps demands that this man be rescued from the tundra immediately!"

Franzisket's argument that the corps had expressly requested the mission in question was probably lost in the general commotion. As the *Staffel* had to remain at operational readiness, the search and rescue mission was given to H.H. Schmidt, who, after being wounded in December 1941, had only been back with the *Staffel* for four weeks. Technically he wasn't supposed to fly because his wounds were slow to heal.

And so Schmidt and Weißenberger were given the task of retrieving the war reporter.

Franzisket vented his anger: "Of course no one will take responsibility for it now, but what difference does it make? Get the man back or else we're in deep shit!"

The dramatic rescue of *Sonderführer* Kuhnke required an all-out effort by the two *Zerstörer* pilots. The crew of Schmidt and Weißenberger flew six missions totaling 337 minutes flying time (five and a half hours) between 21:33 on 13 August and 18:29 on 14 August. Then it was time to sleep, and the next mission began at 12:58 on the 15th. Deserving of special recognition are the Arado crew from the air-sea rescue *Staffel* in Kirkenes and the *Zerstörer* radio operator Gerhard Friedrich, who volunteered both for the *Storch* search flight as well as those carried out by the Ar 196 floatplane, or "paramecium" as it was called by the fighter crews.

The Arado crew, with *Oberfeldwebel* Günter Urtel as pilot, flew 80 kilometers deep into Soviet-held tundra and took the *Sonderführer* on board under the most difficult conditions. The aircraft was then shot down and the crew spent two days making its way through the mosquito-infested swamps, pursued by a Russian reindeer brigade, past the enemy outposts, and finally regained the German lines.

Bitterness rose in the men when they realized that the staffs appeared to be less interested in the death of *Leutnant* von Rabenau and the still uncertain fate of the outstanding radio operator *Unteroffizier* Schröder than they were in Kuhnke and his "red pass". For the time being, however, there was no time for further thinking. They had to find the men who had baled out, and quickly, for the other side surely was not unaware of the incident. Perhaps the Russians were already looking for the involuntary parachutists. Schmidt had Weißenberger explain the exact positions of the bale-outs and von Rabenau's crash site and entered them on the latest 1:100,000 flight charts. Then both pilots established the course and agreed on a division of the search. At the same time emergency kits with maps and food were prepared. Though it was almost midnight, at that time of the year there was still twilight, and it was possible to fly round the clock.

At 21:33 on 13 August 1942 *Hauptmann* Schmidt and his radio operator Friedrich took off from Kirkenes in LN+HR, along with *Leutnant* Weißenberger and his radio operator, *Unteroffizier* Pfeiffer, in LN+PR. They turned on course and disappeared at low level in the direction of the search area. About nine kilometers east of the southern tip of Urd Lake they could make out the smoldering wreck of their *Staffel* comrade's Messerschmitt, which had crashed just a few hours before. From there they had to keep their eyes open, for no one knew what had happened to the two survivors in the difficult country below.

It must then have been more than a fortunate coincidence that *Hauptmann* sighted *Sonderführer* Kuhnke in a narrow lane just a kilometer from the crash site. Kuhnke had set fire to some paper to attract attention. The two search aircraft turned and dropped two smoke cartridges with the emergency kits. Unfortunately the PK reporter was unable to locate the packets. Then the two Bf 110s turned back and at 23:15 landed in Kirkenes.

Less than three hours later they took off again, this time from Petsamo. *Hauptmann* Schmidt described the first mission of the new day as follows:

14/8/42: LN+PR (Lt. Weißenberger), LN+HR (*Hptm*. Schmidt). Takeoff from Petsamo 02:44. Landing Petsamo 04:26. Escort for a Fieseler *Storch* (also provided guidance). No signal observed, located *Sonderführer* K. 2 km SW of his previous position. Dropped 1 x summer emergency equipment and message box with instructions to reach the southern tip of Urd Lake by 10:00 and identify his position with light signals and dye packet. (Discovery observed).

So this time it had worked. Meanwhile the air-sea rescue detachment in Kirkenes was also advised and it provided an Arado 196 to pick up the *Sonderführer*. Back from Petsamo, at 12:07 the aircraft of *Hauptmann* Schmidt and *Leutnant* Weißenberger took off at 12:07 to fly the second search mission of the day. The two machines escorted the Arado, with *Unteroffizier* Friedrich aboard, to the agreed-upon rendezvous point. But Kuhnke wasn't there. Circling low over the difficult terrain, Schmidt for the third time spotted a lone man. Fearing discovery, he was understandably hesitant to give a clear signal. Kuhnke had gone to the wrong lake; he was on the east side of Vezhny Lake. The Ar 196 was quickly redirected. It immediately touched down on the mirror-smooth surface of the lake. A dinghy was sent to collect Kuhnke and the Arado's pilot started the engine again.

But then two MiG-3s suddenly appeared out of nowhere. They roared in at low level and opened fire on the floatplane with their machine-guns. In seconds the two *Zerstörer*, which were watching over the rescue at low altitude, engaged the Russians. Weißenberger got on the tail of one of the enemy fighters at a height of just 50 meters, and as the Russian pilot tried to take evasive action he made contact with the ground. The Soviet fighter crashed about ten kilometers east of Vezhny Lake at 13:24. It was Weißenberger's 22nd victory. *Hauptmann* Schmidt made a head-on pass at the second Russian fighter to prevent it from shooting at the Arado. Neither pilot gave way, and Schmidt's radio operator advised him that the MiG had clipped off the 110's antenna mast. The MiG then began trailing black smoke – probably from a damaged oil cooler – and pulled up into the clouds. The Bf 110 had taken five hits, all around the cockpit, but they were not serious. Schmidt was unable to claim the MiG as a victory as he did not see it go down.

The two heavy fighters then returned to the lake. To their dismay, the *Zerstörer* pilots saw the Arado still sitting on the water on the north shore of the lake, its engine not running. The three men from the Arado and the *Sonderführer* waved from the shore, signaling that the machine could not take off from the lake. The rescue of the PK reporter had now entered a new, uncertain phase. The situation then became critical when six more Russian fighters, Curtiss P-40s and Yaks, approached. This time the German pilots were able to spot the enemy in time and divert them west, away from the recovery site. With insufficient fuel for combat, it was fortunate that a heavy shower moved in, enabling them to disengage from the enemy. The pair landed in Petsamo shortly before 14:00 and immediately arranged for flights of fighters to hold station over the rescue site, however no more enemy aircraft appeared. There followed a third search mission on 14 August. The Schmidt and Weißenberger crews took off from Petsamo at about 17:30 and found the four men left behind in the tundra three kilometers west of the lake's western tip. This time they dropped instructions to Field Outpost 11, which was about 40 kilometers away, directing it to send a patrol in the opposite direction. Meanwhile an intercepted radio transmission had revealed that the Russians had dispatched a reindeer battalion to search for the Germans in the tundra. This was very serious news. The next day, therefore, the two pilots of 13.(Z)/JG 5 carried out a diversionary flight. Again a description from Schmidt's personal papers: "15/8/42: LN+PR (*Lt.* Weißenberger), LN+NR (*Hptm.* Schmidt). Takeoff from Kirkenes 12:50. Landing in Kirkenes 13:53. Diversionary flight on the center east side of Urd Lake (low passes, firing of flares and waggling of wings) to divert attention of possible enemy forces. Flew back along crew's probable march route in the direction of Menyikova Hill, where German patrol waited to receive them. Nothing seen of crew or patrol. Did not search further to avoid attracting attention."

"Fritze" Friedrich wrote: "We got through OK. The air-sea rescue boys were excellent fellows. The mosquitoes made things tough on us though. And once I almost killed Kuhnke. He bellyached after getting mud on his mosquito net. After a long internal struggle I gave him mine, because I felt so sorry for him. The mosquitoes really were a torment. After a while he lost his net again while creeping through the birches. The complaining began as before. I could have hit him. The mosquitoes really could drive one mad."

Sonderführer Kuhnke returned to Propaganda Company 680 in one piece. He wrote a fantastic account in which he was in the middle of all the action. Perhaps he wasn't entirely wrong. An effort like this wouldn't have been made for a mere mortal. And the brave *Unteroffizier* Schröder, *Leutnant* von Rabenau's radio operator? It is no longer entirely clear how he made it. In any case, he completed a difficult cross-country trek through the trackless forests, bypassing enemy outposts, arriving home even before the others made it safely to the German lines.

After that 14th of August 1942 Vezhnye Lake became known as "Arado lake" to the *Zerstörer* crews, and years later the abandoned Ar 196 was still at the north tip of the lake.

Epilogue in Murmansk, one and a half years later. The interrogating Soviet captain said to the prisoner H.H. Schmidt: "So, if you were with the heavy fighters in the summer of 1942, then you must know the name of the general who was shot down in an Me 110."

"?"

"So, you know nothing about it? A floatplane was supposed to pick him up but our brave red falcons foiled the plan."

"The two MiG-3s?"

"Oh, so you do know about it?"

"Yes, I was there. What became of the MiGs?"

"Well, one made a forced landing ten kilometers east of the lake; the other is missing."

"Thank you for the belated victory confirmation. We already know how the forced landing turned out."

It turned out that the Soviet captain had taken part in the search effort by the other side. Later in the conversation, when he learned to his dismay that he hadn't been chasing a general, he asked: "Tell me, why did the German group try to go north around Urd Lake; after all, the next day you dropped emergency kits on the northeast shore. We found them. The southern route would surely have been much easier." Schmidt was very satisfied that their diversionary flights had been a success, and he did not reveal to his adversary that the group had in fact taken the southern route to get home.

Convoy Escort Missions

More and more the *Zerstörer* were called upon to carry out bombing missions themselves, as on Wednesday, 2 September 1942. That day the *Staffel* flew two attacks against Murmashi airfield. During the return flight it lost the crew of *Oberfeldwebel* Frenzel and *Unteroffizier* Hemmenstedt just prior to landing in Kirkenes. Their aircraft was on approach to land when its port engine quit. Frenzel was probably already too low to take corrective action; the Messerschmitt crashed from low altitude and both airmen were killed. The same thing almost happened to *Leutnant* Weißenberger, for he also came back on one engine but managed to make a relatively safe landing in his LN+PR. The *Staffel* lost another crew two days later, when *Unteroffizier* Assmuss was supposed to ferry a Bf 110 F-2 from Pori to Kirkenes. He and his radio operator, *Gefreiter* Härtel, made a fuel stop in Kemijärvi. They took off again and were last heard from at 17:30 from the Sondankylä area. No trace of the aircraft and crew was ever found.

The final months of 1942 again found the *Staffel* operating from the airfields in Rovaniemi, Alakurtti, Petsamo and Kirkenes. On the afternoon of 8 September Theo Weißenberger came home with his 23rd victory. It was to be his last with the *Zerstörer* unit before he joined 6./JG 5 and began his extraordinary rise as a fighter pilot, eventually becoming a leading ace and *Staffelkapitän* of 7./JG 5.

A regrettable accident occurred at the *Zerstörerstaffel*'s based in Kirkenes on Sunday, the 11th of October 1942. In the morning Schloßstein received the *Staffel*'s mission orders, whereupon the aircraft were each armed with two SD 250 bombs and readied for takeoff. For reasons that are unexplained, at about 11:30 the mission was cancelled and the *Staffelführer* subsequently ordered the aircraft unloaded. Then, shortly after 13:00, there was suddenly a terrific explosion which completely destroyed two aircraft and damaged two others. The armorer involved, *Flieger* Kulterer, probably switched the bomb fusing panel back on by mistake and accidentally jettisoned the bombs. The fuses in the bombs had toggle pins, which oscillated for a short while after impact, and the bombs were set off despite the short fall. In any case the effect was devastating. Kulterer was killed in the explosion, and the two engines and other parts of the Bf 110 were hurled more than 20 meters. By an unfortunate coincidence one of the engines landed in the midst of a group of construction troops that happened to be marching by. Twelve men were killed and the others were more or less badly injured.

The new year 1943 also got off to a bad start. *Leutnant* Forst and his radio operator *Unteroffizier* Hitzinger were killed on 5 January. Their Bf 110, LN+RR, developed engine trouble west of Kemijärvi. Forst put the Messerschmitt into a steep turn to the left in an attempt to return to the airfield. At 10:50 the aircraft crashed from a height of 500 meters and both airmen were killed. On 9 February *Unteroffizier* Otto Weißenberger, brother of Theo Weißenberger, made a forced landing after losing both engines. He and his radio operator were both injured but survived. The next day when *Leutnant* Weißenberger, who had since been transferred to 6./JG 5, heard of the accident, he immediately climbed into a *Storch* with *Unteroffizier* Krischkovski and flew to the suspected crash area. This reaction was typical of the 28-year-old *Leutnant*, who never lacked decisiveness, and he did not hesitate to personally look for his brother in hope of rescuing him from the tundra. The first search flight from Alakurtti at 10:18 was unsuccessful, and after an hour and twenty minutes Weißenberger landed at Kemijärvi. He took off again at about 14:30 and this time had better luck. He found the crash-landed Bf 110 about ten kilometers south of Alakurtti, and, after a rather uncomfortable flight, he returned safely to Alakurtti with his brother Otto and his radio operator Wilhelm Pfeiffer.

The mission on 28 February 1943 proved to be a tragic one, from which *Oberleutnant* Maertins and his radio operator *Unteroffizier* Steinbeck would not return. That day the *Staffel*'s target was again the Murmansk railway, but the Russians were waiting. The call "Watch out, fighters!" rang out over the frequency, but the warning came too late for Maertins. His Messerschmitt, LN+SR, was shot up and he was forced to come down in Soviet territory. As far as his comrades could tell, the forced landing went smoothly; unfortunately no one could say anything about the crew's fate. It was later learned that *Oberleutnant* Maertins had been shot before being taken prisoner. *Unteroffizier* Hans Steinbeck, on the other hand, was captured by the Russians and started down the bitter path of a prisoner of war.

Franzisket was more fortunate, perhaps because he was superstitious. He believed that eating before a combat mission was dangerous. Of course a belly full of lentil soup was not exactly good for a long, high-altitude mission. Once, while on a train-hunting mission, the crews made a refueling stop in Kiestinki, where they also filled up on a delicious green pea stew. But not "Zisket"! Hunger and the inviting aroma eventually overcame his reservations and he began to eat. But then he declared "No! I don't eat before a mission!" and pushed away the half-full plate. But then the inevitable happened – over the Murmansk railway Franzisket was hit and came down 80 kilometers deep inside Russian territory. The *Staffel* held station over the crash site. Theo Weißenberger raced to Kiestinki, grabbed a *Storch* and plucked the crew from under the Russian's nose. Franzisket's comment: "If I had finished the plate, you wouldn't have gotten us out!"

And so the flying went on – armed reconnaissance with bombs against the Murmansk railway south of Murmansk down to Kandalaksha almost every day. On 12 March one of these missions resulted in the destruction of an enemy supply train bound for the Karelian Front.

On 14 March a bad weather front hung over German territory. Schloßstein was on a ferry flight and, because of poor visibility, had difficulty letting down to the airfield. The new Bf 110 G-2 made a hard landing and cracked up. Schloßstein and *Feldwebel* Gerhard Friedrich were injured.

The time came when, thanks to deliveries from the western Allies, the Russian air forces were able to make good on their material losses and even form new units. The enemy had undoubtedly grown stronger, and his defensive combat units had turned into an offensive force. Several German bomber formations, especially the torpedo-bomber units, had moved to the Mediterranean, and largely as a result of this the Russians now tried to turn the tables and block the delivery of German supplies to Petsamo. In the months that followed, therefore, escort missions in support of convoys to and from Petsamo dominated the activities of the *Zerstörerstaffel*.

On 1 May a Russian force of ten to fifteen DB-3 twin-engined bombers set out to attack a German convoy defended by the Messerschmitt heavy fighters. Abeam Kvalnes a fight broke out over the rough waters of the Polar Sea, in which a Soviet rear gunner was able to shoot down *Oberfeldwebel* Renke's Bf 110. The Messerschmitt immediately crashed into the sea. A minesweeper rushed to the crash site and recovered Renke's body, but the sailors were unable to rescue radio operator *Unteroffizier* Helmuth Reiher before the aircraft sank beneath the waves.

By the beginning of 1943 the ratio of opposing forces in the far north was about equal, and a battle now began for superiority in the air. In mid-June, in addition to the handful of Bf 110s of 13.(Z)/JG 5, *Luftflotte 5* had a total of about 70 fighter aircraft, of which 56 were reported serviceable. One month later the figure was 88 fighters, 63 of them serviceable. Three times in June, Kirkenes, where the *Zerstörer* unit was still based, was the target of Russian bombing raids. Heavy damage was inflicted on installations, especially in the harbor area. At the same time the *Zerstörerstaffel* was still primarily tasked with guarding the German convoys. Usually part of the *Staffel* picked up the convoys east of Tana Fjord near Berlevaag before escorting them to Petsamo or Kirkenes. Another *Schwarm* waited near Vardö as airborne reinforcements, while the rest sat on the airfield at five-minute readiness.

The Russian bomber formations consisted mainly of Pe-2s or older British Hampden torpedo-bombers and later Douglas Bostons. They came in low over the water and tried to break up the convoys. There were usually victories and losses on both sides. The anti-aircraft guns on the picket boats caused a lot of problems during the chaotic air battles, as they tended to shoot at everything in the air, posing a threat to both hostile and friendly aircraft. More than once, therefore, the *Staffel* posted an officer on the lead boat to coordinate the defense. It wasn't a very easy or pleasant task.

The *Staffel* suffered its next casualties east of Eckerö on 19 June, when the crew of *Unteroffizier* Friedrich and *Unteroffizier* Denzer was shot down by enemy fighters. Both airmen died in the waves. Three days later *Unteroffizier* Karl Herrmann took off on a combat mission. On returning to Kirkenes his aircraft crashed while landing due to pilot error and he and his radio operator, *Unteroffizier* Alois Herrmann, were killed. On 20 July 1943 the crew of *Feldwebel*

Drechsler and *Unteroffizier* Möst came to grief after losing an engine. Drechsler just managed to nurse the aircraft across Varangerfjord, but then he had to make an emergency landing. Just before touching down the Bf 110 dropped like a stone, hit the ground and exploded. The aircraft was completely consumed by fire.

By that date the *Staffel* had lost 28 men killed and four missing, including 16 complete crews, and despite the flow of replacement pilots and radio operators the *Zerstörer* had difficulty dealing with its losses.

Escort flights and bombing missions alternated constantly, as on 24 July 1943. The twin-engined Messerschmitts were in the air shortly before midnight to bomb and strafe Russian coastal artillery position west of the Fischer Peninsula. The operations ended without incident, but on the following Sunday, 25 July, *Oberleutnant* Kohlweiß lost his radio operator. The *Staffel* was once again loitering over a German convoy far out in Varangerfjord when Russian aircraft attacked. An engagement devcloped abeam Vardö in which several cannon shells struck the cockpit of Kohlweiß' machine, fatally wounding *Feldwebel* Robert Hink in the head.

As soon as German supply ships rounded Vardö and turned in the general direction of Kirkenes, they became especially vulnerable to attacks by Soviet aircraft, and occasionally torpedo boats, from the area of the Fischer Peninsula. Once, on or about 1 August, another German convoy arrived off Vardö. A pair of fighters led by *Hauptmann* Treppe had already been over the southbound convoy for ten minutes when, suddenly, the pilots spotted several dots approaching rapidly at low level.

Treppe radioed a warning to his wingman and the convoy. "Indians coming in from the east!" Then they headed towards the enemy aircraft, a formation of Bostons. As soon as the *Zerstörer* approached, the enemy formation split up.

The *Hauptmann* raced after a pair of bombers that had separated from the main body. "My wingman radioed a warning and my radio operator called out too, alerting me to the presence of nine Hurricanes flying in a defensive circle at an altitude of about 500 meters. From a distance I opened fire on the first Boston with cannon and then machine-guns. The enemy aircraft went down, and I had to take evasive action as I flew past. While my radio operator was reporting seeing the crash, and at the same time advising that we had taken several hits, I already had the next Boston in my sights. I used up the rest of my ammunition, but not without bringing it down too. It was a double by a raw beginner. Only then did I realize, from the uncomfortable draft in my cockpit and the frightful stink of gasoline, that we had been hit too. My radio operator grumbled and reported that I had lost my wingman, who was nowhere to be seen. Despite the cold I opened the cockpit window so that I could breathe freely. It was time to head for the coast and then fly along it back to Kirkenes. To make matters worse there was a Nordstau effect on the coast and very poor visibility. We had several anxious moments on account of the gasoline fumes in the cockpit and the poor visibility outside – during which my radio operator quietly cursed to himself, for forced landings in cold water were almost certain death. Landing our shot-up aircraft on the difficult airfield once again stretched our nerves to the breaking point, then the realization of our double victory overwhelmed us. When I made my report to the air commander, he said to me, 'We know all about it – two coastal observers independently observed the crashes of both aircraft and reported them by telephone. My congratulations.' Incidentally, my radio operator never entirely forgave me for flying across the Polar Sea in the direction of the Fischer Peninsula in that situation – especially without a wingman – and as a newcomer attacking so insanely."

In September 1943 the air fleet gave the *Zerstörerstaffel* a special kind of mission. It was one that fell outside the norm and for which therefore extensive precautions had to be taken. The *Kriegsmarine* was moving its heavy cruiser *Lützow*, which had been based in Alta Fjord, back to home waters. The *Zerstörer* of 13.(Z)/JG 5 were supposed to provide air cover for this move, but as the cruiser's route lay far beyond the aircraft's range, it required the *Staffel* to move to Stavanger to cover the southern part of the voyage. While a Ju 52 transported the necessary technical personnel, ten crews flew their Bf 110s via Bodö, Trondheim and Herdla to Stavanger. Not everything went according to plan, however. First there were crashes during stopovers at the unfamiliar airfields, as a result of which only six of the ten aircraft arrived safely in Stavanger. Fortunately there were no casualties. Then the actual escort flight began. The *Zerstörer* did not pick up the German convoy until it was between Trondheim and Bergen, roughly near Stadlandet, and flew close to the coast parallel to the warships. There the next problem cropped up. Despite repeatedly firing recognition signal flares, the aircraft were shot at by the ships' anti-aircraft guns. *Oberleutnant* Ziegenhagen's aircraft was hit in one of its engines and immediately had to break away. The nearest airfield was Herdla, but Schloßstein was the only one familiar with the airbase. He therefore escorted the damaged Messerschmitt there and Ziegenhagen made a safe landing on one engine.

Werner Alt, then an *Unteroffizier* pilot, also took part in the operations and wrote: "The flak didn't stop firing until we had fired the recognition signal. By then we had flown over the ships. A shell had hit my machine on the right side of the nose. Soon afterwards the oil pressure in the starboard engine began dropping. They later found a hole in the oil cooler caused by a shell fragment. I left the *Staffel*, shut down the engine and turned in the direction of Herdla. While flying on one engine one had to extend one leg and apply full rudder to keep the machine straight (the trim was insufficient). It was very strenuous. I had to make a right turn to set up for landing. As turning into the dead engine would surely have resulted in a crash, I started the other engine again (it didn't have much oil left). In any case, my radio operator and I got down safely."

There were no personnel casualties in this unusual operation, but a convoy escort mission north of Vardö on 6 September cost the lives of two members of the *Staffel*. Russian torpedo-bombers attacked the convoy and contact with the enemy aircraft was made abeam Haringsberg. *Oberfeldwebel* Kolodziej, who had chosen to fly as Ziegenhagen's wingman that day, collided head-on with a Russian Hampden, whereupon both aircraft exploded and fell into the sea. Kolodziej and his radio operator, *Unteroffizier* Willi Schipper, died in the collision.

Meanwhile the *Zerstörerstaffel* was back in Kirkenes, where another change occurred. Plans had been made to establish a night-fighter *Staffel* in Norway, and a number of experienced crews were sent to the Reich for night-fighter training. Unfortunately the retraining process in Kitzingen claimed its first victim on 19 October when *Unteroffizier* Widenhorn and *Unteroffizier* Leonhardt crashed during a training sortie. Schloßstein also left Kirkenes and in December handed 13.(Z)/JG 5 over to *Hauptmann* Herbert.

The coming winter would see the *Zerstörer* remain in Kirkenes for the first time and they also spent Christmas 1943 there. The holiday was not exactly as the airmen had hoped and wished for, however. As was learned later, this was because a special *Kriegsmarine* operation against a Murmansk convoy was underway and weather conditions were good. The *Staffel* received a message from the Air Commander North (East) forbidding any Christmas Eve celebrations. For he knew that, for all units, Christmas parties north of the Arctic Circle inevitably involved plenty of alcohol. The *Zerstörerstaffel* was ordered to hold readiness, which extended through the first holiday. The 26th and 27th of December finally brought flying weather, and the *Staffel* received approval to hold its well-deserved party on the second day of Christmas. The men were assured that they would have a rest day on the 27th.

The north wind howled over the barracks, covered in snow with just the roofs sticking out, and the footpaths dug in the man-deep snow. Inside, as the drinks flowed, the men took turns singing Christmas carols and watching merry skits. They were anything but sober.

At about three in the morning on 27 December the phone began ringing. After the incessant ringing was ignored for a while, finally someone picked up the receiver and then handed it to the *Staffelkapitän*. He heard the voice of the operations officer, who relayed to him a three-part operations order:

1. The *Staffel* was to immediately stop the party and go to bed.
2. The Bf 110s were to be loaded with bombs at 06:00.
3. From 08:00 the *Staffel* was to conduct armed reconnaissance in the following sea areas. Any enemy warships were to be attacked and destroyed.

Then followed four numbers, which *Hauptmann* Treppe had to write down. He then asked if they had forgotten the promise that the *Staffel* would be left in peace on the 27th. He argued that low-level attacks against ships by such unpracticed crews with inadequate weaponry made no sense and was pure suicide. The crews would never get close enough to the heavily-armed ships to drop their bombs.

Only then did Treppe learn the facts. The 26th of December 1943 was a black day in the history of the German navy. A destroyer flotilla and the battleship *Scharnhorst* had sortied against an Allied convoy. In the polar night the German warships encountered a powerful enemy task force which sank a destroyer and then the *Scharnhorst* with radar-directed gunfire. The German seamen never saw their attackers and there were few survivors. The mission by the *Zerstörer* of JG 5 was the result of an express order from Hitler and was meant as a reprisal against the Allied naval forces. "Enemy ships are to be sunk when found!"

Sobered, the *Staffelkapitän* issued the necessary orders and sent the men to bed. Then he assembled his most experienced officers in his "command post," his living and bedroom. Together they carried out the laborious task of dividing up the assigned sea area for missions in pairs and calculated the headings and times for each *Rotte*. Then they went to bed, satisfied that they had done everything possible under the circumstances.

The next morning there was thick fog that grounded the *Staffel*. The air commander seemed to be pleased that he didn't have to send his pilots out to sea in the condition they were in, and he summarily cancelled the whole thing. Few of the airmen regretted the decision, despite their great sympathy and sadness over the deaths of so many sailors.

Back in Norway – The End in Stavanger

The new year 1944 began with a transfer. A new unit had been created in Kiestinki under the command of *Major* Wolf, operations officer in the staff of the Air Commander North (East). Several *Jagdstaffeln* of JG 5 had already been attached to the new unit, and now elements of the *Zerstörerstaffel* were to join it as well. For this reason, on about 9 January the *Zerstörer*, under the command of Oberleutnant Ziegenhagen, moved to Kiestinki, where the so-called "*Nahkampfgruppe Süd*" (Close Combat Group South) was located at the time. The unit's mission: intensive attacks against targets on the Murmansk railway. But this was not enough to cut the supply line so vital to the Russians. Though many sections of track had been destroyed and traffic hampered, Murmansk and its rail line kept functioning to the end. The actions by the *Nahkampfgruppe* could do nothing to change this. On 13 January it attacked the railway station in Kusema and was greeted by a storm of anti-aircraft fire. The attack itself dissipated, and only a few machines made diving attacks. Then *Leutnant* Helmut Müller's Messerschmitt took a direct hit. Initially reported missing, Müller's body was finally recovered on 16 January.

This unfortunate opening act also marked the beginning of the end of the *Staffel*'s month-long deployment to Finland. Once assembled back in Kirkenes, 13.(Z)/JG 5 began preparations to move south. The necessary orders arrived on 14 February 1944, and the ground personnel left the base in transport aircraft the same day. *Hauptmann* Treppe and his heavy fighters left Kirkenes for the last time two days later and flew to their new base in Herdla in the south of Norway. The *Staffel*'s activities in Finland were over. The unit's new operational role was not unlike the mission order given to the *Jagdstaffeln* of I./JG 77 in 1941: "Air operations over the sea to defend the Norwegian coast and supply shipping."

The *Staffel*'s new area of operations was the coastal area between Stadlandet in the north and Stavanger Bay in the south. From then on attached to the Fighter Commander Norway, it now faced the Royal Air Force and would very soon receive a taste of its striking power.

The more or less secondary problems which the commander of a flying unit had to deal with in addition to conducting the air war should not go unmentioned. There is the example of the "*Staffelkapitän*'s reserve," a stockpile of spirits and tobacco products of all kinds, which *Hauptmann* Treppe had procured over time. He used this store to provide small rewards to deserving personnel on the occasion of victories, long-distance weddings or similar occasions. At the front ground personnel received three cigarettes daily, pilots seven. *Hauptfeldwebel* Roos, the senior NCO of 13.(Z)/JG 5, repeatedly urged the *Staffelkapitän* to use some of the tobacco products from his "reserve" to make up for this disparity in the allocation of cigarettes. It must be said that Roos was a man with a pronounced sense of justice, and at every opportunity he displayed exemplary moral courage in standing up for those he saw as weak and inferior.

Repeatedly coerced by his men, one day Roos again brought up the topic of the "*Staffelkapitän*'s reserve", but this time *Hauptmann* Treppe tried *General* von Steuben's recipe of convincing instead of ordering. He instructed the senior NCO to report to the mess hall the next morning with all of the *Feldwebel* and *Oberfeldwebel* of the ground personnel.

The large room in the barracks, where all aircrew ate lunch together and where photos of all the fallen members of the *Staffel* hung, soon filled. Treppe had the men gather around the picture of the first fallen and asked an *Oberfeldwebel* radio technician:

"*Oberfeldwebel* Y, did you know this *Gefreiter* X, who was only with the *Staffel* for two weeks before he was killed?"

"Yes, *Herr Hauptmann*, I was still a *Gefreiter* then."

Treppe repeated the question in front of other photos of fallen comrades and finally turned to the men" "Dear comrades, I am – as you know – a non-smoker. But I am the last one who would begrudge you more cigarettes. You all know that the different allocations are ordered by the *Wehrmacht* command. You can see the point of it in X and Y. Both were then *Gefreiter*. For two weeks X received four more cigarettes a day than Y. Then he was shot down. But Y has continued receiving his three cigarettes a day and is now an *Oberfeldwebel*."

The matter of cigarette allocations never came up again.

When *Hauptmann* Treppe went on leave in spring 1944, he placed *Oberleutnant* Ziegenhagen in command of the *Staffel*. At the same time the German troop transport *Monte Rosa* was sailing in convoy southwards along the Norwegian coast. The *Zerstörer* were subsequently ordered to provide air cover for the convoy. It was 30 March 1944. During preparations for the mission Ziegenhagen suddenly fell ill and had to be taken to hospital in Bergen. At Ziegenhagen's suggestion, *Leutnant* Friedrich, radio operator and *Staffel* aide-de-camp, would take over the unit. The *Staffel* had two other officer pilots, however they lacked operational experience. Gerhard Friedrich was supposed to fly as *Oberfeldwebel* Albert Mack's radio operator on this day, but after repeated pleas from *Unteroffizier* Möbius, his regular radio operator, Mack decided to give him the spot – a fateful decision as it would turn out.

Late in the day 18 Beaufighters attacked the German convoy in Stavanger Bay. The *Staffel* shot down several of the enemy and then pursued the British aircraft out to sea as they withdrew. Among the victorious pilots was *Oberfeldwebel* Mack, who shot down a Beaufighter over the bay and then set off in pursuit of the enemy. His aircraft, 1B+EX, was last seen northwest of Utsima. Mack and radio operator Möbius remain missing.

In mid-May 1944 a regrettable error, the kind that happens frequently and often unavoidably during wartime, resulted in problems with the Swedes. A pair of *Zerstörer* flown by *Unteroffizier* Wunderle and *Unteroffizier* Bock were on patrol off the Norwegian coast. After a while they transmitted the following message to the *Staffel* command post: "50 kilometers of Stadlandet, freighter heading for the coast." A call was placed to the "Admiral West Coast" in Bergen. The reply from the operations officer in Bergen: "Not a German ship, the aircraft may attack." The two Messerschmitts made the first strafing pass, but as they pulled up an excited voice came over the frequency: "Man, that's a Swede!"

This incident was just another example of the inadequate coordination between the various elements of the *Wehrmacht*. Not until after the mistaken attack on the Swedish ship, which fortunately only suffered damage to its bridge, was the *Staffel* kept informed of the position of neutral Swedish vessels sailing to and from England. The German naval attaché in Kristiansand inspected the ship involved in the above-mentioned incident. The several cases of spirits he brought with him helped smooth things over and avoid any unpleasant investigations.

Many times the *Zerstörer* were sent on armed reconnaissance missions, during which they scouted the target themselves before attacking, but only once during the entire war was the *Staffel* given a pure reconnaissance mission, and that was three weeks before the Allied invasion of France. A large Allied naval formation, whose composition was uncertain, was operating in the seas northwest of Trondheim. The Bv 138 flying boat that made the report had apparently been shot down immediately afterwards, and the *Fliegerführer Nord (Ost)* issued orders for information about the enemy group's numbers, types and heading to be obtained at all costs, for it was feared that it was an invasion fleet.

The next day, when none of the aircraft sent against the naval force returned, there was great unrest among the senior staffs. At least two BV 138s of the *Fernaufklärerstaffel (See)* and one Ju 88 of the *Fernaufklärerstaffel (Land)* had been lost without having sent a single radio transmission. There was only one solution: the strategically vital reconnaissance would have to be carried out by fast, heavily-armed aircraft. The problem with this was that the crews of such aircraft lacked the training in identifying sea targets to return with accurate information. Nevertheless, the results had to be sent to the OKW immediately.

Ultimately the air commander turned to the *Zerstörerstaffel*, which was then stationed in Trondheim-Lade. As a former bomber pilot with KG 26, *Hauptmann* Treppe had extensive experience in anti-shipping operations and the next night he was ordered to report to *Oberst* Kühl. Treppe remarked of this: "Strictest orders had been received from *Führer* headquarters under threat of court martial, that under no circumstances was the *Zerstörer* flight carrying out the mission to allow itself to become involved in aerial combat. The sole objective was to determine the exact composition of the task force and its heading. This information was to be transmitted by radio during the return flight in case the *Zerstörer* were intercepted before reaching the coast and shot down by superior enemy aircraft."

After receiving detailed instructions, Treppe took his leave of the air commander with the words: "If the weather doesn't let us down, and our fuel allows us to fly far enough out to sea, then *Herr Oberst*, you will have your reconnaissance report by tomorrow morning!"

Early on 14 May 1944 four Bf 110s took off from Lade, stopped in Örlandet to refuel, and then took off for the specified area of sea. Over the coast there was a solid cloud deck reaching to the tips of the mountains, but beneath it visibility was good.

The coast of Norway lay far behind, but there was still no sign of a task force. The crews were uneasy, for – apart from their *Staffelkapitän* – they were not used to leaving the coastline behind and flying to the limits of their endurance over the sea. Of course there was radio silence. The cloud deck dissipated and suddenly before the *Zerstörer* there lay a vast area of water beneath a sunny sky – and right in the middle was the enemy task force they were looking for. It was an imposing sight. Floating in the magnificent dark blue of the ocean, disturbed only by the white wakes of ships, were a large aircraft carrier, two heavy cruisers and one light cruiser, plus a large number of destroyers and torpedo boats, which zigzagged around the larger vessels.

The Messerschmitts immediately made a climbing reversal to reach the safety of the clouds, for aircraft had been seen taking off from the carrier's deck. During this maneuver *Hauptmann* Treppe had been able to identify the ships and determine their course.

The Messerschmitts hadn't reached the clouds when a voice suddenly broke the radio silence: "Indians from behind, Indians from behind!" Some of the carrier's aircraft had obviously been airborne when the Germans appeared. The four Messerschmitts moved in closer, while the gunners tried to ward off their attackers, then the clouds swallowed them up. When they broke out one aircraft was missing, but the carrier aircraft were gone too.

Oberfeldwebel Brüggenthies, the *Staffelkapitän*'s radio operator, had meanwhile transmitted a report on the task force. *Hauptmann* Treppe then called the missing Bf 110: "Blue Four from One, come in please." Finally, after several tries, came a reply: "Blue Four to One. Have been hit. Port engine is out. Can only fly at reduced speed."

Treppe immediately ordered the two aircraft behind him to go on alone, while he formed up with the damaged machine to lead it to the coast for a landing in Örlandet. The *Staffelkapitän* did not land there, instead flying on to Trondheim-Lake, where he immediately went to the air commander's command post.

Finally there was certainty about the enemy task force. It was no invasion fleet; rather it was the usual "heavy group" that the Allies occasionally sent south to guard a convoy sailing to Murmansk along the pack ice.

On the west coast things remained largely quiet until the end of July. Duties alternated between escort missions and alert readiness, and only occasionally was there contact with enemy aircraft. On 18 July 1944 the *Zerstörer* unit left the *Geschwader* formation and became the *10. Staffel* in a newly-formed IV./ZG 26. It did not return to the old *Geschwader* until February 1945, when *Hauptmann* Treppe was ordered to form a new II./JG 5, becoming 7./JG 5. 10./JG 26 was under the direct command of *Hauptmann* Stendel's IV./JG 5. When, after Finland's ceasefire, the *Gruppe* was sent to northern Norway to augment III./JG 5, the *Zerstörer* unit was the only unit available to the Fighter Commander Norway to provide air defense over the southern coastal area. Treppe took half of his *Staffel* to Stavanger, while the rest was stationed in Lister, where *Fähnrich* Kurpiers assumed responsibility for commanding the partial unit in the air.

The final events can be summarized quickly. In Lister there was a constant state of combat readiness, but the *Staffel* was not given permission to take to the air even though the British Mosquitoes made the coastal region unsafe day after day. There wasn't even a scramble when two Mosquitoes attacked the *Staffel*'s base sometime in October. The only victory during this period came on 28 September 1944, when Treppe downed a four-engined anti-submarine aircraft patrolling the seas between Stavanger and Herdla. Not surprisingly, the crews, sentenced to inactivity, became restless. Finally, at the beginning of November, *Leutnant* Friedrich went to Stavanger to discuss the confusing situation with *Hauptmann* Treppe. At the same time new orders were received: the *Staffel* was moving to Trondheim-Lade. *Hauptmann* Treppe was being named *Kommandeur* of IV./JG 26.

A final reorganization took place in February 1945. Under Treppe, in Herdla a new II./JG 5 was created from elements of III./JG 5 and IV./ZG 26. Its organization was as follows:

Kommandeur:	*Hptm.* Treppe
Adjutant:	*Lt.* Friedrich
Technical Officer:	*Lt.* Schmoll
Signals Officer:	*Lt.* Brüggenthies
5. *Staffel*:	*Oblt.* Gayko
6. *Staffel*:	*Lt.* Koch
7. *Staffel*:	*Lt.* Kurpiers

Formed from 10. and 12./ZG 26, 7./JG 5 was in reality JG 5's old *Zerstörerstaffel* back with the unit. By the way, Willi Brüggenthies, in the far north since September 1941, had the highest number of combat missions of any crew in the *Zerstörerstaffel*, with 258. Under *Hauptmann* Riedel, 11./ZG 26 remained attached to the *Geschwader* in Örlandet. In the final weeks of the war the pilots were retrained on the Bf 109 in Stavanger-Sola but saw no action.

With the war nearly over, there was one more tragic accident, which took the life of *Feldwebel* Wunderle from Swabia. Of course the *Staffel* still had several dachshunds, which had been part of the *Staffel* emblem since the unit was formed. After conversion to the Bf 109, taking the dogs along on transfer flights posed a certain space problem, for in the twin-engined Messerschmitt the pilot had flown the aircraft while the radio operator held the dog in his lap. In a single-seater this was impossible. Prior to the move from Trondheim to Herdla on 3 April 1945, *Hauptmann* Treppe expressly forbade his pilots from taking the animals in their Bf 109s. Despite this, *Feldwebel* Wunderle put the dachshund "Lockheed" in his aircraft. When he took off, the dog escaped into the rear fuselage. He must have become caught up in the control cables, for the pilot lost control of the aircraft. It contacted the ground and crashed.

Feldwebel Wunderle was thus the last fatal casualty from the successful *Zerstörerstaffel* of JG 5.

Appendices

Staffel Family Tree

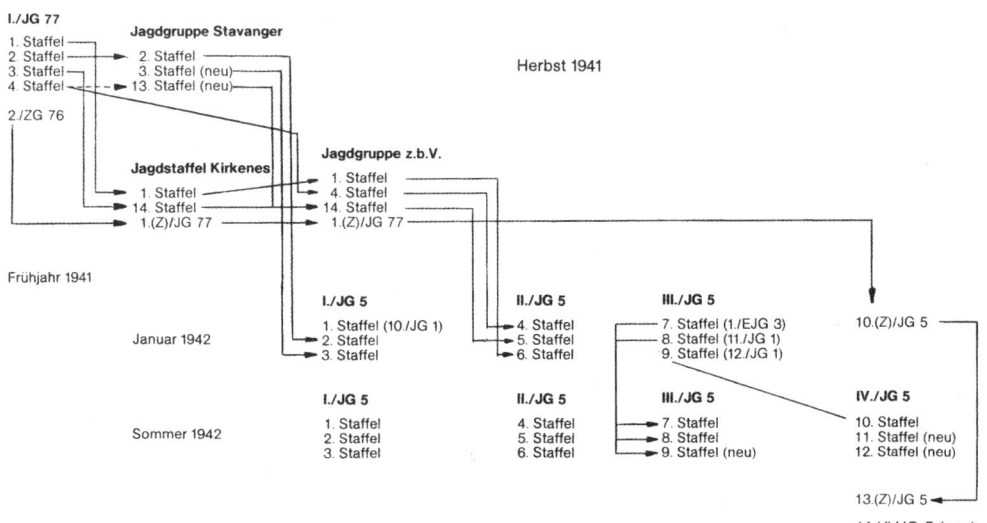

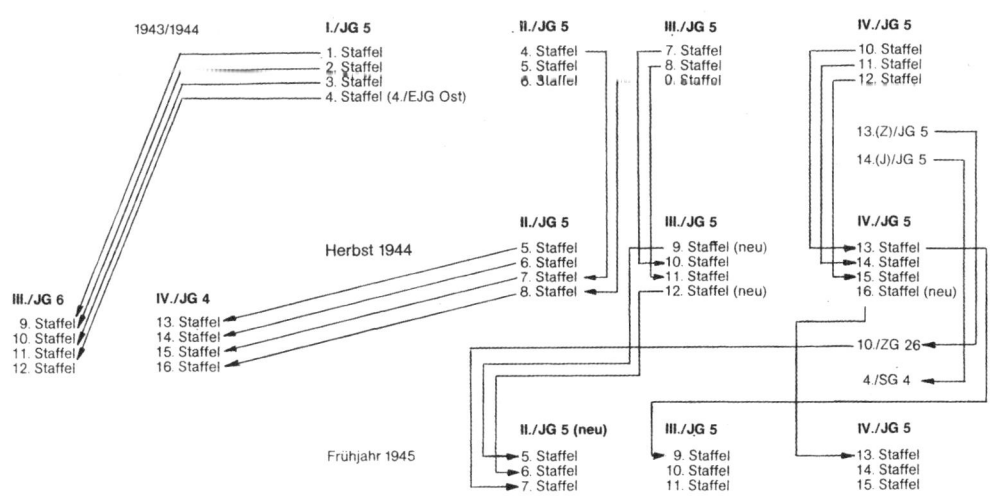

Jagdgeschwader 5

Staffing

I./JG 77 (from *Jagdkommando* 77, *Hptm.* Walter Grommes)
1./JG 77	*Oblt.* Horst Carganico	spring 1941 – 6/41
	from 6/41 = 1./JG 77, JSt. Kirkenes	
2./JG 77	*Hptm.* Gerd von Wehren	spring 1941 – 6/41
	from 6/41 = 2./JG 77, JGr. Stavanger	
3./JG 77	*Lt.* Franz Menzel	spring 1941 – 6/41
	from 6/41 = 14./JG 77, JSt. Kirkenes	
4./JG 77	*Lt.* Gerd Senoner	spring 1941 – 6/41
	Hptm. Hans Christian Schäfer	6/41 – 11/41
	from 11/41 = 4./JG 77, JGr. z.b.V.	

2./ZG 76	*Oblt.* Felix Maria Brandis	spring 1941 – 6/41
	from 6/41 = 1.(Z)/JG 77, JSt. Kirkenes	

Jagdstaffel Kirkenes (1. + 14./JG 77, 1.(Z)/JG 77)
(IV./JG 77)	*Hptm.* Alfred von Lojewski	26/6/41 – 27/6/41
	from 9/41 = *Jagdgruppe* z.b.V.	

Jagdgruppe Stavanger (*Major* Joachim Seegert)
2./JG 77	*Hptm.* Gerhard Büchel	6/41 – 1/42
	from 1/42 = 2./JG 5	
3./JG 77 (new)	*Lt.* Franz Wienhusen	6/41 – 1/42
	from 1/42 = 3./JG 5	
13./JG 77 (new, from elements of 4./JG 77)		
	Lt. Gerd Senoner	6/41 – 9/41
	from 9/41 to 14./JG 77, JGr. z.b.V.	

Jagdgruppe z.b.V. (*Major* Hennig Strümpell, Jafü Nordnorwegen (Ost))
Adjutant	*Lt.* Rudolf Glöckner	
Technical Officer	*Oblt.* Hans Herrmann Schmidt	
Signals Officer	*Lt.* Helmut Schenk	
1./JG 77	*Oblt.* Horst Carganico	9/41 – 1/42
	from 1/42 = 6./JG 5	
4./JG 77	*Hptm.* Hans Christian Schäfer	11/41 – 1/42
	from 1/42 = 4./JG 5	
14./JG 77 (from old 3./JG 77 + 13./JG 77)		
	Oblt. Franz Menzel	9/41 – 1/42
	from 1/42 = 5./JG 5	

1.(Z)/JG 77	*Oblt.* Felix Maria Brandis	9/41 – 1/42
	from 1/42 = 10.(Z)/JG 5	

Geschwaderkommodore and Stab JG 5
Oberstlt. Gotthardt Handrick	1/42 – 6/43
Oberstlt. Günter Scholz	6/43 – 5/44
Major Heinrich Ehrler	5/44 – (2/45)
Oberstlt. Günter Scholz	(2/45) – end of war
(simultaneously Jafü Norwegen)	

Adjutant
Hptm. Brockmann (also operations officer)	5/42 – 6/43
Lt. Rolf Sadewasser	12/42 – 2/43
Hptm. Hermann Segatz (also operations officer)	6/43 – 2/44
Hptm. Rolf Lüder (also operations officer)	2/44 – 2/45

Ia (Operations Officer)
Hptm. von Hahn	10/42 – 43
Hptm. Hermann Segatz	6/43 – 2/44
Hptm. Rudolf Lüder	2/44 – 2/45
Lt. Erwin Naps	2/45 – end of war

Ic (Intelligence Officer)
Oblt. Günther Schwanecke   5/43 – 7/43
Lt. Wolfgang Rost   7/43 –

Technical Officer
Hptm. Bernd Probst   5/42 – end of war

Signals Officer
Lt. Joachim Rutishauser   5/43 – 28/12/42†
Oblt. Knipfer   1/43 – 6/43
Hptm. Karl Schmidt   6/43 – 5/44
Oblt. Kalischeck   5/44 – 2/45

I./JG 5
Major Joachim Seegert   1/42 – 4/42
Hptm. Gerhard von Wehren   4/42 – 2/43
Hptm. Gerhard Wengel   2/43 – 10/1/44†
Oblt. Robert Müller (acting) 10/1/44 – 25/1/44
Major Erich Gerlitz   25/1/44 – 16/3/44†
Major Horst Carganico   26/3/44 – 27/5/44†
Hptm. Theo Weißenberger   4/6/44 – 24/11/44
 from 14/10/44 = III./JG 6

Adjutant
Oblt. Rudolf Müller   –
Lt. Franz von Thienen   –
Hptm. Erich Mikat   –

Technical Officer
Oblt. Hans Dieter Hartwein   –
Lt. Fritz Schütze   – 3/5/43†
Lt. Edgar Habermann   – 8/10/43
Lt. Max Endriß   9/10/43 – 14/10/44

Signals Officer
Lt. Franz Laskovic   42 – 18/2/42
Lt. Udo Schneider   –
Lt. Dr. Hugo Ritter   44 –
Lt. Wendlinger   44 – 14/10/44

Headquarters Company
Oblt. Kurt Bänsch   – 1/6/43
Lt. Vetter ?   –
Hptm. Taucher   – 44
Oblt. Fritz Reß   44 –

Medical Officer
Dr. Otto Stockhammer   –
Dr. Knorr   –

1./JG 5 (from 10./JG 1)
Oblt. Diethelm von Eichel-Streiber   1/42 – 42
Oblt. Wolfgang Kosse   42 – 42
Lt. Max Endriß (acting)   4/43 – 8/10/43
Oblt. Gerd Senoner   6/43 – 25/2/44†
Oblt. Walter Krupinski (acting)   5/44 – 44
Oblt. Lothar Gerlach   – 44
 from 14/10/44 = 9./JG 26

2./JG 5 (from 2./JG 77)
Hptm. Gerhard Büchel	1/43 –
Hptm. Wrobel	– 8/10/43
Oblt. Edgar Habermann	9/10/43 – 12/4/44†
Lt. Friedrich Bölz	4/44 – 4/8/44
Oblt. Gerhard Weyl	8/44 – 10/44
from 14/10/44 = 10./JG 6	

3./JG 5 (from 3./JG 77)
Lt. Franz Wienhusen	1/42 – 11/42
Oblt. Franz Menzel	11/42 –
Lt. Max Endriß	– 4/43
Oblt. Robert Müller	– 17/7/44†
Lt. Alfred Lehner	17/7/44 – 44
Oblt. Klaus Faber	44 –
from 14/10/44 = 11./JG 6	

4./JG 5 (from 4./EJGr. Ost, 8/44)
Lt. Siegfried Dönch	8/44 – 10/44
from 14/10/44 = 12./JG 6	

II./JG 5
Major Hennig Strümpell	1/42 – 4/42
Hptm. Horst Carganico	4/42 – 26/3/44
Hptm. Theo Weißenberger	26/3/44 – 3/6/44
Oblt. Hans Tetzner	4/6/44 – 19/7/44†
Oberstlt. Kurt Kettner	20/7/44 – 25/8/44†
Hptm. Franz Wienhusen	1/9/44 – autumn 44
from autumn 1944 = IV./JG 4	

Adjutant
Oblt. Rudolf Glöckner	1/42 – ?
Oblt. Gerd Weyl	–
Oblt. Günther Schwanecke	7/43 – 1/44

Technical Officer
Lt. Hans-Dieter Hartwein	1/42 – 5/42
Lt. Werner Kunze	– 19/9/42
Oblt. Lorenz Bauer	42 –
Lt. Friedrich Bölz	– 44

Signals Officer
Lt. Franz Laskovic	–
Oblt. Stribny	–
Oblt. Konrad Schlossarzyk	– 43
Oblt. Hedergott	–

Headquarters Company
Hptm. Erich Mikat	– 4/44
Hptm. Georg Mildner	–

Medical Officer
Dr. Merkel	42 –
Dr. Waldemar Ostermann	42 – 44

4./JG 5 (from 4./JG 77)
Oblt. Christian Schäfer	1/42 – 42
Lt. Wolfgang Lamprecht (acting)	–
Oblt. Hans Tetzner	42 – 3/6/44
Hptm. Franz Wienhusen	44 – 44
Oblt. Gerhard Weyl	44 – 44
Oblt. Günther Schwanecke	44 – 8/44
from August 1944 = 7./JG 5	

Appendices

Oblt. Günther Schwanecke	8/44 – 8/9/44
Lt. Josef Kunz	8/9/44 – ca. 10/44
from autumn 1944 = 15./JG 4	

5./JG 5 (from 14./JG 77)
Oblt. Franz Menzel	1/42 – 11/42
Oblt. Franz Wienhusen	11/42 – 31/5/44
Hptm. Wolfgang Kosse	1/6/44 – autumn 44
from autumn 1944 = 13./JG 4	

6./JG 5 (from 1./JG 77)
Oblt. Horst Carganico	1/42 – 11/42
Oblt. Hans Dieter Hartwein	5/42 – 21/8/42†
Oblt. Heinrich Ehrler	21/8/42 – 6/43
Oblt. Theo Weißenberger	9/43 – 26/3/44
Lt. Ernst Scheufele	28/3/44 – autumn 44
from autumn 44 = 14./JG 4	

8./JG 5 (from 9.III./JG 5, 5/7/44)
Oblt. Lorenz Andresen	7/44 – 20/7/44†
Unknown	– autumn 44
from autumn 44 = 16./JG 4	

II./JG 5 (new, 2/3/45 from III./JG 5 and IV./ZG 26)
Hptm. Herbert Treppe	2/45 – end of war

Adjutant
Lt. Gerhard Friedrich	–

Technical Officer
Lt. Schmoll	–

Signals Officer
Lt. Willi Brüggenthies	–

Headquarters Company
Lt. Gerhard Friedrich	–

5./JG 5 (new, from 9./JG 5 "Eismeerstaffel" and IV./ZG 26)
Oblt. Werner Gayko	2/45 – end of war

6./JG 5 (new, from 12.III./JG 5 and IV./ZG 26)
Lt. Karl Heinz Koch	2/45 – end of war

7./JG 5 (new, from IV./ZG 26)
Lt. Kurpiers	2/45 – end of war

III./JG 5
Hptm. Günter Scholz	1/42 – 6/43
Major Heinrich Ehrler	6/43 – 5/44
Hptm. Franz Dörr	5/44 – end of war
Oblt. Rudolf Glöckner (acting)	1944-45

Adjutant
Oblt. Rudolf Lüder	42 – 2/43
Lt. Rolf Sadewasser	2/43 – 8/5/43†
Lt. Lorenz Andresen	5/43 – 43
Lt. Helmut Neumann	– 8/44
Oblt. Kurt Schulze	9/44 – 1/45
Lt. Heinrich von Podewils	1/45 – end of war

Jagdgeschwader 5

Technical Officer
Lt. Friedrich Schumann — 42 – 43
Lt. Schumacher — 43 –
Lt. Bernd von Hermann — – 17/3/44

Signals Officer
Lt. Rudolf Kalischeck — 42 – 43
Lt. Franz Reichenbach — 44 –

Headquarters Company
Hptm. Heinz Hecht — 42 – 45

Medical Officer
Dr. Schulze-Gericke — 42 – 43
Dr. Rentsch — 44 –

7./JG 5 (from 1./EJG 3)
Hptm. Hans Curt Graf von Sponeck — 1/42 – 1/1/43
Oblt. Gerd Senoner — 1/1/43 – 15/6/43
Oblt. Theo Weißenberger — 15/6/43 – 9/43
Oblt. Franz Dörr — 14/9/43 – 5/44
Lt. Walter Schuck — 5/44 – 7/44
 from 7/44 = 10./JG 5
Lt. Walter Schuck — 7/44 – 2/45
Lt. Werner Heinicke — 2/45 – end of war

8./JG 5 (from 12./JG 1)
Oblt. Hermann Segatz — 1/42 – 43
Oblt. Horst Berger — 43 – 8/5/44†
Oblt. Rudolf Glöckner — 5/44 – 7/44
 from 7/44 = 11./JG 5
Oblt. Rudolf Glöckner — 7/44 – 2/45
Lt. Heinrich von Podewils — 2/45 – end of war

9./JG 5 (from 12./JG 1)
Oblt. Herbert Huppertz — 1/42 – 7/42
 from 7/42 = 10.IV./JG 5

9./JG 5 (new, from elements of 7. and 8.III./JG 5)
Hptm. Gerhard Wengel — 7/42 – 2/43
Oblt. Wulf-Dietrich Widowitz — 2/43 – 28/7/43†
Hptm. Hans-Hermann Schmidt — 8/43 – 11/1/44
Lt. Wolfgang Rost — 1/44 – 29/2/44
Oblt. Lorenz Andresen — 3/44 – 7/44
 from 8/44 = 8.II./JG 5

9./JG 5 "*Eismeerstaffel*" (new, summer 1944)
Lt. Werner Gayko — 7/44 – 2/45
 from 2/45 = 5./JG 5 (new)

9./JG 5 (new, from 13.IV./JG 5, March 1945)
Lt. August Schneider — 3/45 – end of war

12./JG 5 (new, July 1944)
Lt. Rudi Linz — 7/44 – 9/2/45
Lt. Karl Heinz Koch — 2/45 – 3/45
 from 3/45 = 6./JG 5 (new)

IV./JG 5
Hptm. Hans Kriegel — – 4/44
Oblt. Rudolf Lüder (acting) — 3/10/43 –
Hptm. Fritz Stendel — 15/5/44 – end of war

Appendices

Adjutant
Oblt. Pfeiffer   42 –
Oblt. Gerhard Beyer   43 – 2/44

Technical Officer
Lt. Joachim Hoffmann   43 – 30/3/44†

Signals Officer
Lt. Wolf Degner   44 –

Headquarters Company
Hptm. Schobelt   –

Medical Officer
Dr. Engelmann   –

10./JG 5 (from 9.III./JG 5, 7/42)
Oblt. Herbert Huppertz   7/42 – 42
Oblt. Hans Schneider   42 – 15/7/44
  from 15/7/44 = 13./JG 5
Oblt. Hans Schneider   15/7/44 – 12/3/45†
  from 3/45 = 9.III./JG 5

11./JG 5 (new, summer 1942)
Unknown   7/42 – 1/44
Oblt. Horst Keim   1/44 – 7/44
  from 15/7/44 = 14./JG 5
Oblt. Horst Keim   7/44 – 8/44
Lt. Helmut Neumann   8/44 – 4/45
Oblt. Heinz Goesmann   4/45 – end of war

12./JG 5 (new, summer 1942)
Hptm. Friedrich-Wilhelm Strakeljahn   7/42 – 2/43
Oblt. Rudolf Lüder   2/43 – 15/2/44
Oblt. Gerhard Beyer   2/44 – 7/44
  from 15/7/44 = 15./JG 5
Oblt. Gerhard Beyer   7/44 – 15/8/44
Unknown
Lt. Keppler   – 5/4/45†
Lt. Schild/*Lt.* Gröne?   – end of war

16./JG 5 (new, autumn 1944)
Lt. Hans Vollet   10/44 – 4/45
Lt. Gillet   4/45 – 11/4/45†
  from 4/45 = 13./JG 5
Lt. Georg Höhn (acting)   14/4/45 –
Oblt. Kurt Schulze   5/45 – end of war

10. Zerstörerstaffel/JG 5 (from 1.(Z)/JG 77)
Oblt. Felix Maria Brandis   41 – 2/2/42†
Oblt. Max Franzisket (acting)   42 – 42
Oblt. Karl-Fritz Schloßstein   2/42 – summer 42
  from summer 42 = 13.(Z)/JG 5
Oblt. Karl-Fritz Schloßstein   summer 42 – 6/43
Oblt. Hans Kirchmeier (acting)   6/43 – 9/43
Hptm. Herbert Treppe   6/43 – 7/44
  from 7/44 = 10./ZG 26
Hptm. Herbert Treppe   7/44 – 11/44

10./ZG 26 attached to IV./ZG 26 (*Hptm.* Treppe) from 11/44
Lt. Gerhard Friedrich (acting)   11/44 – 12/44
Lt. Peter Bäthge   12/44 – 2/4/45†

11./ZG 26
Hptm. von Rochow   11/44 – 12/44
Hptm. Riedel   12/44 – 2/45

12./ZG 26
Lt. Kurpiers   11/44 – 2/45

The new II./JG 5 was formed from IV./ZG 26 and elements of III./JG 5 on 2/45.

14. Jabostaffel/JG 5 (new 2/43)
Hptm. Friedrich-Wilhelm Strakeljahn   2/43 – 4/44
 from 4/44 = 4./SG 4

Operational Aircraft of JG 5

I./JG 77
1941   Bf 109 E-7, Bf 109 T

I./JG 5
1942   Bf 109 F-4, Fw 190 A-3
1943   Bf 109 G-2, Bf 109 G-6, Fw 190 A-2, Fw 190 A-3, Fw 190 A-4
1944   Bf 109 G-2, Bf 109 G-5, Bf 109 G-6, Bf 109 G-14

II./JG 5
1942   Bf 109 E-7, Bf 109 F-4
1943   Bf 109 G-2, Bf 109 G-6
1944   Bf 109 G-6, Bf 109 G-14

III./JG 5
1942   Bf 109 E-7, Bf 109 F-4
1943   Bf 109 F-4, Bf 109 G-2
1944   Bf 109 F-4, Bf 109 G-2, Bf 109 G-6, Fw 190 A-8
1945   Bf 109 G-2, Bf 109 G-14, Fw 190 A-8

IV./JG 5
1942   Bf 109 F-4
1943   Bf 109 G-2, Bf 109 G-6, Fw 190 A-2, Fw 190 A-3, Fw 190 A-4
1944   Bf 109 G-2, Bf 109 G-6, Fw 190 A-2, Fw 190 A-3, Fw 190 F-8
1945   Bf 109 G-14, Fw 190 A-8

13.(Z)/JG 5 (*Zerstörerstaffel*)
1941   Bf 110 E-2, Bf 110 F-2
1942   Bf 110 E-2, Bf 110 F-2
1943   Bf 110 F-2, Bf 110 G-2
1944   Bf 110 G-2

14.(J)/JG 5 (*Jabostaffel*)
1943   Fw 190 A-2, Fw 190 A-3
1944   Fw 190 A-2, Fw 190 A-3

Appendices

The Knight's Cross Holders of JG 5

	Last unit in JG 5	Victories in JG 5	total	Knight's Cross on	Oak Leaves on	
Ofw. Bartels, Heinrich	8.*Staffel*	47	99	13/11/42		KIA 23/12/44, JG 27
Ofw. Brunner, Albert	6.*Staffel*	53	53	3/7/43*		KIA 7/5/43
Major Carganico, Horst	I.*Gruppe*	56	60	25/9/41		KIA 27/5/44
Hptm. Dahmer, Hugo	1./JG 77	25	57	1/8/41		
Lt. Döbrich, Hans	6.*Staffel*	65	65	19/9/43		
Hptm. Dörr, Franz	III.*Gruppe*	122	128	19/8/44		died 10/10/72
Major Ehrler, Heinrich	Kom. JG 5	200	204	21/10/42	2/8/43	KIA 4/4/45, JG 7
Lt. Linz, Rudi	12.*Staffel*	70	70	3/45*		KIA 9/2/45
Lt. Mors, August	1.*Staffel*	60	60	24/10/44*		KIA 8/8/44
Ofw. Müller, Rudi	6.*Staffel*	94	94	19/6/42		missing, POW
Lt. Neumann, Helmut	14.*Staffel*	62	62	12/3/45		
Lt. Norz, Jakob	11.*Staffel*	117	117	26/3/44		KIA, 16/9/44
Oblt. Schuck, Walter	10.*Staffel*	198	206	8/4/44	30/9/44	
Hptm. Strakeljahn, Walter	14.*Staffel* (J)	9	9?	19/8/43		KIA 6/7/44, SG 4
Major Weißenberger, Theodor	I.*Gruppe*	200	208	13/11/43	02/08/43	killed in accident 10/6/50

* awarded posthumously

Aerial Victories of JG 5

While there are quite accurate victory summaries for some other *Jagdgeschwader*, the exact number of victories achieved by *Jagdgeschwader 5* is not known. The *Geschwader* reported its 3,000th victory on 9 October 1944; therefore the total number can be estimated to be about 3,300. Of these victories, which JG 5 scored during its operations on all fronts, about 2,750 can be seen in surviving records (I./JG 77, JG 5 including the *Zerstörerstaffel*).

It is understandably difficult to compile a complete victory list today. The victories of a number of well-known fighter pilots such as *Oblt.* Koch, *Lt.* Kunze, *Lt.* Scheufele, *Oflr.* Schmider and others are missing. Documents were lost, some of the former *Eismeerjäger* can no longer be questioned, some others are reluctant to grant access to documents still in their possession for reasons that we must respect. The following, incomplete victory list can therefore only be seen as a rough overview, and for this reason it would be most welcome to receive from our circle of readers hints, corrections and especially additional information that would contribute to the completion of this summary.

While many *Geschwader* members must reconstruct events from memory, *Major* Theo Weißenberger's log and *Leistungsbuch* survived the turmoil of war, making it possible for us to provide a chronological list of the victories achieved by one of JG 5's most successful pilots.

Perhaps one more comment concerning victories in general: we know that a fighter pilot's accomplishments cannot always be measured by victories alone. Sometimes a pilot with just two victories perhaps possessed more operational experience and prudence than one with far more enemy aircraft to his credit. And if, for example, a pilot returned with one victory in each of ten missions, under certain circumstances – this of course depended on the situation at the front – this might be valued more highly than one who required forty combat missions to achieve the same number of victories.

Uffz. Amend, Hermann	at least 7	II./JG 5	KIA 5/8/44	
Oblt. Andresen, Lorenz	about 9	II./JG 5	KIA 20/7/44	
Uffz. Angerer, Erwin	1	III./JG 5	KIA 5/4/45	
Ofw. Arnold, Heinz	42	III./JG 5	KIA 4/4/45	JG 7
Ofw. Artner, Rudolf	20	III./JG 5		
Uffz. Baasch, Dieter	3	IV./JG 5		
Lt. Bäthge, Peter	at least 1	Z-*Staffel*	KIA 2/4/45	
Lt. Bahr, Hans-Joachim	at least 7	III./JG 5	KIA 13/7/42	
Ofw. Bartels, Heinrich	47	II./JG 5	KIA 26/9/44	JG 27
Ofw. Bauer, Eberhard	2	II./JG 5	KIA 28/2/42	
Lt. Belz, Alfred	2	III./JG 5	KIA 26/9/44	JG 27
Oblt. Berger, Horst	about 30	III./JG 5	MIA 8/5/44	
Uffz. Berger, Kurt	at least 1	I./JG 5	MIA 16/7/44	

Jagdgeschwader 5

Uffz. Bernhardt, Harry	at least 1	IV./JG 5	MIA 7/12/44	
Fw. Beth, Arthur	16	III./JG 5	POW 3/1/44	
Ofw. Beulich, Erich	at least 10	III./JG 5	MIA 14/9/43	
Fw. Beulig	at least 2	I./JG 5		
Ofw. Beyer, Heinz	33	II./JG 5		
Uffz. Binna, Ernst	at least 2	I./JG 5	MIA 7/8/44	
Ofw. Birk, Heinz	14	III./JG 5		
Ofw. Bößenecker, Josef	at least 4	III./JG 5		
Uffz. Bozicek, Franz	5	I./JG 5		
Oblt. Brandis, Felix-Maria	14	Z-Staffel	KIA 2/2/42	
Lt. von Brunn, Klaus	1	IV./JG 5		
Ofw. Brunner, Albert	53	II./JG 5	KIA 7/5/43	
Fw. Buzzi, Bruno	9	IV./JG 5	Died 23/4/71	
Major Carganico, Horst	56	I./JG 5	KIA 27/5/44	
Lt. Carl, Horst	at least 1	III./JG 5	KIA 9/8/44	
Lt. Dahmer, Hugo	25	I./JG 77		
Lt. Dahn, Friedrich	26	II./JG 5	MIA 25/5/42	
Fw. Degner, Franz	at least 12	III./JG 5		
Lt. Döbrich, Hans	65	II./JG 5		
Lt. Dönch, Siegfried	at least 2	I./JG 5	MIA 25/12/44	JG 6
Hptm. Dörr, Franz	128	III./JG 5	Died 10/72	
Ofw. Dreisbach, Heinrich	16	III./JG 5		
Fw. Drößler, Kurt	6	IV./JG 5	KIA 10/4/44	
Fw. Eder, Max	1	IV./JG 5		
Uffz. Ehring	at least 1	I./JG 5		
Major Ehrler, Heinrich	200	Kom. JG 5	KIA 4/4/45	JG 7
Lt. Eichhorn, Günter	7	III./JG 5	POW 2/12/43	
Uffz. Eisermann, Gerhard	at least 1	III./JG 5		
Uffz. Elbracht, Heinz	at least 9	III./JG 5		
Lt. Endriß, Max	1	I./JG 5		
Uffz. Erlinger, Werner	1	II./JG 5	MIA 9/5/44	
Fw. Fahldieck, Erwin	1	II./JG 5	MIA 29/4/43	
Ofw. Felser, Walter	11	IV./JG 5		
Uffz. Fiedler	at least 3	Z-Staffel		
Oblt. Franzisket, Max	at least 4	Z-Staffel		
Lt. Froscheck, Karl-Heinz	at least 2	Jabo-Staffel	MIA 14/2/44	
Lt. Fuhrmann, Günther	at least 1	III./JG 5	MIA 15/9/44	
Oblt. Gayko, Werner	13	III./JG 5		
Lt. Geisen, Walter	7	III./JG 5	MIA 22/6/43	
Oblt. Gerlach, Lothar	at least 1	I./JG 5	MIA 1/1/45	JG 6
Major Gerlitz, Erich	about 1	I./JG 5	KIA 16/3/44	
Oblt. Glöckner, Rudolf	32	III./JG 5		
Uffz. Grams, Willi	at least 2	III./JG 5		
Fw. Graupner, Heinz	at least 1	I./JG 5	KIA 10/4/43	
Uffz. Gerndt	at least 1	III./JG 5		
Oblt. Habermann, Edgar	at least 2	I./JG 5	KIA 11/4/44	
Fw. Halstrick, Heinz	13	IV./JG 5		
Oblt. Hammel, Kurt	11	II./JG 5		
Oblt. Hartwein, Hans-Dieter	16	II./JG 5	MIA 21/8/42	
Uffz. Haus, Willi	1	IV./JG 5		
Lt. Heinicke, Werner	at least 2	III./JG 5		
Uffz. Heinsdorf	at least 1	I./JG 5		
Uffz. Hellwig	at least 1	III./JG 5		
Lt. Helms, Bodo	6	III./JG 5	POW 5/8/42	
Lt. von Hermann, Bernhard	at least 3	III./JG 5	POW 17/3/44	
Ofhr. Höhn	6	III./JG 5		
Lt. Hoffmann, Heinz-Horst	3	Z-Staffel	KIA 15/9/41	
Oblt. Huppertz, Herbert	2	IV./JG 5	KIA 8/6/44	JG 2

230

Appendices

Name	Victories	Unit	Fate
Lt. Jakobi, Alfred	10	II./JG 5	POW 9/4/42
Lt. Junghans, Franz	at least 1	I./JG 5	POW 14/7/44
Fw. Kaddatz, Ernst	at least 1	I./JG 5	KIA 4/4/43
Uffz. Käppler	at least 2	I./JG 5	
Fw. Kaiser, Josef	11	III./JG 5	
Fw. Kalweit, Walter	at least 1	I./JG 5	
Uffz. Kern, Heinz	1	III./JG 5	
Uffz. Kersten, Erich	at least 1	I./JG 77	MIA 29/11/41
Oblt. Kirschmeier, Hans	2	IV./JG 5	KIA 8/10/44
Ofw. Kischnick, Helmut	14	III./JG 5	
Ofw. Klante, Helmut	21	III./JG 5	
Ofw. Klein, Erich	5	I./JG 5	
Fw. Knier, Leopold	5	II./JG 5	
Lt. König, Fritz	1	Jabo-Staffel	
Ofw. Kolodziej, Johann	at least 1	Z-Staffel	KIA 6/9/43
Lt. Koschack, Helmut	at least 4	II./JG 5	MIA 11/43
Hptm. Kosse, Wolfgang	at least 20	II./JG 5	MIA 24/12/44 JG 3
Hptm. Kriegel, Hans	at least 1	IV./JG 5	
Lt. Krippahl, Harry	at least 2	Z-Staffel	MIA 18/6/42
Lt. Kunz, Josef	16	II./JG 5	
Lt. Lehner, Alfred	35	II./JG 5	KIA 4/4/44 JG 7
Fw. Leitner, Franz	at least 3	I./JG 5	KIA 2/4/44
Fw. Lenz, Adolf	1	II./JG 5	
Oblt. Lesch, Heinrich	8	II./JG 5	
Fhr. Von Lilienhoff, Rolf	6	III./JG 5	MIA 21/10/44
Lt. Linz, Rudi	70	III./JG 5	KIA 9/2/45
Uffz. Lork, Heinz	2	III./JG 5	
Ofw. Lübking, August	38	III./JG 5	KIA 22/3/45 JG 7
Lt. Lüdecke, Friedrich	6	II./JG 5	POW 25/1/43
Hptm. Lüder, Rudolf	6	Stab/JG 5	Died 7/9/73
Uffz. Lutzka, Richard	at least 5	III./JG 5	
Ofw. Luy, August	35	III./JG 5	
Ofw. Mack, Albert	at least 1	Z-Staffel	MIA 30/3/44
Lt. Mahlkuch, Hans	about 16	I./JG 77	MIA 23/8/41
Lt. Maul	at least 2	Z-Staffel	
Uffz. Mayer, Ernst	at least 1	III./JG 5	
Fw. Mecke, Erhardt	about 12	II./JG 5	KIA 14/2/45 JG 4
Uffz. Mendl, Arthur	at least 9	II./JG 5	
Uffz. Meyer, Hans	at least 1	I./JG 5	KIA 25/4/44
Lt. Minz, Werner	1	I./JG 77	KIA 24/7/41
Lt. Mors. August	60	I./JG 5	WIA 6/8/44 (Died 8/8/44)
Oblt. Müller, Hans	6	III./JG 5	MIA 17/7/44
Ofw. Müller, Rudolf	94	II./JG 5	POW 19/4/43 (died in captivity)
Ofw. Munding	at least 2	Z-Staffel	
Lt. Neumann, Helmut	62	IV./JG 5	
Lt. Norz, Jakob	117	III./JG 5	KIA 16/9/44
Uffz. Oberländer, Horst	9	II./JG 5	KIA 20/7/43
Uffz. Opitz	at least 1	III./JG 5	
Uffz. Orlowski, Heinz	at least 3	III./JG 5	
Lt. Peters, Walter	at least 2	III./JG 5	KIA 12/12/44
Ofw. Pfränger, Willi	30	II./JG 5	POW 17/5/42
Uffz. Philipp, Kurt	1	III./JG 5	POW 5/8/42
Lt. von Podewils, Heinrich	3	III./JG 5	
Ofhr. Pöllinger, Hans	1	I./JG 5	POW 17/7/44
Lt. Politt, Wolfgang	at least 2	I./JG 5	
Uffz. Preisler, Bela	6	II./JG 5	POW 4/4/43
Lt. Prenzler	at least 1	IV./JG 5	

Jagdgeschwader 5

Ofw. Reinhold, Gerhard		41	II./JG 5	KIA 4/4/45	JG 7
Uffz. Rödig, Rudolf	at least	1	I./JG 5	KIA 1/5/43	
Uffz. Rohde, Peter	at least	1	III./JG 5	MIA 23/4/44	
Uffz. Rolly, Horst		36	II./JG 5	KIA 2/11/44	JG 400
Lt. Rost, Wolfgang		12	III./JG 5	POW 29/2/44	
Ofw. Salwender, Florian		25	II./JG 5	POW 23/4/42 (died in captivity)	
Fw. Schalk, Paul		20	II./JG 5		
Uffz. Scharf, Ludwig		18	II./JG 5	POW 15/9/42	
Fw. Scharwächter, Gustav		1	IV./JG 5	MIA 24/10/44	
Hptm. Schaschke, Gerhard	about	20	*Z-Staffel*	POW 4/8/41 (missing in captivity)	
Uffz. Schattschneider, Helmut	at least	1	II./JG 5	KIA 4/8/42	
Uffz. Scherf, Ralph	at least	1	I./JG 5		
Ofw. Schinzel, Max	at least	1	I./JG 5		
Oblt. Schloßstein, Karl-Friedrich		8	*Z-Staffel*		
Uffz. Schmejkal	at least	2	IV./JG 5		
Hptm. Schmidt, Hans-Hermann	at least	4	III./JG 5	POW 11/1/44	
Lt. Schmidt, Heinrich	at least	3	II./JG 5	KIA 11/12/43	
Lt. Schneider, August		11	IV./JG 5		
Oblt. Schneider, Hans	at least	11	IV./JG 5	KIA 12/3/45	
Gefr. Schöppler, Anton	at least	2	I./JG 5		
Oberstlt. Scholz, Günther		24	*Jafü/Kom.*		
Uffz. Schröder, Rudolf	at least	1	I./JG 5	MIA 16/7/44	
Oblt. Schuck, Walter		198	III./JG 5		
Lt. Schütze, Fritz	at least	2	I./JG 5	KIA 3/5/43	
Uffz. Schumacher, Werner		30	III./JG 5	POW 5/8/42 (died in camp)	
Oblt. Schwanecke, Günther		10	II./JG 5		
Fw. Seez, Emil		1	IV./JG 5		
Hptm. Segatz, Hermann		17	III./JG 5	KIA 8/3/44	JG 1
Oblt. Senoner, Gerd	about	20	I./JG 5	KIA 25/2/44	
Lt. Simme, Fritz	at least	4	IV./JG 5	MIA 15/10/44	
Fw. Sommeregger, Josef	at least	1	I./JG 5	MIA 7/7/43	
Hptm. Graf von Sponeck, Hans Curt	at least	1	III./JG 5		
Ofw. Stebner, Theo	about	9	IV./JG 5	KIA 12/3/45	
Lt. Stephan, Horst	about	3	III./JG 5		
Hptm. Strakeljahn, Friedrich-Wilhelm		9	*Jabo-Staffel*	KIA 6/7/44	SG 4
Uffz. Stoll, Alfred	at least	2	III./JG 5		
Uffz. Suske, Josef	at least	3	III./JG 5	KIA 9/10/44	
Oblt. Tetzner, Hans	about	20	II./JG 5	KIA 19/7/44	
Lt. von Thienen, Franz	at least	1	I./JG 5		
Uffz. Thoms, Bruno	at least	1	II./JG 5		
Ofw. Timm, Oskar	at least	1	III./JG 5		
Hptm. Treppe, Herbert		3	*Z-Staffel*		
Uffz. Tretter, Wilhelm	at least	1	II./JG 5	POW 2/8/42	
Fw. Uhlmann, Martin	at least	3	IV./JG 5		
Lt. Vogel, Karl-Heinz		4	III./JG 5	KIA 16/1/44	
Lt. Vollet, Hans		11	IV./JG 5		
Uffz. Voltmer, Willi		1	IV./JG 5	MIA 14/4/45	
Fw. Weinitschke, Dietrich		18	II./JG 5	POW 12/3/43	
Lt. Weiß, Franz		31	III./JG 5		
Hptm. Weißenberger, Theodor		200	I./JG 5	(killed in accident 10/6/50)	
Oblt. Widowitz, Wulf-Dietrich		36	III./JG 5	(killed in accident 28/7/43)	
Fw. Wiegand, Heinfried	at least	9	III./JG 5		
Hptm. Wienhusen, Franz		12	II./JG 5	KIA 3/12/45	JG 4
Fw. Wiesener, Hans		4	II./JG 5		

Appendices

Uffz. Wirz, Peter	at least 1	III./JG 5	MIA 5/4/45	
Uffz. Woite	at least 1	I./JG 77		
Oblt. Wollenweber, Wolfgang	4	Z-*Staffel*		
Lt. Wollmann, David	21	III./JG 5		
Uffz. Wünsche, Günter	at least 1	I./JG 5		

Victory List of *Major* Theo Weißenberger
(200 victories with JG 5)

No.	Date	Type	Location	Time	Mission	Unit
1	24/10/41	I-153	40 km SE of Lisa	12:35	12	1.(Z)/JG 77
2	24/1/42	I-18	4 km N of Boyaskoye	13:35	39	"
3	24/1/42	Hurricane	6 km SE of Toporny	13:40	39	"
4	25/2/42	Hurricane	S of Grazmaya-Guba	11:15	47	"
5	25/2/42	Hurricane	N of Ruchi railway	11:22	47	"
6	8/4/42	MiG	N of Ristikent	15:20	72	10.(Z)/JG 5
7	12/4/42	LaGG	Lake Vilye W of Lisa	07:11	73	"
8	15/4/42	I-180	10 km W of Murmansk	13:18	74	"
9	15/4/42	MiG	20 km W of Murmansk	17:42	74	"
10	15/4/42	Hurricane	20 km W of Murmansk	17:45	74	"
11	23/4/42	Hurricane	E of Titovka	06:25	77	"
12	25/4/42	Pe-2	10 km S of Motovskiy	07:44	79	"
13	25/4/42	Pe-2	35 km S of Motovskiy	07:49	79	"
14	10/5/42	MiG-3	10 km S of Eina-Guba	16:45	82	"
15	10/5/42	MiG-3	18 km SE of Eina-Guba	16:46	82	"
16	10/5/42	Hurricane	NE corner Lisa Bay	16:48	82	"
17	10/5/42	Hurricane	Vichnaya Bay	16:50	82	"
18	10/5/42	MiG-3	8 km S of Vladimir	16:57	82	"
19	12/5/42	MiG-3	SE of mouth of the Lisa	08:15	83	"
20	15/5/42	Hurricane	20 km W of Murmansk	18:12	89	"
21	1/6/42	Curtiss	SW of Murmashi	15:34	107	"
22	14/8/42	MiG-3	E of Vezhny Lake	13:24	SAR Flight	13.(Z)/JG 5
23	8/9/42	Yak-1	middle of Nyal Lake	15:02	135	"
24	15/9/42	Curtiss	16 km S of Murmashi	14:31	139	6./JG 5
25	22/9/42	Curtiss	15 km SE of Murmashi	14:33	139	"
26	22/9/42	Hurricane	W of Murmashi	14:59	143	"
27	22/9/42	Hurricane	N of Murmashi	15:00	143	"
28	22/9/42	Curtiss	S of Murmashi	15:05	143	"
29	27/9/42	Airacobra	20 km NE of Murmansk	11:36	145	"
30	27/9/42	Hurricane	S of Shongui	15:49	146	"
31	27/9/42	Hurricane	SW of Shongui	15:50	146	"
32	27/9/42	Hurricane	S of Shongui	15:51	146	"
33	27/9/42	Hurricane	E of Shongui	15:56	146	"
34	30/10/42	Curtiss	21 km NE of Murmansk	12:10	154	"
35	30/10/42	Curtiss	NE of Murmansk	12:20	154	"
36	30/10/42	LaGG-3	Murmansk area	12:25	154	"
37	30/10/42	Curtiss	Murmansk area	15:00	155	"
38	30/10/42	Curtiss	Murmansk area	15:06	155	"
39	6/3/43	LaGG-3	Kem/Uzhmana area	10:10	171	"
40	6/3/43	Curtiss	Kem/Uzhmana area	13:09	172	"
41	6/3/43	Curtiss	Kem/Uzhmana area	13:11	172	"
42	6/3/43	Curtiss	Kem/Uzhmana area	13:06	172	"
43	10/3/43	Curtiss	20 km SE of Murmansk	09:59	174	"
44	10/3/43	Curtiss	32 km SE of Murmansk	10:00	174	"
45	10/3/43	Airacobra	31 km SE of Murmansk	10:06	174	"
46	10/3/43	Airacobra	37 km SE of Murmansk	10:07	174	"
47	10/3/43	Airacobra	43 km SE of Murmansk	10:08	174	"
48	10/3/43	Curtiss	45 km SE of Murmansk	10:09	174	"

Jagdgeschwader 5

49	12/3/43	Curtiss	20 km SE of Murmashi	14:17	175	"
50	12/3/43	Curtiss	15 km S of Murmashi	14:18	175	"
51	12/3/43	Airacobra	16 km S of Murmashi	14:19	175	6./JG 5
52	12/3/43	Airacobra	20 km SE of Murmashi	14:32	175	"
53	12/3/43	Airacobra	19 km S of Murmashi	14:35	175	"
54	13/3/43	Pe-2	17 km E of Petsamo airfield	09:35	176	"
55	13/3/43	Pe-2	25 km E of Petsamo airfield	09:36	176	"
56	13/3/43	Curtiss	13 km SE tip of Ura Bay	13:05	177	"
57	13/3/43	Curtiss	S tip of Ura Bay	13:08	177	"
58	14/3/43	Airacobra	W of Urd Lake	14:05	178	"
59	14/3/43	Airacobra	W of Urd Lake	14:08	178	"
60	14/3/43	Airacobra	E of Urd lake	14:11	178	"
61	20/3/43	Curtiss	S edge Murmashi airfield	11:20	181	"
62	20/3/43	Curtiss	7 km SE of Murmashi	11:24	181	"
63	20/3/43	Curtiss	4 km E of Murmashi	11:30	181	"
64	21/3/43	Il-2	S edge Murmashi airfield	09:02	182	"
65	27/3/43	Airacobra	4 km W of Shongui	13:58	185	"
66	27/3/43	Airacobra	8 km SW of Murmashi	13:59	185	"
67	27/3/43	Curtiss	12 km W of Murmashi	14:02	185	"
68	27/3/43	Curtiss	11 km W of Murmashi	14:06	185	"
69	28/3/43	Airacobra	30 km SE Salmijärvi airfield	11:50	187	"
70	28/3/43	Airacobra	45 km W of Murmansk	11:58	187	"
71	28/3/43	Airacobra	33 km NW of Murmashi	12:00	187	"
72	13/4/43	Hurricane	12 km NE of Murmansk	17:05	202	"
73	13/4/43	Hurricane	14 km NE of Murmansk	17:06	202	"
74	13/4/43	Airacobra	17 km NE of Murmansk	17:13	202	"
75	13/4/43	Airacobra	11 km NE of Murmansk	17:14	202	"
76	13/4/43	Airacobra	14 km E of Murmansk	17:15	202	"
77	13/4/43	Airacobra	21 km NE of Murmansk	17:16	202	"
78	19/4/43	Airacobra	24 km NE of Murmansk	11:24	205	"
79	22/4/43	Curtiss	4 km N of Murmansk	12:57	208	"
80	22/4/43	Yak-1	11 km SE of Murmansk	13:10	208	"
81	22/4/43	Yak-1	8 km SE of Murmansk	13:12	208	"
82	11/5/43	Curtiss	7 km SE of Murmashi	16:30	216	"
83	13/5/43	Airacobra	9 km N of Cape Pogan	05:05	218	"
84	13/5/43	Airacobra	10 km E of Cape Pogan	05:07	218	"
85	13/5/43	Airacobra	2 km NE of Cape Pogan	05:08	218	"
86	13/5/43	Airacobra	16 km NW Cape Pogan	05:14	218	"
87	8/6/43	Typhoon	21 km NE of Murmansk	17:15	226	"
88	8/6/43	Typhoon	22 km NE of Murmansk	17:16	226	"
89	8/6/43	Typhoon	20 km NE of Murmansk	17:18	226	"
90	8/6/43	Airacobra	23 km NE of Murmansk	17:21	226	"
91	8/6/43	Typhoon	27 km NE of Murmansk	17:23	226	"
92	22/6/43	Hurricane	3 km E of Kola Station	09:27	235	7./JG 5
93	22/6/43	Hurricane	6 km NE of Kola Station	09:30	235	"
94	22/6/43	Hurricane	2 km E of Kola Station	09:40	235	"
95	23/6/43	Airacobra	50 km N of Makur	07:06	237	"
96	23/6/43	Airacobra	55 km N of Makur	07:07	237	"
97	23/6/43	Airacobra	60 km N of Makur	07:12	237	"
98	4/7/43	Pe-2	18 km N of Vayda-Guba	21:07	242	"
99	4/7/43	Il-2	NW of Fischer Peninsula	21:53	242	"
100	4/7/43	Il-2	NW of Fischer Peninsula	21:54	242	"
101	4/7/43	Il-2	NW of Fischer Peninsula	21:55	242	"
102	4/7/43	Hampden	15 km NW of Pummanki Bay	21:59	242	"
103	4/7/43	Hampden	10 km NW of Pummanki Bay	22:04	242	"
104	4/7/43	Hampden	12 km NW of Pummanki Bay	22:06	242	"
105	18/7/43	Airacobra	28 km E of Zyp Navolok	00:25	249	"
106	18/7/43	Airacobra	30 km SE of Zyp Navolok	00:28	249	"
107	24/7/43	Hurricane	8 km E of Kildinskoye	15:55	253	7./JG 5
108	25/7/43	Airacobra	12 km SE of Kiberg	02:48	254	"
109	25/7/43	Pe-2	15 km SE of Kiberg	02:50	254	"
110	25/7/43	Pe-2	18 km S of Kiberg	02:51	254	"
111	25/7/43	Pe-2	20 km S of Kiberg	02:52	254	"

Appendices

112	25/7/43	Airacobra	35 km SE of Kiberg	02:59	254	"
113	13/10/43	Il-2	31 km WNW of Vayda Guba	12:58	269	6./JG 5
114	13/10/43	Il-2	32 km WNW of Vayda Guba	12:59	269	"
115	3/11/43	Il-2	24 km W of Vayda Guba	13:01	273	"
116	3/11/43	Boston	37 km NW of Vayda Guba	13:11	273	"
117	3/11/43	Boston	31 km NW of Vayda Guba	13:14	273	"
118	3/11/43	Hurricane	7 km W of Vayda Guba	13:29	273	"
119	31/1/44	LaGG-5	10 km SE of Soltsy	14:48	282	"
120	1/2/44	LaGG-5	E of Soltsy	10:50	285	"
121	1/2/44	LaGG-5	12 km NNW of Soltsy	10:51	285	"
122	1/2/44	LaGG-5	9 km NNW of Soltsy	10:53	285	"
123	1/2/44	LaGG-5	7 km N of Soltsy	10:56	285	"
124	1/2/44	LaGG-5	4 km NW of Soltsy	10:58	285	"
125	6/2/44	Il-2	27 km N of Soltsy	12:17	286	"
126	14/2/44	LaGG-3	30 km WSW of Narva	11:45	305	"
127	14/2/44	LaGG-3	31 km WSW of Narva	11:47	305	"
128	14/2/44	Il-2	27 km SW of Narva	11:40	305	"
129	15/2/44	unidentified	18 km S of Lipno	12:15	306	"
130	16/2/44	Yak-9	36 km S of Luga	14:01	308	"
131	16/2/44	Yak-9	38 km S of Luga	14:02	308	"
132	16/2/44	Yak-9	S of Luga	14:04	308	"
133	18/2/44	Yak-9	15 km N of Schimsk	14:14	310	"
134	18/2/44	Yak-9	13 km N of Schimsk	14:15	310	"
135	18/2/44	LaGG-3	17 km NE of Schimsk	16:00	311	"
136	18/2/44	LaGG-3	11 km NE of Schimsk	16:01	311	"
137	27/2/44	Il-2	9 km SE of Irditsa	12:13	316	"
138	27/2/44	Il-2	15 km SE of Idritsa	12:16	316	"
139	27/2/44	Il-2	30 km SE of Idritsa	12:25	316	"
140	28/2/44	Pe-2	18 km NE of Pustoshka	08:33	transfer flight	"
141	16/3/44	Yak-9	5 km S of Nyam Lake	11:53	317	"
142	17/3/44	Yak-9	S of Nyam Station	10:31	318	"
143	17/3/44	Yak-9	N edge of Verkhne-Ivanovka Lake	10:34	318	"
144	17/3/44	Yak-9	SSE of Nyam Station	13:04	319	"
145	20/3/44	Il-2	NNW of Nizhne-Verman	09:51	321	"
146	20/3/44	Il-2	N of Nizhne-Verman	09:53	321	"
147	20/3/44	Il-2	NNE of Nizhne-Verman	09:55	321	"
148	20/3/44	Curtiss	S of Kamenoye Lake	10:00	321	"
149	25/3/44	Yak-9	NE of Nizhne Verman	09:21	323	"
150	25/3/44	Yak-9	S of Kamenoye Lake	09:23	323	"
151	25/3/44	Yak-9	NE of Nizhne-Verman	09:27	323	"
152	25/3/44	Yak-9	NW of Nyam Station	12:00	324	"
153	25/3/44	Yak-9	NW of Nyam Station	12:03	324	"
154	27/3/44	Airacobra	10 km NE Alakurtti airfield	09:17	328	II./JG 5
155	27/3/44	Airacobra	N of Verman Lake	09:19	328	"
156	4/4/44	Yak-9	10 km NE of Nizhne-Verman	18:20	329	"
157	4/4/44	Yak-9	14 km NE of Nizhne-Verman	18:23	329	"
158	4/4/44	Yak-9	15 km NE of Nizhne-Verman	18:26	329	II./JG 5
159	9/4/44	Yak-9	NW of Nizhne-Verman	09:54	332	"
160	9/4/44	Yak-9	N of Nizhne-Verman	09:57	332	"
161	9/4/44	Yak-9	E of Nizhne-Verman	10:08	332	"
162	9/4/44	Yak-9	W tip of Ori Lake	10:12	332	"
163	12/4/44	Yak-9	8 km N of Kaprayevo Station	10:25	333	"
164	12/4/44	Yak-9	9 km NE of Kaprayevo Station	10:26	333	"
165	13/4/44	Yak-9	N edge of Tolvand Lake	16:20	334	"
166	6/4/44	Yak-9	W tip of Tolvand Lake	15:12	337	"
167	15/5/44	Yak-9	15 km SE of Pustoshka	14:21	342	"
168	15/5/44	Yak-9	42 km SE of Ostrov	05:09	344	"
169	15/5/44	Yak-9	45 km SE of Ostrov	11:15	345	"
170	15/5/44	Yak-9	36 km SE of Ostrov	11:37	344	"
171	15/5/44	Yak-9	40 km SE of Opochka	15:29	345	"
172	15/5/44	Yak-9	35 km SE of Opochka	15:32	345	"
173	18/5/44	Yak-9	25 km SE of Ostrov	08:33	350	"
174	18/5/44	Yak-9	25 km SE of Ostrov	08:33	350	"

Jagdgeschwader 5

175	18/5/44	Yak-9	17 km SE of Ostrov	08:41	350	″
176	7/6/44	Thunderbolt	SW Montdidier	09:05	transfer flight	I./JG 5
177	7/6/44	Thunderbolt	SW Montdidier	09:26	transfer flight	″
178	7/6/44	Thunderbolt	SW Montdidier	09:27	transfer flight	″
179	7/6/44	Thunderbolt	near Beauvais	approx.17:15	351	″
180	7/6/44	Thunderbolt	near Beauvais	approx.17:15	351	″
181	8/6/44	Thunderbolt	E of Montdidier	18:50	353	″
182	8/6/44	Thunderbolt	SW of Montdidier	18:54	353	″
183	12/6/44	Thunderbolt	E of Evreux	06:48	355	″
184	12/6/44	Thunderbolt	30 km E of Evreux	06:56	355	″
185	12/6/44	Thunderbolt	Gisors area	07:02	355	″
186	6/7/44	Lightning	7 km S of Cambrai	08:48	362	″
187	6/7/44	Lightning	15 km S of Cambrai	08:49	362	″
188	7/7/44	Thunderbolt	S of Rosieres	18:32	364	″
189	7/7/44	Thunderbolt	S of Rosieres	18:33	364	″
190	7/7/44	Thunderbolt	S of Rosieres	18:36	364	″
191	13/7/44	Typhoon	Trouville-sur-Mer	18:24	368	″
192	13/7/44	Typhoon	Trouville-sur-Mer	18:26	368	″
193	14/7/44	unidentified	15 km S of Bayeux	14:41	369	″
194	14/7/44	Spitfire	16 km N of Lisieux	14:56	369	″
195	19/7/44	Typhoon	N of Lisieux	20:22	373	″
196	19/7/44	Typhoon	N of Lisieux	20:23	373	″
197	19/7/44	Typhoon	NW of Cormeilles	20:25	373	″
198	19/7/44	Mustang	Charleval	20:35	373	″
199	25/7/44	Spitfire	15 km S of Rouen	11:00	375	″
200	25/7/44	Spitfire	SE of Rouen	11:02	375	″

Appendices

Casualties

I./JG 77

18/4/41	*Uffz.* Kind, Helmut	2. *Staffel*	killed
24/4/41	*Oblt.* Reinicke, Horst	2. *Staffel*	missing
19/6/41	*Lt.* Meissel, Eckehard	2. *Staffel*	killed
24/6/41	*Lt.* Leow, Rudolf	3. *Staffel*	killed
24/7/41	*Lt.* Minz, Werner	2. *Staffel*	killed
22/8/41	*Uffz.* Kastens, Wilhelm	1. *Staffel*	open tracing case
4/9/41	*Ofw.* Eisseler, Helmut	2. *Staffel*	killed
12/9/41	*Lt.* von der Lühe, Eckhard	1. *Staffel*	killed
17/9/41	*Fw.* Stiglmair, Josef	1. *Staffel*	missing
24/11/41	*Uffz.* Steinborn, Ernst	3. *Staffel*	killed
13/12/41	*Uffz.* Streb, Günther	3. *Staffel*	killed

13. and 14./JG 77

29/6/41	*Hptm.* von Lojewski, Alfred	14. *Staffel*	POW
2/7/41	*Uffz.* Döpfer, Kurt	13. *Staffel*	killed
2/7/41	*Uffz.* Scheimann, August	13. *Staffel*	killed
5/7/41	*Fw.* Hauser, Paul	14. *Staffel*	open tracing case
9/8/41	*Lt.* Wolter, Horst	14. *Staffel*	killed
23/8/41	*Lt.* Mahlkuch, Hans	14. *Staffel*	open tracing case
31/8/41	*Gefr.* Kobold, Hans	14. *Staffel*	killed
5/10/41	*Uffz.* Keller, Eduard	14. *Staffel*	killed
29/11/41	*Uffz.* Kersten, Erich	13. *Staffel*	missing

***Stab*/JG 5**

28/12/42	*Lt.* Rutishauser, Hans-Joachim		killed
13/5/43	*Lt.* Zeuch, Günther		killed

I./JG 5

30/3/42	*Gefr.* Reichard, Paul	3. *Staffel*	killed
7/4/42	*Lt.* Schuhmann, Ulrich	2. *Staffel*	killed
14/4/42	*Ogfr.* Klesa, Gerhard	2. *Staffel*	killed
14/4/42	*Fw.* Drossel, Alfred	3. *Staffel*	killed
17/5/42	*Fw.* Reitinger, Josef	2. *Staffel*	killed
10/8/42	*Uffz.* Bruns, Martin	1. *Staffel*	killed
21/1/43	*Uffz.* Nelder, Kurt	3. *Staffel*	killed
28/1/43	*Uffz.* Friedmann, Kurt	1. *Staffel*	killed
3/3/43	*Fw.* Gruber, Josef	1 *Staffel*	open tracing case
8/3/43	*Uffz.* Lieber, Rudolf	3. *Staffel*	killed
1/4/43	*Uffz.* Menk, Otto	3. *Staffel*	killed
4/4/43	*Fw.* Kaddatz, Ernst	2. *Staffel*	killed
10/4/43	*Fw.* Graupner, Heinz	2. *Staffel*	killed
30/4/43	*Fw.* Schaub, Herbert	1. *Staffel*	killed
1/5/43	*Uffz.* Rödig, Rudolf	1. *Staffel*	killed
3/5/43	*Lt.* Schütze, Fritz	2. *Staffel*	killed
14/5/43	*Uffz.* Koch, Arnold	3. *Staffel*	killed
7/7/43	*Fw.* Sommeregger, Josef	1. *Staffel*	open tracing case
7/10/43	*Uffz.* Hüllenhütter, Fritz	2. *Staffel*	killed
13/10/43	*Lt.* Assmy, Manfred	2. *Staffel*	killed
10/1/44	*Hptm.* Wengel, Gerhard	*Stab*/I./JG 5	killed
25/2/44	*Oblt.* Senoner, Gerd	1. *Staffel*	killed
16/3/44	*Major* Gerlitz, Erich	*Stab*/I./JG 5	killed
16/3/44	*Fw.* Veleba, Johann	3. *Staffel*	killed
18/3/44	*Gefr.* Hack, Hubertus	1. *Staffel*	killed
2/4/44	*Fw.* Leitner, Franz	2. *Staffel*	killed
8/4/44	*Ofw.* Schulte, Anton	1. *Staffel*	killed
8/4/44	*Ofw.* Glatz, Walter	2. *Staffel*	killed
11/4/44	*Oblt.* Habermann, Edgar	2. *Staffel*	killed
11/4/44	*Ogfr.* Burkhardt, Herbert	*Stab* I./JG 5	killed
24/4/44	*Uffz.* Glienke, Kurt	2. *Staffel*	killed

Jagdgeschwader 5

Date	Name	Unit	Fate
25/4/44	Uffz. Meyer, Hans	3. Staffel	killed
9/5/44	Uffz. Puttrich, Günter	2. Staffel	killed
10/5/44	Uffz. Schrade, Hans	3. Staffel	killed
12/5/44	Gefr. Lieberknecht, Herbert	1. Staffel	killed
19/5/44	Fw. von Ahsen, Heinrich	1. Staffel	killed
27/5/44	Major Carganico, Horst	Stab I./JG 5	killed
27/5/44	Lt. Wiesen, Heinz	3. Staffel	killed
27/5/44	Hptm. Deuschle, Heinz	Stab I./JG 5	killed
27/5/44	Uffz. Schorsch, Hans	2. Staffel	killed
27/5/44	Fw. Reckendorfer, Friedrich	3. Staffel	killed
27/5/44	Gefr. Bollinger, Eberhard	3. Staffel	killed
27/5/44	Gefr. Glöckner, Otto	3. Staffel	killed
28/5/44	Fw. Englert, Ludwig	1. Staffel	killed
28/5/44	Uffz. Doll, Otto	3. Staffel	killed
7/6/44	Ofhr. Fricke, Jürgen	3. Staffel	killed
11/6/44	Uffz. Wenninger, Franz	3. Staffel	killed
12/6/44	Uffz. Tychi, Alfred	1. Staffel	killed
27/6/44	Uffz. Kenter, Hermann	2. Staffel	killed
28/6/44	Ogefr. Höppner, Karl	3. Staffel	missing
1/7/44	Uffz. Seidel, Paul	3. Staffel	killed
1/7/44	Gefr. Jansen, Heinrich	3. Staffel	open tracing case
3/7/44	Lt. Buth, Wolfgang	2. Staffel	killed
5/7/44	Lt. Berneburg, Eckhard	1. Staffel	killed
6/7/44	Uffz. Hiltwein, Kurt	3. Staffel	killed
14/7/44	Fw. Junghans, Franz	1. Staffel	POW
14/7/44	Uffz. Geilert, Johannes	1. Staffel	POW
14/7/44	Fw. Baumgart, Maximillian	3. Staffel	POW
16/7/44	Uffz. Berger, Kurt	2. Staffel	missing
16/7/44	Uffz. Schröder, Rudolf	2. Staffel	open tracing case
17/7/44	Oblt. Müller, Robert	3. Staffel	open tracing case
17/7/44	Uffz. Straube, Manfred	2. Staffel	killed
17/7/44	Ofhr. Pöllinger, Hans	2. Staffel	POW
4/8/44	Lt. Bölz, Friedrich	2. Staffel	open tracing case
6/8/44	Lt. Mors, August	1. Staffel	wounded (died 8/8/44)
7/8/44	Uffz. Binna, Ernst	1. Staffel	missing
20/9/44	Uffz. von Ungern Sternberg, Wolf	3. Staffel	killed
25/9/44	Uffz. Rausch, Siegfried	1. Staffel	killed
27/9/44	Gefr. Seifert, Ferdinand	2. Staffel	killed
3/10/44	Uffz. Schönbach, Peter	1. Staffel	killed

II./JG 5

Date	Name	Unit	Fate
19/2/42	Ogfr. Seibt, Gerhard	4. Staffel	missing
28/2/42	Ofw. Bauer, Eberhard	5. Staffel	killed
23/3/42	Oblt. Grobe, Rudolf	5. Staffel	killed
29/3/42	Ogfr. Hesse, Hermann	5. Staffel	missing
9/4/42	Lt. Jakobi, Alfred	5. Staffel	POW
9/4/42	Fw. Kandziora, Anton	5. Staffel	POW (died in camp)
23/4/42	Ofw. Salwender, Florian	6. Staffel	POW (died in camp)
1/5/42	Uffz. Kanbach, Gerhard	5. Staffel	killed
10/5/42	Uffz. Bausch, Heinz	5. Staffel	open tracing case
17/5/42	Ofw. Pfränger, Willi	6. Staffel	POW
17/5/42	Uffz. Wellner, Karl Heinz	4. Staffel	POW
25/5/42	Lt. Dahn, Friedrich	5. Staffel	open tracing case
29/6/42	Uffz. Kuchlingg, Wilhelm	6. Staffel	open tracing case
2/8/42	Uffz. Tretter, Wilhelm	4. Staffel	POW
4/8/42	Uffz. Schattschneider, Helmut	4. Staffel	killed
21/8/42	Oblt. Hartwein, Hans Dieter	6. Staffel	open tracing case
9/9/42	Ogfr. Hoffmann, Günther	6. Staffel	open tracing case
11/9/42	Fw. Froböse, Erich	5. Staffel	killed
15/9/42	Uffz. Scharf, Ludwig	6. Staffel	POW
19/9/42	Lt. Kunze, Werner	Stab II./JG 5	open tracing case
20/9/42	Fw. Oehme, Johannes	4. Staffel	missing
9/11/42	Ogfr. Luther, Gustav	4. Staffel	open tracing case

Appendices

Date	Name	Unit	Status
9/11/42	*Uffz.* Zeuschel, Erwin	4. *Staffel*	open tracing case
5/1/43	*Fw.* Bigalk, Reinhold	4. *Staffel*	open tracing case
6/1/43	*Fw.* Wirtz, Josef	5. *Staffel*	killed
25/1/43	*Lt.* Lüdecke, Friedrich	6. *Staffel*	POW
19/2/43	*Uffz.* Fenten, Rudolf	6. *Staffel*	POW
12/3/43	*Fw.* Stratmann, Emil	6. *Staffel*	killed
12/3/43	*Fw.* Weinitschke, Dietrich	5. *Staffel*	POW
20/3/43	*Uffz.* Merker, Karl	5. *Staffel*	killed
27/3/43	*Uffz.* Krischkovski, Edmund	6. *Staffel*	POW (died in camp)
4/4/43	*Uffz.* Preisler, Bela	4. *Staffel*	POW
19/4/43	*Ofw.* Müller, Robert	6. *Staffel*	POW (missing in camp)
23/4/43	*Uffz.* Lorenz, Herbert	4. *Staffel*	killed
29/4/43	*Fw.* Fahldieck, Erwin	6. *Staffel*	missing
7/5/43	*Ofw.* Brunner, Albert	6. *Staffel*	killed
11/5/43	*Lt.* Steinmann, Günther	4. *Staffel*	missing
3/6/43	*Lt.* Harder, Gerhard	6. *Staffel*	open tracing case
16/6/43	*Uffz.* Seedorf, Georg	4. *Staffel*	POW
23/6/43	*Lt.* Simon, Herbert	4. *Staffel*	open tracing case
9/7/43	*Uffz.* Grosser, Hans	6. *Staffel*	open tracing case
20/7/43	*Uffz.* Oberländer, Horst	6. *Staffel*	killed
25/7/43	*Oblt.* Leitner, Fritz	*Stab* II./JG 5	killed
11/8/43	*Lt.* Knigge, Herbert	6. *Staffel*	killed
18/8/43	*Fw.* Stolz, Christian	6. *Staffel*	open tracing case
7/9/43	*Uffz.* Caspar, Otto	6. *Staffel*	wounded (died 16/9/42)
20/9/43	*Lt.* Stahlschmidt, Manfred	*Stab* II./JG 5	killed
6/10/43	*Uffz.* Fleischmann, Richard	6. *Staffel*	killed
25/10/43	*Uffz.* Pötter, Hans-Georg	4. *Staffel*	killed
11/43	*Lt.* Koschak, Helmut	II./JG 5	missing
8/12/43	*Uffz.* Weiser, Helmut	5. *Staffel*	killed
11/12/43	*Lt.* Schmidt, Heinrich	5. *Staffel*	killed
24/1/44	*Gefr.* Schnelling, Helmut	4. *Staffel*	open tracing case
24/1/44	*Uffz.* Kindler, Hans	4. *Staffel*	killed
31/4/44	*Uffz.* Haberichter, Richard	4. *Staffel*	missing
1/2/44	*Gefr.* Ludewig, Horst	5. *Staffel*	killed
1/2/44	*Uffz.* Schad, Adolf	6. *Staffel*	killed
3/2/44	*Uffz.* Zimmermann, Wolfgang	4. *Staffel*	open tracing case
24/2/44	*Uffz.* Schrag, Karl	5. *Staffel*	open tracing case
9/4/44	*Uffz.* Wagner, Heinz	6. *Staffel*	missing
9/5/44	*Uffz.* Erlinger, Werner	4. *Staffel*	missing
15/5/44	*Gefr.* Ziersch, Werner	5. *Staffel*	killed
20/6/44	*Uffz.* Scharf, Heinrich	4. *Staffel*	killed
20/6/44	*Fw.* Eichelmann, Helmut	4. *Staffel*	missing
22/6/44	*Uffz.* Demmig, Walter	4. *Staffel*	killed
24/6/44	*Lt.* Meyer, Ortwin	5. *Staffel*	missing
25/6/44	*Uffz.* Siegmund, Gerhard	4. *Staffel*	open tracing case
25/6/44	*Uffz.* Vahle, Johannes	4. *Staffel*	killed
25/6/44	*Uffz.* Scheidt, Emil	9. *Staffel*	missing
7/7/44	*Uffz.* Heines, Herbert	4. *Staffel*	killed
7/7/44	*Ofhr.* Dettmann, Herbert	4. *Staffel*	killed
19/7/44	*Oblt.* Tetzner, Hans	*Stab* II./JG 5	killed
19/7/44	*Fw.* Riemer, Walter	5. *Staffel*	missing
20/7/44	*Oblt.* Andresen, Lorenz	9. *Staffel*	killed
20/7/44	*Uffz.* Steinke, Gerhard	5. *Staffel*	killed
20/7/44	*Uffz.* Baumann, Otto	9. *Staffel*	killed
21/7/44	*Ofhr.* Göldner, Werner	9. *Staffel*	killed
4/8/44	*Ofhr.* Jühnemann, Alexander	5. *Staffel*	killed
4/8/44	*Uffz.* Moses, Heinz	7. *Staffel*	open tracing case
4/8/44	*Uffz.* Drägert, Fritz	7. *Staffel*	missing
5/8/44	*Uffz.* Kraus, Gerhard	7. *Staffel*	open tracing case
5/8/44	*Uffz.* Ohr, Günther	7. *Staffel*	killed
5/8/44	*Ofhr.* Schick, Hermann	6. *Staffel*	killed
5/8/44	*Ofw.* Sels, Heinrich	8. *Staffel*	killed
5/8/44	*Uffz.* Amend, Hermann	8. *Staffel*	killed

Jagdgeschwader 5

5/8/44	*Fhr.* Tengeler, Helmut	8. *Staffel*	missing
9/8/44	*Gefr.* Liebe, Herbert	6. *Staffel*	killed
9/8/44	*Lt.* Carl, Horst	8. *Staffel*	killed
15/8/44	*Uffz.* Thomas, Ernst	6. *Staffel*	killed
16/8/44	*Ofhr.* Jusa, Heinz	7. *Staffel*	killed
16/8/44	*Uffz.* Kortmann, Günther	7. *Staffel*	killed
23/8/44	*Gefr.* Rohfeld, Franz	5. *Staffel*	killed
24/8/44	*Uffz.* Weidner, Max	8. *Staffel*	killed
25/8/44	*Oberstlt.* Kettner, Kurt	*Stab* II./JG 5	killed
25/8/44	*Ofhr.* Papenschütz, Joachim	6. *Staffel*	killed
25/8/44	*Gefr.* Heubel, Rudolf	7. *Staffel*	open tracing case
29/8/44	*Lt.* Strenge, Walter	*Stab* II./JG 5	killed
3/10/44	*Fw.* Kadenbach, Gerhard	6. *Staffel*	killed
16/10/44	*Uffz.* Steiner, Herbert	8. *Staffel*	killed
16/10/44	*Uffz.* Mahnke, Claus	8. *Staffel*	killed
30/10/44	*Uffz.* Seissler, Daniel	5. *Staffel*	killed

III./JG 5

2/4/42	*Gefr.* Pürzl. Adolf	8. *Staffel*	killed
9/5/42	*Lt.* Lechte, Hans	8. *Staffel*	open tracing case
27/5/42	*Ofw.* Sommer, Walter	8. *Staffel*	missing
28/5/42	*Gefr.* Hofinger, Johann	8. *Staffel*	killed
8/7/42	*Fw.* Strasser, Franz	7. *Staffel*	killed
13/7/42	*Lt.* Bahr, Hans-Joachim	8. *Staffel*	missing
5/8/42	*Lt.* Helms, Bodo	7. *Staffel*	POW
5/8/42	*Uffz.* Philipp, Kurt	7. *Staffel*	POW
5/8/42	*Uffz.* Schumacher, Werner	7. *Staffel*	POW (died in camp)
15/9/42	*Uffz.* Braun, August	7. *Staffel*	open tracing case
30/10/42	*Uffz.* Kastner, Adolf	7. *Staffel*	killed
9/11/42	*Uffz.* Betz, Klaus	9. *Staffel*	missing
2/12/42	*Lt.* Erber, Guido	9. *Staffel*	POW
27/12/42	*Uffz.* Schedl, Ludwig	7. *Staffel*	killed
31/12/42	*Uffz.* Gathmann, Dietrich	7. *Staffel*	POW
8/1/43	*Uffz.* Rennemann, Friedrich	8. *Staffel*	POW
21/2/43	*Fw.* Schwippert, Paul	9. *Staffel*	missing
5/3/43	*Lt.* Grosse-Brauckmann, Gerd	9. *Staffel*	killed
14/3/43	*Uffz.* Kern, Alfred	7. *Staffel*	POW (died in camp)
27/3/43	*Uffz.* Riess, Andreas	7. *Staffel*	open tracing case
3/4/43	*Ogfr.* Fritz, Eugen	9. *Staffel*	missing
8/5/43	*Lt.* Sadewasser, Rolf-Viktor	*Stab* III./JG 5	open tracing case
5/6/43	*Lt.* Steinle, Hellmut	9. *Staffel*	open tracing case
12/6/43	*Fw.* Gaehme, Ludwig	7. *Staffel*	killed
14/6/43	*Uffz.* Kimmeskamp, Günther	8. *Staffel*	killed
22/6/43	*Lt.* Geisen, Walter	7. *Staffel*	open tracing case
9/7/43	*Uffz.* Gunthroth, Oskar	9. *Staffel*	killed
28/7/43	*Oblt.* Widowitz, Wulf-Dietrich	9. *Staffel*	killed
10/8/43	*Uffz.* Leibersperger, Alfred	7. *Staffel*	open tracing case
19/8/43	*Fw.* Thomann, Hans	9. *Staffel*	killed
14/9/43	*Ofw.* Beulich, Erich	7. *Staffel*	missing
26/9/43	*Lt.* Schumann, Friedrich	9. *Staffel*	missing
28/9/43	*Uffz.* Link, Hans	9. *Staffel*	POW
2/12/43	*Lt.* Eichhorn, Günter	9. *Staffel*	POW
3/1/44	*Gefr.* Amann, Oskar	7. *Staffel*	killed
3/1/44	*Fw.* Beth, Arthur	7. *Staffel*	POW
11/1/44	*Hptm.* Schmidt, Hans Hermann	9. *Staffel*	POW
16/1/44	*Lt.* Vogel, Karlheinz	7. *Staffel*	killed
16/1/44	*Gefr.* Bergmann, Horst	7. *Staffel*	killed
29/1/44	*Lt.* Walter Klaus	9. *Staffel*	POW
24/2/44	*Uffz.* Bader, Karl-Heinz	8. *Staffel*	killed
28/2/44	*Uffz.* Wagner, Felix	8. *Staffel*	missing
29/2/44	*Lt.* Rost, Wolfgang	9. *Staffel*	POW
5/3/44	*Uffz.* Finzsch, Heinz	8. *Staffel*	missing
8/3/44	*Lt.* Diepen, Hans-Bodo	8. *Staffel*	POW (died soon afterwards)

Appendices

Date	Name	Unit	Fate
17/3/44	Lt. von Hermann, Bernhard	Stab III./JG 5	POW
17/3/44	Fw. Hakenjos, Werner	8. Staffel	killed
23/4/44	Fw. Rohde, Peter	7. Staffel	missing
23/4/44	Uffz. Gorgas, Günter	8. Staffel	open tracing case
8/5/44	Oblt. Berger, Horst	8. Staffel	open tracing case
11/5/44	Uffz. Schneider, Gerd	7. Staffel	POW
11/5/44	Uffz. von Veltheim, Friedrich	7. Staffel	open tracing case
28/6/44	Uffz. Kesseler, Hermann	7. Staffel	missing
29/6/44	Uffz. Hein, Emil	8. Staffel	missing
4/7/44	Gefr. Elken, Friedrich	8. Staffel	missing
9/7/44	Uffz. Freytag, Paul	8. Staffel	killed
17/7/44	Uffz. Hinz, Werner	7. Staffel	killed
21/7/44	Uffz. Mollenhauer, Wilhelm	7. Staffel	killed
28/7/44	Uffz. Mayer, Stephan	8. Staffel	killed
17/8/44	Lt. Schneider, Karl-Heinz	10. Staffel	killed
17/8/44	Gefr. Wien, Günther	9. Staffel	open tracing case
23/8/44	Fiw. Schlammer, Willi	11. Staffel	open tracing case
8/9/44	Uffz. Hirschfeld, Hermann	9. Staffel	killed
15/9/44	Lt. Fuhrmann, Günther	10. Staffel	open tracing case
16/9/44	Lt. Norz, Jakob	11. Staffel	killed
26/9/44	Obfhr. Haschke, Gerhard	10. Staffel	missing
9/10/44	Uffz. Suske, Josef	10. Staffel	killed
12/10/44	Uffz. Hornberger, Gerhard	11. Staffel	open tracing case
12/10/44	Uffz. Heinelt, Rudolf	11. Staffel	open tracing case
17/10/44	Uffiz. Fuchs, Karl-Heinz	9. Staffel	open tracing case
21/10/44	Fhr. von Lilienhof, Rolf	9. Staffel	open tracing case
22/10/44	Fhr. Delbrück, Heinrich	9. Staffel	killed
7/12/44	Uffz. Bernhardt, Harry	10. Staffel	missing
7/12/44	Uffz. Bruscagin, Raimund	11. Staffel	missing
12/12/44	Lt. Peters, Walter	9. Staffel	killed
12/1/45	Uffz. Kirchner, Ludwig	9. Staffel	missing
12/1/45	Fiw. Lieber, Georg	9. Staffel	killed
15/1/45	Uffz. Helbig, Oskar	9. Staffel	killed
15/1/45	Uffz. Zeuner, Waldow	9. Staffel	killed
15/1/45	Uffz. Lehnert, Richard	9. Staffel	killed
9/2/45	Lt. Linz, Rudi	12. Staffel	killed
9/2/45	Fw. Leibfried, Otto	9. Staffel	missing
16/2/45	Fw. Kindt, Wolfgang	10. Staffel	missing
26/3/45	Fw. Jäger, Hermann	10. Staffel	open tracing case
5/4/45	Uffz. Angerer, Erwin	10. Staffel	killed
5/4/45	Uffz. Wirz, Peter	10. Staffel	missing
5/4/45	Ogfr. Ohage, Wilhelm	10. Staffel	missing

IV./JG 5

Date	Name	Unit	Fate
7/7/42	Uffz. Niehaus, Heinz	11. Staffel	killed
18/8/42	Flg. Eiling, Siegfried	12. Staffel	killed
30/8/42	Lt. Löffler, Heinz	12. Staffel	killed
4/9/42	Uffz. Eckhardt, Rudolf	11. Staffel	killed
9/11/42	Uffz. Burkel, Otto	11. Staffel	killed
13/11/42	Fw. Teichgräber, Treuwart	11. Staffel	killed
7/12/42	Uffz. Kahlert, Engelbert	12. Staffel	killed
16/1/43	Uffz. Schmitz, Heinz	10. Staffel	missing (found dead 18/7/43)
21/1/43	Fw. Koch, Ernst	12. Staffel	killed
11/3/43	Uffz. Jasbec, Theobald	12. Staffel	missing
19/3/43	Uffz. Grundhöfer, Karl	12. Staffel	missing
22/3/43	Uffz. Kolle, Franz	10. Staffel	killed
23/3/43	Lt. Kolbe, Hans-Henning	11. Staffel	killed
28/3/43	Uffz. Stavenhagen, Gerhard	12. Staffel	missing (found dead 5/5/43)
24/8/43	Uffz. Kauper, Georg	10. Staffel	killed
30/8/43	Uffz. Neugebauer, Reinhard	11. Staffel	killed
4/9/43	Uffz. Homann, Karl-Ernst	11. Staffel	missing

241

Jagdgeschwader 5

10/10/43	*Uffz.* Nieske, Wolfgang	10. *Staffel*	missing
25/10/43	*Fw.* Wawrzin, Fritz	10. *Staffel*	killed
26/10/43	*Uffz.* Gocht, Walter	11. *Staffel*	killed
16/12/43	Uffz. Sürth, Willi	12. *Staffel*	killed
18/12/43	*Uffz.* Fleischhauer, Paul	12. *Staffel*	missing
27/12/43	*Ofw.* Lindinger, Karl	11. *Staffel*	killed
4/1/44	*Uffz.* Brenner, Josef	12. *Staffel*	open tracing case
6/2/44	*Uffz.* Merkl, Robert	10. *Staffel*	missing (found dead 13/9/44)
21/2/44	*Fw.* Zukunft, Gerhard	11. *Staffel*	killed
26/3/44	*Fw.* Hermann, Hans	11. *Staffel*	missing
30/3/44	*Lt.* Hoffmann, Joachim	*Stab* IV./JG 5	missing
31/3/44	*Ofhr.* Kümpfel, Hubert	12. *Staffel*	killed
10/4/44	*Fw.* Drößler, Kurt	10. *Staffel*	killed
8/5/44	*Uffz.* Brettin, Ernst	10. *Staffel*	open tracing case
8/5/44	*Ofhr.* Otto, Kurt	10. *Staffel*	open tracing case
8/6/44	*Uffz.* Grothe, Walter	12. *Staffel*	killed
19/7/44	*Uffz.* Heinrich, Rudolf	12. *Staffel*	missing (found dead 23/7/44)
30/7/44	*Lt.* Salz, Heinz	11. *Staffel*	killed
30/7/44	*Uffz.* Kwiotkowski, Johann	11. *Staffel*	missing
30/7/44	*Lt.* Mülling, Horst	12. *Staffel*	open tracing case
30/7/44	*Uffz.* Kriekemeier, Hermann	11. *Staffel*	missing
27/8/44	*Oblt.* Beyer, Gerhard	12. *Staffel*	killed
26/9/44	*Uffz.* Thonemann, Kurt	13. *Staffel*	missing
26/9/44	*Uffz.* Hagemeyer, Hermann	13. *Staffel*	open tracing case
8/10/44	*Oblt.* Kirchmeier, Hans	13. *Staffel*	killed
15/10/44	*Lt.* Simme, Fritz	15. *Staffel*	missing
23/10/44	*Uffz.* Hauck, Friedrich	15. *Staffel*	killed
24/10/44	*Fw.* Scharwächter, Gustav	13. *Staffel*	missing
14/12/44	*Ofhr.* Albert, Hans	*Stab* IV./JG 5	killed
5/1/45	*Uffz.* Jünger, Heinrich	14. *Staffel*	killed
11/1/45	*Uffz.* Köhler, Clemens	14. *Staffel*	killed
11/1/45	*Uffz.* Nieft, Werner	14. *Staffel*	killed
12/3/45	*Oblt.* Schneider, Hans	13. *Staffel*	killed
12/3/45	*Ofw.* Stebner, Theo	13. *Staffel*	killed
5/4/45	*Lt.* Keppler	15. *Staffel*	killed
11/4/45	*Lt.* Gillet, Adolf	16. *Staffel*	killed
14/4/45	*Uffz.* Schoppert, Heinz	16. *Staffel*	killed
14/4/45	*Uffz.* Voltmer, Willi	16. *Staffel*	open tracing case
14/4/45	*Gefr.* Bahlmann	13. *Staffel*	killed

14.(J)/JG 5 (*Jabostaffel*)

5/4/43	*Uffz.* Dobner, Kurt	open tracing case
13/4/43	*Uffz.* Wendler, Kurt	killed
11/5/43	*Lt.* Busse, Günther	killed
22/5/43	*Lt.* Biwer, Klaus	killed
18/6/43	*Uffz.* Pohl, Walter	killed
18/6/43	*Fw.* Hünlein, Ewald	killed
18/12/43	*Fw.* Culemann, Helmut	killed
14/2/44	*Lt.* Froschek, Karl-Heinz	open tracing case
43/44	*Oblt.* Koch, Karl	killed

Zerstörer Units

Stab/ZG 26

28/6/41	*Uffz.* Kühn, Kurt	radio operator	killed
7/7/41	*Uffz.* Schneider, Heinz		killed
4/8/41	*Hptm.* Schaschke, Gerhard		POW (missing in camp)
4/8/41	*Uffz.* Widtmann, Michael	radio operator	missing
12/8/41	*Major* Groth, Erich		killed
12/8/41	*Uffz.* Muche, Herbert	radio operator	killed

Appendices

1.(Z)/JG 77

Date	Name	Role	Status
5/7/41	Lt. Weyergang, Dietrich		killed
5/7/41	Uffz. Tigges, Kurt	radio operator	killed
17/7/41	Gefr. Gans, Matthias	radio operator	open tracing case
19/7/41	Lt. Klappenbach, Dietrich		missing
19/7/41	Gefr. Methke, Rudolf	radio operator	missing
15/9/41	Lt. Hoffmann, Heinz-Horst		killed
15/9/41	Gefr. Boehm, Rudolf	radio operator	killed
15/12/41	Lt. Reichel, Eberhard		killed
15/12/41	Gefr. Boehmer, Günther	radio operator	killed

10. and 13. (Z)/JG 5 (*Zerstörerstaffel*)

Date	Name	Role	Status
2/2/42	Oblt. Brandis, Felix Maria		killed
18/6/42	Lt. Krippahl, Harry (10.)		open tracing case
18/6/42	Ofw. Kulik, Erich (10.)	radio operator	open tracing case
13/8/42	Lt. von Rabenau, Hans-Bodo		killed
2/9/42	Ofw. Frenzel, Kurt		killed
2/9/42	Uffz. Hemmenstedt, Paul	radio operator	killed
4/9/42	Uffz. Assmuss, Bruno		missing
4/9/42	Gefr. Härtel, Erwin	radio operator	missing
24/10/42	Uffz. Michels, Karl		killed
5/1/43	Lt. Forst, Walter		killed
5/1/43	Uffz. Hitzinger, Rupert	radio operator	killed
28/2/43	Oblt. Maertins, Oskar		missing
1/5/43	Ofw. Renke, Wolfgang		killed
1/5/43	Uffz. Reiher, Helmuth	radio operator	killed
19/6/43	Uffz. Friedrich, Günther		killed
19/6/43	Uffz. Denzer, Albert	radio operator	killed
22/6/43	Uffz. Herrmann, Karl		killed
22/6/43	Uffz. Herrmann, Alois	radio operator	killed
20/7/43	Fw. Drechsler, Heinrich		killed
20/7/43	Uffz. Möst, Georg	radio operator	killed
25/7/43	Fw. Hink, Robert	radio operator	killed
31/8/43	Gefr. Jettkandt, Siegfried		killed
6/9/43	Ofw. Kolodziej, Johann		killed
6/9/43	Uffz. Schipper, Willi	radio operator	killed
9/10/43	Fw. Mähling, Heinz		killed
19/10/43	Uffz. Widenhorn, Otto		killed
19/10/43	Uffz. Leonhardt, Werner	radio operator	killed
13/1/44	Lt. Müller, Helmut (found dead 16/1/44)		missing
30/3/44	Ofw. Mack, Albert		open tracing case
30/3/44	Uffz. Möbius, Rolf	radio operator	missing

10./ZG 26

Date	Name	Role	Status
2/4/45	Lt. Bäthge, Peter		killed
2/4/45	Uffz. (name not known)	radio operator	killed
3/4/45	Fw. Wunderle, Martin		killed

Ground Personnel Fatal Casualties

Date	Name		Cause
3/3/43	Ogfr. Szameitat, Eberhard	I.	accident Kristiansand
29/1/44	Gefr. Kyas, Engelbert	I.	Ju 52 crash Jagodina
29/1/44	Fw. Lüke, Rudolf	I.	Ju 52 crash Jagodina
29/1/44	Fw. Fuchs, Otto	I.	Ju 52 crash Jagodina
29/1/44	Ogfr. Kristler, Sylvester	I.	Ju 52 crash Jagodina
29/1/44	Ogfr. Brinkmann, Karl-Heinz	I.	Ju 52 crash Jagodina
25/2/44	Uffz. Rodemann, Gerhard	I.	bomb. raid Obertraubling
12/6/44	Ogfr. Haubrock, Karl	I.	bombing raid Montdidier
12/6/44	Ogfr. Möller, Herbert	I.	bombing raid Montdidier
12/6/44	Ogfr. Wetter, Kurt	I.	bombing raid Montdidier
4/9/44	Uffz. Dietze, Helmut	I.	partisans, Mormont, Belgium

Jagdgeschwader 5

Date	Name	Unit	Cause
9/3/42	Gefr. Moser, Fritz	II.	bombing raid Alakurtti
5/4/42	Gefr. Niegel, Alfred	II.	accident Lillehammer
4/8/42	Uffz. Fricke, August	II.	air raid Pontsalenojki
14/9/42	Gefr. Kessler, Wilhelm	II.	illness
13/12/42	Ogfr. Biebricher, Paul	II.	illness
10/4/43	Ogfr. Martens, Walter	II.	accident Salmijärvi
4/6/43	Uffz. Sprink, Josef	II.	illness
6/6/44	Uffz. Chachaj, Walter	II.	Ju 52 crash Pilsen
6/6/44	Uffz. Bobek, Gerhard	II.	Ju 52 crash Pilsen
6/6/44	Ogfr. Wincek, Edmund	II.	Ju 52 crash Pilsen
6/6/44	Ogfr. Ungering, Karl-Heinz	II.	Ju 52 crash Pilsen
6/6/44	Ogfr. Röhl, Klaus	II.	Ju 52 crash Pilsen
6/6/44	Ogfr. Nowara, Bruno	II.	Ju 52 crash Pilsen
6/6/44	Ogfr. Rabenstein, Alfred	II.	Ju 52 crash Pilsen
6/6/44	Ogfr. Dederichs, Hans	II.	Ju 52 crash Pilsen
6/6/44	Ogfr. Haefker, Manfred	II.	Ju 52 crash Pilsen
6/6/44	Ogfr. Müller, Kurt	II.	Ju 52 crash Pilsen
6/6/44	Ogfr. Hirz, Ruppert	II.	Ju 52 crash Pilsen
6/6/44	Ogfr. Rügner, Werner	II.	Ju 52 crash Pilsen
6/6/44	Ogfr. Neubacher, Wilhelm	II.	Ju 52 crash Pilsen
7/6/44	Ogfr. Franke, Heinz	II.	Ju 52 forced landing Montdidier
7/6/44	Ogfr. Reiser, Karl-Ludwig	II.	Ju 52 forced landing Montdidier
22/2/42	Ogfr. Pröhl, Friedrich	III.	Ju 52 crash Reipaa
22/2/42	Ofw. Smolka, Emil	III.	Ju 52 crash Reipaa
22/2/42	Uffz. Schleucher, Johannes	III.	Ju 52 crash Reipaa
22/2/42	Ogfr. Hutzler, Konrad	III.	Ju 52 crash Reipaa
22/2/42	Ogfr. Nebgen, Otto	III.	Ju 52 crash Reipaa
22/2/42	Ogfr. Hochstätter, Peter	III.	Ju 52 crash Reipaa
22/2/42	Gefr. Gocke, Wilhelm	III.	Ju 52 crash Reipaa
22/2/42	Ogfr. Dumberg, Erich	III.	Ju 52 crash Reipaa
22/2/42	Gefr. Plaotz, Johann	III.	Ju 52 crash Reipaa
22/2/42	Ogfr. Hähnel, Manfred	III.	Ju 52 crash Reipaa
28/4/42	Klingenfuß, Friedrich	III.	ambush
28/4/42	Ogfr. Almeroth, Bernhard	III.	ambush
31/12/42	Ogfr. Allgaier, Georg	III.	bombing raid Liinahamari
1/6/43	Ogfr. Stief, Otto	III.	illness
28/7/43	Uffz. Pichote, Herbert	III.	crash, courier flight
25/11/43	Ogfr. Kigler, Johann	III.	air raid Petsamo
10/5/44	Ogfr. Köth, Reinhold	III.	accident Alta Fjord
8/8/42	Flg. Berner, Norbert	IV.	transport Skagerrak
8/8/42	Flg. Beierlein, Helmut	IV.	transport Skagerrak
4/9/43	Uffz. Karger, Gerhard	IV.	accident Trondheim
9/10/44	Ogfr. Meissner, Willi	IV.	bombing raid Salmijärvi
13/12/44	Ogfr. Rackwitz, Werner	IV.	Soyerhaug
13/12/44	Gefr. Boos, Heinrich	IV.	Soyerhaug
13/12/44	Stgfr. Preu, Franz	IV.	Soyerhaug
13/12/44	Ogfr. Walter, Johannes	IV.	Soyerhaug
13/12/44	Fw. Schrödl, Michael	IV.	Soyerhaug
13/12/44	Fw. Lafeld, Willi	IV.	Soyerhaug
13/12/44	Ogfr. Beck, Anton	IV.	Soyerhaug
13/12/44	Ogfr. Schwiede, Gerhard	IV.	Soyerhaug
13/12/44	Ogfr. Oschek, Josef	IV.	Soyerhaug
13/12/44	Ofw. Sekuterski, Georg	IV.	Soyerhaug
13/12/44	Ogfr. Hauberk, Max	IV.	Soyerhaug
13/12/44	Ogfr. Maikranz, August	IV.	Soyerhaug
13/12/44	Flg. Kulterer, Lucas	IV.	Soyerhaug

Appendices

Missing from the Image List of the German Red Cross Tracing Service

7/43	*Uffz.* Amschler, Hans	I. *Gruppe*
3/45	*Stgfr.* Cordes, Günther	II. *Gruppe*
4/45	*Gefr.* Wanner, Carl	II. *Gruppe*
11/43	*Gefr.* Kosla, Sepp	III. *Gruppe*
8/44	*Uffz.* Scheidt, Emil	III. *Gruppe*
8/44	*Uffz.* Slabig, Johann	III. *Gruppe*
12/44	*Uffz.* Klotz, Hermann	III. *Gruppe*
2/45	*Ogfr.* Beverfoerden, Helmut	III. *Gruppe*
3/45	*Sold.* Härtel, Kurt	III. *Gruppe*
3/45	*Ogfr.* Kaiser, Hermann	III. *Gruppe*
4/45	*Stgfr.* Diedrich, Hans	III. *Gruppe*
4/45	*Gefr.* Hauptmann, Herbert	III. *Gruppe*
2/44	*Funker* Frank, Gerhard	IV. *Gruppe*
2/45	*Ogfr.* Morigl, Alfred	IV. *Gruppe*
3/45	*Ogfr.* Bröker, Heinz	IV. *Gruppe*
3/45	*Oblt.* Kohrt, Fritz	IV. *Gruppe*
3/45	*Ogfr.* Ruft, Georg	IV. *Gruppe*
3/45	*Ogfr.* Wieland, Karl	IV. *Gruppe*
4/45	*Sold.* Haase, Karl-Heinz	IV. *Gruppe*
4/45	*Gefr.* May, Herbert	IV. *Gruppe*

Pilots Whose Unit Association Is Not Known

19/1/45	*Gefr.* Hochfellner, Friedrich	crashed near Aalborg,
19/1/45	*Gefr.* Kolbe, Alfons	buried in
19/1/45	*Fhr.* Günther, Alfred	Frederikshaven

Jagdgeschwader 5

JG 5 from January 1942 (aircrew)

Unit	Area of Operations	Killed	Missing	Captured	Wounded	Unit Leaders	Tracing Cases
Stab/JG 5		2					
I./JG 5	Norway/Denmark	18	2		12		2
	Rumania/Bulgaria	1			5	1	
	Defense of the Reich	25			14	4	
	France (invasion)	10	7	4	18	2	4
	Reich	4					
		58	9	4	49	7	6
II./JG 5	Northern Front	23	25	14	37	1	16
	Defense of the Reich	29	10		20	3	4
		52	35	14	57	4	20
III./JG 5	Northern Front	33	39	16	20	5	18
IV./JG 5	Norway	38	18		25	2	6
14.(J)/JG 5	Northern Front	7	2		2		2
10. + 13.(Z)/JG 5	Polar Sea/Northern Front	23	7	1	15	1	3
JG 5	**(total)**	**211**	**110**	**35**	**168**	**19**	**55**

Appendices

Total *Geschwader* Losses (from unit reports)

Unit	Killed	Missing	Captured	Wounded	Unit Leaders	Tracing Cases
I./JG 77	8	3				1
13. + 14./JG 77	4	4	1		1	2
Stab/JG 5	2					
I./JG 5	58	9	4	49	7	6
II./JG 5	52	35	14	57	4	20
III./JG 5	33	39	16	20	5	18
IV./JG 5	38	18		25	2	6
14.(J)/JG 5	7	2		2		2
ZG 76	4	1	1		1	
1.(Z)/JG 77	6	3				1
10. + 13.(Z)/JG 5	23	7	1	15	1	3
10./ZG 26	2					
	238	**121**	**37**	**168**	**21**	**59**

359 killed or missing (59 of them open tracing cases)
37 captured (of these, at least 7 went missing or died in captivity)
168 wounded
    of these: 6 *Gruppenkommandeure*   killed or missing
                  15 *Staffelkapitäne*   or captured
396 casualties from the flying personnel (not counting wounded)
at least
71 casualties among the ground personnel
20 missing (according to German Red Cross search list*)
3 casualties (pilots) with uncertain unit association
490 personnel casualties in total

* not included in the number of tracing cases given above.

Photo Section

Runway of the small island airfield of Herdla off Bergen, winter 1940-41.

The Bf 109T-2 was originally designed for use as a carrier-based fighter. Here a T-2 has ended up on its nose. The extended wingspan is clearly visible in this view.

Members of the ground personnel of JG 77. This photo was taken on the Pernambuco en route from Stavanger to Kirkenes, June 1941.

Uffz. Siegfried Lösch of 1./JG 5 in his Fw 190A-3.

Stavanger-Sola, 6/8/41. Lt. Jakobi (right) of 13./JG 77 after his first victory. In the center is Major Strümpell.

Lt. Senoner suffered a head wound in the same action. Here he is seen wearing the bandage that was applied as soon as he landed.

Hptm. von Wehren, Kommandeur of I./JG 5 from April 1942 to February 1943.

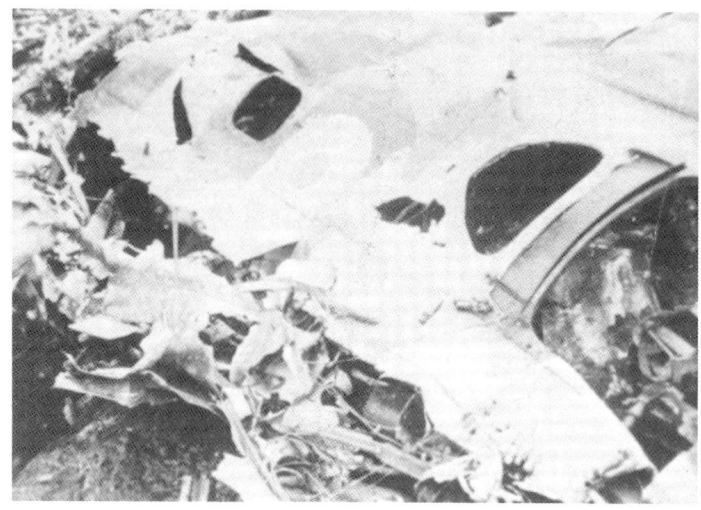

The remains of the Boeing B-17C of No.90 Squadron RAF shot down by Lt. Jakobi near Kristiansund on 8 September 1941. This was the first Fortress to be shot down by a German fighter pilot.

Left: Uffz. Bruns (killed on 10/8/42) and Fw. Grub in Trondheim-Lade.

Right: Lt. Franz Laskowic was I./JG 5's signals officer. This photo was taken in Stavanger in 1941.

Left: Officers of III./JG 5. Hptm. Hecht (H.Q. Comp.), Gruppenkommandeur Scholz and Medical Officer Dr. Schulze-Gericke (left).

Ensuring a smooth flow of supplies to Petsamo was one of the most difficult tasks faced by III./JG 5's headquarters company. In the photo is the supply base in Rovaniemi, the so-called "Elk home", where Fw. Albert Schwarz (below right) served.

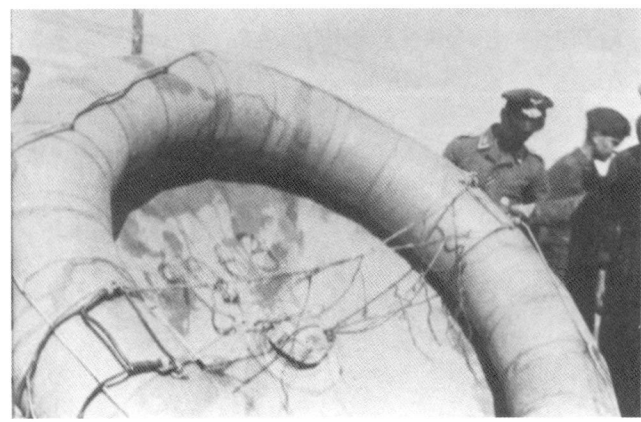

Lister airfield: personnel of JG 5 examine the inflatable dinghy from a Hudson shot down by Lt. Hammel on 30/8/41.

Far left: Lt. Karl Hammel with I./JG 77. He later served with II./JG 5.

Left: Fw. Framm transmitting the daily situation report in I./JG 77's command post in Lister, 1941.

Below: Oblt. Kosse, Staffelkapitän of 1./JG 5. He later became a unit leader in IV./JG 3 and was killed in action against heavy bombers on Christmas Day 1944. Left: Wolfgang Kosse in his Focke-Wulf in Norway.

Generaloberst Stumpff, commander of Luftflotte 5 from May 1940 until the end of November 1943.

Generalmajor Holle, Air Commander North (East).

Generalmajor Roth, Air Commander Lofoten.

Far left: Generalleutnant Harmjanz, commanding general of the Luftwaffe in Norway.

Left: General Schulz, commanding general of the Luftwaffe in Finland.

4./JG 77 in Stavanger-Sola. Seated in the front row: Uffz. Woite (2nd from left), Lt. Ehrler, Lt. Jakobi, Staffelführer Lt. Senoner (6th, 7th and 8th from left) and Hptm. Bachmann (6th from right), who later became Senior NCO of II./JG 5.

3./JG 5's command post in Herdla. On the left is a hangar which has been camouflaged to look like a farmhouse.

This photograph was taken on the island airfield of Herdla, off Bergen. The Bf 109 is Oblt. Wienhusen's "Yellow 1".

Accounting officer Uffz. Peemüller, Staffelkapitän Oblt. Wienhusen, Hptfw. Schurig and Ofw. Jaacks.

1.(Z)/JG 77 was also based in Herdla. Here Lt. Brandis is seen after his third victory in the summer of 1941.

Riddled by bullets, the workshop wagon on Herdla airfield following the low-level raid by the RAF on 27 December 1941.

Ofhr. Habermann in the cockpit of his aircraft after scoring his 2nd victory on 27 December 1941.

One of I./JG 5's Fw 190A-3s, spring 1943.

I./JG 5 operated this Fw 58 Weihe (Harrier) in the air-sea rescue role. The photo shows the aircraft and its crew in Herdla. From l. to r.: Gefr. Geiger (radio operator), Ogfr. Amschler (flight engineer), Ogfr. Mühlberger (pilot).

The Kommodore of Jagdgeschwader 5, Oberstlt. Gotthardt Handrick. He had previously served as Kommodore of JG 26 and after leaving JG 5 in June 1943 he became commander of the 8th Fighter Division in Vienna.

Below: Major Günther Scholz, seen here with the Air Commander Lofoten, Generalmajor Roth, in 1943.

Major Heinrich Ehrler, Geschwaderkommodore of JG 5 and one of the highest-scoring fighter pilots on the Polar Sea Front.

Four views of Kirkenes: the airfield prior to expansion in October 1941, the bay, and the runways, clearly visible from an altitude of about 6000 meters.

Ofw. Dahmer, the Geschwader's first Knight's Cross wearer, in July 1941. He was awarded the Knight's Cross on 1 August 1941 after 25 victories.

Hptm. Carganico was decorated with the Knight's Cross on 25/9/41 after his 27th victory. He was shot down and killed near St. Dizier, France on 27 May 1944. He had scored a total of 60 victories by the time of his death.

JG 5's command post with telephone exchange (in the foreground) in Petsamo.

Hptm. Probst, the Geschwader technical officer, writing the daily serviceability reports.

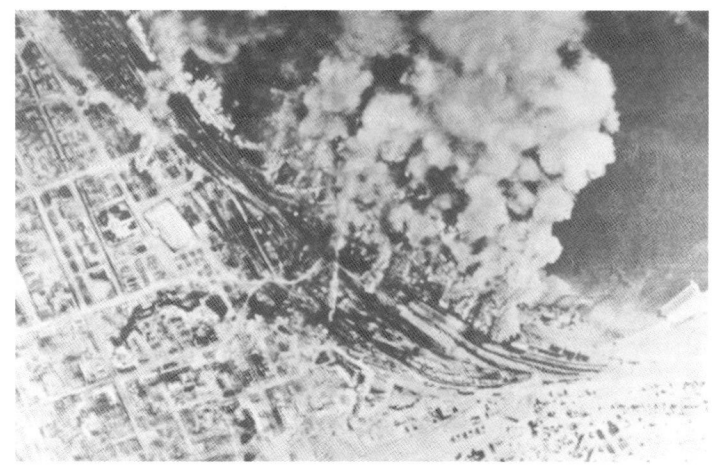

An air raid on harbor installations in the port of Murmansk, the Luftwaffe's number one target in the north. Well aware of the city's strategic importance, with its ice-free port and starting point of the Murmansk railway, the Russians built up a powerful defense. Despite persistent air attacks and offensives by the army, the Germans were never able to take Murmansk.

A Ju 87 of I./StG 5, which was based in Petsamo.

En route to the front. German bomber units were in the air almost daily, attacking the enemy's Polar Sea port on Kola Bay.

A Ju 88 reconnaissance aircraft of F/124 on approach to Kirkenes air base.

The airfield in Kirkenes was defended by anti-aircraft guns. In the background is a Ju 52 air ambulance.

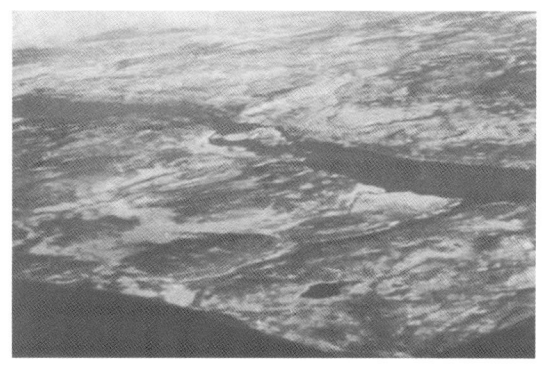

Lisa Bay, a frontline area for many months, photographed during a convoy escort mission.

Hptm. Segatz, operations officer and Geschwader adjutant from the summer of 1943.

Major Strümpell, first Kommandeur of II./JG 5.

Uffz. Rudolf Müller, Alakurtti, 1942. He was the first of the great aces in the far north and was a member of 6./JG 5, the so-called "Staffel of experts". After a total of 94 victories, on 18 April 1943 he was captured by the Russians near Bolshoye Lake. His fate as a prisoner of war remains a mystery to this day.

Oblt. Menzel, Staffelkapitän of 5./JG 5.

Hptm. Carganico after his 50th victory. Oblt. Mikat passes him the honor plaque. The base commander, Oberstlt. van Aaken, Fw. Brunner and Prüfmeister Brunsch (from right) are the first to congratulate him. Petsamo, June 1942.

Fw. Salwender, one of the successful pilots of the 6. Staffel, was captured by the Russians on 23 April 1942. He had previously shot down a Hurricane for his 25th victory. Salwender baled out over Murmansk and later died in captivity.

The landing field in Kirkenes during winter. A Ju 88 may be seen about to take off.

A frequent visitor to Kirkenes was a DeHavilland DH 89 air ambulance, which the Luftwaffe inherited from the Finns.

Mission briefing in Petsamo. Hptm. Lüder assigns roles. Summer 1942.

Men of III./JG 5's ground personnel. Their capable support and assistance played an acknowledged role in the success achieved by German fighter pilots on every front.

Uffz. Beth of the 8. Staffel and his aircraft "Yellow 14". On 3 January 1944 Beth was shot down near Murmashi and taken prisoner by the Russians. He was held for almost five years before returning home.

8./JG 5 in Petsamo. Oblt. Segatz (center) poses with Fw. Rudi Linz (left) and Uffz. Heinrich Bartels, both of whom later won the Knight's Cross.

Summer 1941, Petsamo. Three of the early aces of the far north. From left: Oblt. Carganico, Fw. Salwender, Lt. Dahmer.

Two rare photos taken during the action in which Fw. Froböse of 5./JG 5 was shot down on 11/9/42. A pair of Soviet fighters attack. Inferior to their German counterparts in technology and training when the fighting began in the far north, the Russian pilots caught up quickly and soon became an opponent not to be underestimated in aerial combat.

A Bf 109 of III./JG 5 visits Herdla airfield on the west coast of Norway.

Hptm. Graf von Sponeck, Staffelkapitän of 7./JG 5, and Gruppenadjutant Oblt. Lüder (with back to the camera) in front of the command post.

Oblt. Dörr before a scramble in Petsamo. In September 1943 Dörr took over the 7. Staffel and in May 1944 became Kommandeur of the III. Gruppe.

Pre-mission briefing in Petsamo, summer 1942. From left: Hptm. Scholz, von Sponeck, Lt. Lüder, Ofw. Dörr, unidentified. On the left is the tail of the aircraft of the Gruppenkommandeur, Hptm. Scholz.

The Polar Sea coast. Snow-covered coastal bluffs, ice-covered sea, endless expanses. The pilots of JG 5 saw winter scenes such as this every day.

Major Ehrler, who became Kommandeur of the III. Gruppe in June 1943, after returning from a successful mission.

Air fleet commander Generaloberst Stumpff during a visit to II./JG 5 in 1942. Here Ehrler and Weißenberger greet the high-ranking visitor.

The successful "hunters of Murmansk". From left: Weißenberger, Ehrler, Müller. 6./JG 5, winter 1942-43.

The enemy was also active in the air. Soviet Il-2 close-support aircraft and Kittyhawk fighters attack Petsamo airfield at low level. Winter 1943-44.

Getting German convoys safely to Petsamo became increasingly difficult. Soviet heavy guns positioned on the southwest corner of the Fischer Peninsula (in background) opened fire on the ships. Stukas and Zerstörer attacked the enemy positions, while the Jagdstaffeln kept the Russian fighters at bay. The biggest action took place around midnight on 12-13 August 1942. Do 18 flying boats laid smoke around the ships. Over on the Fischer Peninsula there were flashes – the Soviet artillery. Stukas dive-bombed the positions while the Zerstörer strafed – until finally the ships were out of the danger zone.

Westbound German convoy near Berlevaag.

Barracks complex in Alakurtti, Karelia. Alakurtti and Pontsalenjoki were Luftflotte 5's operational bases in the area of Kandalaksha and the Louhi front.

Uffz. Weinitschke of 5./JG 5 seen leaving the Fieseler Storch after his dramatic recue from the tundra. Weinitschke was shot down over Murmashi on 26 March 1942. Two days later he was spotted and picked up by the crew of the rescue aircraft.

Right: On 12 March 1943, almost exactly a year after he was shot down the first time, Fw. Weinitschke again fell prey to a Soviet fighter. The second time, however, he was captured and became a prisoner of war.

Far right: Lt. Lesch. He and Ofw. Bauer tried to rescue Uffz. Weinitschke after he was shot down on 26 March 1942.

Oblt. Franz Menzel, Staffelkapitän of 5./JG 5.

Three photos of Petsamo during winter. On the right is Savior Mountain, a landmark of the base. Reindeer were almost part of the airfield's inventory. Lt. Rost, the Staffelführer of 9./JG 5, may be seen in the center photo, taken in early 1944. In the bottom photo is Lt. Werner Kunze, technical officer of II./JG 5.

Landscapes in the far north, solitary but with an appealing beauty. A freighter in the northern fjord on its way to Kirkenes. Idyllic scenes on the Kemijoki near Kemi.

I./JG 77 in Petsamo, summer 1941. From l. to r.: unidentified, Uffz. Keppler, unidentified, Ofw. Dahmer, unidentified, Hfw. Zedernhofer (senior NCO), unidentified, Fw. Stratmann, Fw. Mutzel, Lt. Tetzner.

The later Staffelkapitän of 7./JG 5, Oblt. Hans Dieter Hartwein, in conversation with air fleet commander Generaloberst Stumpff. In the center is Lt. Glöckner.

In August 1941 the western powers began sending war materiel to their Russian allies, mainly in convoys to Murmansk and Arkhangelsk. The first big convoy battles in the Polar Sea were fought in the summer of 1942. On the German side KG 26 and KG 30 bore the brunt of the fighting, which was extremely costly for both sides. At 10:30 on 28 May 1942, reconnaissance aircraft of 1.(F)/124 located convoy PQ 16.

Below: German bombers attack a convoy (probably PQ 17) from high altitude.

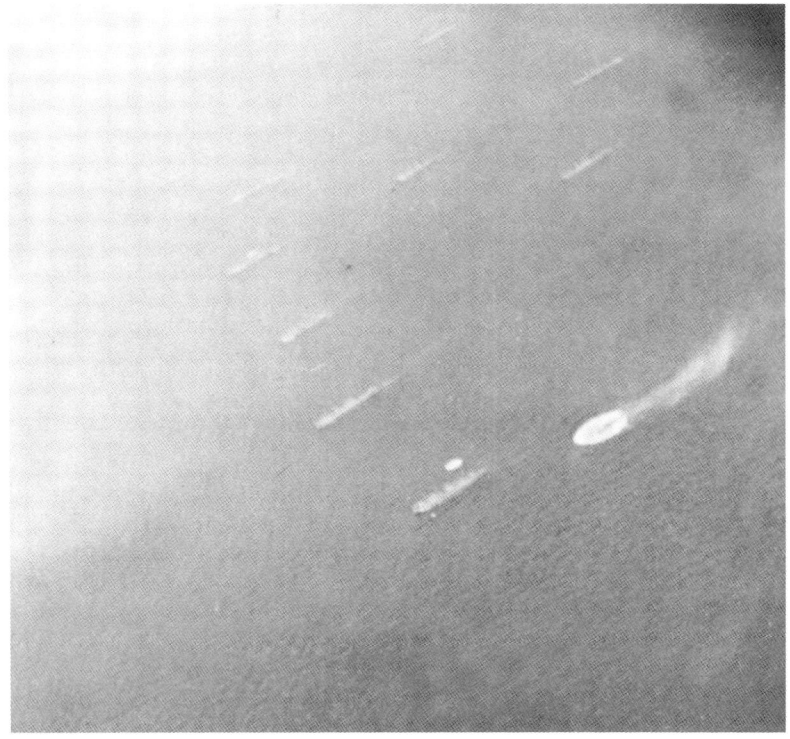

Top and center: A burning tanker photographed from an aircraft of 1.(F)/22. It was part of PQ 18, which lost a total of 13 ships to U-boats and torpedo-bombers.

The Zerstörerstaffel also took part in missions against the convoys. Shown here is a Bf 110 after an attack.

During the long winter months the "black men" of the ground personnel were hard pressed to maintain the aircraft and keep them serviceable. Petsamo, winter 1943.

Uffz. Alfred Kern of 7./JG 5 in front of his aircraft "Yellow 11". Kern was forced down south of Urd Lake on 14 March 1943 and was taken prisoner. He died in captivity.

The Air Commander North (East), Oberst Holle, in Petsamo. Behind him is the air base commander, van Aaken. Second from the right is Hptm. Scholz, Kommandeur of III./JG 5.

Top left: After landing, Major Scholz, Kommandeur of III./JG 5, describes a just-completed combat.

The aircraft of Gruppenkommandeur Scholz bearing 29 victory bars (center and below), Petsamo, 1943. He led the Gruppe until May 1944, when he was named Kommodore of JG 5, succeeding Handrick.

Uffz. Arthur Mendl of 5./JG 5.

Honor guard on the occasion of the awarding of the Knight's Cross to Ofw. Müller (far left), October 1942. From the right are: Uffz. Döring, Lt. Widowitz, Uffz. Weinitschke, Fw. Stratmann, Oblt. Tetzner.

The first two great aces of 6./JG 5, Ofw. Rudolf Müller and Lt. Heinrich Ehrler. Ehrler is seen in the photo on the right while receiving the Knight's Cross in Curtiss in October 1942.

Expansion of the air base in Rovaniemi. The airfield was home to the Zerstörerstaffel for a long time (photo below).

Signpost in Rovaniemi, home of the Army Commander in Norway, Generaloberst von Falkenhorst. The 20th Mountain Army Headquarters was later formed from this command in Finland.

Panoramic view of Rovaniemi on the Kemi River (Kemijoki).

Christmas in Petsamo, 1943. "Kalanag" (Dr. Schreiber) performs magic tricks for members of the III. Gruppe. From r. to l.: Lt. Vogel, Lt. Diepen, Lt. Rost, Lt. Dörr (standing), Hptm. Schmidt (center).

Reichsminister Prof. Dr. Speer was a Christmas guest in the far north. From l. to r.: Chief Conductor Börries, Oberst Kühl, Speer, Hptm. Treppe.

The city of Kirkenes (above) and part of the harbor (below).

A familiar scene in the far north: Lapps on the shore of Kirkenes' north fjord.

A Do 24 of the air-sea rescue Staffel which crashed near Kirkenes.

An unusual visitor – a German U-boat off Kirkenes.

The officer corps of II./JG 5 in Jakobstadt, April 1944. From l. to r.: Oblt. Schwanecke (4. Staffel), Oblt. Hedergott (signals officer), Lt. Tetzner (Staffelführer 4./JG 5), Oblt. Glöckner (adjutant and operations officer), Hptm. Weißenberger (Gruppenkommandeur), Stabsintendant Spindler, Hptm. Mikat (commander of the headquarters company), Lt. Scheufele (Staffelführer 6./JG 5), Stabsarzt Ostermann (medical officer), Lt. Bölz.

Oblt. Glöckner, Stabsarzt Ostermann and Hptm. Weißenberger.

Last action by the crew chief – assisting the pilot in putting on his life vest. Oblt. Schwanecke just prior to takeoff.

On 2 April 1944 Schwanecke shot down three Il-2 close-support aircraft trying to attack the Pontsalenjoki airfield. One of these aircraft came down in the immediate vicinity of the air base.

One of the few photos with the former commander of the I./JG 5 headquarters company, Oblt. Fritz Reß, who died in 1974. From l. to r.: Oblt. Gerlach, Lt. Endriß (T.O.), Oblt. Reß, Lt. Steinicke.

A rare snapshot taken in Petsamo. A Russian Il-2 close-support aircraft photographed while attacking the airfield at low level.

From bed into aerial combat – scramble in pajamas. Oblt. Glöckner returns to Petsamo with a victory. On the right is Lt. Suberg.

9./JG 5 in Petsamo, 1 September 1943. From l. to r.: Uffz. Stoll, Lt. König, Lt. Gayko, Staffelkapitän Hptm. Schmidt, Fw. Schuck, Lt. Stephan, Fw. Thimm, Uffz. Amend and the two Staffel mascots, "Mischka" and "Rolf".

Mechanics working on the engine of a Bf 109 G-6. Sitting is Hptm. Schmidt's crew chief, Uffz. Fischbach.

A pair of Messerschmitts flown by Hptm. Schmidt and Fw. Schuck photographed while flying escort for Generaloberst Stumpff's transport.

Below: Inside 9./JG 5's "cloud cabin" in Petsamo. The Staffel marked its victories on the fin and rudder taken from a downed Russian Pe-2.

Bottom right: Lt. Wolfgang Rost of 9./JG 5 became a prisoner of war on 29/2/44.

Messerschmitt Bf 109T flown by Lt. Alfred Jakobi of 13./JG 77, Stavanger, September 1941.

Messerschmitt Bf 109G-2 flown by Oblt. Heinrich Ehrler of 6./JG 5. Petsamo, March 1943.

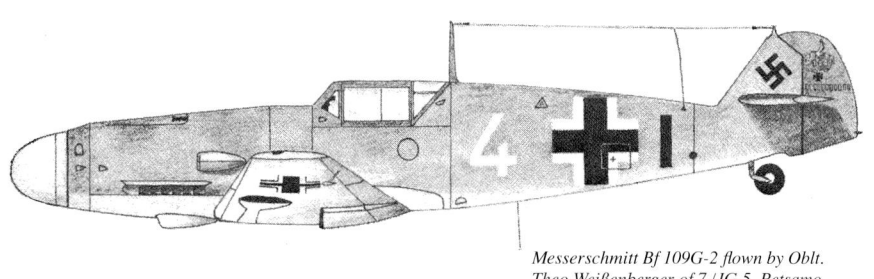

Messerschmitt Bf 109G-2 flown by Oblt. Theo Weißenberger of 7./JG 5. Petsamo, July 1943.

Messerschmitt Bf 109G-2 flown by Uffz. Felix Wagner of 8./JG 5. Petsamo, February 1944.

Messerschmitt Bf 109G-6 flown by Hptm. Horst Carganico of II./JG 5. Alakurtti, March 1944.

Messerschmitt Bf 110E-2 flown by Lt. Hans-Bodo von Rabenau of 13.(Z)/JG 5. Kirkenes, August 1942.

22 March 1944. Oblt. Schwanecke has just completed his 400th operational flight.

General Schulz, the Luftwaffe's commanding general in Finland, inspects 4./JG 5. From l. to r.: Oblt. Schwanecke, General Schulz, Lt. Weitzberg, Ofhr. Schmieder, Uffz. Ofhr, Uffz. Drägert, Uffz. Erlinger (Schwanecke's wingman), Hptfw. Bachmann.

Easter 1944 in Pontsalenjoki. 4. Staffel mission briefing. From l. to r.: Lt. Vetter, Oblt. Schwanecke, Ofhr. Schmieder, Lt. Weitzberg, Uffz. Ohr, Uffz. Erlinger, Uffz. Drägert.

Bombs for the Murmansk railway on Kandalaksha Bay. A Ju 87 waits to be bombed up at Alakurtti.

After a total of seven victories in the north, on 2/12/43 Lt. Günther Eichhorn was shot down by Russian anti-aircraft fire and became a prisoner of war.

Fw. August Mors went with Hptm. Weißenberger to I./JG 5 in the Defense of the Reich in the summer of 1944. On 8 August he succumbed to severe wounds sustained in aerial combat the previous day. Mors was awarded the Knight's Cross posthumously.

Ofw. Heinrich Bartels of 8./JG 5 joined the Eismeergeschwader in the spring of 1942 and went on to score 47 victories with the unit. He was awarded the Knight's Cross in November 1942. Transferred to JG 27 in 1943, Bartels was killed on 23 December 1944 after his 99th victory.

Lt. Friedrich Lüdecke was shot down by Russian anti-aircraft fire on 21 January 1943 and baled out. The Staffel reported him missing, and newspapers in Germany even carried an obituary for the "fallen" Leutnant. In fact, however, Lüdecke had been captured by the Russians.

Walter Schuck was one of the Geschwader's most successful pilots alongside Ehrler and Weißenberger. He scored his 150th victory on 23 August 1944. Schuck ultimately led 10./JG 5 and in the spring of 1945 he joined Jagdgeschwader 7, where he scored seven victories flying the Me 262. Schuck was awarded the Oak Leaves in September 1944 after 171 victories.

"Jockel" Norz was another rising ace of the Polar Sea Front. He had achieved 117 victories by 16 September 1944, when he was killed in a crash after his engine failed on approach to land in Kirkenes.

III./JG 5 mourns Lt. Norz. His remains were buried in the military cemetery in Parkkina. Lt Schuck is holding the black cushion bearing Norz's decorations.

The Northern Lights over Petsamo. The Northern Lights were probably the most striking natural phenomenon seen by the men in the far north: a colorful display of impressive beauty.

Two Bf 109s in their snow blast pens. The temperature was approximately minus 30 degrees.

This is the aircraft of Lt. Heinicke of 7./JG 5. The damage behind the cockpit was inflicted by enemy gunfire during an air battle over the Polar Sea. Despite the damage Heinicke landed safely in Kirkenes.

Oblt. Theo Weißenberger in May 1944 as Gruppenkommandeur of II./JG 5. In June 1944 Weißenberger went to the invasion front in France as Kommandeur of the I. Gruppe with 175 victories to his credit. Within the next few weeks he shot down another 25 enemy aircraft. Weißenberger scored his 200th victory on 25 July 1944.

Photographs of I./JG pilots and aircraft are rare. Here is one taken in Sofia showing Lt. von Podewils of 3./JG 5, January 1944/

A gathering of aces of the III. Gruppe. From l. to r.: Schuck, Dörr, Ehrler and Norz. Between them, these four fighter pilots achieved about 600 victories on the Polar Sea Front.

Lt. Rudi Linz from Ilmenau, Thuringia. He was killed in action off the west coast of Norway on 9/2/45, by which time had a total of 70 victories to his credit.

Anlage 1
zu Nr. 431

7./Jagdgeschwader 5   O.U., 5.7.43
―――――――――――――   ―――――――――
(Truppenteil)   (Ort, Datum)

Abschußmeldung, Zerstörungsmeldung

1. Zeit (Tag, Stunde, Minute) und Gegend des Absturzes: 4.7.43, 21.54 Uhr, etwa 7 km nord- westlich der Nordspitze der Fischerhalbinsel, Quadrat 37 Ost 1022 E
   Höhe: 200 m
2. Durch wen ist Abschuß / Zerstörung erfolgt? Lt. Theo Weißenberger (100. Abschuß)
3. Flugzeugtyp des abgeschossenen Flugzeuges: Il-2
4. Staatsangehörigkeit des Gegners: russisch
   Werknummern bzw. Kennzeichen: Sowjetstern
5. Art der Vernichtung:
   a) Flammen mit dunkler Fahne, Flammen mit heller Fahne;
   b) Einzelteil weggeflogen, abmontiert (Art der Teile erläutern), auseinandergeplatzt; Teile von Flächen und Rumpf
   c) zur Landung gezwungen (diesseits oder jenseits der Front, glatt bzw. mit Bruch);
   d) jenseits der Front am Boden in Brand geschossen.
6. Art des Aufschlages (nur wenn dieser beobachtet werden konnte):
   a) diesseits oder jenseits der Front; auf See
   b) senkrecht, flachem Winkel, Aufschlagstand, Staubwolke;
   c) nicht beobachtet, warum nicht?
7. Schicksal der Insassen (tot, mit Fallschirm abgesprungen, nicht beobachtet).
8. Gefechtsbericht des Schützen ist in der Anlage beigefügt.
9. Zeugen: Fw. Drößler
   a) Luft: ./.
   b) Erde:
10. Anzahl der Angriffe, die auf das feindliche Flugzeug gemacht wurden: 1
11. Richtung, aus der die einzelnen Angriffe erfolgten: hinten
12. Entfernung, aus der der Abschuß erfolgte: 30 m
13. Takt. Position, aus der der Abschuß angesetzt wurde: aus Linkskurve
14. Ist einer der feindlichen Bordschützen kampfunfähig gemacht worden? ./.
15. Verwandte Munitionsart: Pak, Sek, B-Patr., Spreng-, Panzer- und Brandspreng
16. Munitionsverbrauch: 400 Schuß Kanonen, 900 Schuß M.G. für 6 Abschüsse
17. Art und Anzahl der Waffen, die im Abschuß gebraucht wurden: 3 M.G. 151/20, 2 M.G. 17
18. Typ der eigenen Maschine (z. B. Me 109 E mit 2 Kanonen und 2 MG.): Bf 109 G-2 mit 3 M.G. 151/20 und 2 M.G. 17
19. Weiteres taktisch oder technisch Bemerkenswertes: ./.
20. Treffer in der eigenen Maschine: ./.
21. Beteiligung weiterer Einheiten (auch Flak): ./.

Deipenberg.
(Unterschrift)
Leutnant und Staffelführer

Zu Ziffer 5—7 ist Zutreffendes zu unterstreichen.

2143a Dr. A + Istg. Heidelberger Gutenberg-Druckerei GmbH. III. 43.

Attachment 1 from the victory claim for Lt. Theo Weißenberger's 100th victory. On 4 July 1943 Weißenberger shot down seven enemy aircraft within the space of an hour: a Pe-2, three IL-2s and three Hampdens. The report indicates that he was flying a Bf 109 G-2 armed with two underwing cannon that day.

In autumn 1944 II./JG 5 became IV./JG 4. This rare photo was taken in Reinsdorf. From l. to r.: Uffz. Dittrich, Hptm. Wienhusen (killed near Aachen on 3/12/44), Oblt. Schleef (killed near Bad Dürkheim on 31/12/44), Lt. Morio.

Uffz. Walter Giese, formerly of 6./JG 5, on his BF 109G-14/AS in Riesa-Leutewitz, October 1944.

Lt. Ernst Scheufele, Staffelführer of 6./JG 5 (later 14./JG 4). On 3 December 1944, while flying with the Gruppe under Hptm. Wienhusen, Scheufele was shot down by anti-aircraft fire near Aachen. He was subsequently taken prisoner by the Americans.

Two photos from a Russian prisoner of war camp (Elabuga on the Kama River). Lt. Jakobi of 5./JG 5 managed to preserve these images despite all the searches and the chaos of war.

Summer 1972: a helicopter of the Finnish Air Force recovering a Bf 109 discovered in Lapland. Unfortunately it cannot be established who the pilot of the downed aircraft was.

Far left: Lt. Werner Kunze, technical officer of II./JG 5, failed to return from a mission in the Murmashi area on 19/9/42 and is still listed as missing.

Left: Oblt. Robert Müller of I./JG 5, posted missing in France on 17/7/44.

En route stop in Schwerin during I./JG 5's transfer from Denmark to Rumania. From l. to r.: General Galland, Hptm. Wengel, Oblt. Gerlach, Oblt. Senoner. October 1943.

Lt. Linz (right), Staffelführer of 12./JG 5, and Fw. Bößenecker gaze at the tally of victories on the rudder of Linz's Fw 190.

Hptm. Carganico and Hptm. Wienhusen of II./JG 5 in the far north.

The 10. Staffel in Gossen, April 1945. From left to right: Uffz. Rubenbauer, Uffz. Schilling (back row); Uffz. Baasch, Uffz. Angerer, Fhr. Lork, Fw. Rübeling, Fw. Krumbholz, Uffz. Peters (middle row); Ofw. Wollmann, Uffz. Wirz, Ogfr. Ohage, Fw. Reber (front row).

Fw 190A-8s of 9./JG 5 in Herdla, spring 1945.

Right: Uffz. Opitz and a member of the ground crew on the wing of his Fw 190 in Herdla.

Far right: Oblt. Hans Schneider, Kapitän of 13./JG 5, killed on 12/3/45.

The 16. Staffel's dispersal in Rygge, March 1945. The unit's Bf 109G-14s wear the black and yellow Geschwader band on the aft fuselage.

The end in Lister. A rare document. The entire 13. Staffel, photographed on 8 May 1945, the day of the German surrender.

POWs in the French camp in Mulsanne, 1945. From l. to. R.: (starting in back row) Lt. Amm, Lt. Schneider, Lt. Villing, Lt. Reichenbach, Lt. Pork, Oblt. Tpetschork, Lt. Schmoll, Oblt. Schulze, Oblt. Schulze, Lt. von Podewils, Lt. Richter, Lt. Degner, Lt. Hecker, Lt. Schüler, Lt. Krumrey, Lt. Kurpiers, Lt. Herrmann, Lt. von Brunn, Lt. Schneider, Lt. Hellwig.

The Zerstörerstaffel, roughly October 1942, with Oblt. Kirchmeier, Oblt. Schloßstein, Oblt. Franzisket, Lt. Schwab, Oblt. Maertins and Lt. Maul.

The tail of a Bf 110 whose identity is as yet unclear. It was probably an aircraft of the Stabsschwarm of ZG 76 (Hptm. Schaschke) or an aircraft of 1.(F)/124, a reconnaissance unit based in Kirkenes.

Oblt. Schloßstein's Bf 110 being refueled in Rovaniemi, winter 1941.

Right: Hptm. Gerhard Schaschke of the Zerstörerstaffel/JG 5. He was shot down on 4 April 1941 and captured by the Russians. He is still listed as missing. Schaschke had 20 victories to his credit when he was shot down.

Far right: Lt. Brandis, Staffelführer of 1.(Z)/JG 77, after his tenth victory.

Dachshund dogs were a part of the Zerstörerstaffel throughout its operational life. A dachshund was chosen as the Staffel emblem, which adorned the noses of the unit's Bf 110s.

Zerstörer pilots in Kirkenes. From l. to r.: Lt. Diedrich, Lt. Tetzner (later Kommandeur of II./JG 5), Lt. Hoffmann, Lt. Franzisket.

Lt. Kirchmeier, Lt. Kinder of the mountain infantry, Lt. Franzisket.

This captured bus served as the Zerstörerstaffel's first command post in Kirkenes.

The flight control barracks in Kirkenes, 1941. In the foreground is the air raid bunker.

Right: Above the bay in Kirkenes was the so-called "Zerstörer camp".

Below: The Zerstörerstaffel taking off on a mission. Kirkenes airfield, summer 1942.

Bottom right: The crew of Hptm. Schmidt and Uffz. Friedrich at the Zerstörer dispersal in Kirkenes, summer 1942. With round the clock missions, a catnap in a deck chair was often the only sleep the crews got.

"Smile please!" for a photo for the folks at home. From l. to r.: Hptm. Schmidt, Major Strümpell, Gefr. Hermann, Lt. Glöckner.

LN+OR, the aircraft of Hptm. Schmidt and Lt. Reichel's LN+KR.

The Zerstörerstaffel also suffered some painful losses. On 2 February 1942, Oblt. Brandis (bottom left) crashed onto the ice of Pyav Lake in bad weather and was killed. His radio operator, Herbert Baus, was seriously injured

Lt. Reichel (right) and his radio operator Boehmer were killed in a crash near Rovaniemi airfield on 15 December 1941.

The "Zerstörer camp" in Kirkenes photographed from a Fieseler Storch.

Fw. Gerhard Friedrich, longtime radio operator of Hptm. Schmidt and one of the very few non-flying personnel to command a Staffel.

A Schwarm of Bf 110s during a mission in the area of Ura Bay.

16 October 1941: Bf 110s of the Zerstörerstaffel prior to a transfer flight to Petsamo to escort a unit of Ju 88s from there to Varlamovo.

Lt. Brandis again, here with the dachshund "Lockheed" in front of the base mess.

An Ar 196 after landing on Vezhny Lake. The photo was taken during search operation "Sonderführer Kuhnke". 16 August 1942.

The crash site of Lt. von Rabenau's Bf 110, in which the Sonderführer was flying. While Kuhnke and the radio operator were able to parachute to safety, von Rabenau stayed with the aircraft and was killed when it exploded on impact.

Sonderführer Kuhnke of Propaganda Company 680. The Zerstörerstaffel took part in the three-day operation that resulted in his rescue.

The Rotte of Oblt. Schmidt and Lt. Koch during an escort flight over Kirkenes Fjord, 17 October 1941.

Sunset over Vardö. A Bf 110 on its way to provide air cover for a German submarine.

The entire Staffel in the air.

A pair of Bf 110s over the Polar Sea.

Generaloberst Stumpff visits the Zerstörerstaffel in Kirkenes. From r. to l.: Stumpff's aide-de-camp (name not known), Oblt. Kirchmeier, who was leading the Staffel in Hptm Schloßstein's absence, General Roth (above); Hptm. Treppe, Generaloberst Stumpff, General Roth, air commander Lofoten (left).

The Zerstörerstaffel over the fjord.

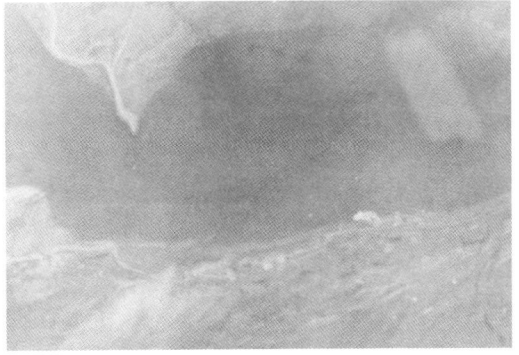

Photo taken from a Bf 110 during a bombing raid on the pier on Mottka Bay, 28 August 1943.

Lt. Bäthge (left) reports to Staffelkapitän Hptm. Treppe after landing. Bäthge had just shot down a four-engined bomber. October 1944.

In good spirits despite a wounded hand. Lt. Bäthge, who failed to return from a mission on 2 April 1945.

Mission debrief. In the middle of the photo is Fw. Wunderle from Swabia. At the beginning of April 1944 he was killed in an accident soon after taking off.

Below: Hptm. Treppe after shooting down a four-engined bomber over the sea between Stavanger and Bergen.

Bottom right: The dachshund emblem on the nose of one of the Zerstörerstaffel's Bf 110s.